BMW 2500 - 2800 - 3.0 & BARVARIA 1968 - 1977

Covers all six-cylinder carbureted and fuel-injected models including: 2500 - 2800 - 2800 CS - Barvaria 3.0 CS - 3.0 Sedan - 3.0 Coupe - 3.0 Si

A Floyd CLYMER Publication by: www.VelocePress.com
Copyright 2024 Veloce Enterprises

PREFACE

TRADEMARKS & COPYRIGHT

BMW ® is the registered trademark of Bayerische Motoren Werke GmbH. This publication is not sponsored by or endorsed by the trademark owner. We recognize that some words, model names and designations, for example, mentioned herein are the property of the trademark holder. We use them for identification purposes only. This is not an official publication however; it may include non-copyright works of the trademark holder.

INTRODUCTION

Welcome to the world of digital publishing ~ the book you now hold in your hand was printed using the latest state of the art digital technology. The advent of print-on-demand has forever changed the publishing process, never has information been so accessible and it is our hope that this book serves your informational needs for years to come. If this is your first exposure to digital publishing, we hope that you are pleased with the results. Many more titles of interest to the classic automobile and motorcycle enthusiast, collector and restorer are available via our website at www.VelocePress.com. We hope that you find this title as interesting as we do.

NOTE FROM THE PUBLISHER

The information presented is true and complete to the best of our knowledge. All recommendations are made without any guarantees on the part of the author or the publisher, who also disclaim all liability incurred with the use of this information.

INFORMATION ON THE USE OF THIS PUBLICATION

This manual is an invaluable resource for those interested in performing their own maintenance. However, in today's information age we are constantly subject to changes in common practice, new technology, availability of improved materials and increased awareness of chemical toxicity. As such, it is advised that the user consult with an experienced professional prior to undertaking any procedure described herein. While every care has been taken to ensure correctness of information, it is obviously not possible to guarantee complete freedom from errors or omissions or to accept liability arising from such errors or omissions. Therefore, any individual that uses the information contained within, or elects to perform or participate in do-it-yourself repairs or modifications acknowledges that there is a risk factor involved and that the publisher or its associates cannot be held responsible for personal injury or property damage resulting from the use of the information or the outcome of such procedures.

WARNING!

One final word of advice, this publication is intended to be used as a reference guide, and when in doubt the reader should consult with a qualified technician.

CONTENTS

Fuel	1
Ignition	13
Cooling	17
Engine	23
Clutch	43
Transmission	47
Drive axle	65
Brakes	81
Front suspension	95
Steering	103
Electrical	118
Heat & Air Conditioning	145
Body	161
Specifications	171
Lubrication Chart	188
Fuel Injection	189
Detailed Wiring Diagrams 1970-1976	195

FUEL SYSTEM .. EMISSION CONTROL

INDEX

	Page
CARBURETORS	1
Synchronizing	1
Cleaning	2
Choke flap adjustment	3
Fast idling speed adjustment	3
Stage 2-vacuum adjustment	4
Accelerator pump adjustment	5
HEAT-SENSITIVE CHOKE VALVE	5
Operation	5
CARBURETOR	5
Removing	5
Replacing	6
Float replacing	6
Float needle valve replacing	6
Choke housing replacing	6
Insulating flange replacing	7
FUEL PUMP	7
Checking pressure and float needle valve for sealing	7
Cleaning	7
Removing and refitting	7
INSULATING FLANGE AND PUMP PUSHROD	7
Replacing	7
Overhauling	7
WARM AIR REGULATING FLAP	8
Adjusting	8
AIR FILTER CASING COMPLETE	8
Removing and installing	8
EXHAUST EMISSION CONTROL SYSTEM	9

	Page
Description	9
Checking automatic choke carburetor	9
Adjust idle speed mixture with exhaust tester	9
Increased idling speed	9
THROTTLE CLOSURE DELAY SYSTEM	10
Description	10
THROTTLE DIAPHRAGM UNIT	10
Testing	10
88FUEL EVAPORATION CONTROL SYSTEM	10
Descritpion	10
EXCESS FUEL RETURN VALVE	10
Description	10
DASHPOT	10
Testing	10
Adjustment	10
VACUUM CONTROL VALVE	11
Operation	11
Testing	11
TEMPERATURE CONTROLLED VACUUM SOLENOID	11
Testing	11
VACUUM SOLENOID VALVE	11
Testing	11
EGR SYSTEM	11
Description	11
EGR system test	11
EGR VALVE	11
Cleaning	11
EXHAUST GAS FILTER	11
CRANKCASE VENTILATION	11
Description	11

CARBURETORS

Synchronizing

It is essential that valve clearance, dwell angle and ignition timing settings are correct and engine at working temperature. Detach air filter housing complete. Carefully screw both mixture regulating screws in to their fullest extent and then screw out by approximately 1½-2 turns. For synchronization with Moto-Meter 28.10.1004 only, unscrew stud.

The rotary spindle should not be sprung against the stop. The adjusting screw is only required for carburetor synchronization, ignition timing adjustment and for checking the centrifugal advance. On no account should engine idling be influenced by the adjusting screw.

Disconnect tie-rod on rear carburetor and start the engine. At 900 rpm, synchronize the position of the throttle butterflies of the two carburetors by means of the idling adjustment screws. With Moto-Meter, plunger in column must be at the same height for both carburetors. With synchronizing unit made by Messrs. Korinth, Steinheim/Main, pointer positions on both scales must be identical.

Set engine to maximum running speed with the two mixture regulating screws. Correct engine idling to 900 rpm. This procedure should be repeated until the engine speed is 900 rpm. The last setting should always be carried out at the mixture regulating screw.

FUEL SYSTEM

Adjust length of tie-tod until the engine speed does not change when engaged. Check synchronization at 1700 rpm and if necessary readjust tie-rod. Screw out adjusting screw until there is play between rotary spindle and stop.

Refit complete air filter housing. The engine speed will drop by about 100 rpm when the filter housing is fitted. Set mixture regulating screw for maximum engine running speed.

Cleaning

Detach and refit air filter housing. Detach fuel hose. Remove stud and fixing bolts for carburetor cover. Slacken screw of tie-rod. Lift off carburetor cover.

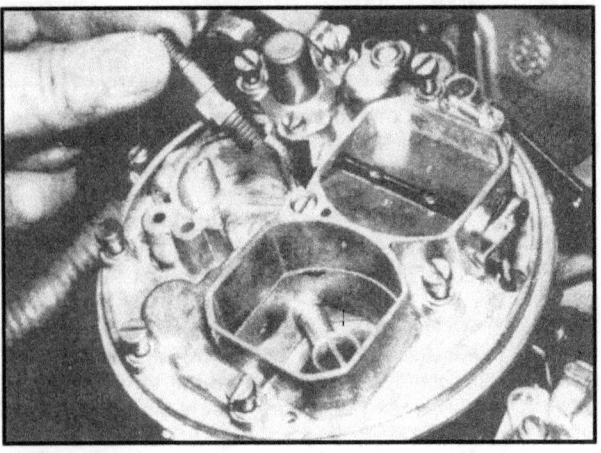

Fitting instructions: When the choke flap is closed the toggle lever should rest flat on the circlip.

Extract idling jet and detach mixture block.

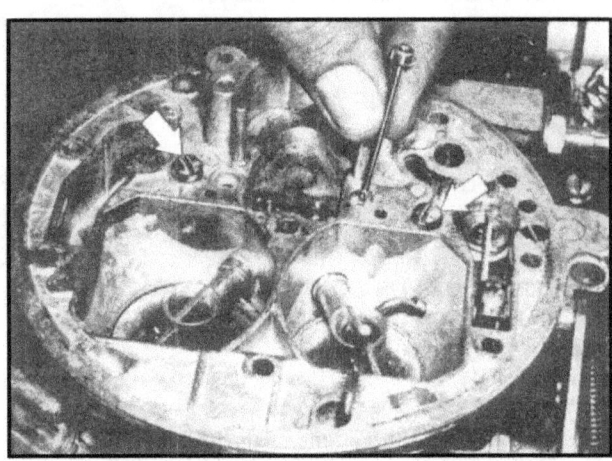

Clean main jets, pump intake valve, pump pressure valve and float chamber. Remove and clean air compensating jets, choke tubes and pump piston.

1. Main jets
2. Pump intake valve
3. Pump pressure valve

FUEL SYSTEM

Fitting instructions: Do not confuse air compensating jets and choke tubes. First stage on right in direction of travel.

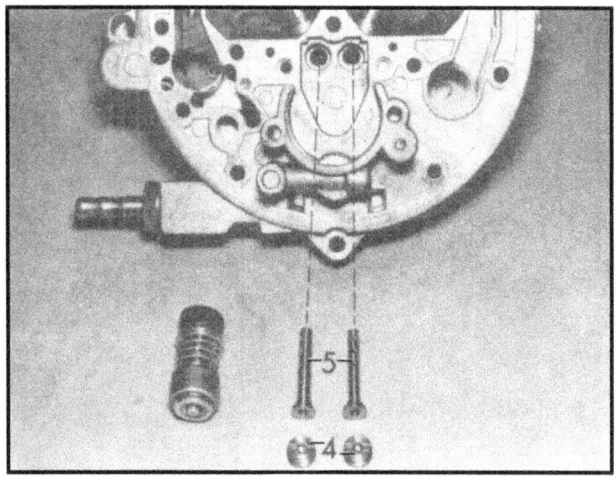

4. Air compensating jets
5. Choke tubes

Choke flap adjustment

Detach choke cover. Close choke flap by hand. Slacken screw in toggle joint. Adjusting screw will be against top recess of setting plate. Secure toggle joint on tie-rod with a clearance (A) 1.5 mm/0.0591" between tie-rod and follower. Then press clamp ring against toggle joint so that no play is present.

1. Tie-rod
2. Follower
3. Toggle joint on tie-rod
A = 1.5mm/0.0591"

Setting screw will be at top recess of setting plate. Push tie-rod up and follower against tie-rod. Set choke flap opening at the lobe facing downwards by means of the adjusting screw.

1. Tie-rod
2. Follower

4. Adjusting screw

Fast idling speed adjustment

It is essential that the engine is at working temperature, air filter housing detached and engine idling synchronized to 900 rpm. With the engine stationary disconnect tie-rod at rear. Lift accelerator linkage of rear carburetor approximately 1/8 inch. Close choke flap by hand until there is a gap of 2.4 mm (0.094 in.). Check with twist drill at lobe of choke flap facing downwards.

FUEL SYSTEM

By means of this procedure the stop lever in the automatic choke will be set to stage 2. Release choke flap. Start engine without depressing accelerator. Idling speed should be 1400 rpm. Shut off engine to make corrections. Push accelerator linkage to full throttle position. Unscrewing adjusting screw – slower idling. Screwing in – faster idling. One turn of the adjusting screw corresponds to approximately 300 rpm.

Repeat procedures until idling speed is 1400 rpm. Lift accelerator linkage approximately 1/8 in. so that the adjusting screw can disengage at the setting plate. Set front carburetor in the same sequence. Re-engage tie-rod and set stop lever in the automatic choke of both carburetors to stage 2. Release choke flaps. Start engine without depressing accelerator. Fast idling speed must then be 1800-2000 rpm.

Stage 2 – vacuum box adjustment

Stage 2 is controlled from the vacuum box. Throttle flap opening of stage 2 is set to an air throughput (A) (0.05 mm/0.002 in. gap) corresponding to main jet 130 ± 10. If the throttle flap opening is too small, the throttle flap sticks.

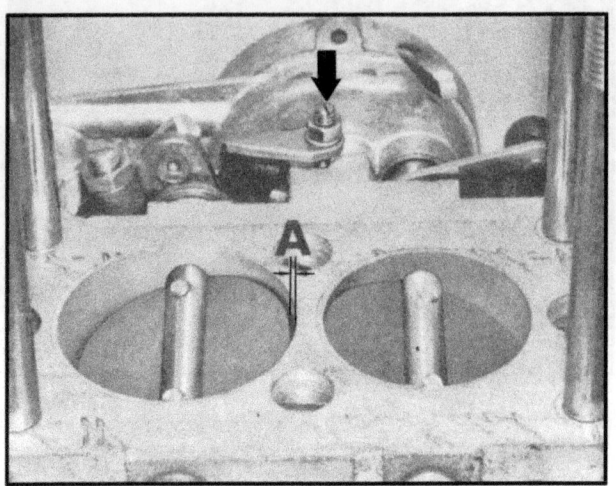

Adjust the throttle butterfly with the spring stop pin to 0.3 mm (0.12 in.) preload. Loosen the lock nut. Screw in the adjusting screw until the spring stop pin just touches the locking lever. Screw the adjusting screw by a further 1/3 turn. Coat the adjusting screw with Loctite and tighten the lock nut. If the preload dimension exceeds 0.3 mm (0.12 in.), the roller will jam in the gate.

Only applicable when renewing diaphragm: Disengage tie-rod. Detach cover. Extract spring and diaphragm. Relaxed spring length – 46 mm (1.81 in.)–BMW2500, 72 mm (2.83 in.)–BMW2800. Check tie-rod adjustment. A 66 mm (2.598 in.)–BMW2500 and 2800.

FUEL SYSTEM

Accelerator pump adjustment
Detach carburetor cover. Slacken pressure screw. Extract pre-atomizer. Check injection unit.

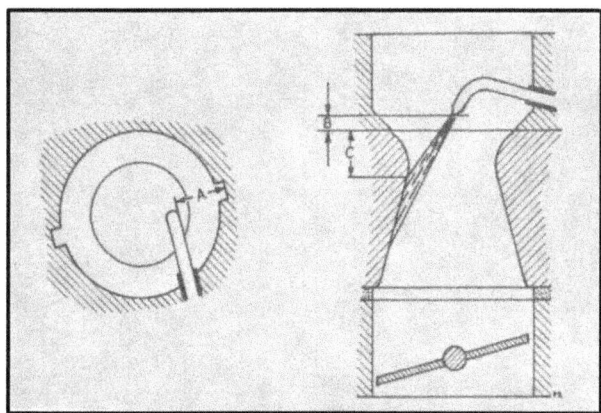

A   (0.433 + 0.039 in.)
B   (0.059 in.)
C–D   (0.393 ÷ 0.590 in.)

To check injection volume, use 7020 measuring vessel. Adjust injection volume by bending at the nominal adjustment point. The pump plunger can only be exchanged as a complete unit.

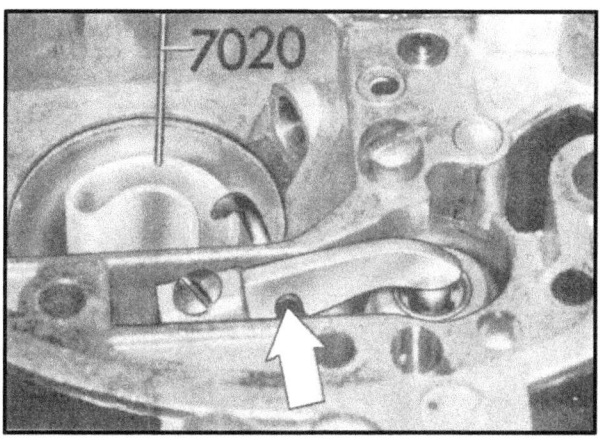

HEAT-SENSITIVE CHOKE VALVE
Checking
Take off the cover. At +59°F the valve should be open or lifted away from its seat. At temperatures below +59°F, switch on the ignition. After about 1 minute the bimetallic spring should have raised the valve by 1–2 mm (0.04-0.08 in.). If the valve does not lift, the resistance is defective or there is no current at the flat plug. The valve seat has been correctly set in an air-conditioned room. This setting must not be altered.

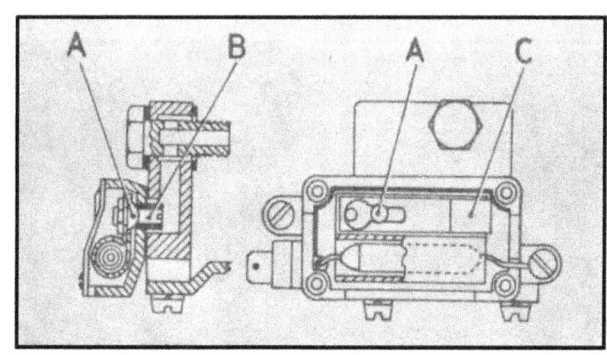

A.   Valve   B.   Valve seat   C.   Bimetallic spring

Operation
Position of choke plate is controlled by a bi-metal spring which responds to coolant temperature and an electrical heating coil. Cut-in point of the heating element is controlled by two heat sensors. One sensor is located on intake manifold, and applies current to choke heater at temperatures above 63°F. The other sensor is in water jacket of intake manifold heating system. It sends current to choke heater at coolant temperatures above 113°F. Choke operates normally when outside temperature is below 63° and coolant is below 113°.

CARBURETOR
Removing
Detach complete air filter housing. Remove fuel and vacuum hoses. Disconnect tie-rod. Detach choke cover.

FUEL SYSTEM

Fitting instructions: Engage follower in bi-metal spring. Notch on choke housing must line up with projection on choke body. Remove nuts from studs. Pull off carburetors. Check flange gasket, graphited side towards inlet manifold. Synchronize carburetors.

Replacing
Drain off cooling water.

Fitting instructions: Bleed cooling system.

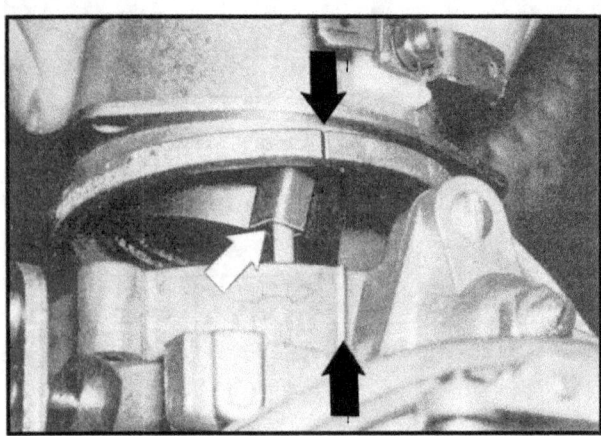

Detach and refit air filter housing complete. Remove fuel, vacuum and water hoses. Pull off cables. Disconnect pushrod.

Detach carburetor.

Fitting instructions: Fit graphited side of flange gasket towards inlet manifold.

Check pushrod setting (A) – 40 mm (1.574"). Synchronize.

Float replacing
Detach carburetor cover and mixture block. Undo bracket. Extract float.

Float needle valve replacing
Remove and refit float. Unscrew float needle valve. Sealing washer thickness will alter the fuel level.

1. Sealing washer thickness

Choke housing replacing
Drain off cooling water.

Fitting instructions: Bleed cooling system.

FUEL SYSTEM

Detach cover. Remove sealing washer. Pull off cables. Remove choke housing.

Fitting instructions: Engage follower in bi-metal spring. Notch on choke housing must line up with projection on choke body.

Insulating flange replacing

Disconnect pushrod and tie-rod. Remove tie-rod. Remove flange gasket. Detach throttle butterfly unit. Replace insulating flange.

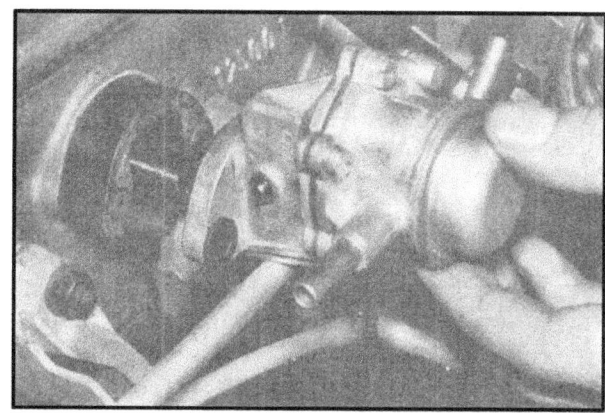

2 & 3. Tie rod
1. Pushrod

INSULATING FLANGE & PUMP PUSHROD
Replacing

Remove fuel pump. Pump pushrod length and insulating flange thickness with gaskets may not be altered.

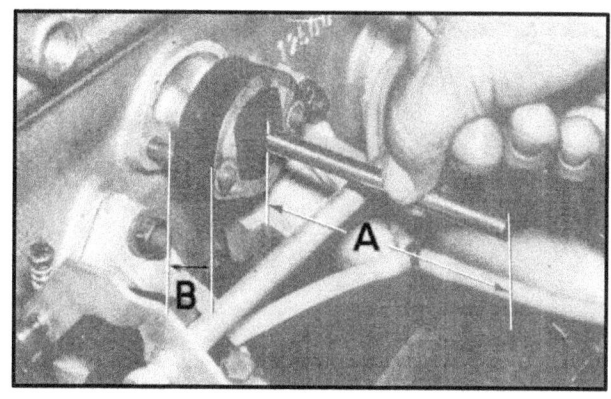

A. Pushrod length
B. Flange thickness with gaskets

FUEL PUMP
Checking pressure and float needle valve for sealing

For fuel pump pressure – test gauge between main line and fuel pump. For float needle valve – test gauge between fuel pump and carburetor.

Cleaning

Remove and refit air filter housing complete. Remove and refit screw plug with mesh filter.

Overhauling

Mark pump top and bottom sections. Detach top section. Remove inlet valve. Inspect sealing face. Check outlet valve for proper operation. Strip bottom section. Replace diaphragm. Locate diaphragm in correct fitting position with setting gauge 5125.

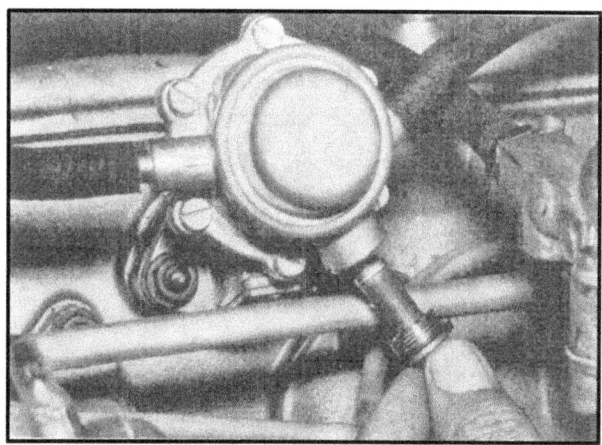

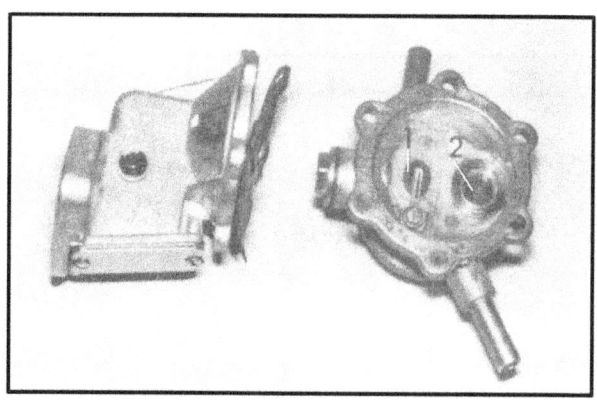

1. Inlet valve
2. Outlet valve

Removing and refitting

Remove and refit air filter housing complete. Remove fuel hoses. Detach fuel pump.

FUEL SYSTEM

WARM AIR REGULATING FLAP
Adjusting

Intake air pre-heating is controlled automatically by the actuating element. The flap must move easily if the warm air regulating mechanism is to function correctly. Check by detaching the thrust rod, if necessary coat the bearing points in the attachment section with a branded multi-purpose grease.

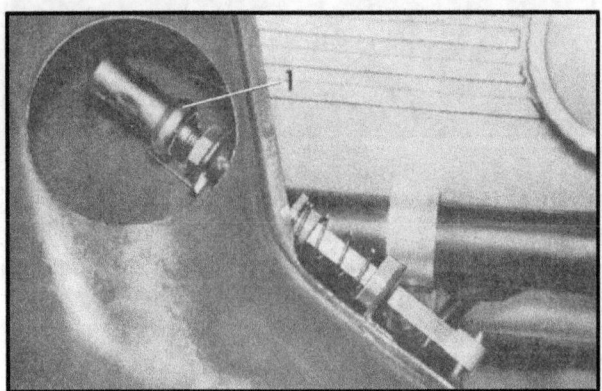

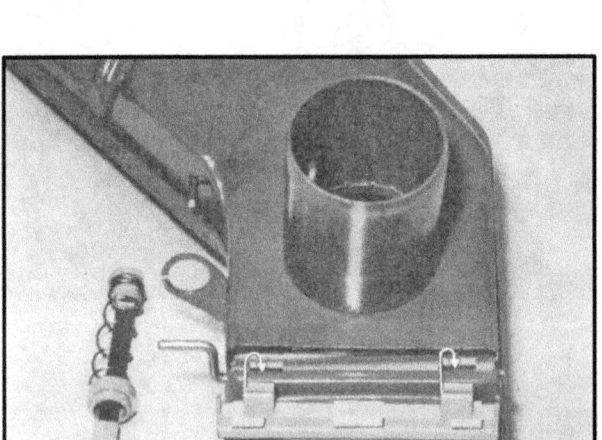

To adjust the flaps, place the cold air stub pipe together with the actuating element in a water bath at +59°F for approximately 5 minutes. The flap should just touch its upper stop. Correct by moving the actuating element after loosening the nut.

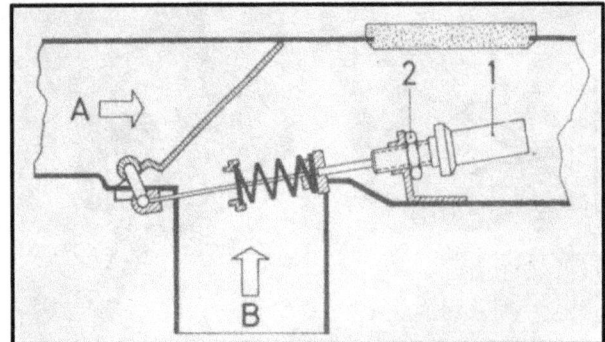

1. Actuating Element   A Cold air inlet
2. Nut   B Warm air inlet

AIR FILTER CASING COMPLETE
Removing and installing

Take off cover and detach air filter casing from carburetors. Pull off the breather hoses. Check condition of sealing rings and replace if necessary. If the air filter elements are clogged with dirt, strike lightly to free and blow through from the inside with compressed air at maximum 5 atmg (70 psi).

1. Sealing ring

FUEL SYSTEM

EXHAUST EMISSION CONTROL SYSTEM

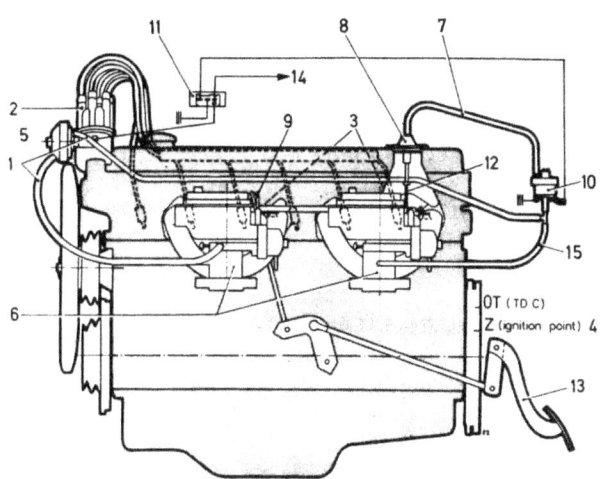

1. Vacuum hose
2. Distributor
3. Main idle adjustment screw (not shown)
4. Distributor points
5. Distributor vacuum hose
6. Carburetor
7. Vacuum hose
8. Dashpot
9. Throttle linkage
10. Magnetic switch
11. Speed sensitive electronic control
12. Adjustment pad
13. Accelerator pedal
14. Ignition lock
15. Vacuum hose

Automatic choke carburetor
Checking

The notch on the choke housing must be opposite the second ridge (in a clockwise direction) on the choke block.

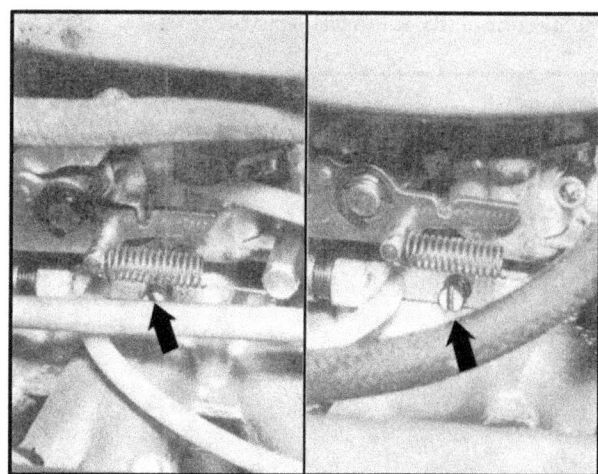

Idle mixture screw

Adjust idle mixture with exhaust tester

Zero and connect the tester. With the air cleaner in position and the engine idling, use the two mixture regulating screws to obtain a CO mixture value of 1.5 – 2.5%. The engine should continue to run smoothly and evenly.

Increased idling speed

The increased idling speed must still be less than the shift speed. Pull off the vacuum hose and accelerate the engine. After the engine speed has again dropped, it should settle at 1500 – 1600 rpm. To correct, loosen nut and turn damper until the engine speed is 1500 – 1600 rpm. After completing the adjustment, reconnect the vacuum hose. The adjusting pad must lift away from the accelerator linkage.

EXHAUST EMISSION CONTROL SYSTEM
Description

A car fitted with this system can be identified by a plate inside the engine compartment, on the left side front wheel housing.

Emmision control is accomplished through modification of standard engine components. A double acting vacuum unit connected to the distributor eliminates spark advance in the lower speed ranges, during idling and during deceleration. A speed sensitive relay is used in conjunction with a magnetic switch to control distributor movement. During deceleration a diaphragm system delays throttle closure.

The intake manifold has been modified to allow some exhaust gases to recirculate back (EGR system) into the intake manifold where they mix with the incoming fuel mixture. This system was adapted to the 3.0 models starting with the 1972 models.

Fumes from the gas tank are lead to the second carburetor where they are drawn into the engine and burned. They flow from the gas tank through a storage tank and charcoal filled canister before entering the carburetor. In addition, excessive fuel in the carburetors is returned to the fuel tank through the excess fuel return valve. Crankcase fumes and vapors are prevented from entering the atmosphere, by being drawn into the air cleaner and into base of carburetor. This system is maintenance free.

FUEL SYSTEM

1. Vacuum hose
2. Nut

If engine will not return to slow idling speed: the vacuum hoses are leaking, the diaphragm in the closure damper is leaking, the solenoid valve is not grounded (earthed), the solenoid valve is not operating, the engine speed sensor switch is defective or, the connection at the engine speed switch is incorrect. To check the solenoid switch, pull off cable. Connect the test lamp to the cable and the solenoid switch. Run the engine up to over 2000 rpm. The solenoid switch is not faulty if the test lamp lights up.

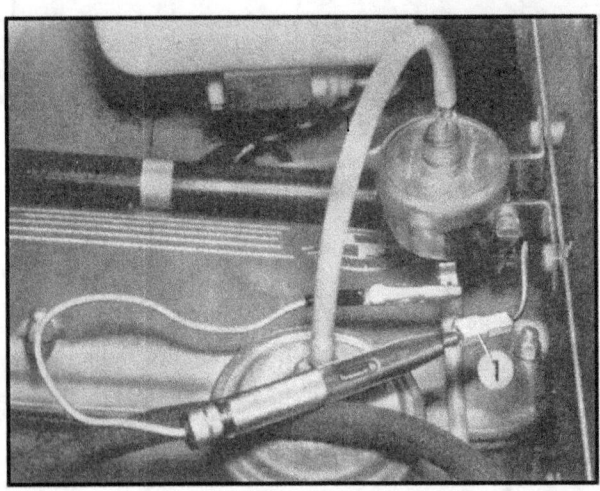

Connect test lamp to earth (ground and to plug green/blue lead. Run the engine at over 2000 rpm. If the test lamp does not light up, the engine speed sensing switch is defective.

THROTTLE CLOSURE DELAY SYSTEM
Description

To control emissions during decleration, throttle plate is held slightly opened by means of a vacuum operated diaphragm unit. At a speed of over 1920 ± 100 RPM speed sensing relay actuates two way valve to vent vacuum diaphragm unit to atmosphere. A spring, in vacuum unit, then causes carburetor linkage to open throttle 3-4°. As engine speed drops below 1800 ± 100 RPM, relay interrupts flow of current to valve. This allows intake manifold vacuum to retract plunger of vacuum unit and return throttle to idle position.

If system does not function correctly and throttle diaphragm unit is adjusted properly, disconnect vacuum line from throttle diaphragm unit and check for vacuum. If vacuum is present but plunger does not operate, replace throttle diaphragm unit. If no vacuum is present, check for leaky hoses and connections and make sure speed relay is properly grounded. Unplug lead to two way valve and connect voltmeter. With engine speed above 2000 RPM, if reading is 12 volts, replace valve. If reading is 0 volts, replace speed relay.

THROTTLE DIAPHRAGM UNIT
Testing

Disconnect vacuum hose from unit. By means of throttle linkage, accelerate engine to 2500 RPM. Gradually decrease throttle opening until contacting set screw. Speed obtained should be 1800 ± 50 RPM. If adjustment is required, loosen diaphragm unit clamp and turn unit until proper speed is obtained. Recheck for proper adjustment.

FUEL EVAPORATION CONTROL SYSTEM
Description

The system consists of a purge system leading from fuel tank to hose of crankcase ventilation system. Between the fuel tank and the crankcase ventilation system is a vapor storage tank and an activated carbon canister. Because of the sealed filler cap, all vapor in gas tank must pass into engine where it is burned. Provision is made for all excess fuel to return to the gas tank. As the system is designed and installed it requires no routine maintenance. Any component that looks damaged should be repaired or replaced.

EXCESS FUEL RETURN VALVE
Description

This valve returns excess fuel to fuel tank to avoid excessive overheating of fuel which prevents vapor lock. This promotes a more consistant idle mixture to reduce exhaust emissions.

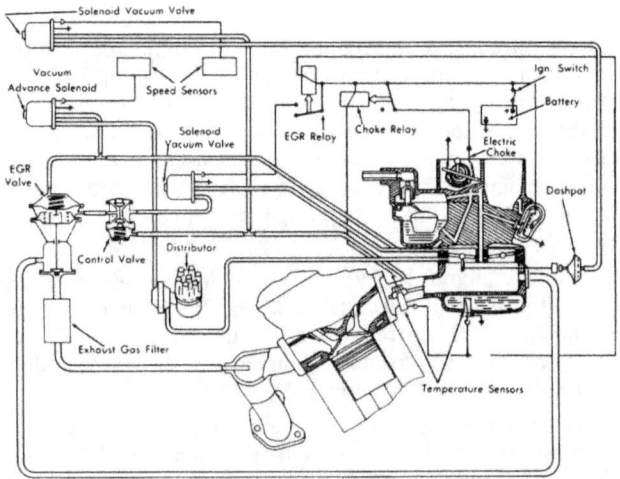

DASHPOT
Testing

Step on accelerator and release quickly. RPM must return to idle with a certain delay. If not, adjust dashpot.

FUEL SYSTEM

Adjustment
With vacuum hose removed from dashpot, idle speed must increase to 1700 ± 50 RPM. If necessary, adjust by turning dashpot in bracket. Reinstall vacuum hose and test dashpot system.

VACUUM CONTROL VALVE
Operation
When manifold vacuum is high, valve closes off vacuum to EGR valve. During periods of acceleration, control valve opens allowing vacuum to operate second stage of EGR valve.

Testing
Ensure that all vacuum connections are correct. Remove red vacuum hose from carburetor and connect to vacuum source. Engine speed should not decrease. Disconnect blue vacuum hose from second stage of EGR valve and feel for vacuum. If vacuum is present, valve is defective. With engine at idle, blow through blue hose, air should flow freely. *NOTE—Do not use pressurized air.* Reconnect vacuum hoses and disconnect white vacuum hose from dashpot. Turn dashpot until plunger is free of throttle lever and reconnect vacuum hose. Remove white vacuum hose from carburetor and connect to secondary venting hose and plug loose end of secondary vent hose. Start engine and detach white hose from intake manifold to control valve. A considerable speed drop must occur and blue hose connected to EGR valve must be under vacuum. If not, replace control valve.

TEMPERATURE CONTROLLED VACUUM SOLENOID
Testing
This valve is controlled by the temperature sensor mounted in the intake manifold water passage. When coolant temperature is below 113° F., solenoid closes vacuum flow to vacuum control valve. This prevents second stage from operating, thereby improving cold driving.

VACUUM SOLENOID VALVE
Testing
Ensure that valve is open to vacuum flow when de-energized. Connect solenoid to 12 volt power source, valve should close.

EGR SYSTEM
Description
This system recirculates a small amount of exhaust gases into intake manifold during low engine loads and a larger amount as loads and acceleration increase to reduce NOX emissions. A dual diaphragm valve begins to open valve disc at about 1900 rpm. The first stage is controlled by carburetor throttle position. The second stage responds to pressure in the intake manifold. When second stage is opened, valve is completely open. The valve is mounted on firewall.

EGR System Test
Connect infra-red exhaust gas analyzer and allow engine to idle. Lift diaphragm of EGR valve with finger or dull tool, using care not to damage diaphram. Idle speed must drop about 500 RPM and CO reading remain steady or increase slightly. If CO reading decreases, or if engine stalls, air leaks exist in system. Remove black vacuum hose from caburetor and connect to secondary venting hose of crankcase ventilation system and plug loose end of secondary venting hose. First stage of EGR valve must open and RPM should drop about 150-200 RPM. Now, remove red vacuum hose from carburetor and connect to secondary venting hose. Remove white vacuum hose from control valve on firewall. Again RPM should decrease 150-200 RPM. If either test fails, valve is defective and must be replaced.

EGR VALVE
Cleaning
If tests indicate EGR valve requires cleaning, remove major deposits from valve using suitable tool. If sharp tools are used, use care not to damage diaphragm or scratch valve. Complete cleaning operation using a suitable solvent and brush.

EXHAUST GAS FILTER
Replace the exhaust gas filter every 12,000 miles of operation.

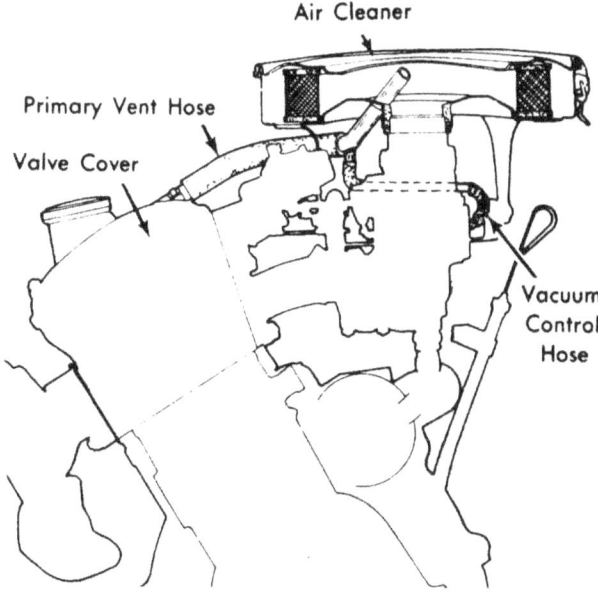

Crankcase ventilation system

CRANKCASE VENTILATION
Description
System prevents crankcase fumes from entering atmosphere, by drawing them into engine to be burned. Two hoses, one from valve cover to air cleaner; the other from primary hose to carburetor. The second hose has a control orifice in it. The system is maintenance free, but any hose that looks cracked or damaged should be replaced.
Illustration 6

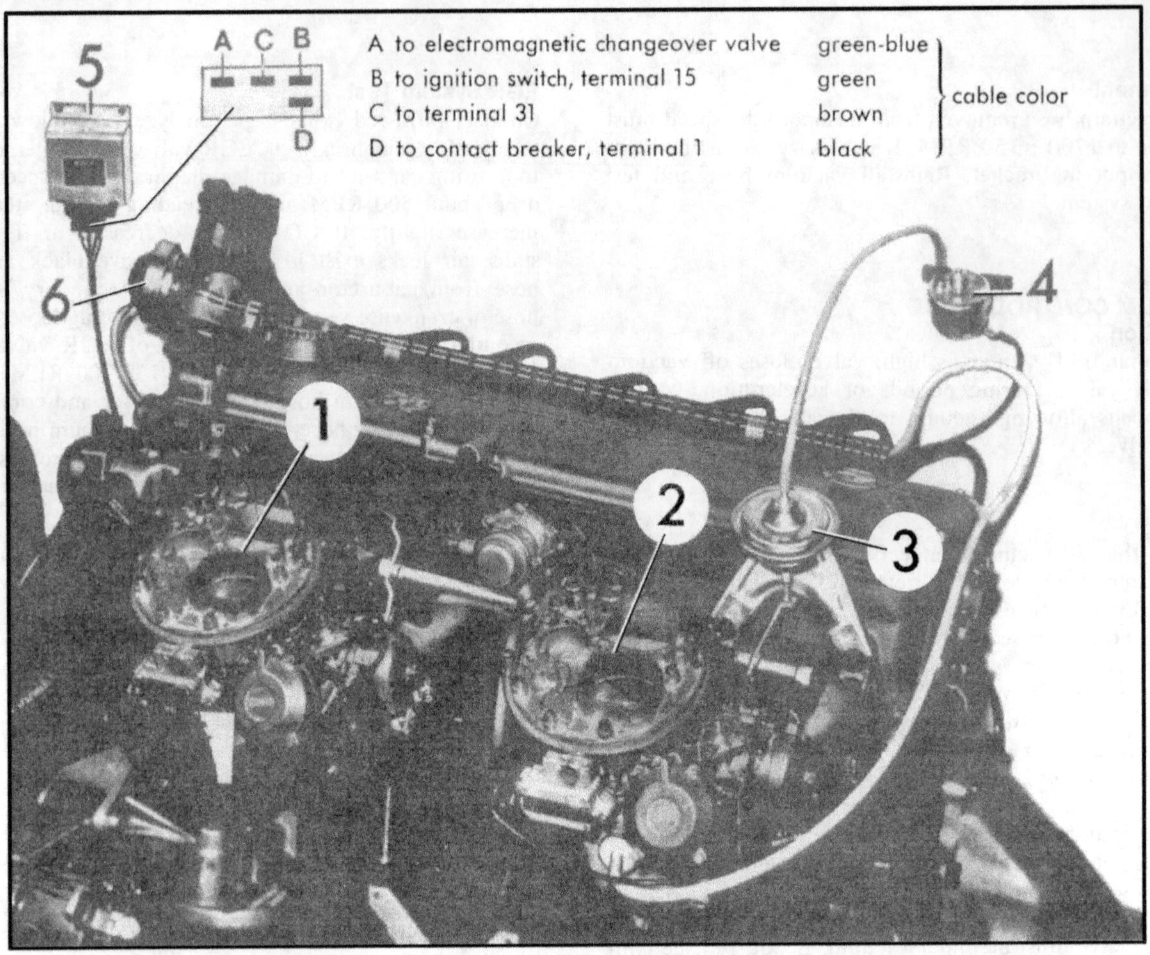

FUEL SYSTEM

A to electromagnetic changeover valve	green-blue
B to ignition switch, terminal 15	green
C to terminal 31	brown
D to contact breaker, terminal 1	black

cable color

Twin 35/40 INAT carburetors with exhaust emission control system

1 Front carburetor
2 Rear carburetor
3 Closure damper
4 Electromagnetic changeover valve
5 Electronic switch
6 Distributor with double acting vacuum box

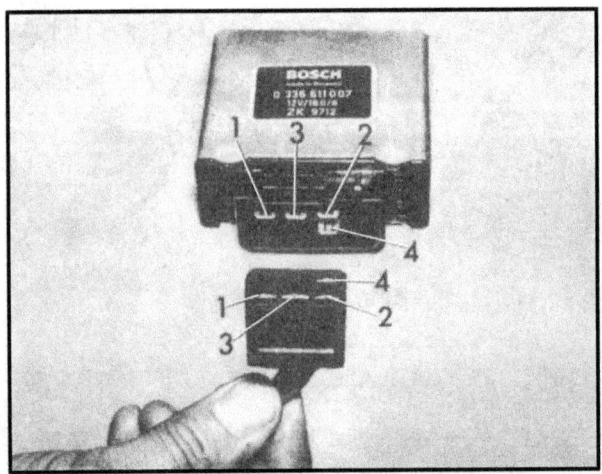

Checking plug connection to engine switch
1. green/blue
2. green
3. brown
4. black

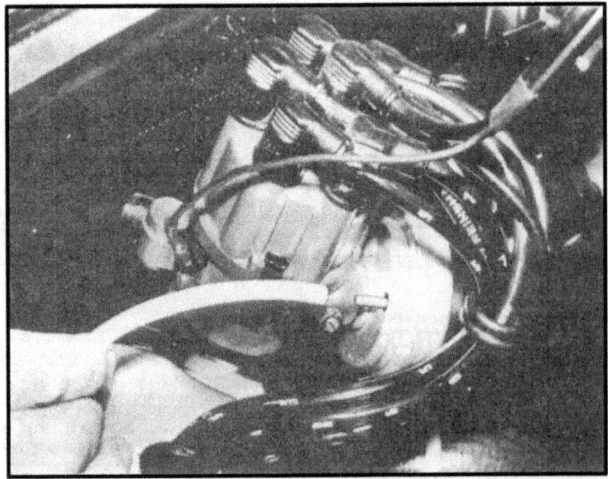

Ignition retarding
Checking

All vacuum hoses remain connected. The engine should run at a speed of 900 rpm. Ignition should occur between TDC and 5° ATDC, that is to say the TDC (OT) mark on the flywheel should still be visible in the inspection hole. The TDC mark on automatic transmissions is a short peg on the flywheel. On the earlier version without short TDC peg, mark the TDC on the flywheel with a colored pencil. Correct by moving cam. When the vacuum hose is removed, the engine speed should rise.

IGNITION

INDEX

	Page		Page
TIMING (ENGINE)	13	Removing and installing	14
Adjusting	13	Replacing contact breaker points	14
DISTRIBUTOR	13	Overhauling	14
Checking (engine tester)	13		

TIMING (ENGINE)
Adjusting

Satisfactory contact breaker points and correct dwell angle are essential for accurate ignition timing.

Connect the dwell angle tester and turn engine over on starter. Set dwell angle to the minimum value by rotating contact bracket.

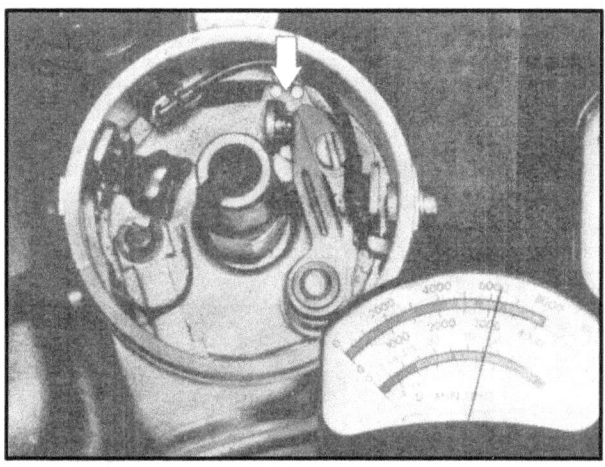

Pull the vacuum hose away from vacuum chamber and set engine to run at 1700 rpm at working temperature. After ignition timing has been carried out, screw out adjusting screw until there is no play between rotary spindle and stop.

Switch off the dwell angle reading with the thumb wheel. Illuminate the ball mark on the flywheel with the timing light. On automatic transmissions: long peg is ignition firing point, short peg is TDC. Turn the distributor until the pointer on the clutch housing indicates the center of the ball mark.

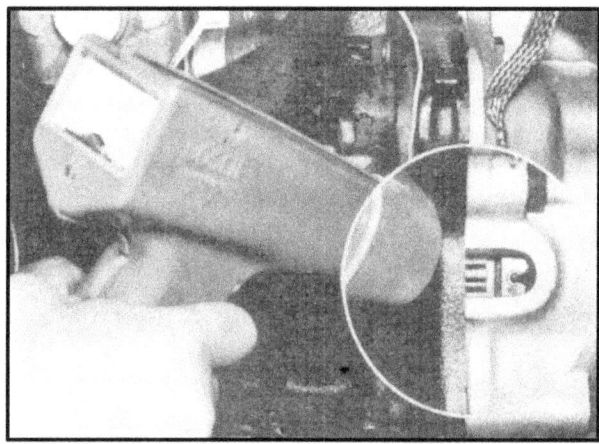

DISTRIBUTOR
Checking (engine tester)

Make visual check on service condition of contacts. Check distributor rotor for resistance. Resistance of suppressed rotor approximately 5000 Ohms.

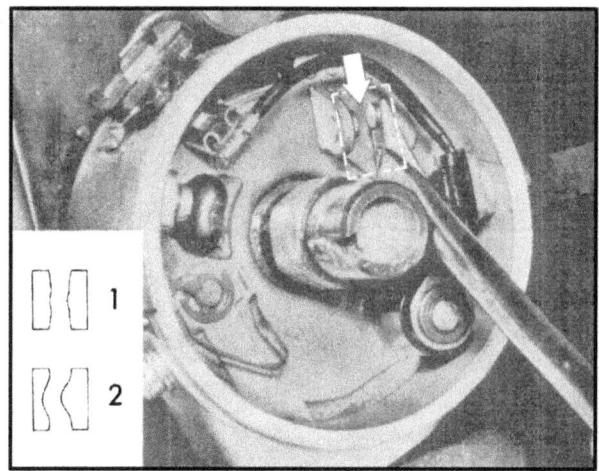

1. Permissible
2. Unsatisfactory, must be replaced.

IGNITION

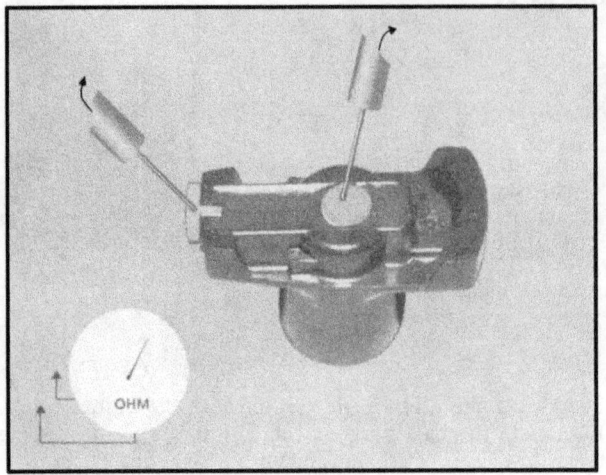

A-Distance to turn distributor when reinstalling

Removing and installing

Take off the distributor cap. Pull off the cable from terminal 1, then pull off the vacuum hose. Move the piston in cylinder 1 to TDC, so that the notch on the distributor rotor is aligned with the notch on the distributor body. Loosen the clamp bolt and pull out the distributor.

On vehicles with exhaust emission control system a distributor with double acting vacuum box is installed. Hose A leads to vacuum connection on carburetor. Hose B leads to the electromagnetic changeover valve.

Replacing contact breaker points

Pull off the flat connector and slacken the screw. Extract the contact breaker points.

When installing: Clean grease from new points. Soak the felt pad with engine oil. Grease the cam and follower on the contact breaker arm with Bosch Ft 1 v 4 grease. Adjust ignition timing.

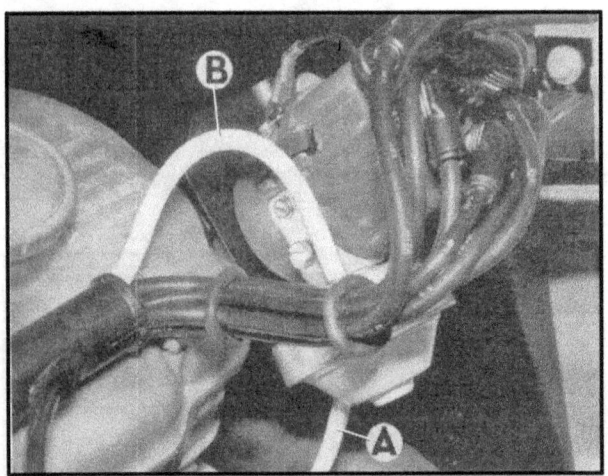

A-Vacuum advance hose
B-Vacuum retard hose

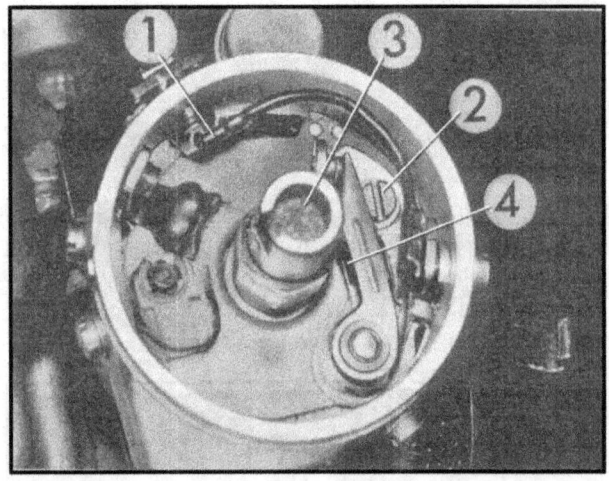

1. Flat connector
2. Screw
3. Felt pad
4. Cam and follower

When installing: Turn the distributor rotor back through approximately 1.4 inches from the notch in the distributor body anti-clockwise.

Engage the distriburor drive in the camshaft drive.

Overhauling

Take off the vacuum box. Remove the contact breaker plate. Using two screwdrivers, pull the cam upwards until the circlip snaps out off the groove. Do not pull out the lubricating felt pad or the circlip beneath it will escape. Drill out the taper pin with a 3 mm drill.

IGNITION

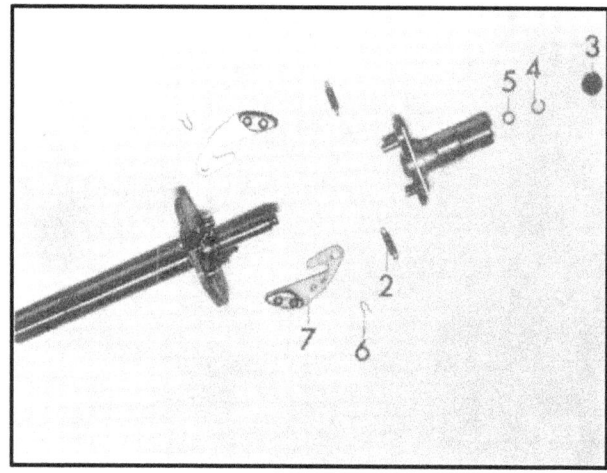

Pull out the distributor shaft with centrifugal weights and cam. Check bearing bushes and replace if necessary. Detach springs, lubricating felt pad, circlip, washer and cam. Remove keepers and centrifugal weights.

2. Springs
3. Felt pad
4. Circlip
5. Washer
6. Keepers
7. Centrifugal weights

When installing: Lubricate the cam with engine oil and the centrifugal weights with Bosch Ft 1 v 22 grease before installing.

If the retainers or springs are replaced, check the centrifugal advance curve on the distributor test bench and adjust if necessary.

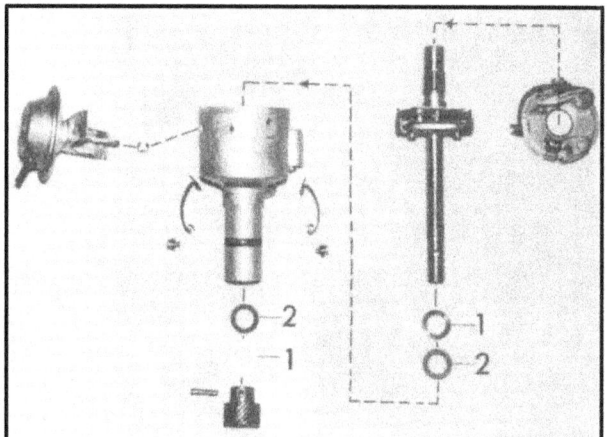

1. Thrust washer
2. Insulating washer

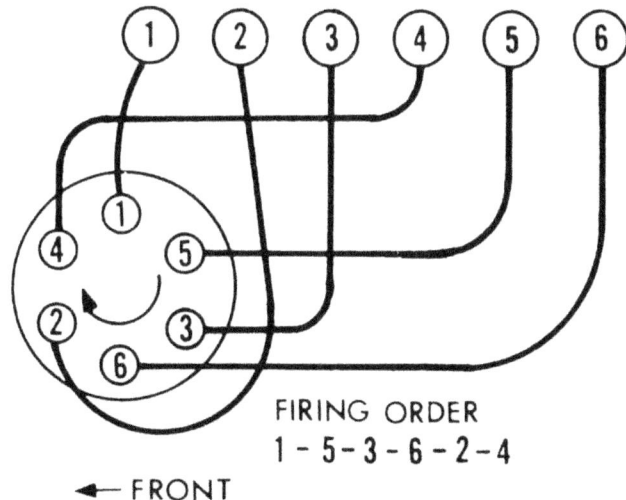

Firing order

NOTES

COOLING SYSTEM

INDEX

	Page		Page
COOLING SYSTEM	17	Replacing	18
Checking for leaks	17	FRONT LEFT OR RIGHT EXHAUST PIPE	19
RADIATOR	17	Removing and installing	19
Removing and installing	17	FRONT AND REAR EXHAUST MUFFLERS	19
EXHAUST SYSTEM COMPLETE	18	Removing and installing	19
Removing	18	REAR EXHAUST MUFFLER	19
Bleeding the cooling system	18	Replacing	19
GASKET BETWEEN EXHAUST MANIFOLD AND EXHAUST PIPE	18	FRONT EXHAUST MUFFLER	19
		Replacing	19

COOLING SYSTEM
Checking for leaks
Fix test gauge on compensating tank. With hand pump induce a pressure of approximately 1 atm (14.22 psi) in the cooling system. The cooling system is completely free of leaks if there is no pressure drop after 1-2 minutes.

Fix filler cap and test gauge on union. Induce pressure with hand pump. The opening pressure must agree with the figure shown on the filler cap.

RADIATOR
Removing and installing
Remove filler cap. Drain off water. Detach hose. Remove hoses. Detach support. Lift out radiator.

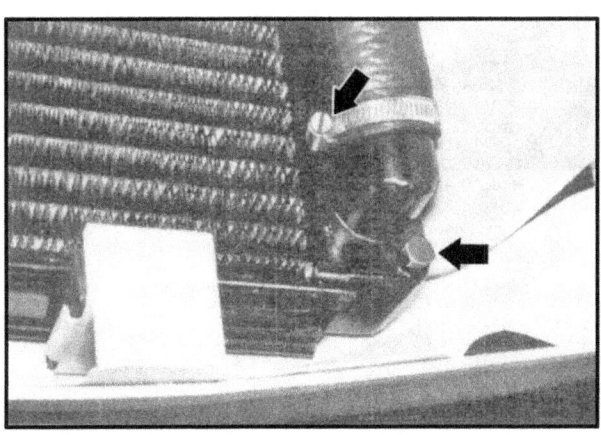

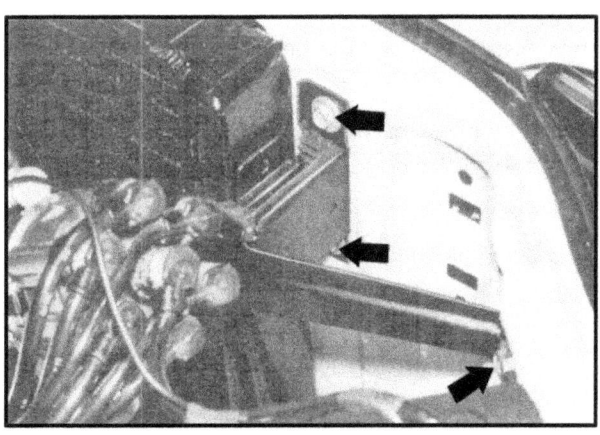

18 COOLING SYSTEM

When installing: Retainer stay must press on mounting on radiator. If the radiator incorporates a transmission oil cooler, detach the feed and return lines.

When installing: In the event of transmission damage, the transmission oil cooler in the side coolant tank must be flushed through with washing petrol or mineral oil immediately after removal. The radiator should then be propped up so that the transmission oil cooler can dry before the radiator is re-installed.

Bleeding the cooling system
Loosen the bleed screw. Run the engine at a fast idle speed until water emerges free from air bubbles. Add water to the equalizing reservoir to maintain the level while bleeding the cooling system.

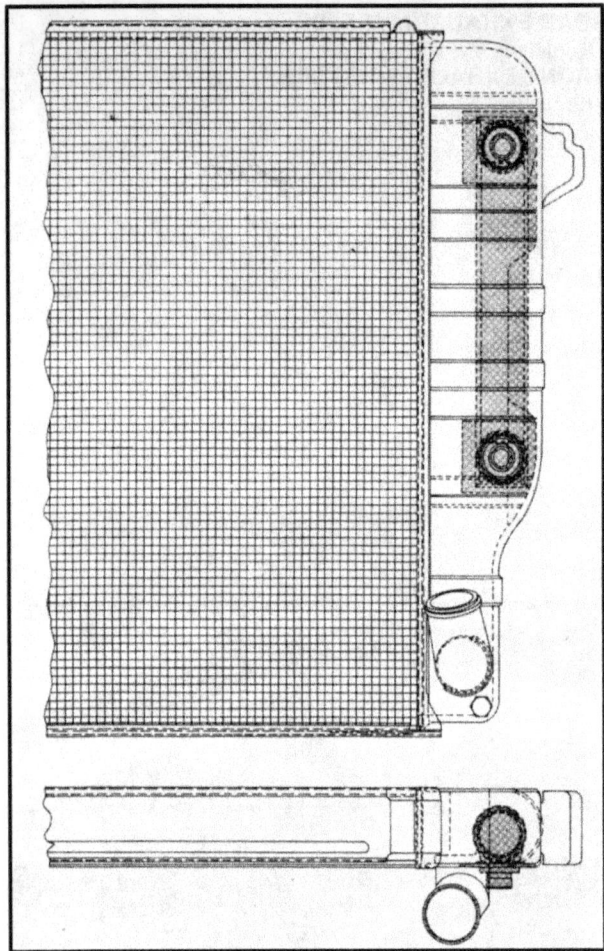

GASKET BETWEEN EXHAUST MANIFOLD AND EXHAUST PIPE
Replacing
Detach the pipe clip. Remove the exhaust pipe.

When installing: Coat the threaded pins with Molykote paste.

Detach the retaining rings from the rear muffler.

EXHAUST SYSTEM COMPLETE
Removing
Detach exhaust pipes from exhaust manifold.

When installing: Coat the threaded pins with Molykote paste.

Detach the pipe clip. Remove the retaining rings from the rear exhaust muffler.

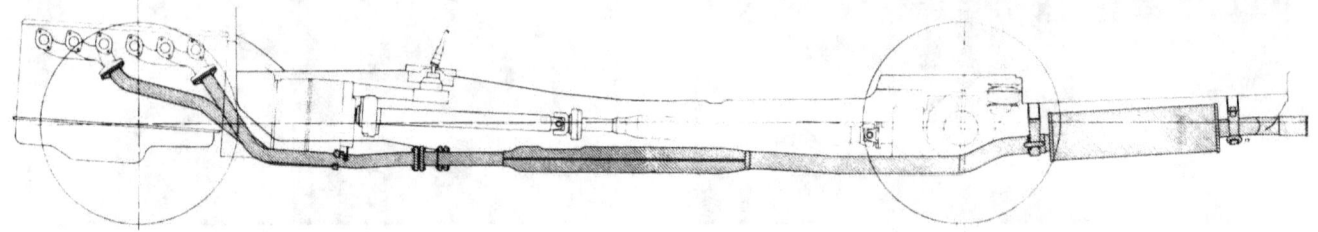

COOLING SYSTEM

FRONT LEFT OR RIGHT EXHAUST PIPE
Removing and installing

Separate the exhaust pipe from the exhaust manifold. Remove the pipe clip and triangular flange.

When installing: Check condition of sealing rings.

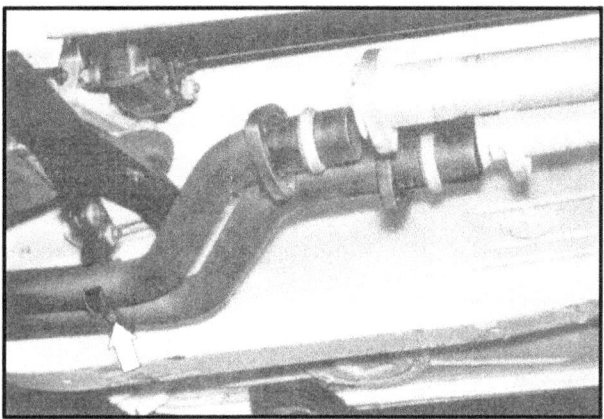

Remove the retaining rings from the rear muffler.

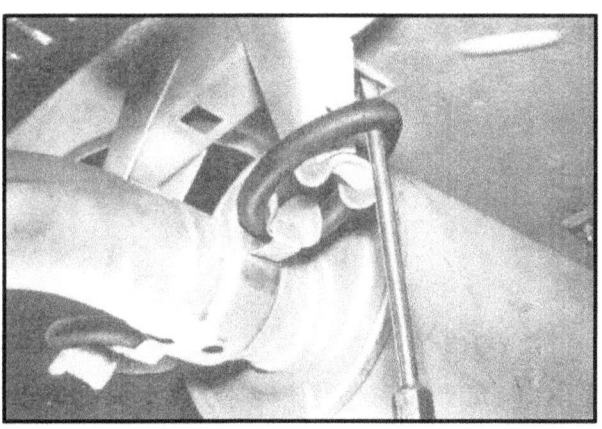

FRONT AND REAR EXHAUST MUFFLERS
Removing and installing

Detach the triangular flanges. Remove the retaining rings. On coupe models detach the triangular flanges. Unscrew the rear exhaust muffler. Unscrew the rear exhaust pipe.

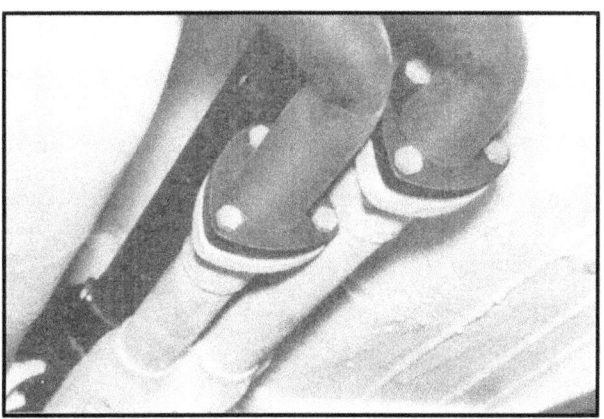

REAR EXHAUST MUFFLER
Replacing

Remove the front and rear exhaust mufflers. Cut round the outer pipe just behind the welded seam (A approximately 10mm/0.4 in.) until the inner pipe with the rear exhaust muffler can be pulled out. Push the new rear exhaust muffler into the outer pipe. Install the exhaust system but do not tighten the triangular flanges. Align the rear exhaust muffler so that the tail pipe is horizontal. Tack weld the outer and inner pipes together. Remove the exhaust system. Weld all round the front and rear exhaust mufflers. Re-install the exhaust system.

On coupe models remove front and rear mufflers. Detach both U-bolts. Separate the rear exhaust muffler from the front muffler and the rear exhaust pipe. Install the new rear exhaust muffler. Reinstall the exhaust system.

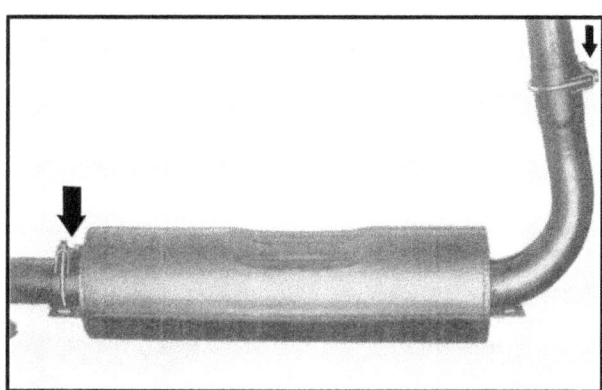

FRONT EXHAUST MUFFLER
Replacing

For procedure, see "rear exhaust muffler – replacing." On coupe models for procedure, see "rear exhaust muffler – replacing." Do not remove rear exhaust pipe.

NOTES

ENGINE

INDEX

	Page		Page
ENGINE	23	CHAIN TENSIONER PISTON	34
Removing and installing	23	Removing and installing	34
EXCHANGE ENGINE	23	TIMING CHAIN (UPPER AND LOWER TIMING CASE REMOVED)	34
Installing	23	Removing and installing	34
ROCKER COVER	24	TENSIONER RAIL/GUIDE RAIL (TIMING CASE COVER REMOVED)	35
Removing and installing	24	Replacing	35
CYLINDER HEAD	24	TIMING GEAR SET	35
Removing and installing	24	Replacing	35
CYLINDER HEAD GASKET	26	ROCKER SHAFTS	35
Replacing	26	Removing and installing	35
ONE VALVE GUIDE–(VALVE REMOVED)	26	VALVE OPERATING CLEARANCES	36
Replacing	26	Adjusting	36
VALVE SEATS AND VALVES (CYLINDER HEAD REMOVED)	26	VALVES (ROCKER SHAFTS REMOVED)	36
Regrinding	26	Removing and installing	36
CYLINDER HEAD SEALING FACE – (CYLINDER HEAD DISMANTLED)	26	OIL PUMP	36
Skimming	26	Removing and installing	36
OIL SUMP	26	ROLLER CHAIN FOR OIL PUMP DRIVE	37
Removing and installing		Replacing	37
Engine installed	26	OIL PUMP	37
Engine removed	27	Dismantling and reassembling	37
UPPER TIMING CASE COVER	27	GUIDE TUBE FOR OIL DIPSTICK	37
Removing and installing	27	Replacing	37
UPPER AND LOWER TIMING CASE COVER	28	WATER PUMP	38
Removing and installing	28	Removing and installing	38
OIL SEAL IN TIMING CASE COVER (ENGINE INSTALLED)	28	Reconditioning	38
Replacing	28	FAN	39
OIL SEAL IN ENGINE END COVER (CLUTCH SIDE)–(FLYWHEEL REMOVED)	28	Removing and installing	39
Replacing	28	FAN CLUTCH	39
CRANKSHAFT	29	Removing and installing	39
Removing and installing	29	COOLANT THERMOSTAT	39
Replacing	30	Removing and installing	39
BALL BEARING ON CRANKSHAFT	30	THERMOSTAT HOUSING	39
Replacing	30	Removing and installing	39
STARTER RING	30	COOLANT THERMOMETER SENSOR	39
Replacing	30	Replacing	39
FLYWHEEL	31	FRONT INTAKE MANIFOLD WITH CARBURETOR	40
Removing and installing	31	Removing and installing	40
TORQUE CONVERTER DRIVING DISC	31	FRONT INTAKE MANIFOLD	40
Replacing	31	Replacing	40
VIBRATION DAMPER WITH HUB	31	REAR INTAKE MANIFOLD WITH CARBURETOR	40
Removing and installing	31	Removing and installing	40
VIBRATION DAMPER	31	REAR INTAKE MANIFOLD	41
Replacing	31	Replacing	41
ONE CONNECTING ROD (PISTON REMOVED)	31	COVER ON FRONT INTAKE MANIFOLD	41
Replacing	31	Removing and installing	41
ONE SMALL END BUSH (CONNECTING ROD REMOVED)	32	COVER ON REAR INTAKE MANIFOLD	41
Replacing	32	Removing and installing	41
ONE PISTON	32	FRONT EXHAUST MANIFOLD	41
Removing and installing	32	Removing and installing	41
CAMSHAFT	33	REAR EXHAUST MANIFOLD	41
Removing and installing	33	Removing and installing	41
Replacing	33	RIGHT ENGINE MOUNTING	41
		Replacing	41
		LEFT ENGINE MOUNTING	41
		Replacing	41

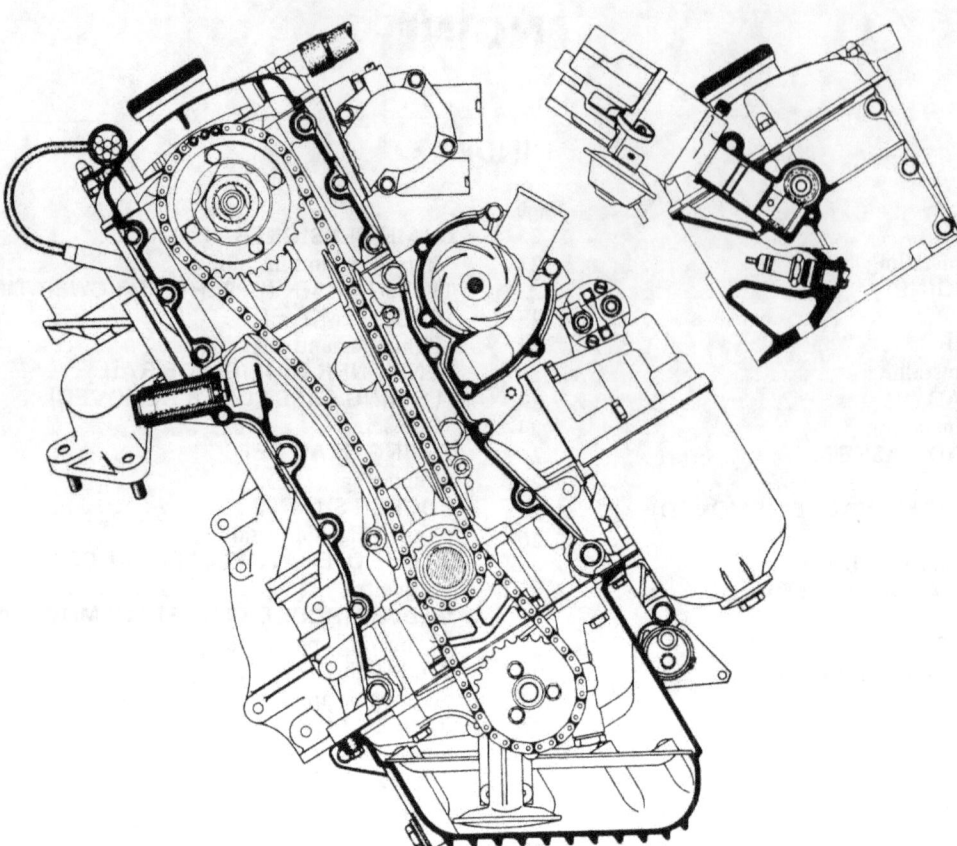

Cross-section showing timing chain

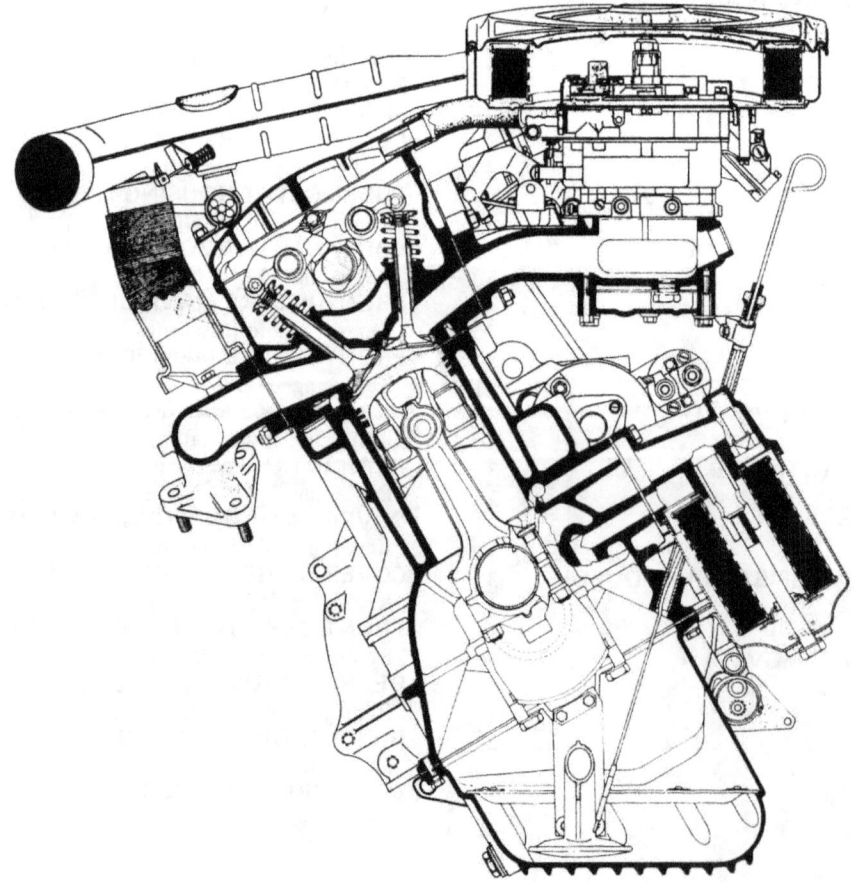

Cross-section through cylinder

ENGINE

Removing and installing

Disconnect the negative lead from battery. Remove and install engine compartment lid. Bleed cooling system. Remove and install radiator. Remove the screenwash tank and detach the air filter. Pull leads 1 and 4 away from thermometer element. Disconnect the earth (ground) lead from the rocker box and detach the fan. Remove the vacuum and fuel hoses and pull the lead off the automatic choke and the oil pressure switch. Disconnect the earth (ground) strap and detach the water hoses. Disconnect the lead from the solenoid switch. Detach lead and plug connection from alternator.

1-4. Leads

Detach accelerator linkage. Loosen both engine mountings. Remove lower apron on the front paneling. Only on vehicles with hydraulically assisted steering, detach high pressure pump at rear. Detach high pressure pump at front.

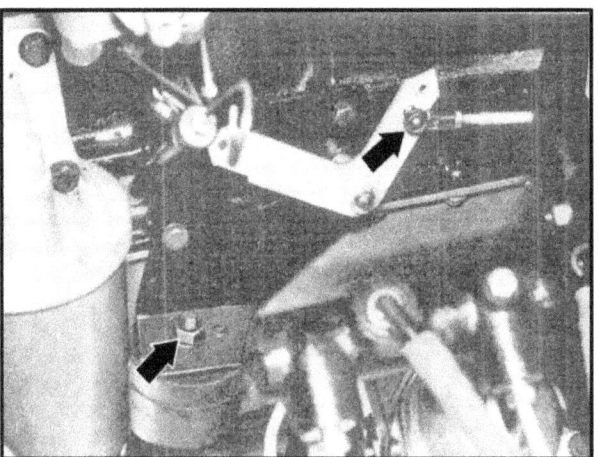

When installing: It should be possible to depress the V belt by 0.2—0.4".

Attach hoist 7000 at the front of the engine. Attach hoist 7000 at rear of engine. Remove gearbox. Push back sleeve. Remove circlip. Extract slave cylinder towards front. Take out the throwout lever with throwout fork from clutch housing.

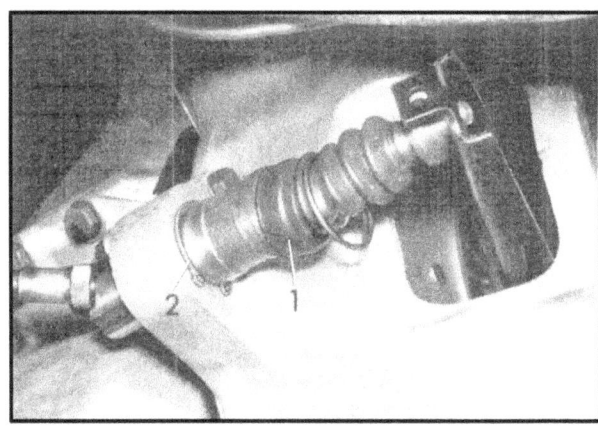

1. Sleeve
2. Circlip

When installing: Coat contact faces on throwout fork with Molykote Longterm 2 paste.

Raise the engine and swing out to the right.

EXCHANGE ENGINE
Installing

Change over the water hoses and studs for the air filter housing. Install the old support bracket, cover plate and clutch housing. Install the old engine mounting bracket on the right and then the left with the carburetor linkage. If high pressure oil pump is installed, take off the fan. Transfer the old belt pulley for the high pressure pump. Note the installed position of the driving disc.

1. Support bracket
2. Cover plate
3. Clutch housing

When installing: Make sure that the piston is in position inside the heat-sensitive element.

1. Driving disc
2. Piston

Tilt the alternator upward. Transfer the old bearing block. Fill the exchange engine with running-in oil.

ROCKER COVER
Removing and installing

Take off the air filter housing and the ignition cable tube. Remove the rocker cover.

When installing: Tighten screws in the order 1—9.

Screw tightening sequence

CYLINDER HEAD
Removing and installing

Detach the ground strap from the battery and drain the coolant.

When installing: Bleed the cooling system.

Pull off the fuel hose from the fuel pump. Detach the accelerator linkage and pull off cables. Detach the vacuum hose for the brake servo unit from the intake manifold. Take off the retaining bracket for the oil dipstick. Detach hoses.

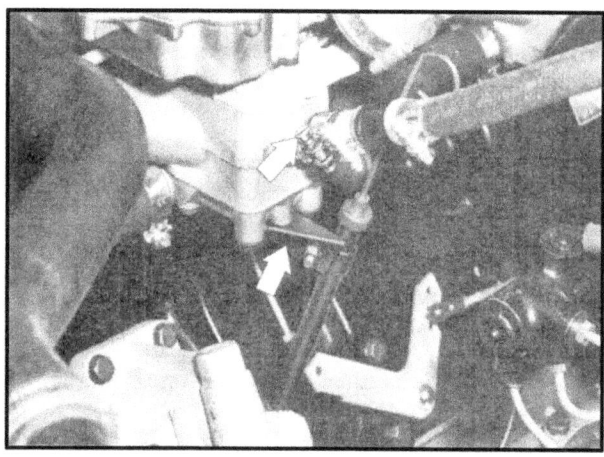

1. Pin

Turn the engine to bring the piston in cylinder 1 to the TDC position. The rotor finger will now point to the notch in the distributor body. Remove the upper timing case cover. Remove the chain tensioner piston. Bend back the locking tabs. Take off the chain sprocket.

Remove the pipe clip. Loosen the triangular flanges on the exhaust muffler. Separate the exhaust pipes from the exhaust manifolds.

When installing: Use new gaskets.

Coat the stud threads with Molykote paste. Loosen the cylinder head bolts. Prevent the rocker shafts from moving or turning by inserting retaining pins and remove the cylinder head.

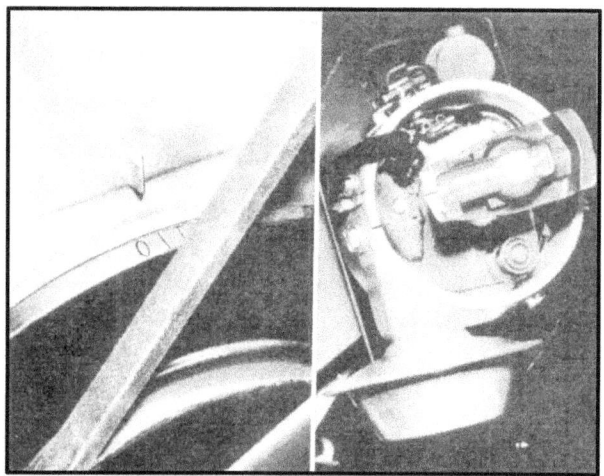

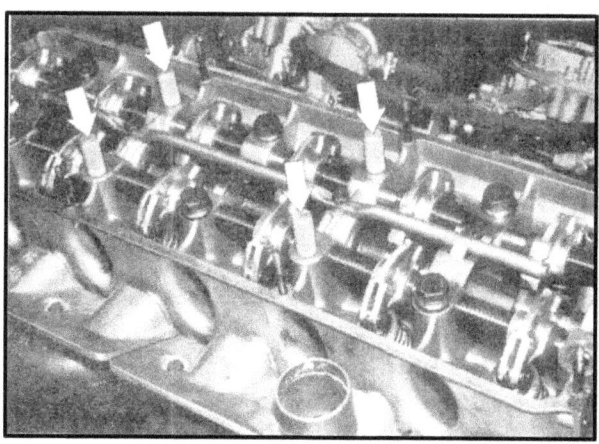

When installing: Tighten the bolts in the order 1–14 in 3 stages.

When installing: Mount the chain and sprocket so that the pin is at the bottom left. The hole in the sprocket must line up with the threaded hole and the cast-in projection.

Warm up the engine to operating temperature. After the test run, allow to cool down to 95°F. Finally tighten cylinder head bolts in 3 stages. No oil should be present in the blind holes or else there is a risk that the bolts may be tightened to the prescribed torque without exerting the correct pressure on the cylinder head. In addition, the crankcase threads may strip.

When installing: Always use a new cylinder head gasket.

Adjust valve clearances. Adjust engine idle speed and mixture.

CYLINDER HEAD GASKET
Replacing
Remove the cylinder head. Make sure the sealing faces on the cylinder head and crankcase are absolutely clean.

When installing: Use only genuine BMW cylinder head gaskets with accurately stamped holes for the passage of coolant. Coat the cylinder head gasket with Atmosit in the region of the timing case mating surface. If necessary, skim the cylinder head sealing face.

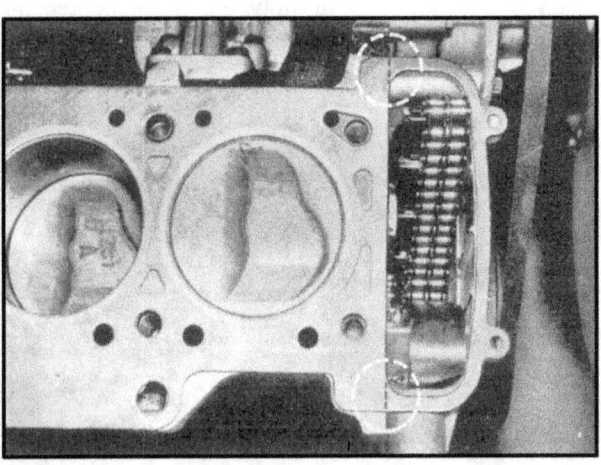

ONE VALVE GUIDE – (VALVE REMOVED)
Replacing
Check valve guide for wear. If the permitted wear limit has been exceeded, drive the valve guide out into the combustion chamber using drift 609, but without heating. Examine the hole in the cylinder head. If the permitted diameter has been exceeded, the hole must be remade out and an oversize valve guide installed. Heat the cylinder head. Press the valve guide into the combustion chamber from the camshaft side. The taper slot should be on the camshaft side. The drilling in drift 610 determines the installed depth 0.591 – 0.02 in. Ream out the valve guide to the prescribed internal diameter.

VALVE SEATS AND VALVES
(CYLINDER HEAD REMOVED)
Regrinding
If the minimum rim thickness is no longer present the valve must be replaced. After regrinding, the valve seats must not show any chatter marks.

When installing: check valve sealing with the gasoline test.

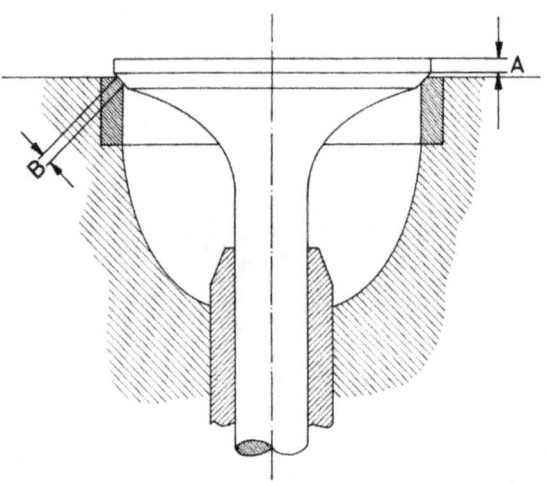

A. Minimum rim thickness
   Inlet – 0.059 ± 0.0039
   Exhaust – 0.086 ± 0.0039

B. Valve seat width
   Inlet – 0.063 – 0.079
   Exhaust – 0.079 – 0.095

CYLINDER HEAD SEALING FACE –
(CYLINDER HEAD DISMANTLED)
Skimming
When skimming the cylinder head, the original total thickness must not be reduced by more than 0.02 in. When the cylinder head is skimmed, the upper timing case cover must be remachined accordingly.

OIL SUMP
Removing and installing
Engine installed
Take off the front lower apron and drain engine oil. Take off the stabilizer. Loosen the alternator. Take off the high pressure oil pump – the hoses remain connected. Remove the screw. Loosen the bearing block until the oil sump can be detached. Partly detach the support bracket and loosen the oil sump. Turn the crankshaft until connecting rod 6 is above the sump joint line. Lower the front of the sump, turn the rear towards the support bracket and remove.

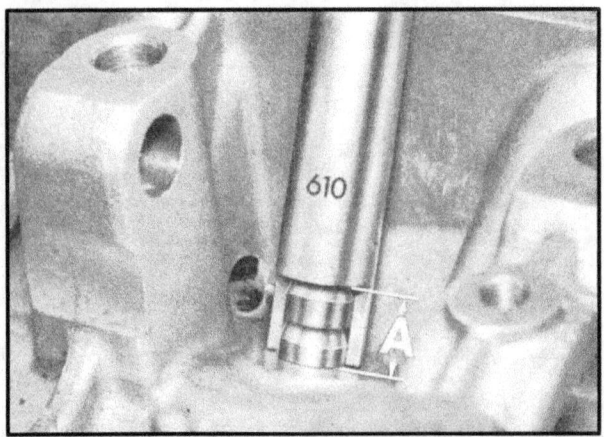

A = 0.591 – 0.02 in.

ENGINE 27

1. Screw

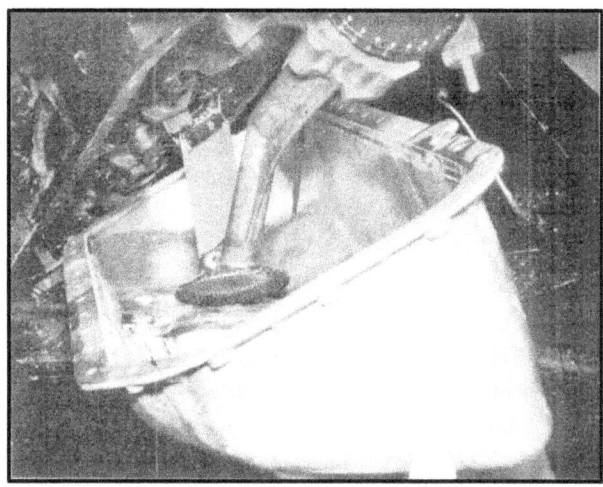

Engine removed
If a high pressure oil pump is fitted, loosen the bearing block. Detach the oil sump.

When installing: Clean the mating surfaces. Coat the junctions with the timing case cover and end cover with Atmosit.

UPPER TIMING CASE COVER
Removing and installing
Take off the distributor cap. Pull off cable 1 and vacuum hose. Take off the rocker cover and take off the thermostat housing cover. Remove the thermostat.

When installing: The hoop and arrow on the thermostat point forward.

Bleed the cooling system. Bring the piston in cylinder 1 to TDC. The distributor rotor will point to the notch in the distributor body. Loosen the timing case cover.

When installing: Screw up bolts 1 and 2 lightly at first. Next tighten bolts 3–8 in sequence, then tighten bolts 1 and 2.

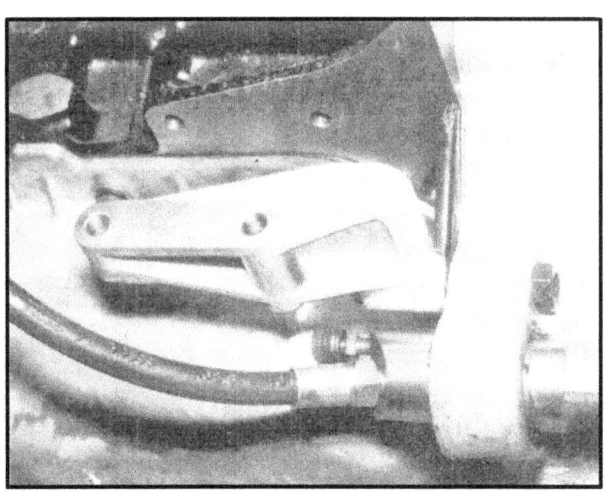

When installing: See removal procedure with engine removed.

ENGINE

Press the rotor arm in a clockwise direction. Take off the timing case cover with the helical gear.

When installing: Insert the helical gear into the camshaft.

Press the rotor arm away from the notch in the distributor body in an anti-clockwise direction. Coat the mating surface between the cylinder head and timing case cover with Atmosit and install the timing case cover. Check ignition timing.

1. Helical gear
A = 1.38 in.

OIL SEAL IN TIMING CASE COVER (ENGINE INSTALLED)
Replacing

Remove the front panel lower apron and loosen the alternator. Protect the radiator block with a card. Prevent the engine from turning by locking the teeth of the flywheel gear ring through the clutch housing inspection hole. Then loosen the nut. Pull off the vibration damper complete with the hub and lift out the oil seal.

When installing: If the hub is severely grooved, insert the oil seal so that the sealing lips are located in front of or behind the groove.

UPPER AND LOWER TIMING CASE COVER
Removing and installing

Remove the upper timing case cover and the chain tensioner piston. Loosen the alternator. Take off the fan clutch. Take off the vibration damper with hub and remove the timing case cover.

When installing: Coat the mating surfaces between oil sump and crankcase with Atmosit.

OIL SEAL IN ENGINE END COVER (CLUTCH SIDE)—(FLYWHEEL REMOVED)
Replacing

Drain the engine oil and loosen the oil sump. Lever the gasket carefully away in the region of the joint between the end cover and the oil sump. Take off the end cover.

When installing: Coat the junction between the end cover and oil sump joints with Atmosit.

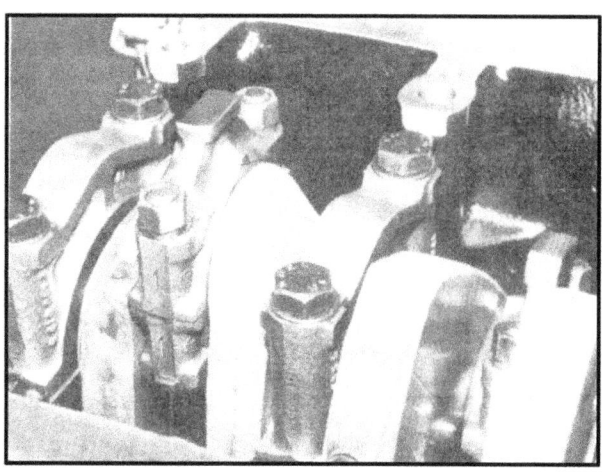

Take off the main bearing caps and lift out the crankshaft.

When installing: Do not interchange the bearing caps accidentally.

Bearing 1 is at the chain sprocket end. Attach the oil pump mounting together with bearing cap 4.

Drive the oil seal out of the end cover.

When installing: Press in the oil seal until it seats firmly.

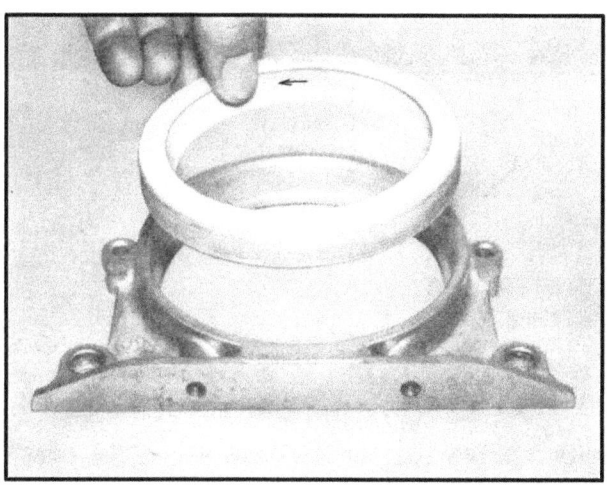

4. Bearing cap

CRANKSHAFT
Removing and installing

Remove the engine and attach the crankcase to the engine stand with assembly plate 7001. Take off the clutch, the cylinder head and remove the timing chain. Take off the oil pump. Before removing the crankshaft, measure axial play. If the maximum permitted play is exceeded, examine the main bearings. Remove the flywheel and take off the end cover.

When installing: Coat the junction between the end cover and oil sump joints with Atmosit.

Remove the big end bearing caps in the TDC position.

When installing: Each connecting rod and bearing cap is marked to indicate the corresponding cylinder. Connecting rod 1 is at the chain sprocket end. The cylinder reference or machining numbers must always be on the same side.

When installing: Install the main bearing caps so that the grooves coincide.

ENGINE

Replacing

Remove Woodruff key and take out the O-ring. Remove the chain sprocket using 7006 puller. Install the old ball bearing. The crankshaft is Tenifer treated and must be reground at the factory. The new bearing shells must be matched to the corresponding bearing journal diameter, that is to say the same red or blue color code spots must be present on both bearing shells and crankshaft.

Crankshaft distinguishing marks:

Blanked number on crank throw cheek
12 50 039 BMW 2500
12 50 042 BMW 2800

When installed:

BMW 2500: flush threaded journal
BMW 2800: stepped threaded journal

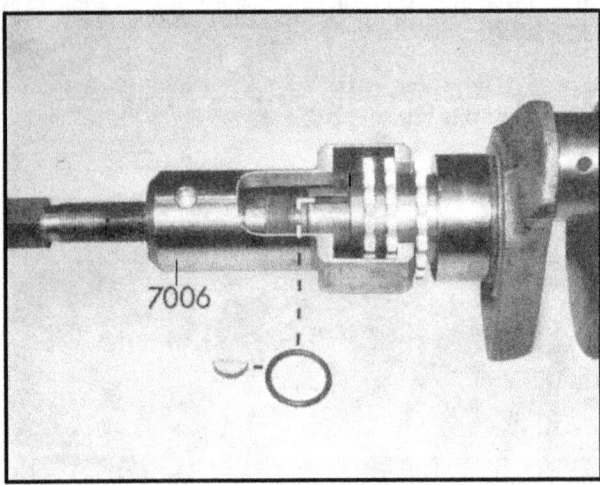

Check bearing play with Plastigage Type PG1. Check each bearing separately. The bearing surface must be oil-dry. Take the measurement at crankshaft top or bottom dead center and tighten the bearing cap to the prescribed torque. Do not disturb the crankshaft while measuring. Read off bearing play by comparing the width of the compressed plastic strip with the reference scale.

BALL BEARING ON CRANKSHAFT
Replacing

Using the Kukko extractor, remove the ball bearing complete with cover plate, felt ring and cap.

When installing: Pack the ball bearing with a branded multi-purpose grease, drip point at least 355°F. Insert the cover plate with the embossed side outwards. Soak the felt ring in hot tallow. Bed down the bearing cap until it seats firmly.

1. Ball bearing
2. Cover plate
3. Felt ring
4. Bearing cap

STARTER RING
Replacing

To simplify splitting, drill the starter ring 0.315 in. under a tooth gap with a 15/64 in. drill. Split the starter ring with a chisel next to the drilled hole.

When installing: Heat the new starter ring to 390 – 445°F using thermochrome pin.

Chamfered side of teeth on engine side. Drive the starter ring firmly against its seating with a brass drift.

ENGINE

FLYWHEEL
Removing and installing

Remove the clutch and check flywheel axial runout. Prevent the flywheel from turning with retaining catch 7007. On version without locating sleeves, mark the installed position of the flywheel in relation to the crankshaft (dynamic ignition timing mark). Loosen the expansion bolts. Always install new expansion bolts, using Loctite LT red. Take off the flywheel.

When installing: The friction face may be skimmed if necessary. However, the metal thickness at the friction face must not be less than 0.532 in.

TORQUE CONVERTER DRIVING DISC
Replacing

Remove the transmission. Prevent the flywheel from turning with retaining catch 7007. Loosen the expansion bolts and install the new driving disc.

VIBRATION DAMPER WITH HUB
Removing and installing

Loosen the alternator. Prevent the flywheel from turning by locking it in position through the clutch housing inspection hole. Loosen the nut and pull off the vibration damper. If the engine is installed, detach the front panel lower apron. Protect the radiator block with a card.

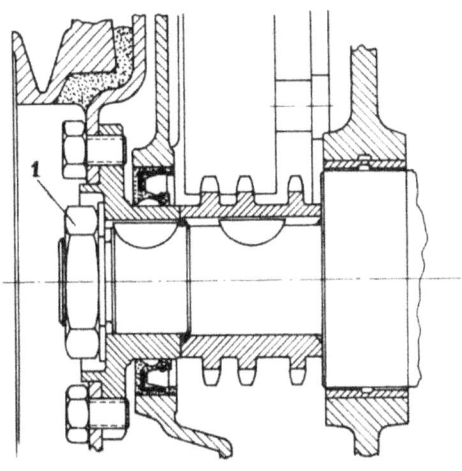

1. Nut

VIBRATION DAMPER
Replacing

Loosen the alternator. Line up the OT (TDC) marking on the vibration damper with the cast projection on the timing case cover and remove the damper.

ONE CONNECTING ROD (PISTON REMOVED)
Replacing

Within any one engine, install only connecting rods of the same weight group with a total tolerance of 0.141 oz. not including bearing shells. The weight group can be identified from the color coding. If the color coding is not

visible, a further connecting rod should be removed and the weights compared. Install the big end bearing shells in the connecting rod. Place Plastigage Type PG 1 onto an oil-dry big end bearing journal. Attach the connecting rod to the crankshaft. The machining numbers must all be on the same side of the engine. The oil drill way in the big end should face towards the timing chain. Tighten the bearing cap to the prescribed torque. Do not disturb either connecting rod or crankshaft. Take off the bearing cap. Determine bearing play by comparing the width of the compressed plastic strip with the reference scale.

ONE SMALL END BUSH
(CONNECTING ROD REMOVED)
Replacing
Press out the old small end bush.

When installing: Press in the new bush with the gap at 90° to the oil drill way.

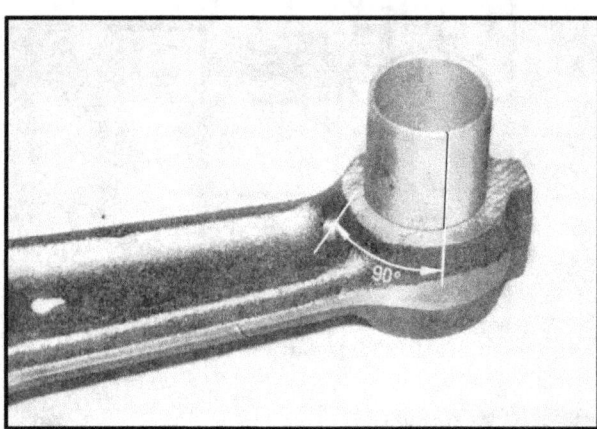

Open out, clean and de-burr the oil drill ways. Ream out the small end bush. The gudgeon pin must pass through the small end bush if light pressure is exerted. Check connecting rods for deviation from parallel.

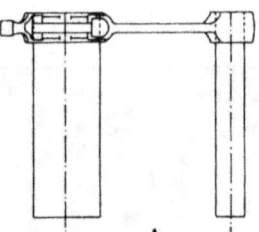 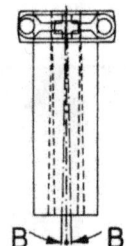

(A) maximum permitted distortion
(B) align if necessary.
   A. 150−0.04 mm (5.9055−0.0016 in.)
   B. 0° − 30'

ONE PISTON
Removing and installing
Take off the cylinder head and remove the oil sump. Take off the connecting rod big end bearing cap with the rod at BDC.

When installing: Both connecting rod and bearing cap are marked to indicate the correct cylinder.

Connecting rod 1 is at the chain sprocket end. The cylinder reference or machining numbers must always be on the same side. Press out the piston and connecting rod upwards.

When installing: The piston ring end gaps should be displaced through 180° in relation to one another. The arrow on the piston crown should point towards the timing chain end.

Remove the gudgeon pin.

When installing: The gudgeon pin is matched to its piston and should not be interchanged.

The oil drill way in the connecting rod small end boss should be on the side indicated by the arrow on the piston. Use only pistons of identical make and weight group. The weight group is indicated by a + or − stamped on the piston crown. Check piston installed clearance. Measure piston ring flank clearance. Remove the piston rings and check end gaps.

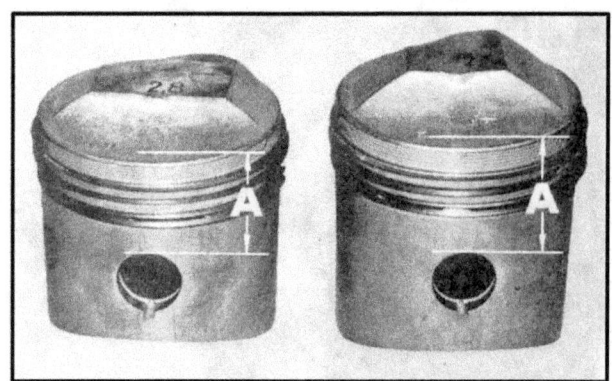

Piston distinguishing features:

BWM 2500   A 36 mm (1.417 in.)
BMW 2800   A 32 mm (1.260 in.)

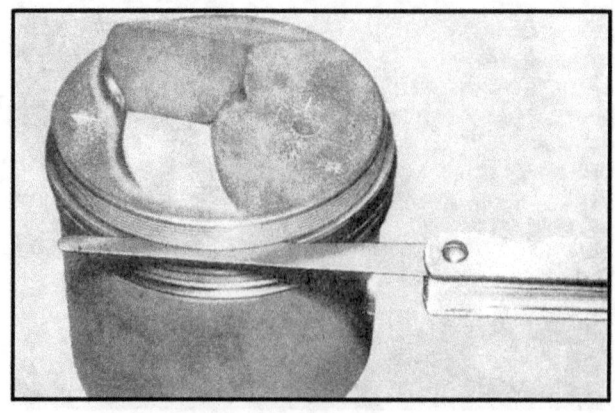

When installing: Install the piston rings, rectangular section ring, stepped ring, equal chamfer ring with the word TOP uppermost, towards the piston crown.

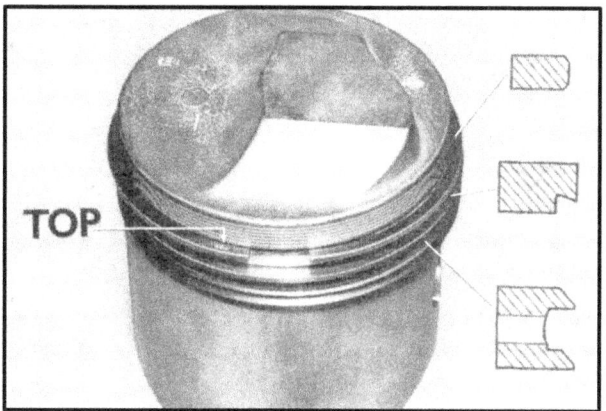

Rectangular section ring
Stepped ring
Equal chamfer ring

CAMSHAFT
Removing and installing
Remove the cylinder head and mount on assembly jig 7003. Take off the fuel pump. Pull out the push rod. Take off the oil pipe. The side of the oil pipe marked 2 must face forwards and measure 6.496 ± 0.0197 in. long from the riser centerline to the pipe end. The opposite side of the pipe is 6.102 ± 0.0197 in. long. Failure to install the pipe correctly may lead to incorrect lubrication and camshaft damage. Note the installed positions of sealing rings 3 and 4. Reset the inlet valves of cylinders 2 and 4 to maximum valve clearance. Failure to observe this precaution will lead to damaged valve. Assemble clamp frame 7003. Detach guide plate from cylinder head. Pull out the camshaft.

When installing: With the guide plate installed, the camshaft must turn easily.

Before detaching the clamp frame, turn the engine over until cylinder 6 is on valve overlap. The threaded hole in the flange must line up with the cast projection.

1. Push rod
2. Oil pipe
3. Sealing ring
4. Sealing ring

When installing: Adjust valve operating clearances.

Replacing
Remove the camshaft. Install the chain sprocket flange on the new camshaft.

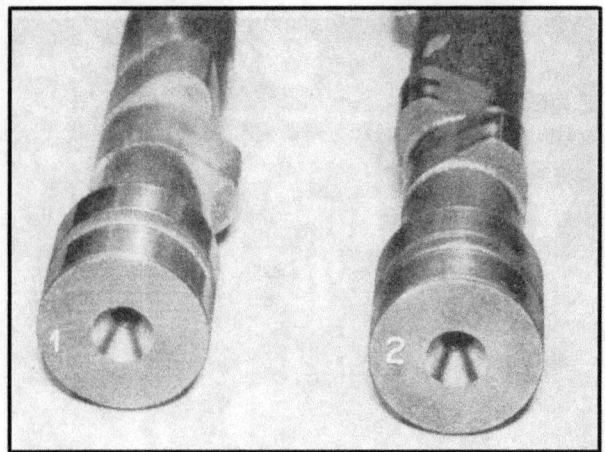

Camshaft identification:
1 BMW 2500
2 BMW 2800

When installing: Check camshaft axial play and if necessary replace the guide plate.

CHAIN TENSIONER PISTON
Removing and installing
Unscrew the end cap. The end cap is subject to powerful spring pressure. Take out the spring and the piston.

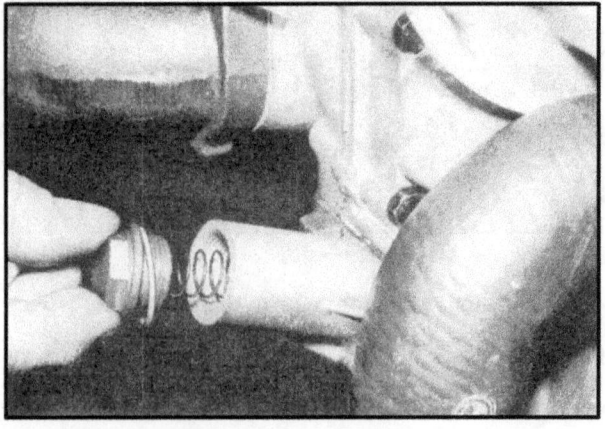

When installing: Check piston installed length A and relaxed length of spring B. The taper-wound end of the spring should be adjacent to the end cap.

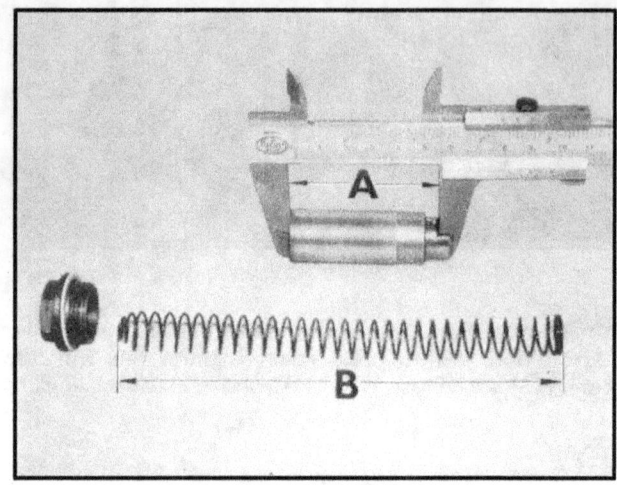

A. Installed piston length
B. Relaxes spring

Check that the bleed slots are not obstructed by blowing through with compressed air. If the bleed slots are not accessible, press out the valve. Clean the bleed slots.

When installing: The convex radius on the flat washer faces the ball. The flat washer must not obstruct the bleed slots.

To bleed the piston, take off the rocker cover. Install the piston and spring. Screw the end cap in a few turns. Fill the oil chamber with engine oil. Move the tensioner rail sideways with a screwdriver until oil emerges from the end cap. If unusual noises are heard from the chain, the cause may be as follows: Piston incompletely bled, piston seized, blocked bleed slots, defective ball valve in piston, excessive or inadequate spring pressure or incorrect piston installed length.

TIMING CHAIN (UPPER AND LOWER TIMING CASE COVERS REMOVED)
Removing and installing
Move the piston in cylinder 1 to the TDC position. The distributor finger should point to the notch on the distributor body.

When installing: Adjust ignition timing.

Open the keeper plates and take off the chain sprocket. Mark the timing chain on 1 face to ensure the same direction of rotation when a run-in timing chain is re-installed. Take off the timing chain.

When installing: The upper threaded hole in the flange must be aligned with the oil spray line. The timing chain is pre-stretched. Replacement before 30,000 miles should not be necessary.

ENGINE

TENSIONER RAIL/GUIDE RAIL
(TIMING CASE COVER REMOVED)
Replacing

Lift out the lock washer. Take off the tensioner rail. To remove the guide rail, detach the chain sprocket from the camshaft. Take off the timing chain. Lift out lock washers. Pull off the guide rail.

1. 2. 3. Lockwasher

TIMING GEAR SET
Replacing

Remove the timing chain. Remove the oil sump and take off the oil pump chain sprocket. Lift out Woodruff key and O-ring. Pull off the chain sprocket with 7006 puller.

When installing: Adjust oil pump drive chain tension with shim plates until the chain can be pressed in with light thumb pressure. Note correct installed position of shim plates with oil drill way. Attach oil pump to mounting plate so that no internal stresses result.

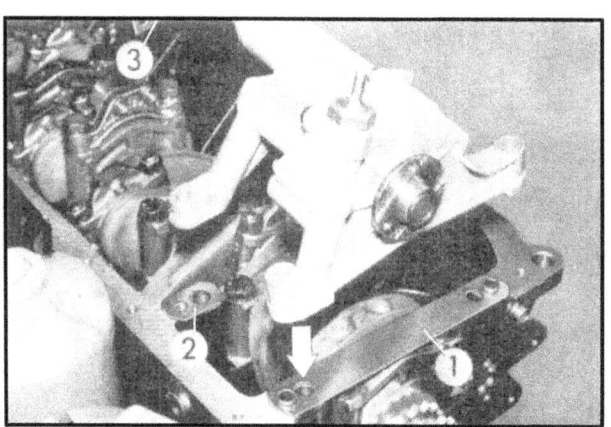

1. 2. Shim plates
3. Mounting plate

ROCKER SHAFTS
Removing and installing

Remove the camshaft. Push back the thrust rings and the rockers. Lift out the circlips. Unscrew and remove the end plugs. Screw extractor device 7004 into the rocker shaft. Remove the aligning pin. Strike the front rocker shafts firmly with the device to remove.

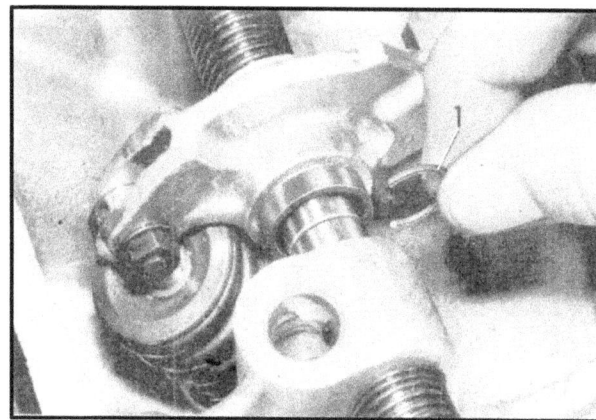

1. Circlip

When installing: Replace grooved rocker shafts. Align the rocker shafts so that the cylinder head bolts can pass through the milled recesses. Insert the aligning pins.

Installation sequence:
3. Spring
4. Washer
5. Rocker
6. Thrust ring

36 ENGINE

To remove the rear rocker shafts, take off the end cover.

When installing: Note self-sealing washer. Only use Cobritol gaskets.

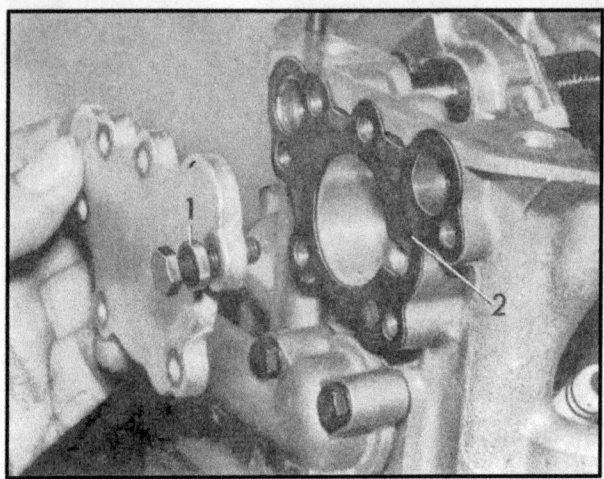

1. Self-sealing washer
2. Cobritol gaskets

Replace all rockers with loose pads. Loose pads can be detected by excessive noise from valve gear.

VALVE OPERATING CLEARANCES
Adjusting

Remove the rocker cover. To adjust valve clearances, turn the engine with device 7008. The valve clearances should be adjusted in the firing order 1−5−3−6−2−4−, at TDC on the compression stroke for each cylinder. To adjust the valve clearance, loosen the nut between the valve and the eccentric.

1. Nut between valve and eccentric

VALVES (ROCKER SHAFTS REMOVED)
Removing and Installing

Place the cylinder head in assembly jig 7003. Remove the spark plugs. Remove the valve caps. Take off the spring cups and springs.

When installing: Use only springs color coded green.

The valve spring is wound to a progressive rate. The side with coils closer together (color coded) should be closer to the cylinder head. To prevent damage to the valve caps or valve guides, the valve stem must be de-burred. Replace damaged valve caps or else oil consumption will be excessively high.

When installing: Before installing the valve caps, cover the annular grooves with Scotch tape.

OIL PUMP
Removing and installing

Remove the oil sump. Take off the chain sprocket. Detach the oil pump from its support and from the crankcase.

When installing: Adjust chain tension with shim plates so that the chain can be depressed with light thumb pressure.

Note the installed position of shim plates with an oil drill way. Shim plates must be of the same thickness. Loosen the retaining plate on the oil pump, align and tighten so that all tension is removed.

1 & 2 Shim plates

ROLLER CHAIN FOR OIL PUMP DRIVE
Replacing
Take off the oil sump. Remove the timing chain. Remove the chain sprocket from the oil pump. Take off the roller chain.

When installing: Adjust chain tension.

OIL PUMP
Dismantling and reassembling
Loosen the threaded union. Take out the coil spring and piston. The relaxed spring length must not be altered. Take off the oil pump cover. Check clearance between the outer rotor and the pump body. If the maximum permitted clearance has been exceeded, replace the pump body. Check the gap between the inner and outer rotors. If the maximum permitted gap has been exceeded, replace outer and inner rotors.

Check clearance between the rotor sealing face and the pump housing. If the maximum permitted clearance has been exceeded, replace the pump housing. Pull off the outward flange with an extractor, do not force or lever off.

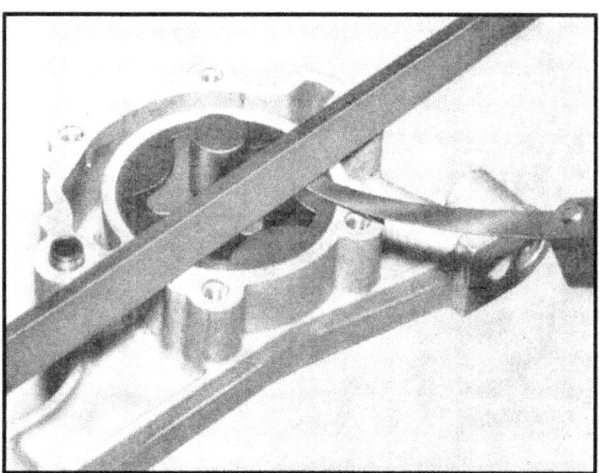

When installing: The distance from the flange to the inner rotor is 1.744 ± 0.004 in.

A = 1.744 ± 0.004 in.

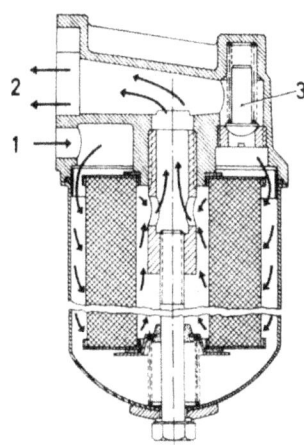

1. Oil supply from pump
2. Filtered oil to lubrication points
3. Pressure relief valve

GUIDE TUBE FOR OIL DIPSTICK
Replacing
Install the clip on the new guide tube. Drive the guide tube into the crankcase. Length A = 8.583 ± 0.004 in. must be maintained. Failure to observe this precaution

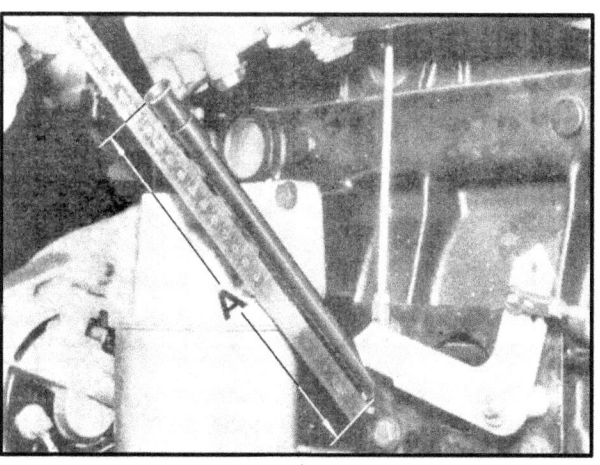

A = 8.583 ± 0.004 in.

38 ENGINE

will lead to false readings on the oil dipstick. This will lead to the engine being filled with an incorrect quantity of oil.

WATER PUMP
Removing and installing
Remove the fan clutch. Take off the belt pulley and the strap. Loosen the hose connections. Take off the water pump.

When installing: Use a new gasket.

Reconditioning
Pull off the hub.

When installing: The double shoulder flange side faces the water pump.

Extract the Seeger circlip. Press the impeller wheel off its shaft and press the water pump bearing out of the housing. Force the axial seal out of the housing.

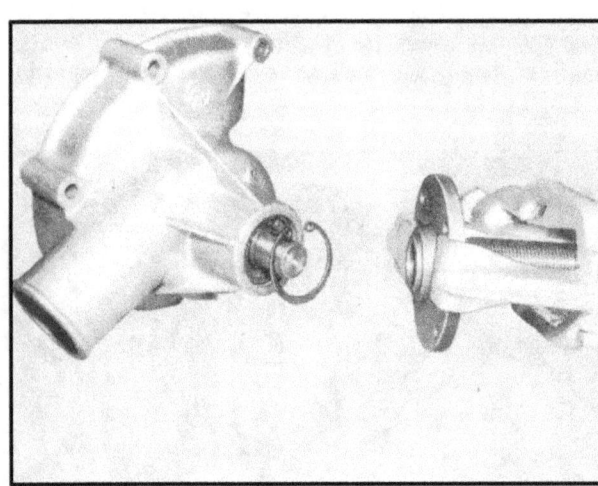

When installing: Press on the impeller wheel after coating with Loctite AVV. Distance B = 0.035 ± 0.008 in. must always be observed.

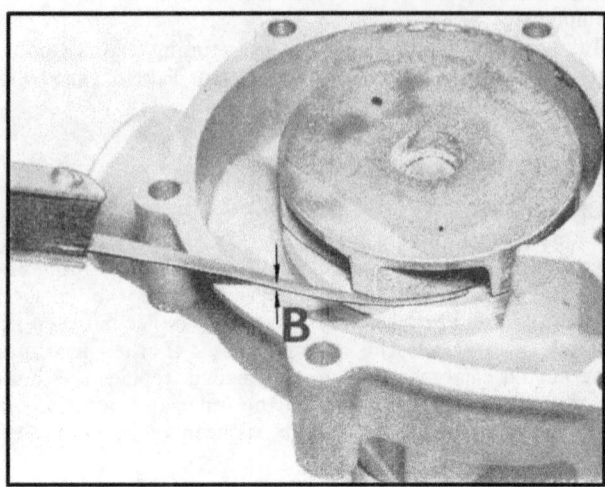

B = 0.035 ± 0.008 in.

Press in the water pump bearing until it seats firmly. Press on the hub.

Distance A = 98.8 mm (3.89 in.)

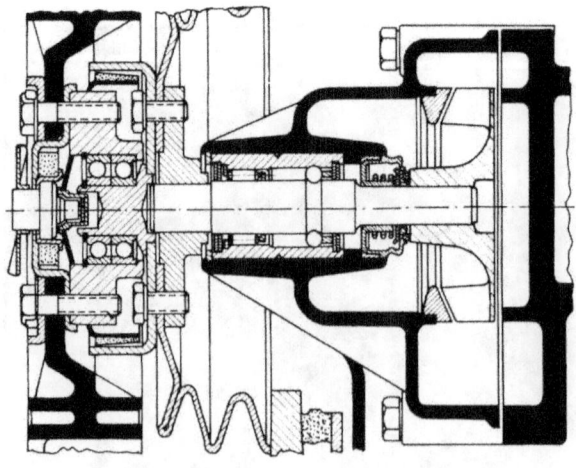

Layout of fan and water pump

FAN
Removing and installing
Remove the radiator. Fold back the tab plates and remove the fan. Use only M6 x 25 mm bolts or else the fan clutch may become jammed.

When installing: Make sure that the plunger is in position in the heat-sensitive element.

1. Plunger

FAN CLUTCH
Removing and installing
Remove the fan. Take off the driving disc and take out the clutch drum.

When installing: Always replace the fan clutch as a complete unit.

The actuating element is matched precisely to the driving disc. If a replacement fan clutch is temporarily unavailable, the existing clutch can be locked in action by means of 2M 6 x 30 mm bolts. The fan will then be driven by the engine at all times. To prevent serious imbalance, the two locking bolts should be inserted on opposite sides of the clutch.

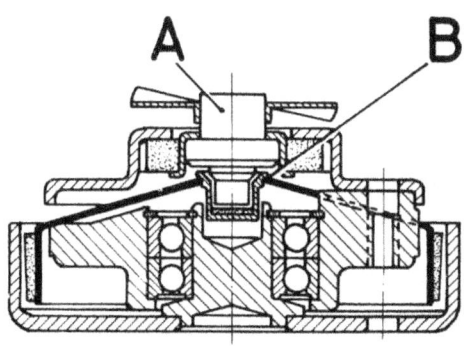

A. Actuating element
B. Driving disc

COOLANT THERMOSTAT
Removing and installing
Partly drain the coolant.

When installing: Bleed the cooling system.

Take off the cover. Take out the thermostat. Check thermostat in hot water bath to establish start of opening movement.

When installing: The loop and arrow point forwards in the direction of travel.

THERMOSTAT HOUSING
Removing and installing
Partly drain the coolant. When installing, bleed the cooling system. Loosen the hose clips. Pull off the cable for the thermometer. Remove the thermostat housing.

COOLANT THERMOMETER SENSOR
Replacing
Partly drain the coolant.

When installing: Bleed the cooling system.

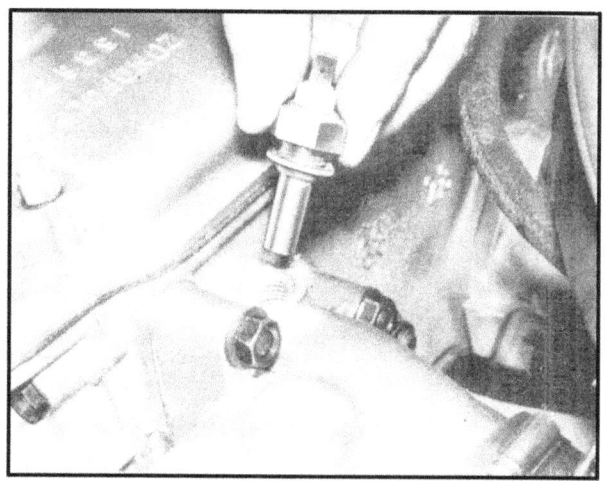

FRONT INTAKE MANIFOLD WITH CARBURETOR
Removing and installing

Partly drain the coolant.

When installing: Bleed the cooling system.

Remove the air filter casing. Take off the fuel and vacuum hoses. Detach the accelerator linkage and connecting linkage. Take off the support bracket.

When installing: The rotary shaft must have a certain amount of axial movement.

1. Accelerator linkage
2. Connecting linkage
3. Support bracket

Pull off cable from the automatic choke mechanism. Detach vacuum hose for the brake servo. Detach water hoses from the cover and the automatic choke mechanism cover. Loosen the support bracket for the oil dipstick. Detach the intake manifold from the cylinder head. Make an imprint of the attachment flanges on an inking plate. Adjust engine idle speed and fuel/air mixture.

4. Cable
5. Vacuum hose
6–9 Water hoses

FRONT INTAKE MANIFOLD
Replacing

Remove intake manifold with carburetor. Detach the carburetor.

When installing: The graphited side of the flange gasket faces towards the intake manifold. Transfer the screw-in union to the new manifold.

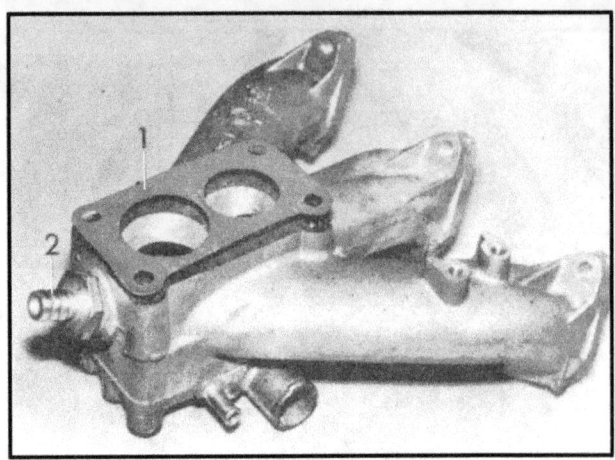

1. Flange gasket
2. Screw-in union

REAR INTAKE MANIFOLD WITH CARBURETOR
Removing and installing

Detach the negative lead from the battery. Partly drain the coolant.

When installing: Bleed the cooling system.

Detach the air filter casing. Loosen the fuel and vacuum hoses. Detach thrust rod. Take off mounting block.

When installing: The rotary shaft must have a degree of axial movement.

Pull off cable at automatic choke mechanism and remove the cover. Take off the coolant hoses. Detach the intake manifold from the cylinder head.

4–6 Coolant hoses

When installing: Make an imprint of the attachment flanges on an inking plate.

Adjust engine idle speed and fuel/air mixture.

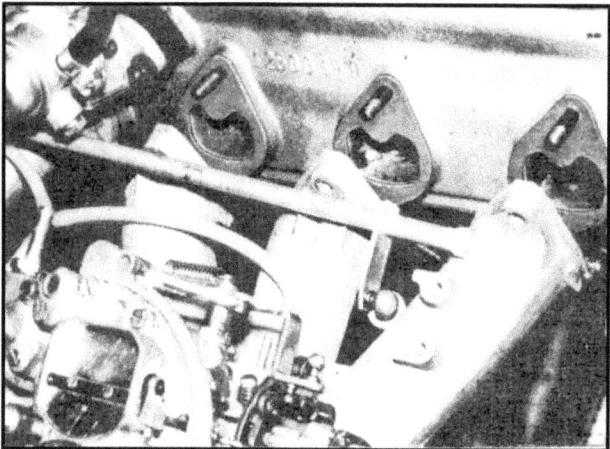

REAR INTAKE MANIFOLD
Replacing

Take off the intake manifold with carburetor. Detach the carburetor.

When installing: The graphited side of the flange gasket faces the intake manifold.

COVER ON FRONT INTAKE MANIFOLD
Removing and installing

Partly drain the coolant.

When installing: Bleed the cooling system.

Loosen the oil dipstick retaining clip. Detach the coolant hoses. Unscrew the nut retaining the carburetor. Take off the cover.

When installing: Be sure to use a new gasket.

COVER ON REAR INTAKE MANIFOLD
Removing and installing

Take off the negative lead from the battery. Partly drain the coolant.

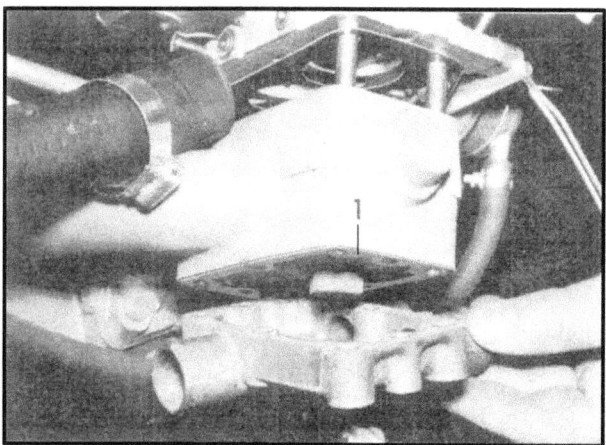

1. Gasket

When installing: Bleed the cooling system.

Take off the air filter casing. Detach the connecting linkage. Take off the coolant hoses. Unscrew the nuts securing the carburetor. Loosen the cover retaining bolts. Pull up the carburetor. Take off the cover.

When installing: Use a new gasket.

FRONT EXHAUST MANIFOLD
Removing and installing

Take off the air filter casing. Remove the cover plate. Detach the exhaust manifold from the cylinder head and from the exhaust pipe. Remove the pipe clip from the exhaust pipe support. Take off the exhaust manifold.

When installing: Note that the gasket hole is not central.

REAR EXHAUST MANIFOLD
Removing and installing

Detach the coolant tank and take off the cover plate. On cars with automatic transmission, detach the oil filler pipe retaining bracket. Detach the exhaust pipes from both front and rear exhaust manifolds. Take off the exhaust pipe clip at the exhaust pipe holder and remove the exhaust manifold from the cylinder head.

When installing: Gasket hole is not central – see front exhaust manifold.

RIGHT ENGINE MOUNTING
Replacing

Loosen the engine mounting at the support bracket and on the front axle beam. Raise the engine with lifting beam 7000 until the engine mounting can be taken out.

When installing: The anti-rotation block must engage in the hole on the support bracket and against the front axle beam.

LEFT ENGINE MOUNTING
Replacing

Remove front apron lower panel. Loosen the engine mounting at the support bracket and front axle beam. Raise the engine with lifting beam 7000 until the engine mounting can be removed.

When installing: The anti-rotation device must engage in the support bracket and front axle beam.

NOTES

CLUTCH

INDEX

	Page		Page
CLUTCH HOUSING	43	CLUTCH MASTER CYLINDER	45
Removing	43	Removing and refitting	45
CLUTCH	43	CLUTCH SLAVE CYLINDER	45
Removing and installing	43	Removing and refitting	45
CLUTCH THROWOUT MECHANISM	45	CLUTCH HYDRAULIC SYSTEM	46
Removing and installing	45	Bleeding	46

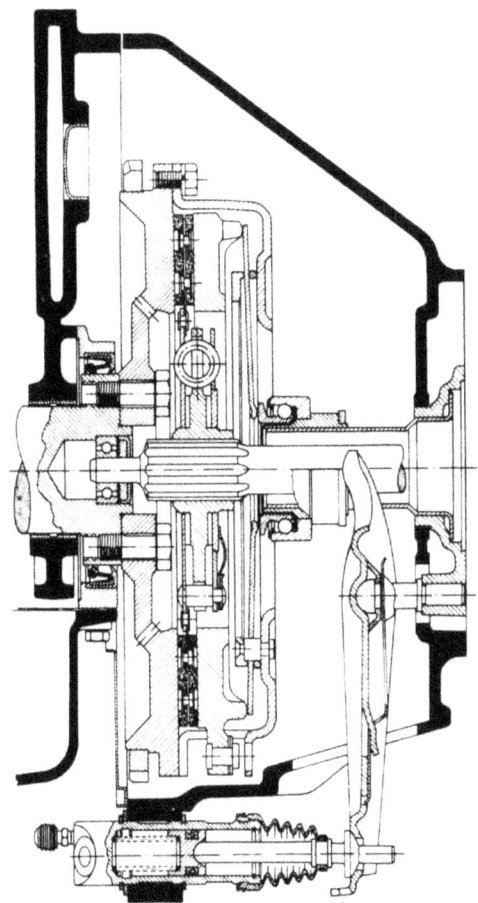

Clutch—layout

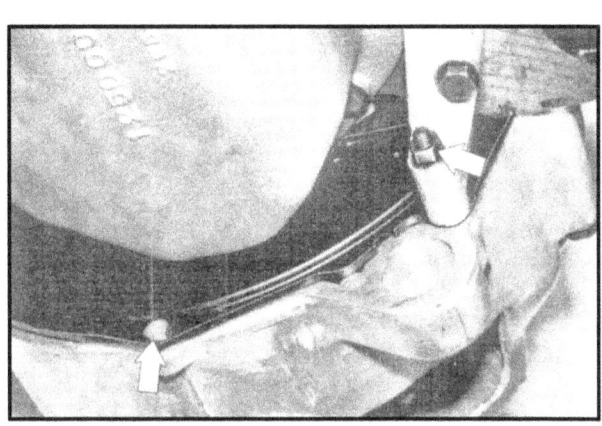

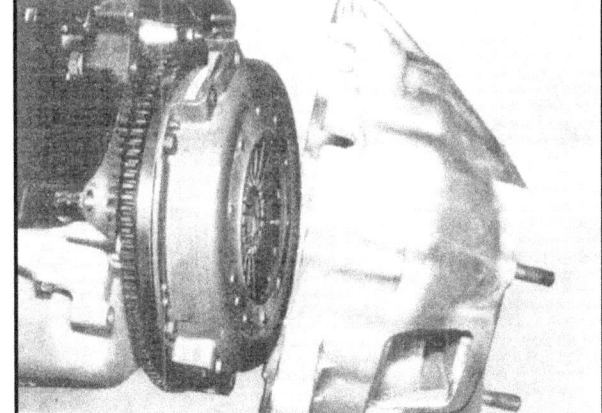

CLUTCH HOUSING
Removing
Remove gearbox and push back the sleeve. Lift out the circlip. Extract slave cylinder forwards.

Fitting instructions: Note rotation lock.

Release the clutch housing and remove the cover plate. Detach the clutch housing.

CLUTCH
Removing and installing
Remove clutch housing and check runout from plane of diaphragm spring ends. Slacken the clutch fixing screws one after the other by 1 – 1½ turns until the clutch is no longer under tension. Remove fixing bolts, clutch and drive plate. Avoid dropping clutch and drive plate as this may cause distortion.

CLUTCH

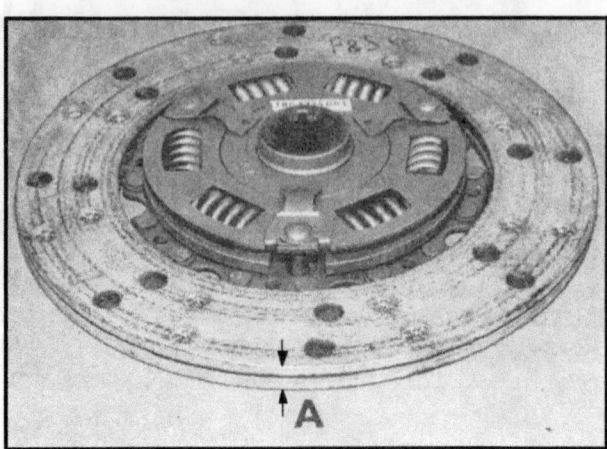

A – Checking for wear

When installing locate clutch in dowel pins. Tighten fixing bolts one after the other by 1 – 1½ turns. Note color coding on clutch. Check bearing on transmission drive shaft for freedom of movement. Lightly smear splines on drive shaft with Molykote Longterm 2. Drive plate must slide smoothly.

Center drive plate in flywheel, using centering mandrel 603. Check drive plate with lining for lateral runout.

Check for cracks, wear and burn spots. Pressure face must be flat. Check rivet joints for wear and firm seating. Exchange clutches with loose or worn rivet heads. Check spring connection between pressure plate and cover. Exchange clutch if any rivets are loose.

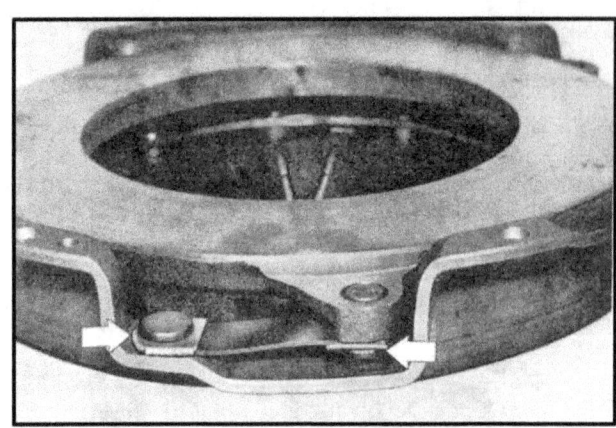

Check drive plate in situ for wear. Press throwout lever up to stop in direction of travel. In new condition the travel at the pushrod will be 17 – 19 mm (0.669-0.748 in.). If dimension is less than 0.19 in., replace drive plate.

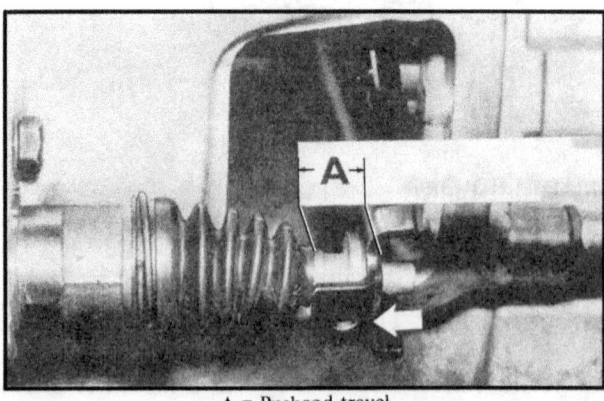

Check drive plate for wear and cracks, and torsion damper for proper seating of spring units and cracks.

A = Pushrod travel

Operation check: At idling speed it should be possible to engage reverse gear after three to five seconds without any tooth noise.

CLUTCH THROWOUT MECHANISM
Removing and refitting
Remove the gearbox. Remove and refit clutch slave cylinder. Lift spring over ball pin flange. To fit, the angle seal must be between ball pin and throwout lever.

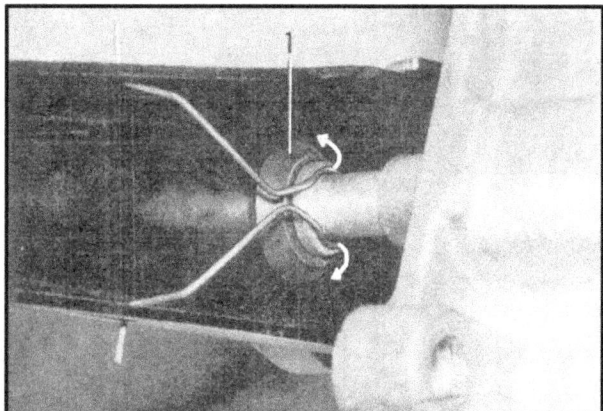

1. Angle seat

Extract throwout mechanism with throwout lever sideways. Disengage throwout mechanism from retaining springs.

Fitting instructions: Smear retaining springs, angle seal and ball pin with Molykote Longterm 2.

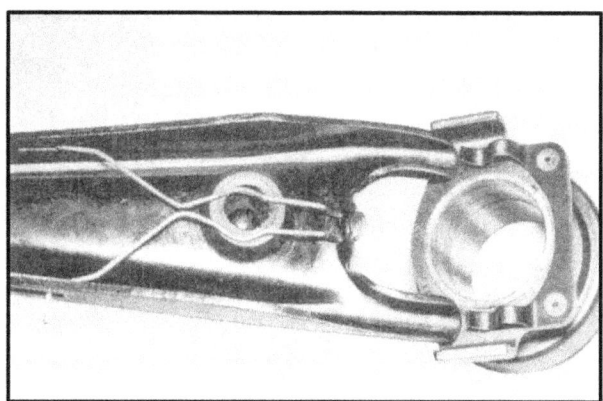

CLUTCH MASTER CYLINDER
Removing and refitting
Detach dashboard paneling on bottom left-hand side. Extract brake fluid in compensating reservoir as far as connection of filler pipe. Pull filler pipe out of master cylinder.

Fitting instructions: Insert sealing plug so that no air can be sucked in.

Release pipe from master cylinder. Detach pushrod on clutch pedal. Remove screws.

Fitting instructions: Smear bolt with Molykote Longterm 2.

Adjust pedal travel with pushrod. Bleed clutch hydraulic system.

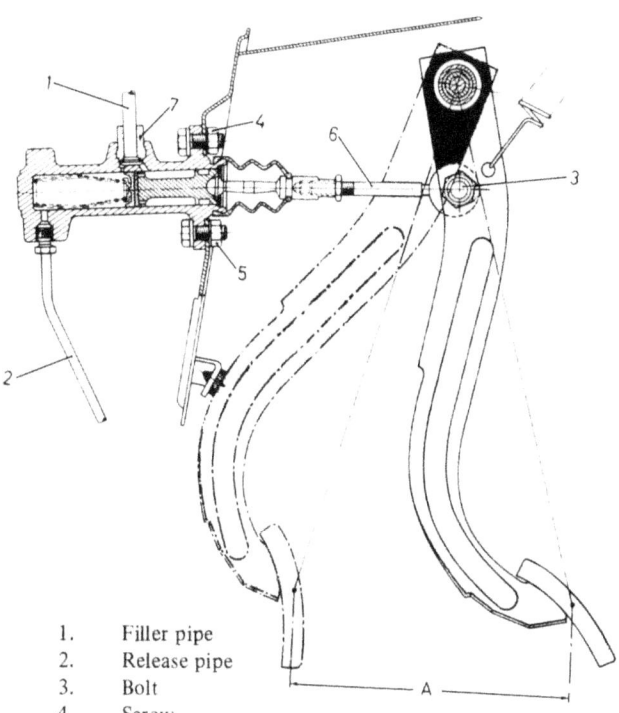

1. Filler pipe
2. Release pipe
3. Bolt
4. Screw
5. Screw
6. Push rod
7. Sealing plug
A. Pedal travel

CLUTCH SLAVE CYLINDER
Removing and refitting
Push back the sleeve and lift out the circlip. Extract slave cylinder forwards.

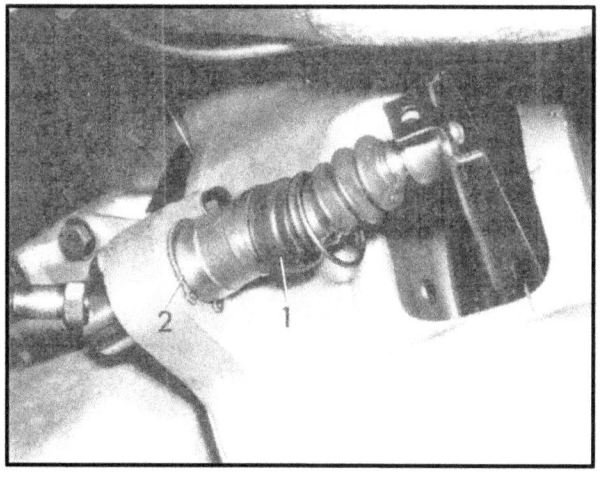

1. Sleeve
2. Circlip

46 CLUTCH

Fitting instructions: Smear ball face of pushrod with Molykote Longterm 2.

Note rotation lock.

Replacing
Extract brake fluid as far as connection of filler pipe at compensating reservoir. Remove and refit clutch slave cylinder. Detach and refit pressure hose.

Fitting instructions: Bleed clutch hydraulic system.

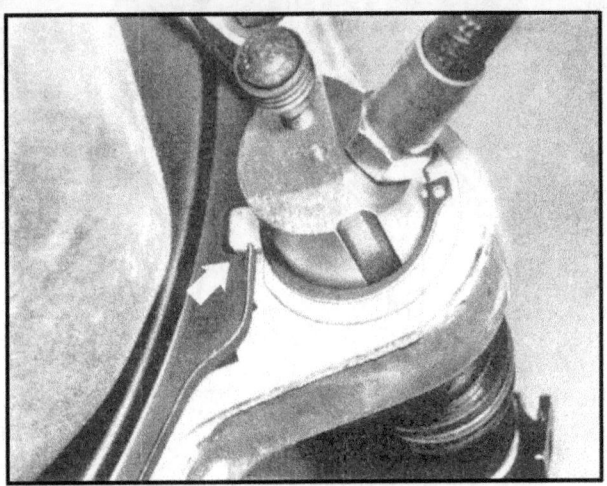

CLUTCH HYDRAULIC SYSTEM
Bleeding
Connect the bleeding device. Open the bleed screw on the clutch slave cylinder until no further air bubbles emerge.

TRANSMISSION, MANUAL

INDEX

	Page
GEARBOX	47
Removing	47
Overhauling	47
Stripping	47
Synchromesh	50
Assembly	51
GUIDE SLEEVE FOR CLUTCH THROWOUT MECHANISM	52
Replacing	52
RADIAL SEALING RING FOR DRIVING SHAFT	52

	Page
Replacing	52
RADIAL SEALING RING FOR DRIVE FLANGE	52
Replacing	52
SPEEDOMETER PINION	52
Removing	52
SHIFT LEVER	53
Removing and refitting	53
RUBBER RINGS IN SHIFT LEVER	53
Replacing	53

GEARBOX
Removing

Remove and refit selector lever. Disconnect exhaust pipes at exhaust manifold.

When installing: Smear studs with Molykote Paste G.

Detach exhaust bracket.

When installing: First, tighten pipe clip, then exhaust bracket.

Disconnect universal shaft.

When installing: Do not damage sealing cap.

Check location for free running; if necessary grease with Longterm 2. Slacken threaded sleeve. Detach center bearing support. Push off universal shaft from gearbox.

When installing: Tension center bearing support in direction of travel (A = 0.078").

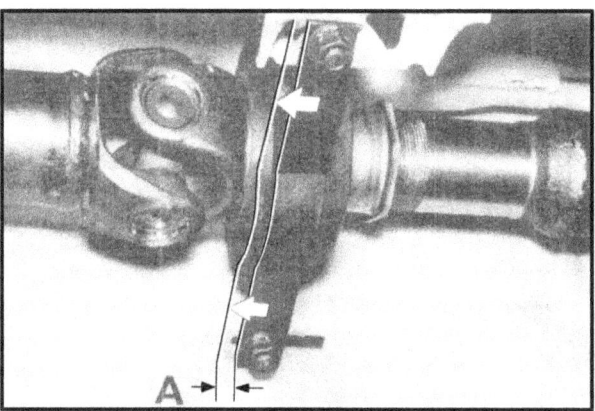

A = 2mm – 0.078"

Remove speedometer shaft. Pull off cable from reversing light switch. Disconnect gearbox from clutch housing at flange fitting. Support engine between front axle brackets. Slacken rubber bushes at gearbox. Detach cross-member. Gently extract gearbox. Lift spring over ball pin flange.

When installing: Angle seal must be between ball pin and throwout lever.

Overhauling
Stripping

Secure gearbox to fixture 7002. Detach shift support from shift arm. Only in the case of defective torsion spring, remove locking bar with torsion spring and spring.

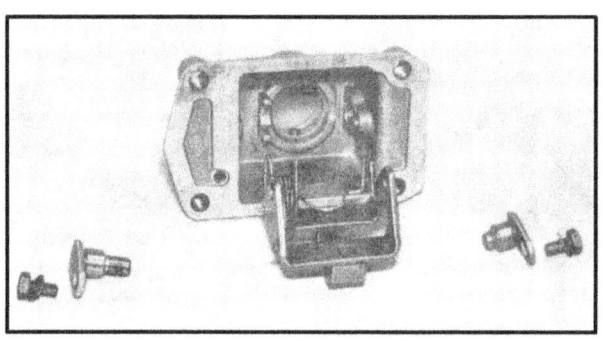

MANUAL TRANSMISSION

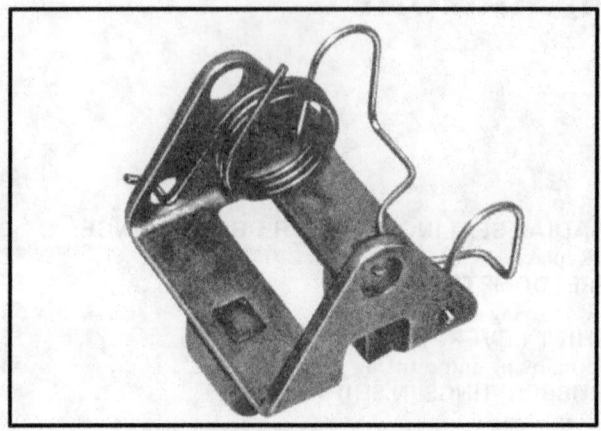

Fitting position of torsion spring and spring

Insert locking bar with torsion spring with the long pin on the torsion spring side. Fit spring with long side towards torsion spring. Release the selector arm and detach the vibration damper. Slide off the guide piece. Detach guide flange and check guide sleeve for wear. Note shims. Lift out the circlip. Note shims. Extract ball bearing – Rillex 6306 long. Note shims. Remove bearing pin 3rd/4th gear. Detach front of housing.

When installing: Use grease when inserting pressure spring and slide piece.

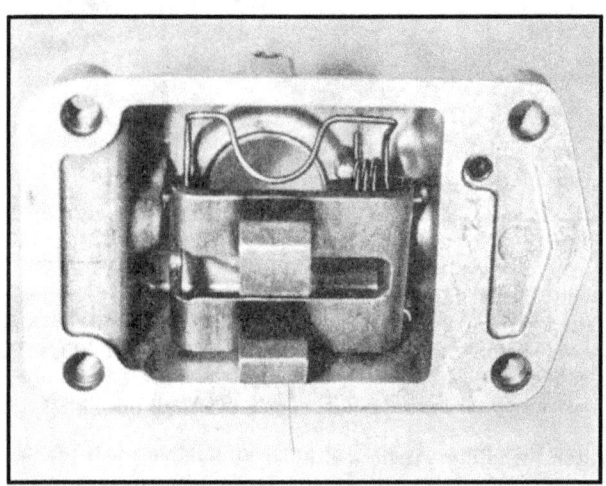

MANUAL TRANSMISSION 49

Extract shift rails for 3rd and 4th and 1st and 2nd gears forwards. Extract shift rail for reverse gear to the rear.

When installing: Deep shift rod cutout should be towards shift lever side.

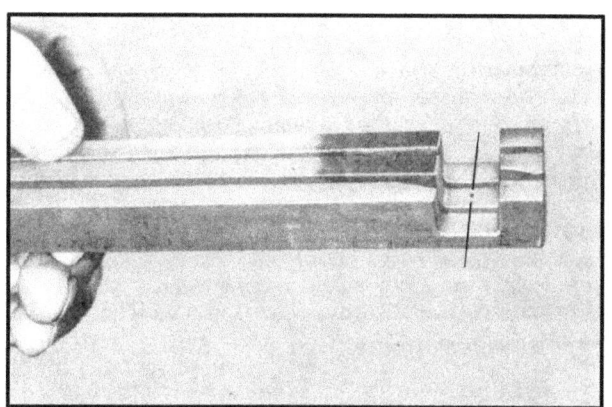

Engage 1st gear. Remove selector fork 3rd and 4th gears. Lift out locking plate.

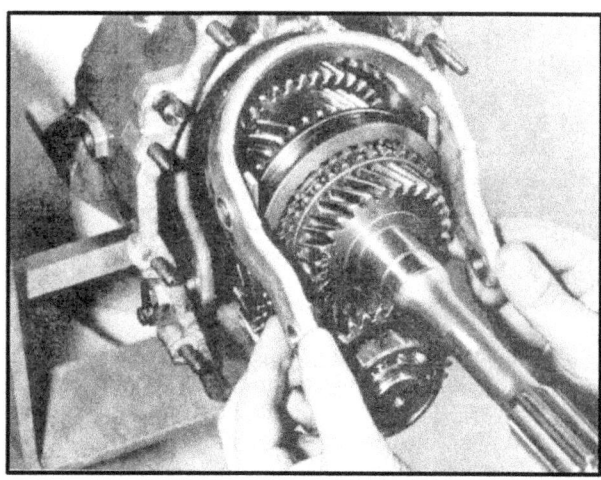

When installing: Chisel locking plate over into drive flange groove.

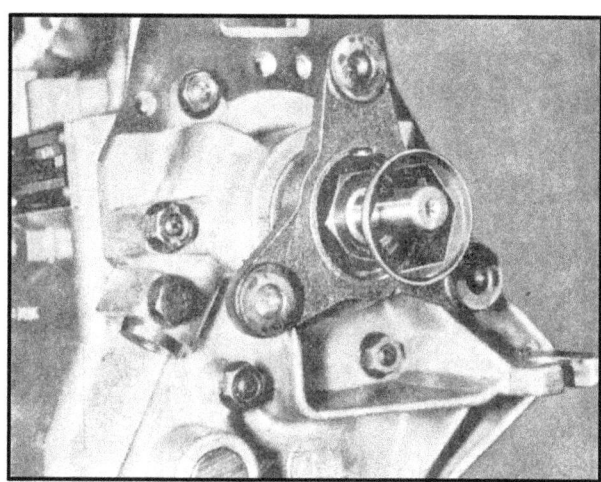

Unscrew flanged nut — retaining spanner 604. Pull off drive flange and detach cover. Note shims. Pull off the speedometer pinion and washer. Next, pull off the ball bearing from layshaft Rillex 6305. Remove layshaft and driving shaft with roller rim and synchromesh. Renew pinion set 3rd and 4th gear. Lift out the circlip and pull off the ball bearing. Press off pinion 4th gear. Lift out circlip. Press off pinion 3rd gear. Pressure required approximately 11,025 lbs.

When installing: Only use C3 bearings.

Heat gear pinions to 302-356°F. Take up play between ball bearing and circlip with shims. To engage 2nd gear, remove bearing pin for selector fork 1st and 2nd gears.

Remove selector fork for reverse gear. Press selector fork for 1st and 2nd gears against stop. Extract reverse gear pinion.

MANUAL TRANSMISSION

When installing: Inclined side of tooth should face toward housing.

1. Selector fork for reverse gear

Press drive shaft out of ball bearing or pull ball bearing off drive shaft — Rillex 6306 long. Note shims. Remove the drive shaft and selector fork for 1st and 2nd gears. Press

off reverse gear pinion and 1st gear pinion. Pull off needle bearing and lift out locking ring. Remove synchromesh ring. Press off synchromesh and 2nd gear pinion. Pull off needle bearing. Lift out circlip. Press off synchromesh and 3rd gear pinion.

1. Needle bearing
2. Locking ring
3. Synchromesh ring

Synchromesh

It is advisable to replace the synchromesh rings when carrying out a gearbox repair. Push sliding sleeve of synchromesh. Detach pressure pieces and synchromesh springs.

When installing: Sliding sleeve 2st and 2nd gears: continuous uniform tooth formation. Synchromesh boss the same height on both sides. Sliding sleeves 3rd and 4th gear: teeth interrupted. Synchromesh boss flatter on side towards 4th gear.

Stagger synchromesh spring ends. Place synchromesh in synchromesh ring and engage pressure pieces in synchromesh springs. Push pressure pieces into the somewhat flatter teeth in the synchromesh ring for 1st and 2nd gears.

MANUAL TRANSMISSION 51

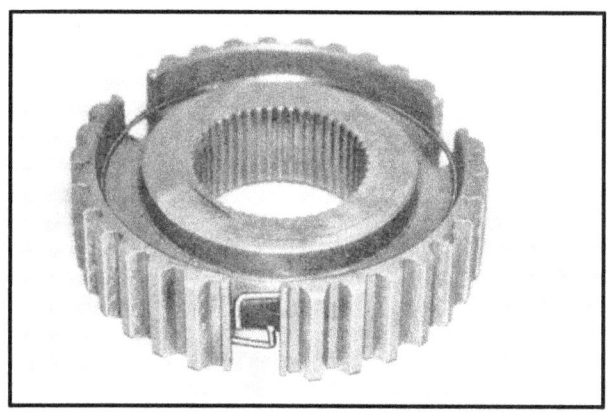

Assembly

Place needle bearing and 3rd gear pinion in position. Insert synchromesh ring in synchromesh on the thicker boss side and press on. Fit circlip so that no play is present. Place needle bearing and 2nd gear pinion in position. Insert synchromesh ring in preassembled synchromesh. Press on synchromesh and fit locking ring so that no axial play is present. Insert synchromesh ring in synchromesh. Place needle bearing and first gear pinion in position. Press on reverse gear pinion with thick boss facing outwards. Insert locking ring in new C3 ball bearing and press in ball bearing to its fullest extent. Remove ball bearing. Fit ball bearing with shim D thickness as calculated. Use grease when refitting stop pin and pressure springs. Position selector fork 1st and 2nd gears in shift sleeve. Press drive shaft into ball bearing in housing.

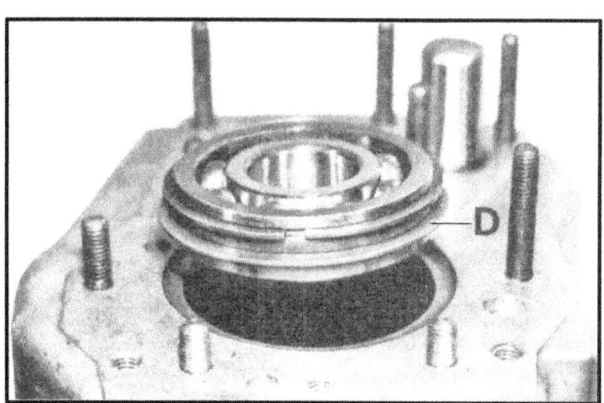

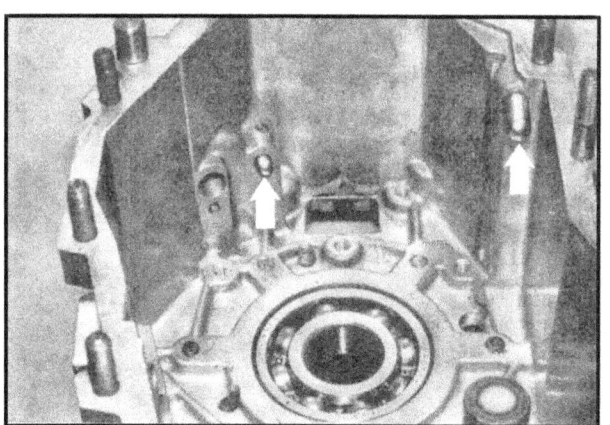

Engage 2nd gear. Press selector fork against stop. Position reverse gear pinion with relieved tooth face side towards housing approximately 0.394" on to reverse gear shaft. Insert selector fork for reverse gear and secure. Fit bearing pin for selector fork 1st and 2nd gears. Press 2nd gear into neutral position. Fit synchromesh springs with spring ends offset. Engage pressure pieces. Press sliding sleeves onto synchromesh. Position roller rim on drive shaft. Insert synchromesh ring. Fit driving shaft. Insert layshaft and support. Heat ball bearing inner race to approximately 194°F, push on to layshaft and press into housing. Allow ball bearing to project (dimension D = approximately 0.196").

Measure distance A with gasket in position. Measure dimension B. Calculate thickness of shim C as follows: Shimming accuracy ±0.06 (0.002"). Fit washer and speedometer pinion. Stick shim C on to speedometer cover with grease. Fit cover and drive flange.

Calculate thickness of shim C as follows:

Example: $A = 3.0\ (0.118")$
$\underline{B = 3.6\ (0.141")}$
$C = 0.6\ (0.023")$

52 MANUAL TRANSMISSION

Secure selector fork 3rd and 4th gears. First of all insert bearing pin on left in direction of travel. Fit all shift rails. Fit front of housing, vibration damper and shift arm. Shim clearance between ball bearing inner race and circlip to zero. Place gasket in position. Secure shim F in guide flange with grease. Place shim C on ball bearing. Secure guide flange.

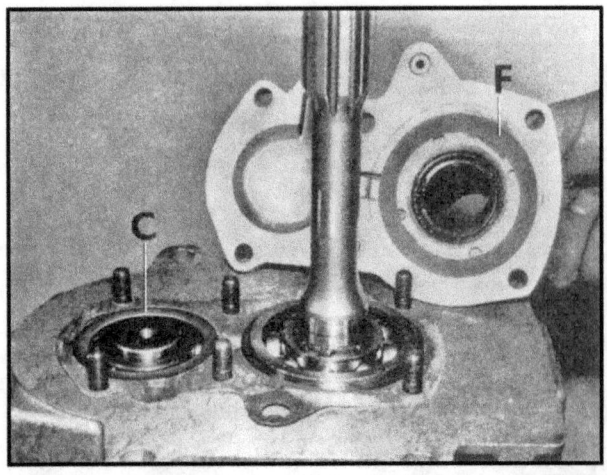

GUIDE SLEEVE FOR CLUTCH THROWOUT MECHANISM
Replacing

Press guide sleeve out of guide flange. Replace radial sealing ring. Refit guide flange to ball bearing. Fit guide sleeve using sealing compound.

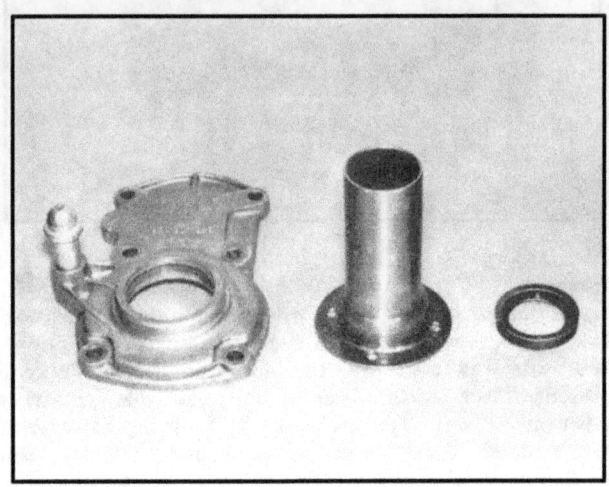

RADIAL SEALING RING FOR DRIVING SHAFT
Replacing

Remove guide flange. Lift out radial sealing ring.

When installing: Open side should face towards gearbox.

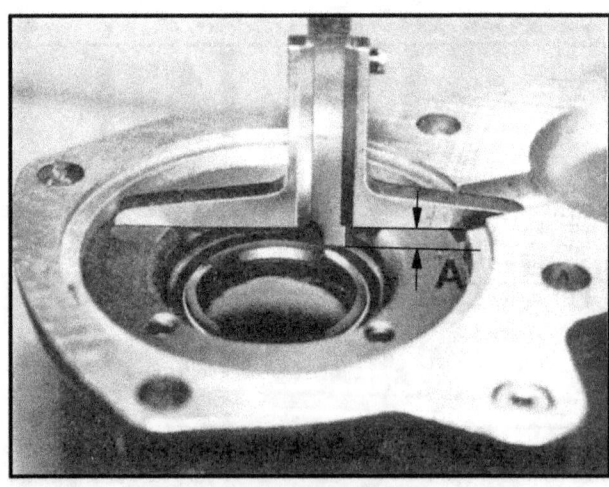

A = 4.5mm – 0.177"

RADIAL SEALING RING FOR DRIVE FLANGE
Replacing

Remove drive flange. Lift out radial sealing ring.

When installing: Drive in radial sealing ring until flush.

SPEEDOMETER PINION
Removing

Detach speedometer shaft. Remove bush and speedometer pinion.

When installing: Check string seal.

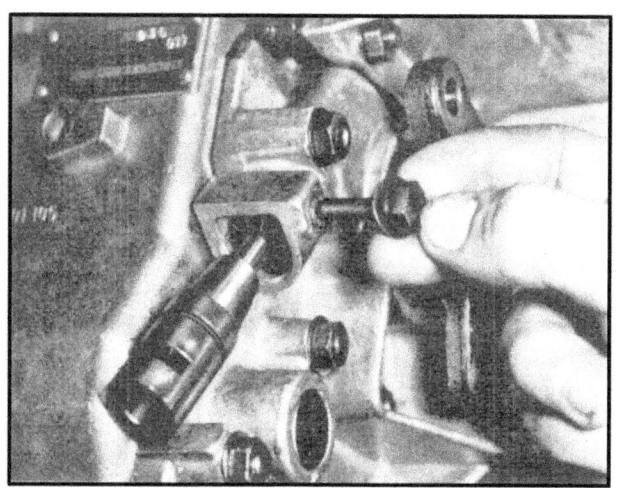
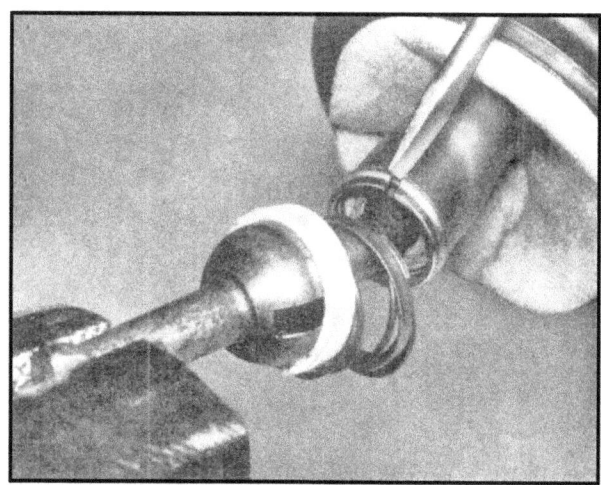
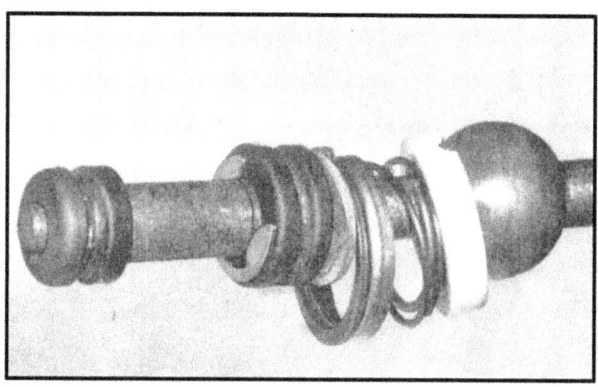

SHIFT LEVER
Removing and refitting
Push up gaiter and foam insert. Lift out circlip. Extract shift lever.

When installing: When inserting shift lever ball use Longterm 2.

RUBBER RINGS IN SHIFT LEVER
Replacing
Remove and refit shift lever. Lift out wire snap ring. Pull off shift lever. Pull off rubber ring. Lift out circlip. Replace rubber rings.

NOTES

TRANSMISSION, AUTOMATIC

INDEX

	Page
DESCRIPTION	55
GEARSHIFT	55
Adjusting	55
ACCELERATOR CABLE	57
Adjusting	57
TRANSMISSION	57
Removing and installing	57
EXCHANGE TRANSMISSION	59
Installing	59
OIL SUMP	59
Removing and installing	59
OIL FILLER PIPE	60
Removing and installing	60
CONVERTER DOME	60
Removing and installing	60
TRANSMISSION COVER	60
Removing and installing	60
OIL SEAL FOR OUTPUT FLANGE	61
Removing and installing	61
O-RING FOR SPEEDOMETER DRIVE BUSH	61
Replacing	61
O-RING FOR SELECTOR LEVER	61

	Page
Replacing	61
TORQUE CONVERTER OIL SEAL – (TORQUE CONVERTER REMOVED)	61
Replacing	61
PAWL FOR PARKING LOCK	61
Replacing	61
THROTTLE CABLE	62
Replacing	62
NOTCHED PAWL	62
Removing and installing	62
TORSION SPRING FOR THROTTLE CABLE – (CONTROL UNIT REMOVED)	62
Replacing	62
TORQUE CONVERTER	63
Removing and installing	63
Replacing	63
TRANSMISSION SELECTOR LEVER	63
Removing and installing	63
TRANSMISSION RUBBER MOUNTING	64
Replacing	64
GEAR LEVER WITH MOUNTING	64
Removing and installing	64

DESCRIPTION

The 3-HP-20 transmission is fully automatic. It is provided with a torque converter and Simpson planetary gear train.

In selector lever position P, the transmission output shaft is locked mechanically by the parking pawl. The engine must be started with the selector lever in position O or P. No power is transmitted to the rear wheels. The lever should remain in position A under normal driving conditions in order to obtain the best possible fuel consumption.

The transmission can be made to change down early by operating the kickdown control with the accelerator pedal. Selector lever position 2 prevents undesirable upward changes from 2nd to 3rd gear on hills. In addition, engine braking is improved. Selector position 1 is particularly suitable for continuous engine braking effect on severe gradients. The selector lever may be moved to position 1 or 2 at any road speed. The transmission will then no longer change up into the next higher gear.

GEAR SHIFT
Adjusting

Engage the selector lever on the transmission in position O. Detach the shift rod from the shift lever. Alter the length of selector rod B until the gear selector lever is touching point C on the gate. Now give eyebolt D, 3 complete turns to shorten the selector rod. Reinstall the shift rod and lock into position. Loosen screws E and F and adjust the selector lever position indicating switch.

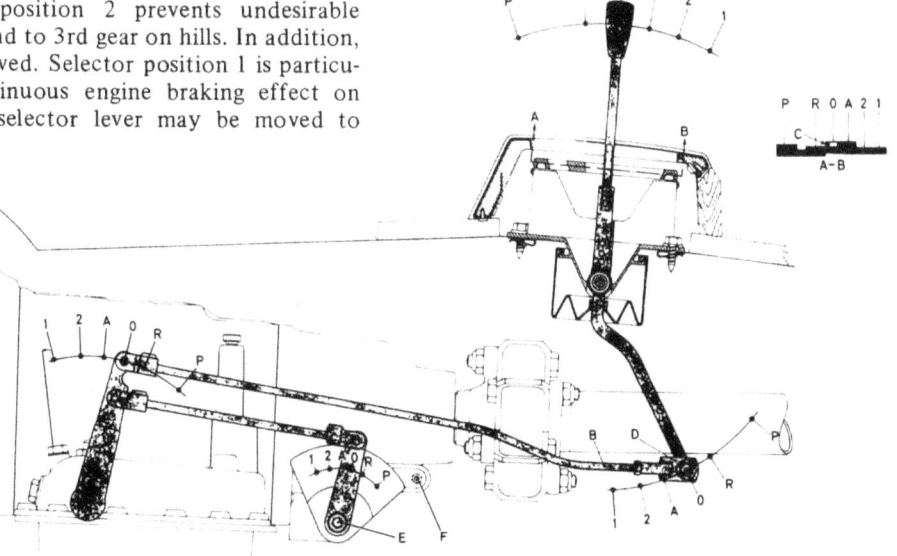

Power flow diagram

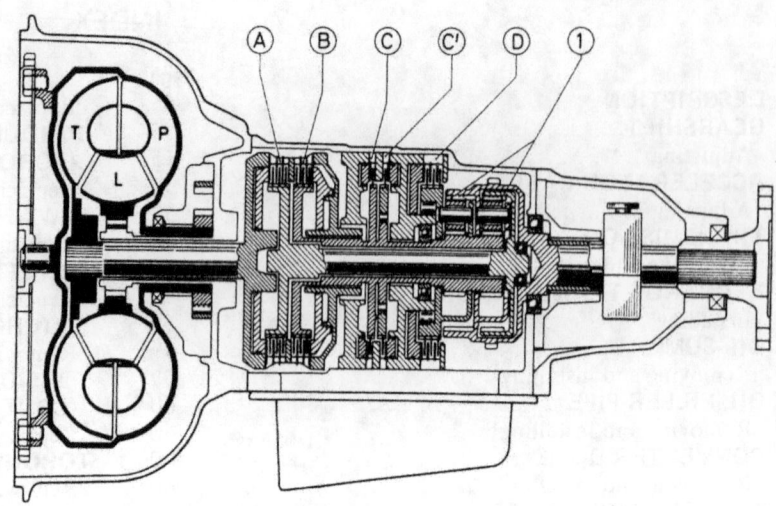

Neutral

Clutches A, B, C, C' and D are disengaged.
All pinions in planetary gear set (1)
can turn freely on their shafts.

1st gear

Clutch A is engaged. On traction the planetary gear carrier bears against freewheel 3, on the overrun it turns freely on the freewheel.

With the selector lever in position 1 or 2, clutch D is also engaged in 1st gear in order to permit engine braking.

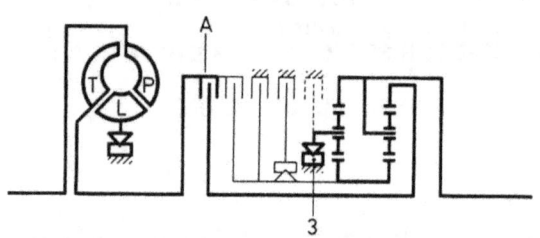

2nd gear

Clutches A, C and C' are engaged.
Freewheel 3 is overrun. The hollow shaft is blocked by freewheel 2. This locks the two sun wheels.

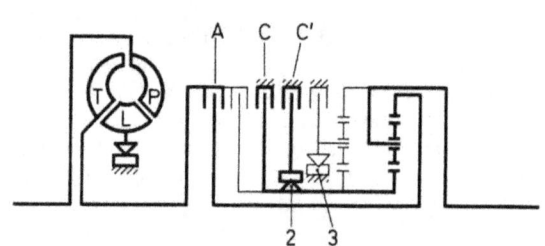

3rd gear

Clutches A, B and C' are engaged. Freewheels 2 and 3 are overrun. The complete planetary gear set turns as a unit in the ratio 1 : 1.

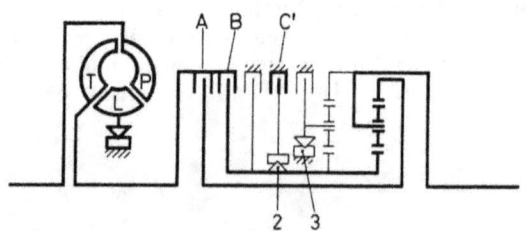

Reverse gear

Clutches B and D are engaged. By locking the planetary gear carrier the direction of rotation of the output shaft is reversed.

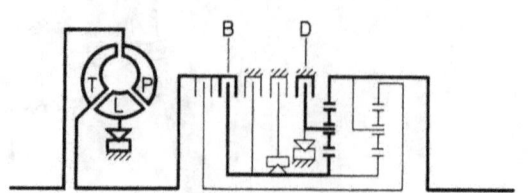

AUTOMATIC TRANSMISSION

ACCELERATOR CABLE
Adjusting

When the accelerator cable is adjusted, the shift points will be affected. Take off the air filter casing. Adjust tension element to length. Detach thrust rod with throttle cable. Move the throttle butterflies with reverse motion lever to the full throttle position. When doing so, make sure that the tension element is not pulled out to the kickdown position.

Pull up the throttle cable as far as the full throttle pressure point. By pulling up the cable several times, the full throttle pressure point will be clearly detectable. In this position the hole in the cable end yoke must be exactly aligned with the hole in the angled lever. If this is not the case, the adjusting screw on the cable end yoke must be turned until the two holes are aligned.

Attach the throttle cable to the angled lever. Move the throttle butterflies to the full throttle position and press the accelerator pedal plate against the kickdown stop. Adjust the length of thrust rod so that the ball end can be placed in position without altering the settings of the throttle butterflies or accelerator pedal plate. To check the setting, press the accelerator pedal plate against the kickdown stop. The throttle butterflies must be fully open before the tension element comes into action.

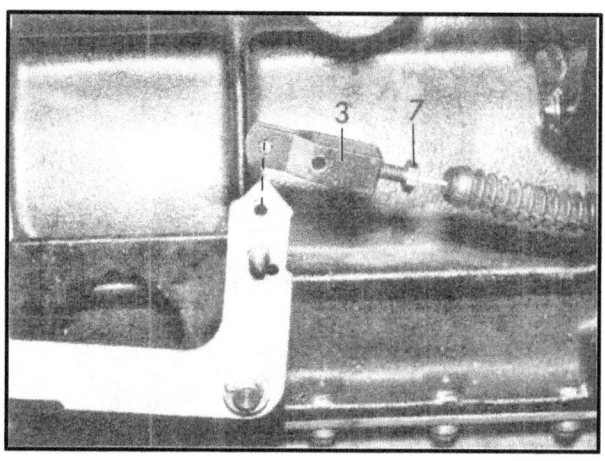

3. Throttle cable
7. Adjusting screw on cable end yoke

TRANSMISSION
Removing and installing

Detach the negative lead from the battery. Take off the air filter casing. Detach the throttle cable from the angled arm and the thrust bearing.

When installing: Drain the oil. Do not reuse oil drained from the transmission.

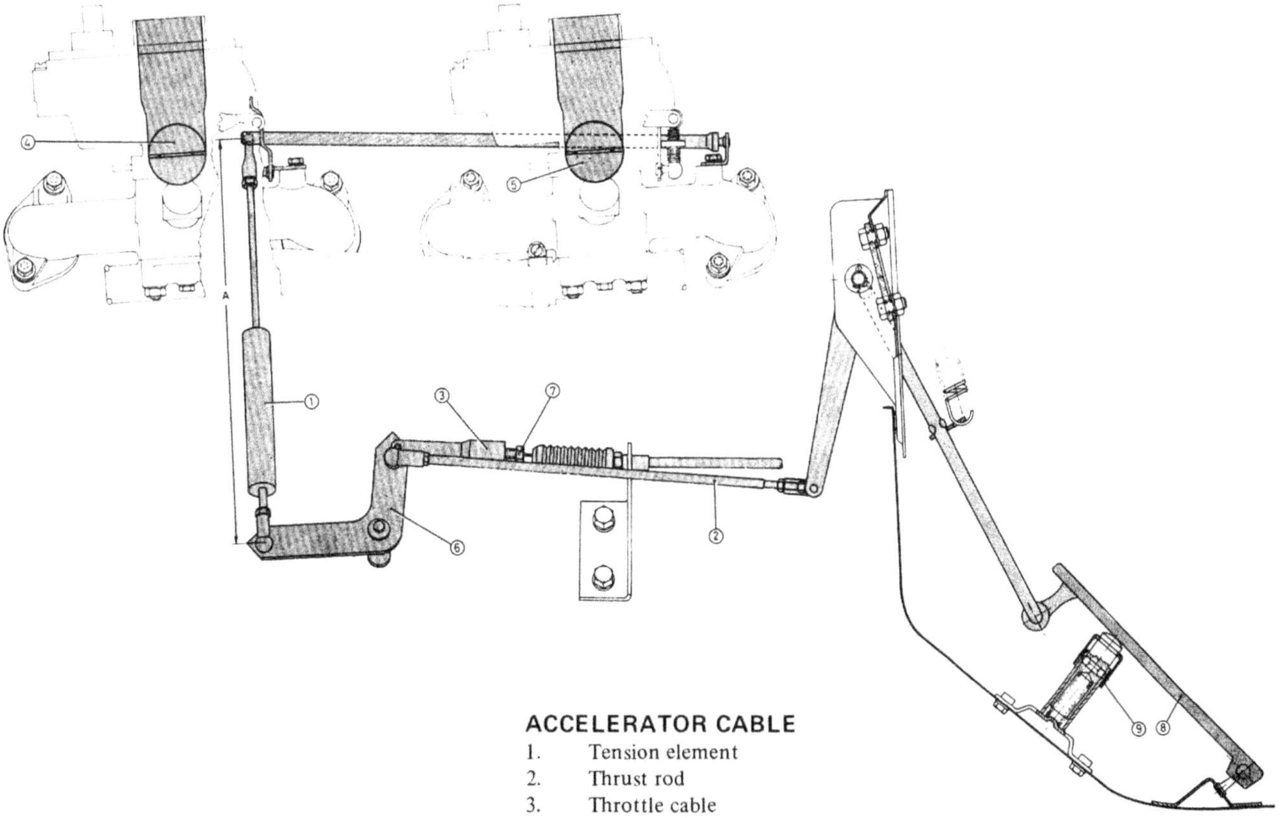

ACCELERATOR CABLE
1. Tension element
2. Thrust rod
3. Throttle cable
4 & 5 Butterflies
6. Reverse motion lever

58 AUTOMATIC TRANSMISSION

When installing: If the oil has a burned smell or is discolored black, the transmissios must be dismantled. If the oil has a metallic grey color, aluminum or iron particles have become dislodged from the transmission. Unlike iron particles, aluminum cannot be retained by a magnetic drain plug.

Remove the oil filler pipe. Plug the opening.

When installing: Replace the O-ring if required.

5. Threaded bush

Swing down the propeller shaft and pull the center bearing away from the centering journal. Pull off the stop buffer. Remove the speedometer drive shaft. Pull off the electric cables for the reversing lights. Detach the crossbeam from the body shell and the transmission mounting. Allow the engine oil sump to rest on the front axle beam.

Support the transmission with a car jack and stand 7060. Detach the earth (ground) strap. Separate the transmission from the engine. Pull the transmission away from the engine, at the same time pressing the torque converter into its housing.

When installing: The torque converter is in the correct installed position when the guide journal is below the edge of the housing. If this is not the case, turn the torque converter slightly while guiding it into the primary pump.

Remove the complete exhaust system.
Detach the oil pipes from the engine and transmission. Separate the multi-pin plug. Loosen the support bracket and remove the cover plate. Separate the torque converter at 4 points from the driving disc. Detach thrust rod from the selector lever and the flexible coupling at the output flange. Loosen the threaded bush. Detach the center bearing mounting.

1. Multi-pin plug
2. Support bracket
3. Cover plate

When installing: Pre-load the center bearing mounting by 2 mm (0.08 in.) in the direction of travel.

6. Stop buffer
7. Speedometer drive shaft
8. Electric cables

AUTOMATIC TRANSMISSION

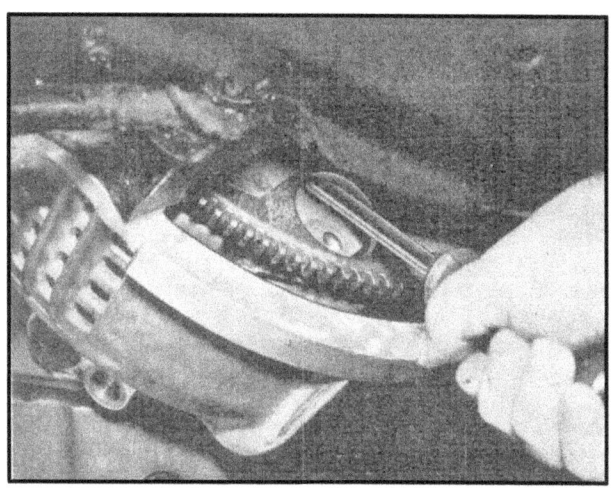

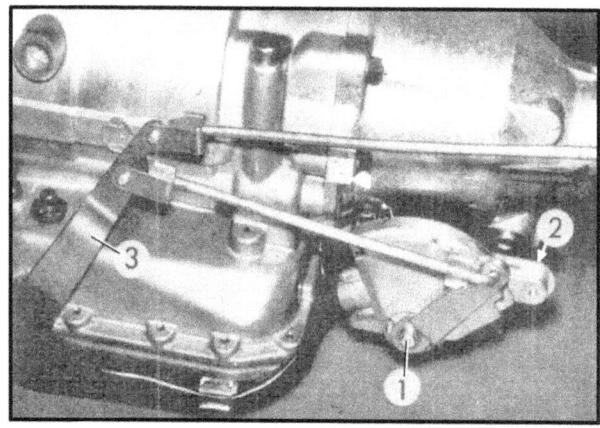

1-2. Screws
3. Selector arm

When installing: Examine the driving disc for cracks and replace if necessary. To replace, lock the flywheel into position with retaining device 7007.

Transfer the exhaust support bracket and the gearbox mounting. Transfer the sleeve for engine-transmission centering. Install the O-ring. Remove the transit plugs from the oil cooler connection.

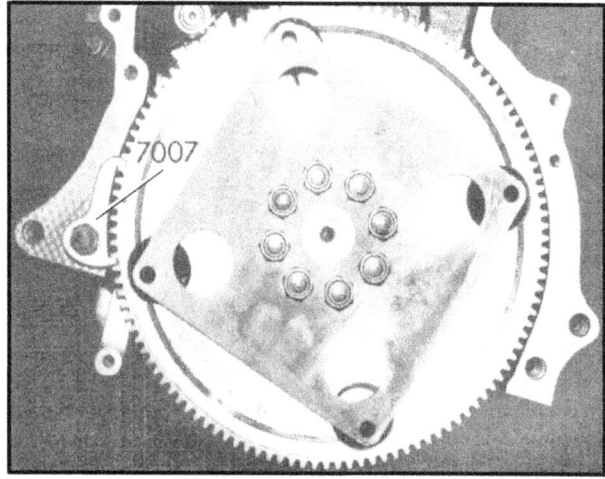

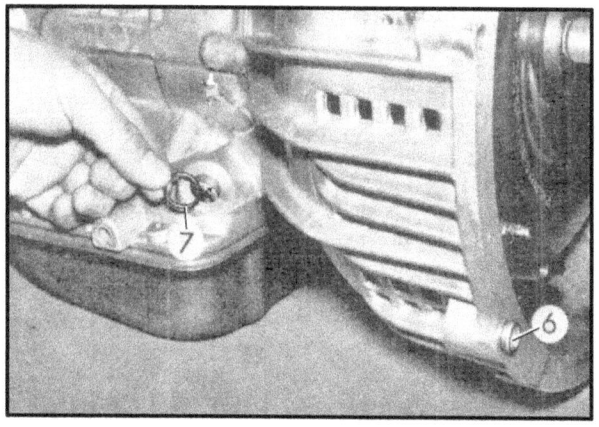

6. Sleeve
7. O-ring

OIL SUMP
Removing and installing
Drain the oil. Do not re-use oil drained from the transmission.

EXCHANGE TRANSMISSION
Installing
Remove the transmission. Whenever installing an exchange transmission, always flush out the oil cooler and hose connections thoroughly with gasoline or petroleum spirit. The 3 HP-20 transmission for the BMW 2500 and 2800 models differ in their conversion ratios and converter diameters. BMW 2500 torque converter — blue spot, BMW 2800 torque converter — red spot. Detach the transit retaining bar. The transmission code number on housing cover and the number underneath is the transmission series number. Transfer the linkage and switch for the selector lever indicator to the exchange transmission. With the transmission installed, loosen screws and adjust the switch for the selector lever indicator such that with the selector arm fully engaged, the correct transmission position is illuminated on the instrument panel scale.

When installing: If the oil has a burned smell and is discolored black, the transmission must be dismantled. If the oil has a metallic grey color, it contains aluminum or iron particles. Unlike iron particles, aluminum cannot be trapped by means of a magnetic drain plug. Place the vehicle on a flat, level surface. With the selector lever in position P and the engine at normal operating temperature, add oil while the engine is idling. When the oil is cold, the level must be approximately ¼ above the minimum marking on the oil dipstick. Quantity of oil between minimum and maximum markings approximately ½ quart.

If oil level is too high, severe foaming, losses by dilution,

AUTOMATIC TRANSMISSION

and temperature rise during fast driving will occur. If oil level too low, valve chatter, foaming, engine overspeed on corners will occur. Loosen the exhaust support bracket. Detach the oil sump.

When installing: Attach the clips and spacing washers on the left side.

Check condition of gasket and replace if necessary. Use only genuine BMW gaskets.

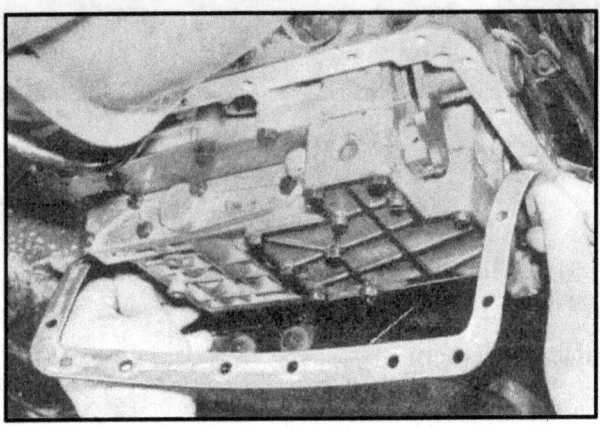

OIL FILLER PIPE
Removing and installing

Detach the oil filler pipe from the cover plate and pull out of the transmission casing.

When installing: The lower end of the oil filler pipe must be de-burred to prevent damage to the O-ring when installing. Check condition of O-ring and replace if necessary.

CONVERTER DOME
Removing and installing

Remove the torque converter. Attach the transmission to support bracket 6002-1. Unscrew the nuts. Lift out the torque converter dome.

When installing: Use only genuine BMW gaskets.

The thrust washer (1) must rest on the needle roller cage.

1. O-ring

TRANSMISSION COVER
Removing and installing

Remove the complete exhaust system. Separate the propeller shaft from the output flange and center bearing mounting. Swing the propeller shaft down and pull out of the center ring journal.

When installing: Pre-load the center bearing journal by 2mm (0.08 in.) in the direction of travel.

Pull off the stop buffer. Lift out the keeper plate.

When installing: The nose on the keeper plate must be engaged in the groove on the output flange.

Retain the output flange in position with locking wrench 604. Place centering bush 607 on to the centering journal. Loosen the shouldered nut. Pull off the output flange. Support the transmission. Detach the speedometer drive shaft. Loosen the transmission cross-beam.

Detach the selector lever switch, exhaust pipe mounting and transmission cover.

When installing: Note the installed position of the cover plate for the pawl.

1. Drive worm
2. Driving plate
3. Section rings

Pull off the speedometer drive worm.

When installing: The shoulder on the worm faces the centrifugal governor.

Loosen the driving plate and swing down. Pull off the centrifugal governor hub.

When installing: Thoroughly oil the square section rings.

Press the driving plate firmly into the groove on the output shaft before tightening. Detach the bearing flange. Always use a new gasket when re-installing.

When installing: Attach the shims to the bearing flange with grease.

AUTOMATIC TRANSMISSION 61

Driving plate

OIL SEAL FOR OUTPUT FLANGE
Removing and installing

Remove the complete exhaust system. Detach the propeller shaft from the output flange and center bearing mounting. Swing down the propeller shaft and pull out of the centering journal.

When installing: Pre-load the center bearing mounting by 2 mm (0.08 in.) in the direction of travel.

Pull off the stop buffer. Lift out the keeper plate.

When installing: Make sure that the keeper plate is firmly located in the slot on the output flange.

Prevent the output flange from moving with locking tool 604. Place centering bush 607 on to the centering journal. Loosen the shouldered nut. Pull off the output flange. Extract the oil seal using 7051 extractor.

When installing: Drive in the oil seal with drift 7053.

Pack the cavity between the sealing lips with branded multi-purpose grease. Do not drive in the oil seal as far as it will go. Always stop when distance A = 3 mm (0.12 in.).

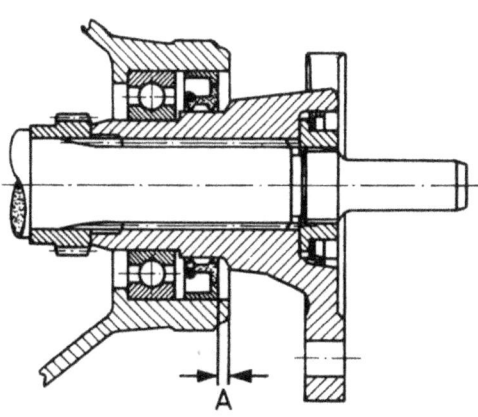

A = 3mm (0.12 in.)

O-RING FOR SPEEDOMETER DRIVE BUSH
Replacing

Detach the speedometer drive shaft. Remove the speedometer drive bush. Replace the O-ring.

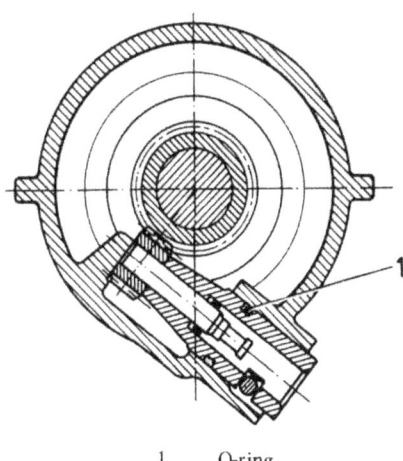

1. O-ring

O-RING FOR SELECTOR LEVER
Replacing

Remove the selector lever. Replace the O-ring.

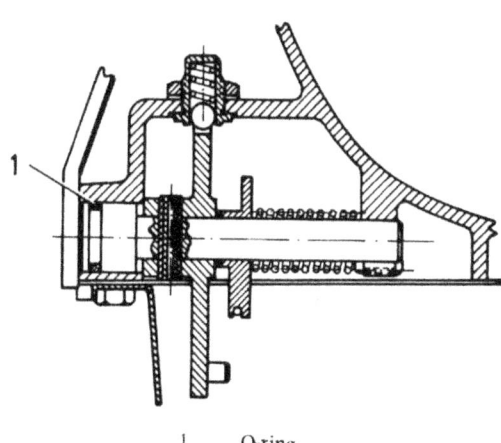

1. O-ring

TORQUE CONVERTER OIL SEAL – TORQUE CONVERTER REMOVED
Replacing

Extract the oil seal with 7051 puller. Drive in the oil seal with plunger 7052 until it is seating firmly.

PAWL FOR PARKING LOCK
Replacing

Detach the connecting rod. Separate the two halves of the multi-pin plug. Take off the selector lever position switch. Remove the speedometer drive shaft. Take off the control unit. Remove the angled lever with torsion spring.

62 AUTOMATIC TRANSMISSION

1. Angled lever
2. Torsion spring

When installing: Note installed position of angled lever, torsion spring and cam.

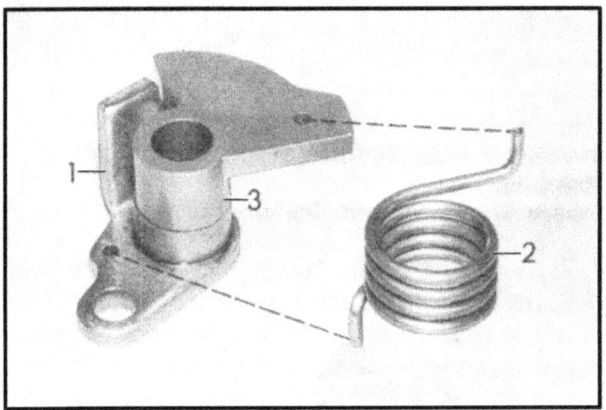

1. Angled lever
2. Torsion spring
3. Cam

Take off the cover plate. Pull the pin out of the housing with an M6 bolt.

When installing: Use a new O-ring.

Take out the pawl with washer and torsion spring.

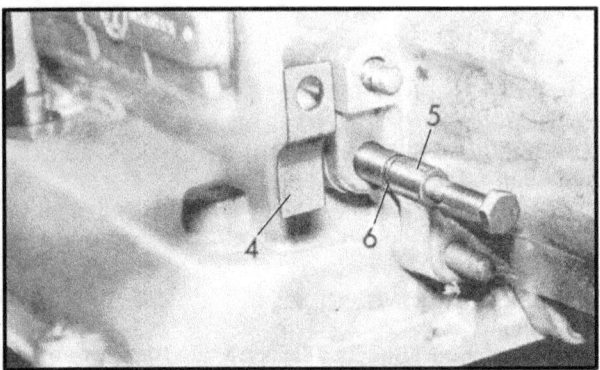

4. Cover plate
5. Pin
6. O-ring

THROTTLE CABLE
Replacing
Disconnect the yoke end. Remove the throttle cable from the thrust mounting.

When installing: Adjust throttle cable.

Set the selector lever to position O. Press the throttle cam forward and detach the cable from the cam. Unscrew the throttle cable from the housing. Use a new sealing ring.

NOTCHED PAWL
Removing and installing
Remove the transmission selector lever. Disconnect the spring clip. Remove the pawl from the connecting rod. Check that the ball can move freely in the engagement sleeve. Transmission ratios are determined by the notches in the pawl.

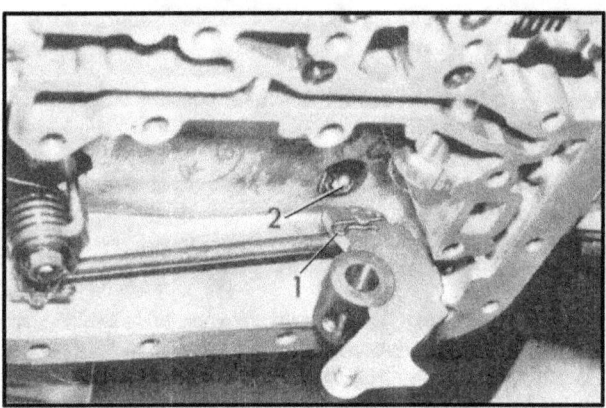

1. Spring clip
2. Ball

TORSION SPRING FOR THROTTLE CABLE – (CONTROL UNIT REMOVED)
Replacing
With the transmission selector lever in neutral, drive out the locking pin. Pull the transmission selector lever out into the transmission tunnel. Take off the torsion spring.

AUTOMATIC TRANSMISSION

When installing: Detach the throttle cable.

Place the short hook on the torsion spring round the throttle cam. The point of the cam should face the rear of the car. Place the long hook on the spring in the slot on the housing. Push the transmission selector lever back in as far as possible. Turn the throttle cam anti-clockwise until the throttle cable can be hooked into place.

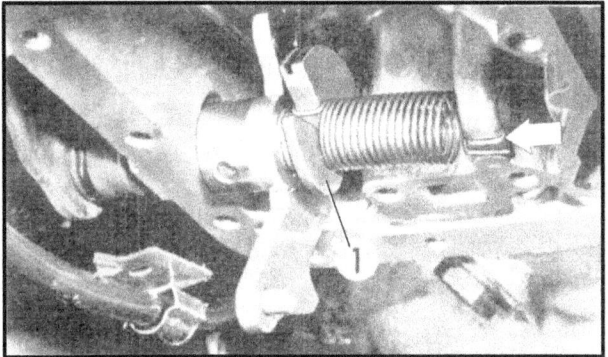

1. Throttle cam

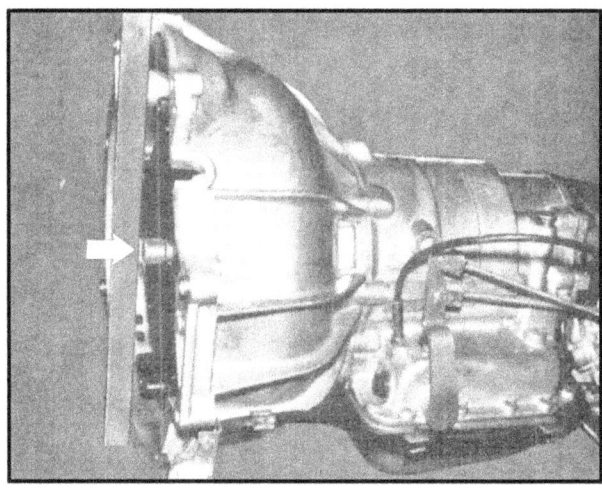

Replacing
Remove the torque converter. The torque converter must not be cleaned with the usual solvents used in the workshop, and should be replaced in the event of transmission damage or a torn oil mesh filter. BMW 2500 torque converter: blue spot; BMW 2800 torque converter: yellow spot. Replace the torque converter if, the running surface on the converter shaft is damaged, the drive lugs are fractured, the welded lugs are torn away, or if the stator or turbine impeller cannot be turned by hand.

Depth of weld lugs:
A = 0.79 in – BMW 2500
A = 0.55 in – BMW 2800

TORQUE CONVERTER
Removing and installing
Remove (install) the transmission. Using assembly handles 6028 carefully pull the torque converter away from the primary pump. Transmission fluid will escape.

When installing: Check torque converter for leakage with test device 7055 and 7.1 psi compressed air line.

Turn the torque converter slightly and insert the 2 hooks into the slots on the primary pump. The torque converter is correctly installed when the guide journals are below the edge of the housing.

TRANSMISSION SELECTOR LEVER
Removing and installing
Remove the control unit. Disconnect the selector rod and connecting rod. With the transmission in neutral, drive out the locking pin. Support the transmission. Detach the cross-beam from the transmission. Take off the rear exhaust system. Lower the transmission on to the front axle beam. In this position, tie up the rear exhaust system. Swing the transmission selector lever down to the rear and pull out of the housing.

AUTOMATIC TRANSMISSION

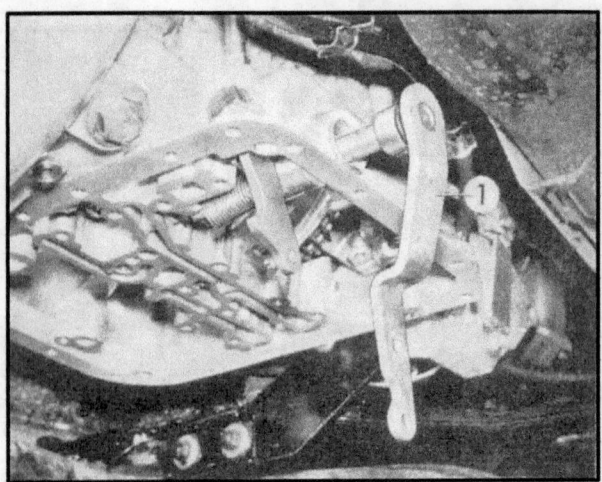

1. Transmission selector lever

When installing: Note position of locating pin in slot.

GEAR LEVER WITH MOUNTING
Removing and installing

Lift out the lock washer. Remove the shift rod. Pull off the knob. Remove the floor of the stowage compartment. Take off the screen plate. Separate the gate carrier from the transmission tunnel.

When installing: Check condition of rubber gasket.

Coupe only, lift away rocker switches (wires remain attached). Loosen screws holding screen plate.

Take off knob and screen and remove gate plate. Detach the shift rod. Pull away the rubber seal and remove bolt. Pull out gear lever upwards.

When installing: Coat pivot bush with Molykote G paste.

When installing: The washer is in front of the notched pawl. Install the throttle cam and torsion spring.

2. Washer

TRANSMISSION RUBBER MOUNTING
Replacing

Support the transmission with stand 7060. Take off the cross-beam. Lower the transmission until the rubber mounting can be removed by loosening with a cranked open-ended spanner.

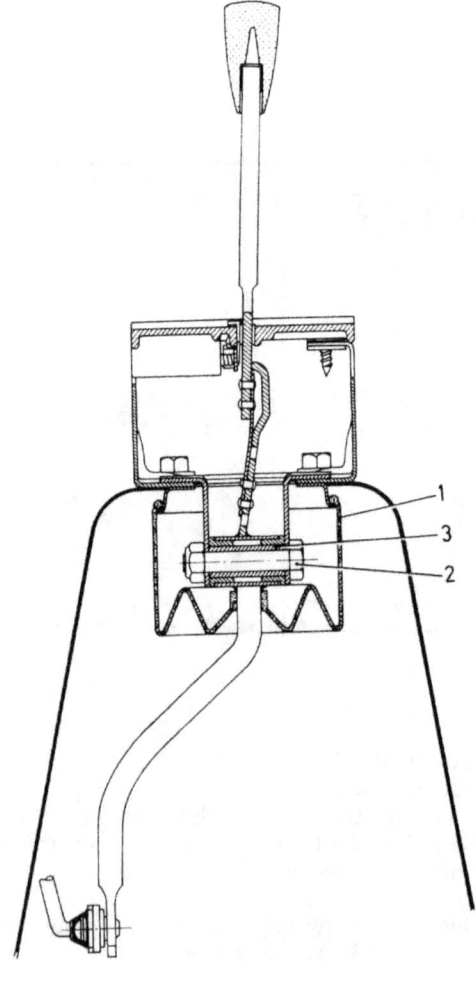

1. Rubber seal
2. Bolt
3. Pivot bush

DRIVE AXLE & DRIVELINE

INDEX

	Page
FINAL DRIVE	65
Removing and refitting	65
SHAFT SEALING RING FOR DRIVING FLANGE	66
Replacing	66
DRIVE FLANGE	66
Removing and installing	66
CROWNWHEEL AND PINION –	
(FINAL DRIVE REMOVED)	67
Replacing	67
Contact pattern setting –	
Gleason tooth profile	70
Klingenberg (Palloid tooth profile)	71
DIFFERENTIAL PINIONS	71
Replacing	71
DIFFERENTIAL HOUSING COMPLETE	72
Removing and refitting	72
LIMITED SLIP DIFFERENTIAL	72
General	72
Checking operation in installed condition	72
Removing and installing	72
Replacing	72
Dismantling and reassembling	73
RUBBER BEARING FOR REAR AXLE DRIVE	74
Replacing	74
Renewing gaiter	74
REAR AXLE BRACKET COMPLETE	74
Removing and refitting	74
Replacing with the rear axle bracket completely removed	75
SUSPENSION ARMS	75
Removing and installing	75

	Page
Replacing both flanblocs	75
Checking	75
RUBBER BEARINGS ON REAR AXLE BRACKET	75
Replacing	75
DRIVE FLANGE	75
Removing and installing	75
REAR AXLE SHAFT	75
Removing and refitting	75
WHEEL BEARINGS AND SHAFT SEALING RINGS	75
Replacing	75
SPRING/SHOCK ABSORBER STRUTS	76
Removing and installing	76
CENTERING CUP	76
Removing and installing	76
SLEEVE FOR SPRING/SHOCK ABSORBER STRUT	76
Replacing	76
COIL SPRING	77
Removing and refitting	77
Replacing	77
PROPELLER SHAFT	77
Removing and refitting	77
Replacing	77
LOCATING RING	77
Replacing	77
RUBBER COUPLING	77
Replacing	77
PROPELLER SHAFT CENTER BEARING	77
Replacing	77
GROOVED BALL BEARING	77
Replacing	77

FINAL DRIVE
Removing and refitting
Disconnect propeller shaft and remove drive shafts.

Support the final drive and detach from final drive bracket. Remove fixing bolt from rubber bearing.

DRIVE AXLE

SHAFT SEALING RING FOR DRIVING FLANGE
Replacing

Remove (install) final drive. Remove (install) differential housing complete. To secure the final drive on mounting bar 6003-1, remove oil drain plug. Mark installed position of driving flange. Lift out locking plate.

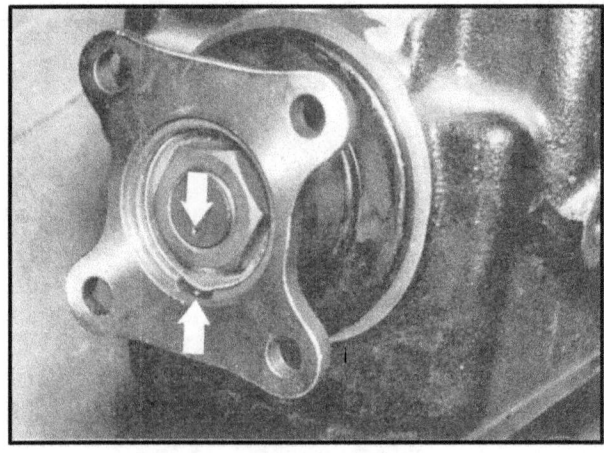

When installing: Lock flanged nut with locking plate in the groove in the driving flange. Determine coefficient of friction, and note. Hold driving flange with locking tool 7012 and slacken flanged nut. Press out the drive pinion. Lift out shaft sealing ring. Check running face of shaft sealing ring on driving flange. If the running face is considerably worn, renew driving flange. Fit drive pinion with new clamp bush. Attach 6057 puller to Kukko 22/1 and pull the front taper roller bearing onto the drive pinion with it. Note: If the taper roller bearing is heated in the oil bath, bearing adjustment — coefficient of friction measurement — must be delayed until the taper roller bearing has completely cooled.

Pack shaft sealing ring with grease and insert flush. Install driving flange. Set drive pinion bearing to the coefficient of friction determined before stripping — plus 5 cmkp for the new shaft sealing ring. The flanged nut must be tightened to at least 108.5 lb/ft. If 108.5 lbs/ft is not reached, or the coefficient of friction is not exceeded the clamp bush must be renewed and measuring procedure repeated.

Example:

Coefficient of friction before stripping	14 cmkp
New shaft sealing ring	+ 4 cmkp
Drive pinion bearing to be set to	18 cmkp

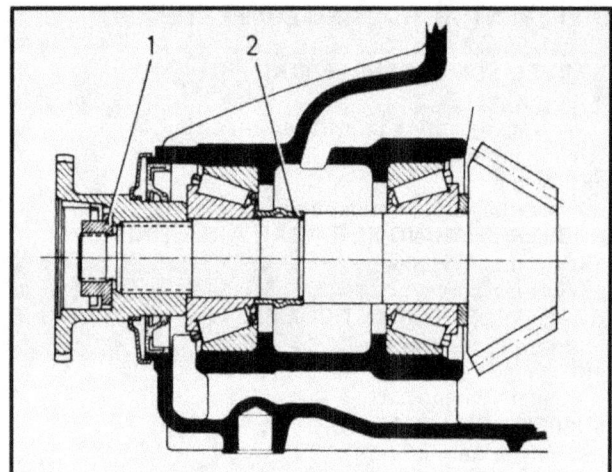

1. Flanged nut
2. Clamp bush

DRIVE FLANGE
Removing and installing

Disconnect halfshaft and hold drive flange with locking tool 7012 and slacken fixing bolt. Pull off drive flange with extractor 7011. If the final drive loses oil severely, the cause may be a vent pipe incorrectly pressed in. Vent passages must be at 90° to the crownwheel.

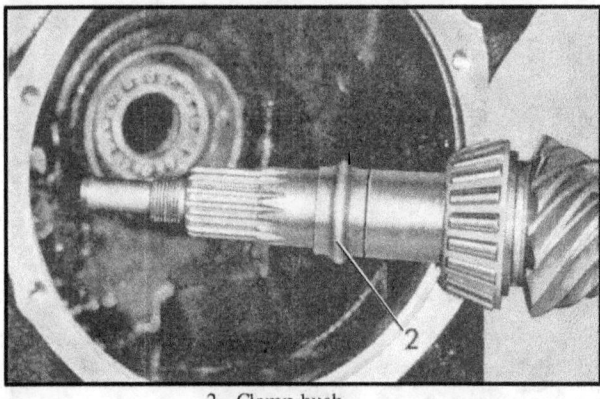

2. Clamp bush

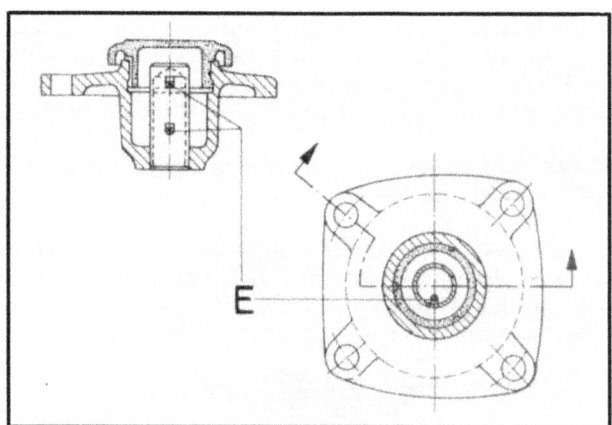

E   Vent passages

To replace the string seal on housing cover, remove (install) drive flange and remove the cover. Lift out string seal.

Replace the shaft sealing ring for drive flange by lifting out the shaft sealing ring.

When installing: Pack shaft sealing ring with grease and flush.

Replace the grooved ball bearing for the drive flange by extracting the thrust bearing.

When installing: Use only C3 bearings.

CROWNWHEEL AND PINION – (FINAL DRIVE REMOVED)
Replacing

Number of teeth of pinion set fitted is stamped on housing. Remove the drive flange with extractor tool 7011. Remove cover. Remove differential complete.

Fitting instructions: Before fitting, insert spacer tubes in differential housing.

Lift out locking plate.

Fitting instructions: Lock flanged nut with locking plate in groove in driving flange.

Lock driving flange with locking tool 7012 and slacken flanged nut. Press out drive pinion. Lift out shaft sealing ring. Extract taper roller bearing. Extract the bearing outer races of the drive pinion with extractor tool 6053.

The crownwheel and pinion have been matched on special machines for maximum operating silence. The matching number P has been electrically inscribed on crownwheel and pinion. Crownwheel and pinions with differing

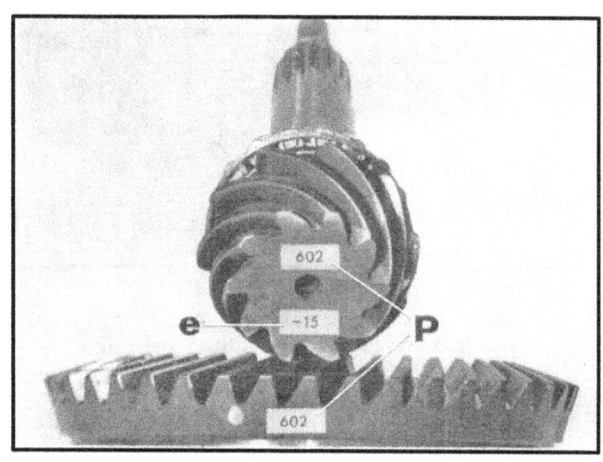

matching numbers should never be assembled together. The figure E, accompanied by a + or − sign is the variation from the basic setting dimension E in hundredths of a mm and is required for ascertaining the thickness of shims x.

e + = add to E
e − = subtract from E

Crownwheel and pinions sets have Klingelnberg (Palloid) and Gleason tooth profiles. With the Klingelnberg Tooth profile the tooth spine on the drive pinion is the same both outside and inside. Klingelnberg sets are stamped with the letter K on both crownwheel and pinion. With the Gleason tooth profile the tooth spine on the crownwheel is wider on the outside than on the inside. Gleason sets are marked H or F on crownwheel and pinion.

Press on taper roller bearing and measuring plate 1.594" thick. To facilitate fitting, coat bearing inner race with grease. Installing position of plate, chamfered inside diameter should face towards drive pinion. Press front taper roller bearing on to drive pinion with insertion tool 6057 and Kukko 22/1. Fit driving flange without shaft sealing ring. Set drive pinion taper roller bearing to 22 ± 1 cmk..Place measuring block on front face of the drive pinion.

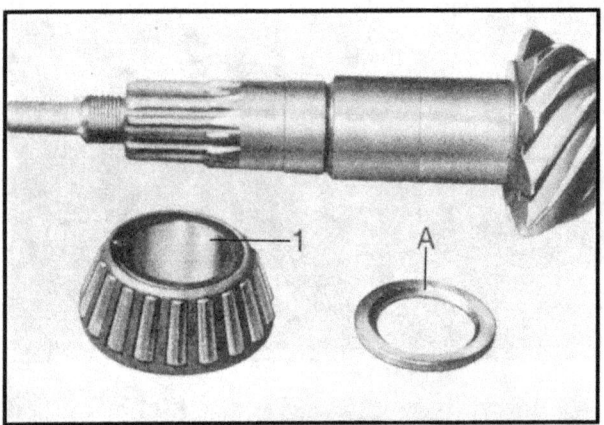

A. 1.594" thick

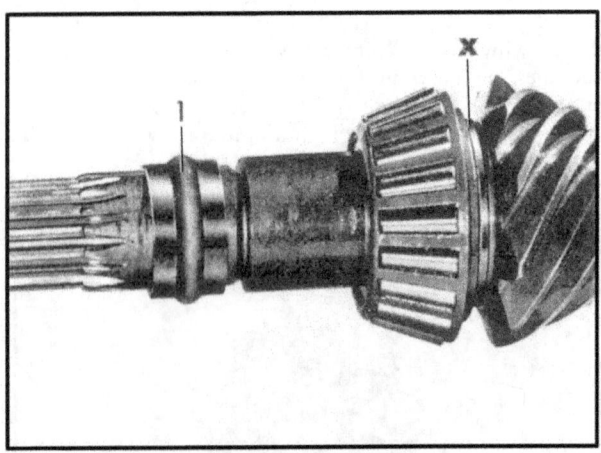

Remove drive pinion. Pull off taper roller bearing with Rollex HM 89449. Fit drive pinion with shim X as calculated and a new clamp bush. The chamfered inside diameter of the shim X should face towards the drive pinion. Pack shaft sealing ring with grease and fit flush.

Secure driving flange with flanged nut. Set drive taper roller bearing to 22 ± 1 cmkp +.4 cmkp for the shaft sealing ring. If the coefficient of friction is exceeded, the clamp bush must be renewed and the measuring procedure repeated. Release crownwheel from differential housing.

Fitting instructions: Fit crownwheel cold. Use Loctite AVV when fitting bolts.

Extract taper roller bearing with Rollex LM 503349. Press on taper roller bearing cold. Pull bearing race out of housing with extractor tool 6053. Mark shim. Pull bearing race out of cap. Mark shim. Extract O ring.

If the new crownwheel and pinion set has the same tooth profile as the one removed, the old shims can be fitted. This will facilitate rapid checking of coefficient of friction, tooth flank play and tooth contact characteristics. If a crownwheel and pinion set with a different tooth profile is fitted, for basic setting with the Gleason tooth profile shims of thickness 0.551−0.669" should be used and with the Klingelnberg tooth profile a thickness of 0.866−0.944".

1. Gleason tooth profile shim

Fit bearing outer race and one shim in the cover with extractor tool 6053. Turn the drive flange fixing bolt against the differential pinion shaft. Fit differential housing without crownwheel. Tighten cover fixing bolt uniformly at 14.5 ± 36.2 lb/ft and measure coefficient of friction. Determine gap and subtract from the shim in the cover. Example: Shim is 0.866". Gap − 0.012". Shim should be 0.748".

DRIVE AXLE 69

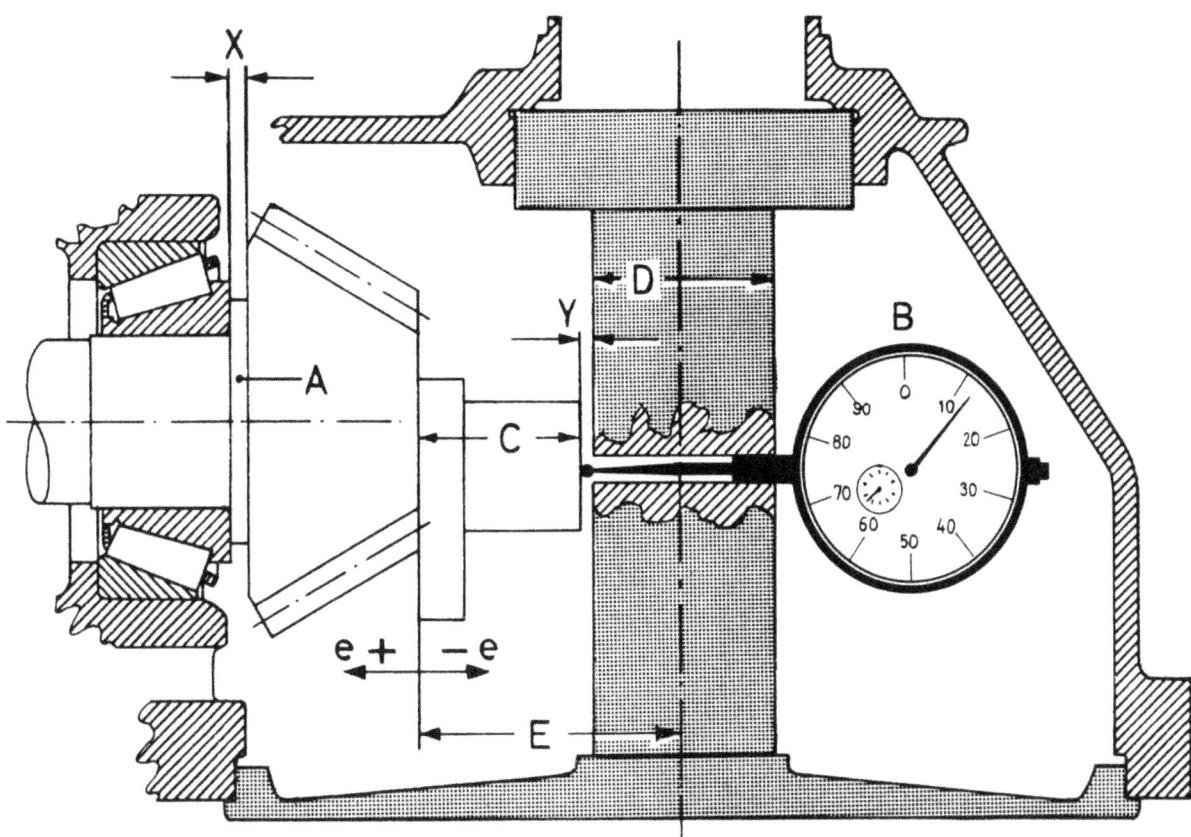

Example I

1. E   59.00 mm (2.323")
   e+   0.15 mm (0.006")

   E theoretical
               59.15 mm (2.328")

2. C   38.00 mm (1.496")
   +D : 2   20.00 mm (0.787")
               58.00 mm (2.283")

3. Depression
   dial gauge   4.00 mm (0.157")
   Less measured
   value B   3.12 mm (0.123")

   Clearance Y   0.88 mm (0.034")

4. Sum C, D   58.00 mm (2.283")
   +Y   0.88 mm (0.346")

   E actual   58.88 mm (2.629")

5. E theoretical
               59.15 mm (2.328")
   E actual   58.88 mm (2.629")

   a   0.27 mm (0.106")

6. Measuring
   plate A   4.05 mm (0.159")
   −a   0.27 mm (0.010")

   Shim X   3.78 mm (0.149")

If E theoretical is greater than E actual, a'should be subtracted from the measuring plate A.

If E theoretical is less than E actual, a'should be added to the measuring plate A.

Permissible thickness tolerance of shim X
with Klingelnberg
tooth profile ±0.03 mm (0.0012")
with Gleason
tooth profile ±0.04 mm (0.0016")

Example II

1. E   61.85 mm (2.434")
   e−   0.12 mm (0.004")

   E theoretical
               61.73 mm (2.430")

2. C   38.00 mm (1.496")
   +D : 2   20.00 mm (0.787")
               58.00 mm (2.283")

3. Depression
   dial gauge   7.00 mm (0.275")
   Less measured
   value B   3.12 mm (0.122")

   Clearance Y   3.88 mm (0.152")

4. Sum C, D   58.00 mm (2.283")
   +Y   3.88 mm (0.152")

   E actual   61.88 mm (2.436")

5. E theoretical
               61.73 mm (2.430")
   E actual   61.88 mm (2.436")

   a   0.15 mm (0.006")

6. Measuring
   plate A   4.05 mm (0.159")
   +a   0.15 mm (0.006")

   Shim X   4.20 mm (0.165")

70 DRIVE AXLE

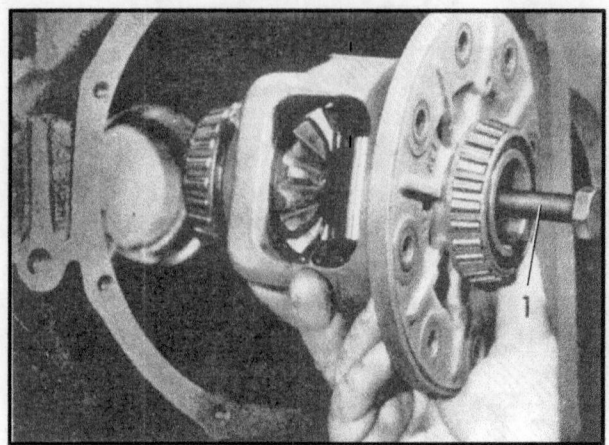

1. Drive flange fixing bolt

Fit the shim as calculated. Fit cover and again check coefficient of friction. Fix crownwheel in differential housing. Insert screws using Loctite AVV and tighten at recommended torque. Fit crownwheel. Remove breather housing. Fix dial gauge holder and measure torsional flank play. To take a tooth contact pattern, smear the crownwheel with engineer's blue, rotate several times in both directions and brake with a piece of hardwood.

The torsional flank play and the contact pattern will be altered by shims 1 and 2. Shims 1 and 2 should be changed until torsional flank play and contact pattern are correct. Alteration of shim thickness by 0.004" will produce a change in torsional flank play of approximately 0.002". On no account should the total thickness of shims 1 and 2 be changed.

Contact pattern setting Gleason tooth profile

By shifting the crownwheel the flank play will be altered; in addition the contact pattern will be shifted in longitudinal tooth direction. By shifting the drive pinion the contact pattern is displaced upwards along the tooth, the flank play alters however only slightly. In addition you should note the four basic incorrect contact patterns which usually occur in combination; recognition will facilitate practical adjustment operations.

For high narrow contact pattern (tip contact) on crownwheel, move drive pinion towards crownwheel axis and if necessary correct torsional flank play by moving the crownwheel away from the drive pinion. For low, narrow contact pattern (base contact) on crownwheel, move drive pinion away from crownwheel axis and if necessary correct torsional flank play by advancing the crownwheel. For short, contact pattern over small area at tooth edge (toe contact) of the crownwheel, move crownwheel away from drive pinion. If necessary move drive pinion nearer to crownwheel axis. For short contact pattern at long edge of tooth (heel contact) of crownwheel, move crownwheel towards drive pinion. If necessary move drive pinion away from crownwheel axis.

Correct contact pattern no load — A

Under load the contact pattern shifts outward slightly. — A^1

Tip contact — 1.

Base contact — 2.

Toe contact — 3.

Heel — 4.

DRIVE AXLE

Klingelnberg (Palloid) tooth profile

The contact pattern must be present at the forward and reverse flanks of the drive pinion at approximately the center of the tooth length and tooth height.

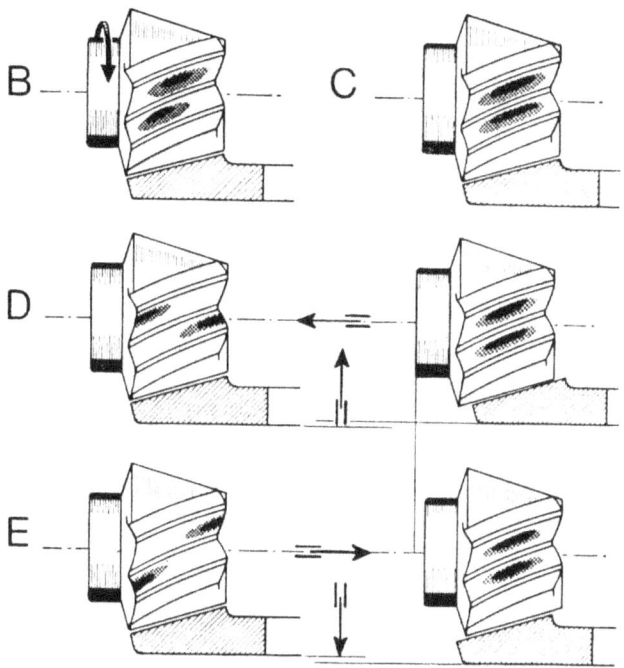

B Contact pattern unloaded
C Contact pattern under load
D By fitment of a thicker shim X behind the drive pinion the contact pattern of the forward face shifts towards the larger drive pinion diameter, whilst on the reverse flank it approaches the smaller drive pinion.

For other alternatives see diagram E.

DIFFERENTIAL PINIONS
Replacing

Drive out clamp sleeve and differential pinion shaft. Unscrew both differential pinions with drive flange. Extract rear axle shaft pinions with cup springs and shims.

1. Clamp sleeve
2. Differential pinion shaft

3. Rear axle shaft pinion
4,5. Differential pinions
A. Differential housing with measuring plate

Fitting instructions: Fit rear axle shaft pinions into differential housing with measuring plate and differential pinions. Fit drive flange and determine coefficient of friction. At initial fitting maximum coefficient of friction 7.23 lb/ft may rise to 14.5 lb/ft at the tight spots. The measuring plate should be changed until the correct coefficient of friction is reached.

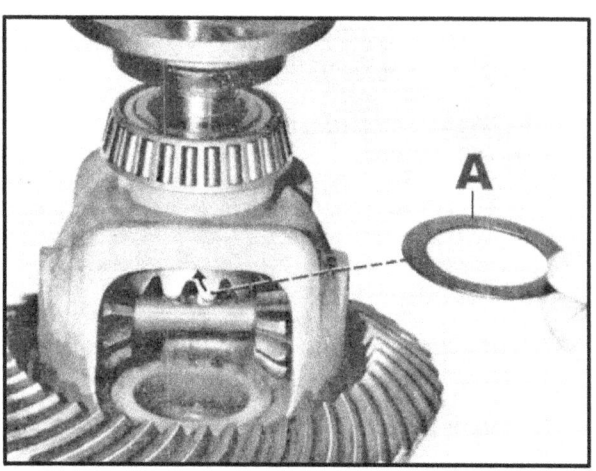

A. Measuring plate

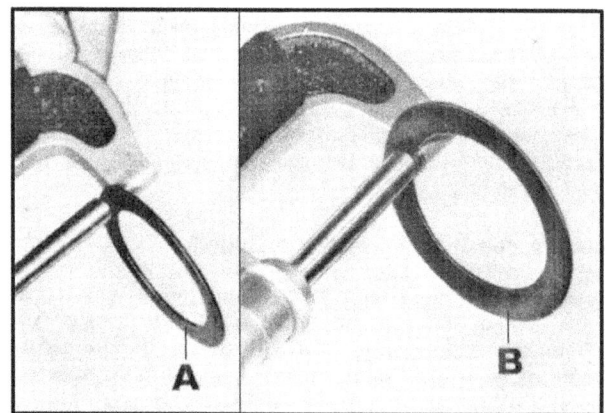

Determine thickness of measuring plate A and cup spring B

DRIVE AXLE

0.002–0.433" should be deducted in each case so that the cup spring does not lock. Calculation of shim thickness C should be carried out for the second rear axle shaft pinion in the same way. Fit rear axle shaft pinions with cup spring B and shim C. Note! Internal dishing of cup spring B should face towards the rear axle shaft pinion.

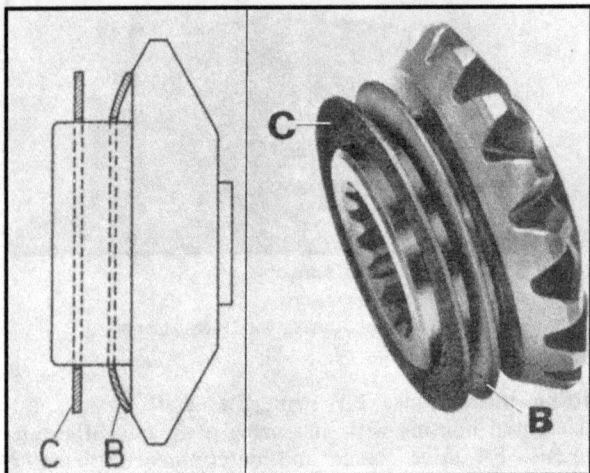

To determine shim thickness C:

Example:

A		1.80 mm (0.708")
–B		1.10 mm (0.433")
		0.70 mm (0.027")
–D		0.05 mm (0.002")
C		0.65 mm (0.025")

DIFFERENTIAL HOUSING COMPLETE
Removing and refitting
Fix rear axle drive on mounting bar 6003-1. Lock drive flange with retaining tool 7012 and unscrew fixing bolt. Extract drive flange with extractor tool 7011. Remove the cover and check O-ring and if necessary renew. Extract differential housing complete.

Fitting instructions: Before fitting, insert spacer tubes into differential housing.

LIMITED SLIP DIFFERENTIAL
General
The limited slip differential has the following advantages: A single rear wheel has much less tendency to spin if it loses contact with the surface while passing over a bump. Wheelspin when starting or driving over surfaces of markedly variable quality is also avoided. When cornering rapidly, the inner wheel can spin if no limited slip differential is installed. In heavy rain at high speed, wheelspin due to aquaplaning is resisted. The risk of skidding when a change in surface is encountered at high speed is reduced.

Checking operation in installed condition
Repair shop floor must be level. Run left rear wheel of vehicle onto roller stand 7023. Fully release the handbrake. Select 1st gear and accelerate. The limited slip differential is functioning correctly if the vehicle can be driven off the roller stand 7023. Limited slip differentials coded S 40 are equipped with molybdenum coated inner plates.

Removing and installing:
Detach the halfshafts from the final drive. Hold driving flange with retaining key 7012. Loosen the attachment screws. Pull off the driving flange with 7011 puller. Drain the oil. Take off the cover.

When installing: Check O-ring and replace if necessary.

Remove the limited slip differential.

Replacing
This procedure is identical with 'Limited slip differential – subsequently installing.' Exceptions at start of procedure – remove differential housing, detach crownwheel from differential housing. Remove final drive. Remove limited slip differential. Detach crownwheel from limited slip differential.

When installing: Install crownwheel without heating.

Clean screw threads carefully and install screws with Loctite AVV. Pull off taper roller bearing with Rollex 503 349 tool.

When installing: Press on taper roller bearing without heating.

Install the new limited slip differential without the crownwheel. Tighten the cover screws evenly to 14.5 ± 3.6 lb/ft. Measure friction loading. If the friction value is below the nominal value, measure the gap and determine the thickness of the shim needed.

Adjust flank backlash and contact pattern with suitable shims. Move shims from one side to the other until both tooth backlash and contact pattern are correct. Never alter the total thickness of the shims. If the contact

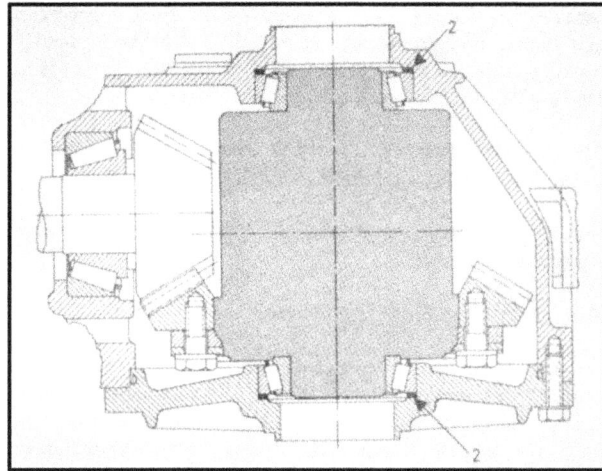

2. Shims

pattern cannot be correctly adjusted, the setting must be altered with shim plate X. (See Contact Pattern Setting.) Before loosening the shouldered nut, check friction loading. Always install a new clamp bush after stripping. Adjust the input bevel pinion bearing to the same friction loading as determined before disassembly. The shouldered nut must be tightened to at least 108 lb/ft. If this cannot be reached or if the value is too easily exceeded, replace clamp bush and repeat the measurement procedure.

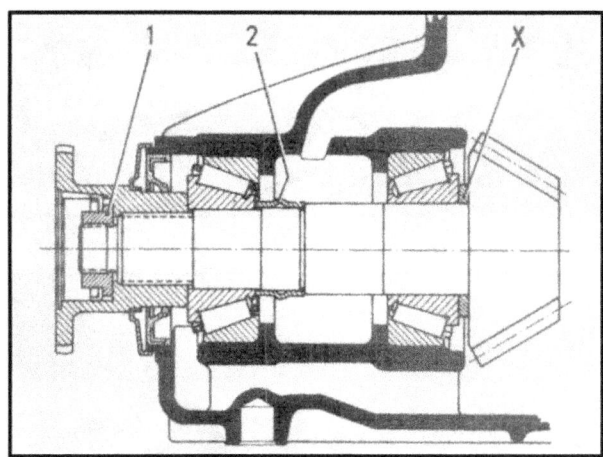

1. Shoulder nut
2. Clamp bush
x. Shim plate

Dismantling and re-assembling
Detach the crownwheel.

When installing: Install the crownwheel without heating. Carefully clean the screw threads. Insert the screws with Loctite AVV.

Remove the screws holding the housing cover. Screw in temporarily two M 6 x 30 mm screws and use them to force the cover away from the housing. Invert the housing and allow the plates to slip out. If necessary, strike the outside of the housing lightly. Take out the thrust washer for the rear axle shaft pinion. When installing, the oil grooves on the thrust washer face the base of the housing. The thrust washers are used to adjust the friction loading of the bevel pinions.

Remove the spacer, outer plate and molybdenum coated inner plate.

When installing: The inner plates are used to adjust the installed clearance of the complete plate set from the housing.

Coat all rubbing surfaces with Molykote G or LM 348 paste. Since the housing has now been modified, conversion to spacer type plate set is not permitted.

Recess in lower housing now 0.138 in; previously 1.075–1.146 in.

Installed position of components for version with crosscut pattern plates — thrust ring, outer plate, crosscut plate, smooth inner plates, crosscut plate, and outer plate. If noise is generated, repair by replacing the crosscut and inner plates by a set consisting of molybdenum coated inner plates and additional outer plates as spacers. Installed clearance is adjusted by means of the inner plates, exactly as in the version using the thick spacer ring.

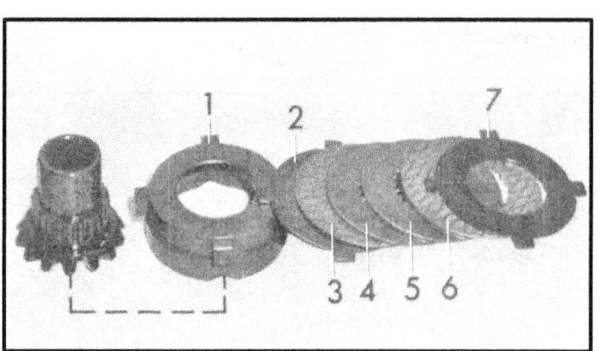

Sequence of plates

Molybdenum coated (2)

1. Thrust ring
2. Inner plate (2)
3. Outer plate
4. Outer plate
5. Outer plate
6. Outer plate
7. Outer plate

Previously

1. Thrust ring
2. Outer plate
3. Crosscut pattern
4. Inner plate
5. Inner plate
6. Crosscut pattern
7. Outer plate

Lift off the thrust ring. Remove the rear axle shaft pinion. Remove the differential pinions complete with shafts. Continue to take down the differential as described above. Examine all components for score marks. The thrust rings must move freely in the housing. The guide lugs on the thrust ring and the outer plates must not be distorted or worn. The inner plates must move easily on the splines. The splines must not be damaged or worn. Replace worn thrust washers and plates.

74 DRIVE AXLE

When installing: Measure depth of housing. Install the plate set on the housing cover and preload to 220 lbs. Measure installed length down to housing cover. Adjust installed clearance with inner plates of suitable thickness.

B Installed length

Insert the complete plate set into the housing. The oil grooves on the thrust washer must face the housing cover. Attach the housing cover with the crownwheel. Check operation. With one rear axle shaft pinion prevented from turning, the other should turn when not more than 50 cmkp load is applied. Adjust the friction loading with the thrust washers.

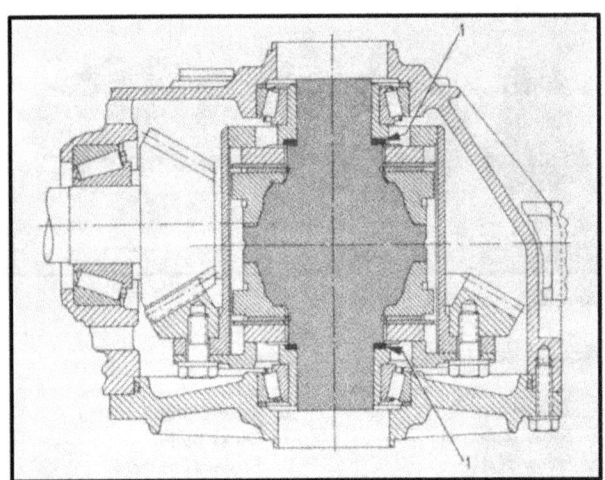

1. Thrust washer

RUBBER BEARING FOR REAR AXLE DRIVE
Replacing
Support rear axle drive. Remove rubber bearing from rear axle drive. Remove rubber bearing from body.

Renewing gaiter
Tap off sealing cover, lift out circlip. Release clip on gaiter. Press off joint. Pull off gaiter. Pack joint and agiter with 4.2 oz. Shell-Retinax AM.

Fitting instructions: Internal dishing of axial clamp ring should face towards joint.

Clean grease off contact faces with gaiter. Smear gaiter with sealing compound EC 750 M – 2 G 51. To facilitate tightening of the clips, drill two holes 0.078" diameter.

REAR AXLE BRACKET COMPLETE
Removing and refitting
Remove handbrake lever. Prevent brake fluid from escaping from compensating reservoir with two pointed wooden rods 0.236" diameter. Jack up vehicle on hoist. Pull handbrake cable out of protective sleeve.

Fitting instructions: Adjust handbrake cable so that the brakes lock evenly up to the 5th click.

Remove silencer and resonator. Remove propeller shaft and brake lines.

When installing: Bleed rear brake.

Lower vehicle until the rear wheels rest on the shop floor. Support rear axle drive with jack. As an additional aid place a block of wood (19.7 x 2.8 x 1.4") on the lifting plate of the jack. Remove final drive from rubber bearing. Unscrew locknuts. Slacken tie rods and swing out sideways. Detach suspension strut shock absorbers at control arm.

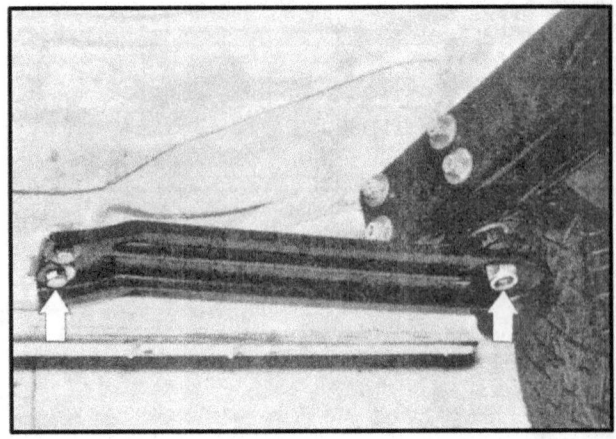

When installing: Tighten bolts in normal position.

Lift vehicle. Run out rear axle.

DRIVE AXLE

Replacing with the rear axle bracket completely removed
Support the control arm. Detach rubber bearing.

When installing: Center rubber bearings and finally tighten on vehicle.

Slacken control arms.

When installing: Tighten bolts in normal position.

Detach rear axle bracket from final drive. Carry out optical check of rear wheel alignment in normal load position, and if necessary correct by moving rear axle mounting bracket sideways.

SUSPENSION ARMS
Removing and installing
Remove handbrake lever. Prevent brake fluid escaping from compensating reservoir by means of two pointed wooden rods (0.236") in diameter. Support the body and detach the wheel. Pull handbrake cable out of protective tube and disconnect brake line.

When installing: Bleed brake and detach halfshaft.

Detach suspension strut/shock absorber from suspension arm.

When installing: Tighten bolt in normal load position.

Detach suspension arm from rear axle bracket.

When installing: Tighten bolts in normal load position.

Replacing both Flanblocs
Press out Flanblocs with suitable drift.

Fitting instructions: Smear Flanblocs with Poliglykol. Flanged side should always be on the outside.

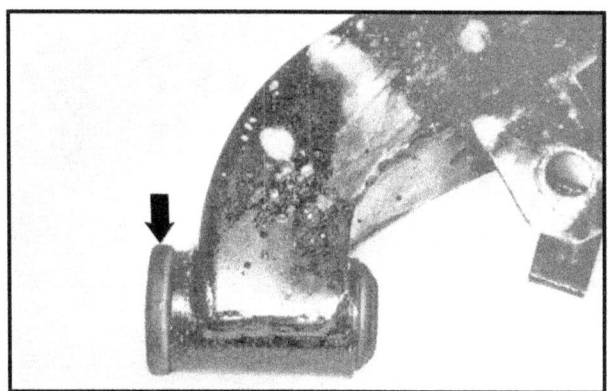

Checking
Press out Flanblocs. Secure drive flange on test unit 6007. It must be possible for the test mandril to pass easily through the locating hole. Realignment of the suspension arm is only permissible if no cracks or other defects are visible. Support rear axle bracket. Detach thrust stay.

RUBBER BEARINGS ON REAR AXLE BRACKET
Replacing
Support rear axle bracket. Remove rear seat and tie rod. Drive out milled screw. Detach rubber bearing from rear axle bracket.

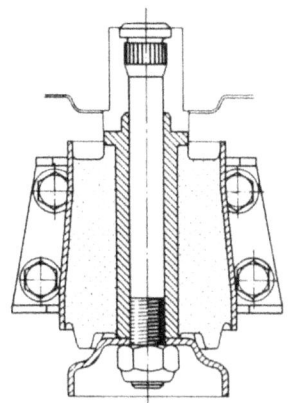

DRIVE FLANGE
Removing and refitting
Disconnect drive shaft flange. Lift out locking plate. Remove flanged nut. Pull off drive flange.

When installing: Lock flanged nut in drive flange groove with locking plate.

REAR AXLE SHAFT
Removing and refitting
Detach brake stirrup – brake line should remain connected. Detach brake disc. Remove drive flange. Unscrew flanged nut. Drive out rear axle shaft. Check spacer ring. Badly worn spacer rings should be renewed.

WHEEL BEARINGS AND SHAFT SEALING RINGS
Replacing
After 60,000 miles it is advisable to renew the wheel bearings even if they appear to be serviceable when examined. Drive out wheel bearing and shaft sealing ring outwards. Check seating faces of wheel bearings for traces of slip on the hub. Drive in outer ball bearing to fullest extent. Only use C3 bearings. The space between wheel bearing and shaft sealing ring must be free of grease. On the other hand the sealing lips should be packed with Retinax A.

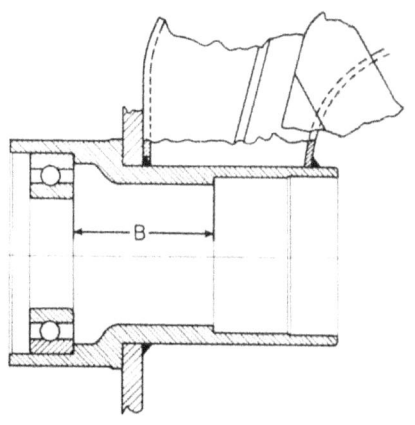

76 DRIVE AXLE

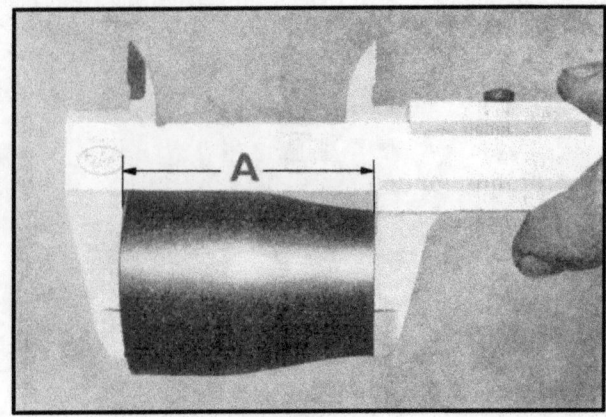

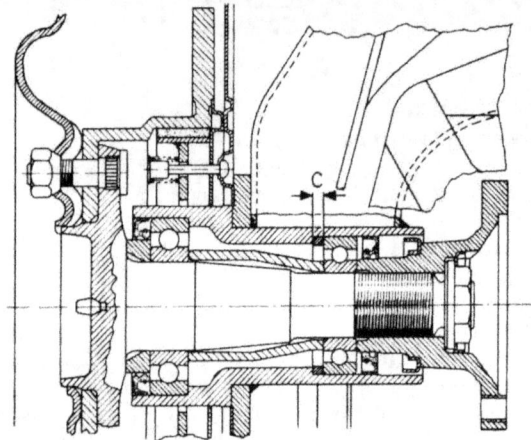

To determine thickness of spacer ring C.

Example: A   2.500"
          B   2.307"

               0.192"
         -D   0.004"

          C   0.188"

D recommended end float = 0.002–0.004".
Fit wheel bearing with spacer ring C as calculated and 35 g (1.2 oz.) Retinax A per wheel bearing.

SPRING/SHOCK ABSORBER STRUTS
Removing and installing

The spring/shock absorber strut has the function of a strap. Angle of inclination of halfshaft 18°.

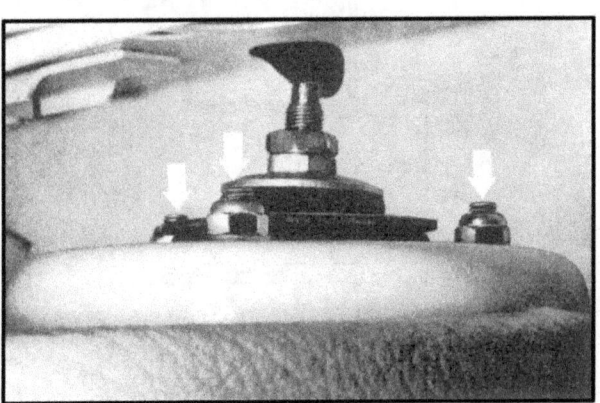

When installing: Tighten bolt in normal load position.

Only change spring/shock absorber struts with suspension arm under load. Release centering cup from wheel arch.

CENTERING CUP
Removing and installing

Remove spring/shock absorber struts. Compress coil spring with spring compressor 6035 until it is possible to detach the centering cup. Check rubber bearing and renew if necessary. Tighten nut to its fullest extent.

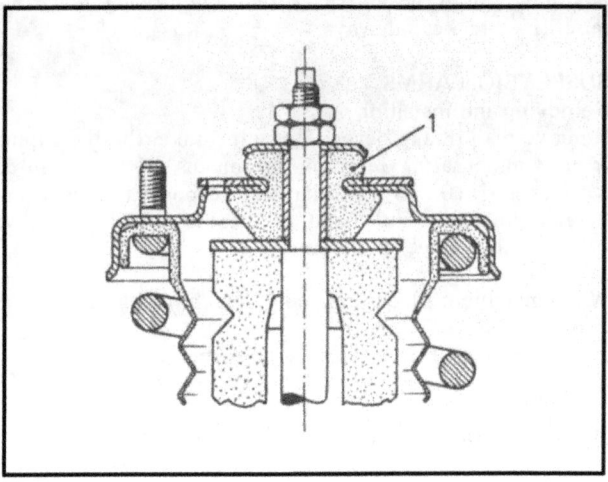

1. Rubber bearing

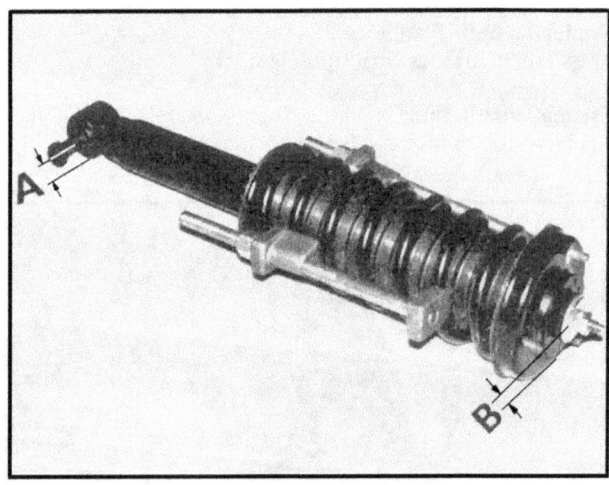

A. Equal on both sides
B. 2.362"

Fitting instructions: Before releasing the coil spring, align the centering cup with its lower seating.

SLEEVE FOR SPRING/SHOCK ABSORBER STRUT
Replacing

Remove coil spring.

When installing: Align centering cup before releasing coil spring.

DRIVE AXLE

COIL SPRING
Removing and refitting
Remove or refit spring/shock absorber strut. Remove or refit centering cup.

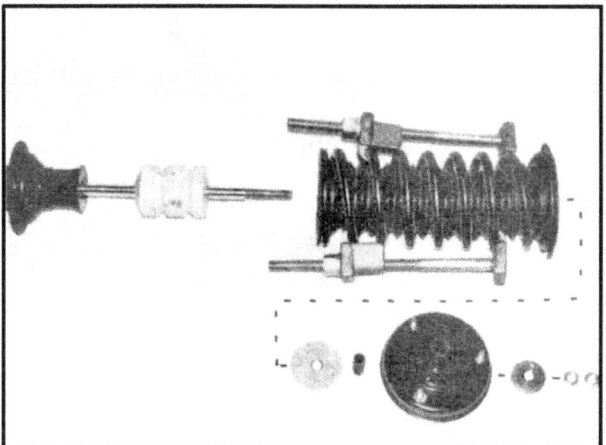

Replacing
Remove or refit coil spring. Spring code, spring length and wire thickness must be the same on the left and right hand sides of the car. Refit sleeve.

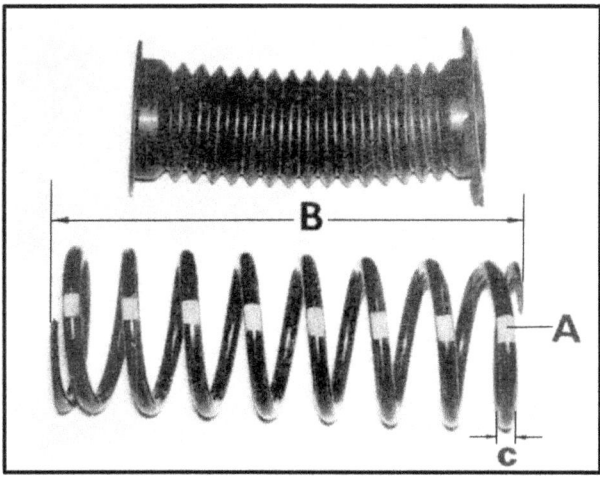

A. Spring code
B. Spring length
C. Wire thickness

PROPELLER SHAFT
Removing and Refitting
Remove exhaust silencer and resonator. Separate propeller shaft from rear axle drive. Remove propeller shaft with rubber coupling. Detach center support bracket.

Fitting instructions: Tension center support (A = 0.0079") in direction of travel.

A=0.079

Bend propeller shaft downwards and pull out from centering peg on gearbox.

When installing: Do not damage sealing cap. Check locating ring for freedom of movement.

Replacing
The propeller shaft is balanced as an assembly and should therefore only be replaced complete. Tighten screw bush after fitment has been completed.

LOCATING RING
Replacing
Press off sealing cap. Lift out circlip. Extract ball cup, locating ring, washer and spring.

Fitting instructions: Pack locating unit with approximately (0.212 oz.) Molykote Longterm 2.

RUBBER COUPLING
Replacing
Remove strap after fitment has been completed.

PROPELLER SHAFT CENTER BEARING
Replacing
Mark propeller shaft before dismantling. Slacken screw bush. Remove circlip and dust cap.

When installing: The internal dishing of the circlip should face towards the dust cap.

Press off bearing support less dust cap.

GROOVED BALL BEARING
Replacing
Press out grooved ball bearing.

When installing: Smear grooved ball bearing socket with water.

DRIVE AXLE

Rear suspension
Independent, with semi-trailing arms pivoting on no-maintenance rubber bushes. Delta-shaped box-section rear axle beam for semi-trailing arms and final drive, bolted to body shell at 3 points by means of rubber mountings with built-in longitudinal compliance. Coil springs and rubber auxiliary springs, total wheel travel 7.9" (200 mm), double-acting telescopic hydraulic shock absorbers.
Torsion bar anti-roll stabilizer mounted in no-maintenance rubber bushes.

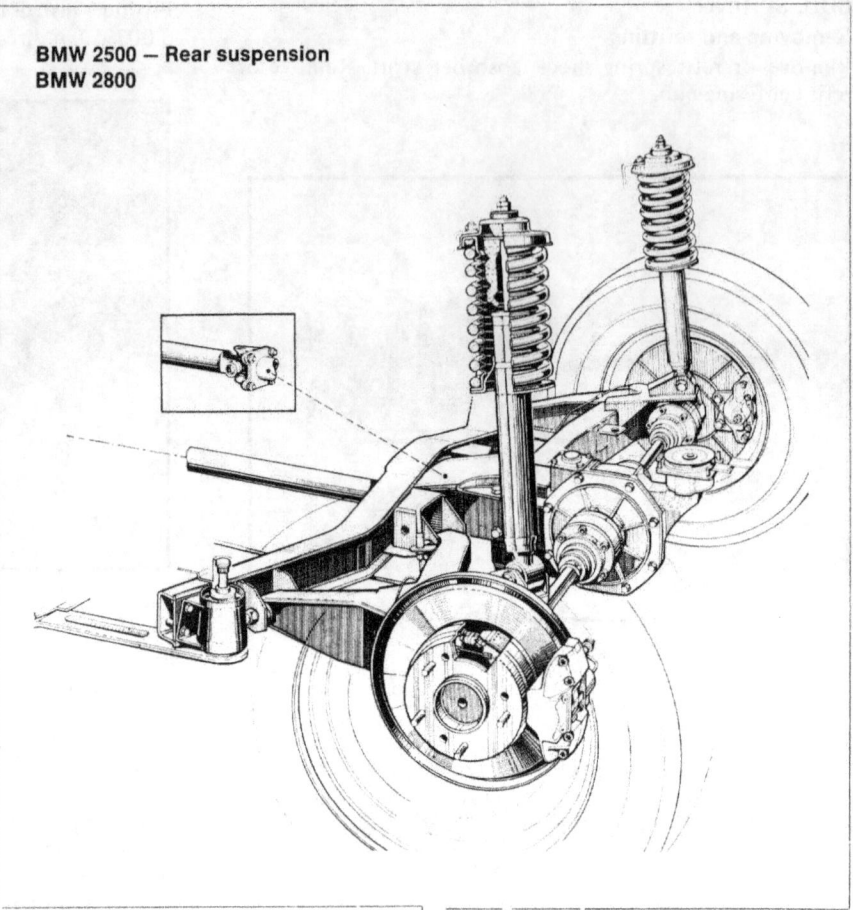

BMW 2500 — Rear suspension
BMW 2800

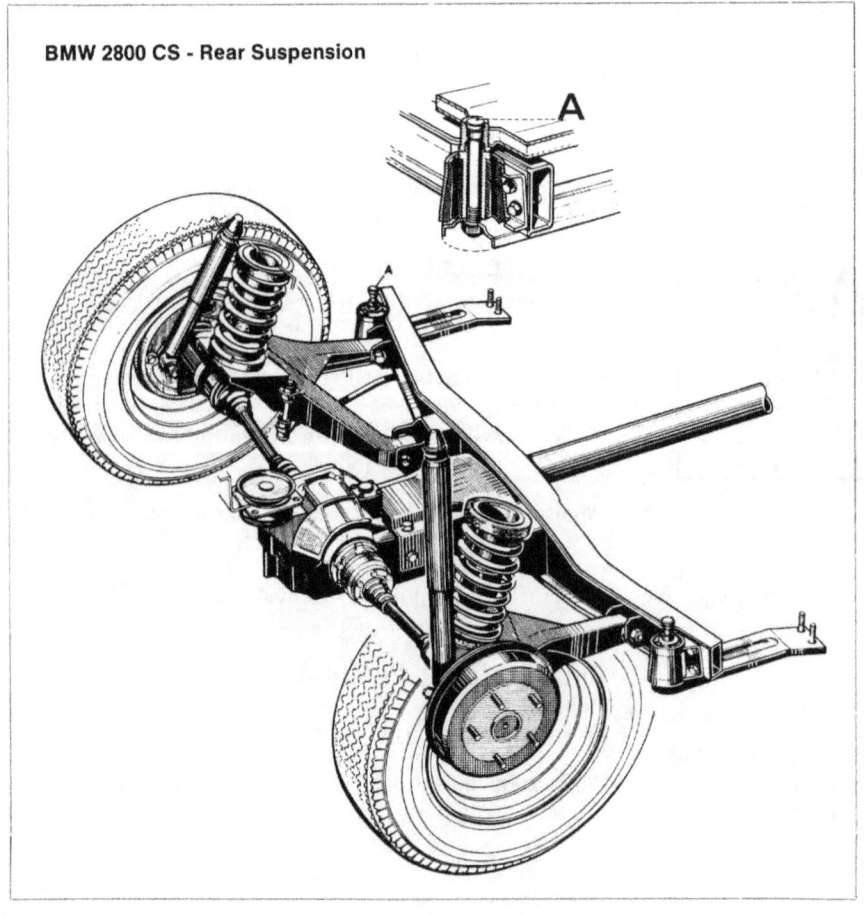

BMW 2800 CS - Rear Suspension

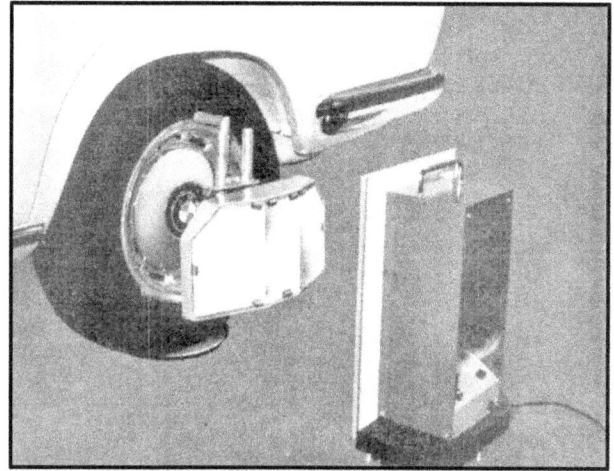

32 00 054 Rear axle optical alignment

The following conditions must be fulfilled before wheel alignment is carried out:
1. Good, even tire tread.
2. Correct tire pressures.
3. Rims in good condition.
4. Correct wheel bearing play.
5. Vehicle in normal load position:
   2 x 65 kg (143 lb.) on the rear seats,
   1 x 65 kg (143 lb.) on the front seats.
   30 kg (66 lb.) in luggage compartment on left, fuel tank full.

Use the optical alignment device to determine actual values.

Enter these values on the alignment chart.

For nominal values, see technical data.

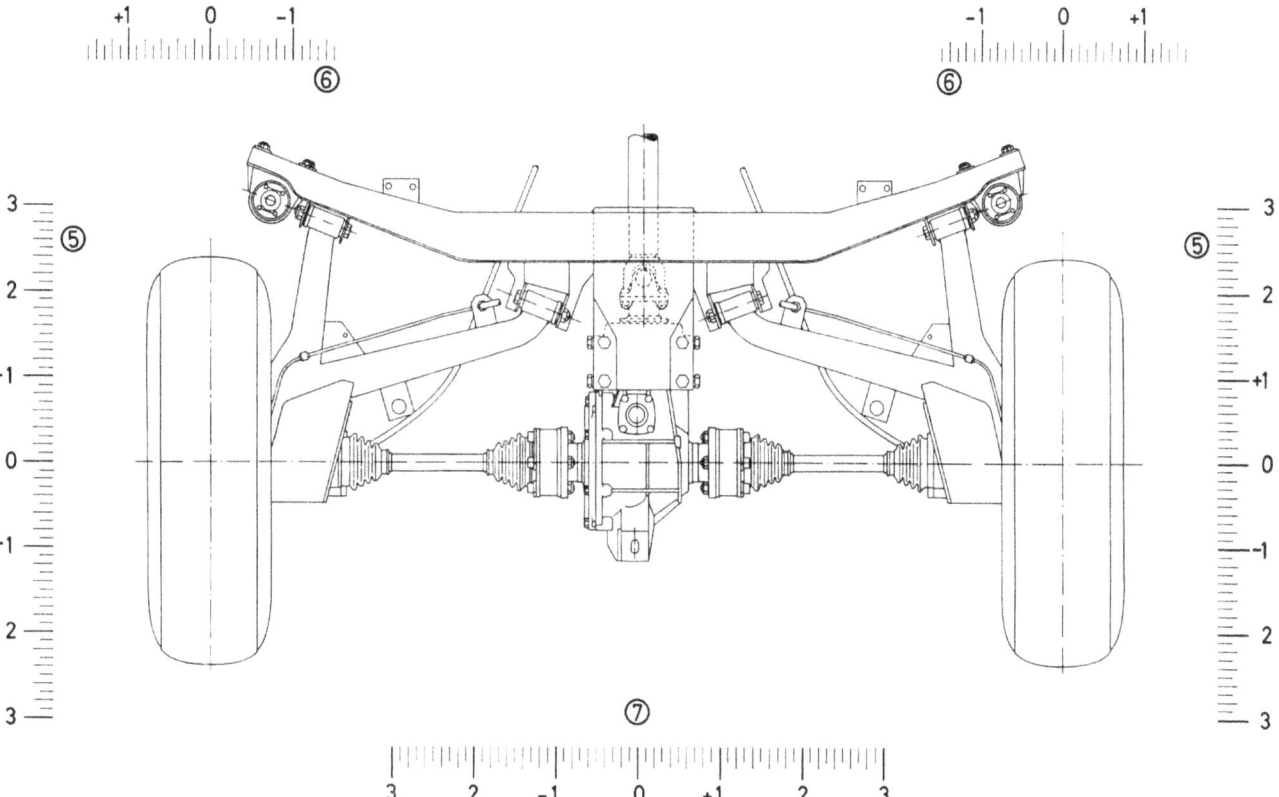

Trouble shooting:

⑤ Camber variation
a) Defective rubber bush on rear axle beam,
b) Defective rubber bush on final drive,
c) Defective Silentbloc bushes in trailing arm,
d) Rear axle beam distorted,
e) Trailing arm distorted,
f) Floor panel assembly distorted.

⑥ Incorrect rear wheel position
a) Rear axle beam moved to one side,
b) Floor panel assembly distorted.

⑦ Incorrect track
a) Rear axle beam distorted,
b) Trailing arm distorted,
c) Defective Silentbloc bushes in trailing arm,
d) Defective rubber bushes at rear axle beam,
e) Spring compression too high.

NOTES

BRAKES

INDEX

	Page
BRAKE SYSTEM	81
Bleeding	81
HANDBRAKE	82
Adjusting	82
FRONT BRAKE PADS	82
Removing and installing	82
Replacing	82
FRONT FIXED CALIPER	83
Removing and installing	83
Replacing	83
Overhauling	83
FRONT BRAKE DISC	84
Removing and installing	84
Checking runout and thickness variation	84
REAR BRAKE DRUM	84
Removing and installing	84
REAR BRAKE SHOES	84
Relining	84
Removing and installing	84
REAR WHEEL BRAKE CYLINDER	85
Removing and installing	85
Overhauling	85
REAR BRAKE PLATE	85
Replacing	85
Removing and installing	85
REAR BRAKE PADS	85
Replacing	85
REAR FIXED CALIPER	86
Removing and installing	86
Replacing	86
Overhauling	86
REAR BRAKE DISC	86
Removing and installing	87
REAR BRAKE DISC SHIELD PLATE	87
Removing and installing	87
MASTER CYLINDER	87
Description	87
Removing	88
Overhauling	88
STOP LIGHT SWITCH	89
Replacing	89
BRAKE FLUID RESERVOIR	90
Replacing	90
CONNECTING HOSE BETWEEN RESERVOIR AND MASTER CYLINDER	90
Replacing	90
ONE FRONT BRAKE HOSE	90
Replacing	90
BRAKE PRESSURE LIMITER	90
Removing and installing	90
Checking	90
BRAKE UNIT WITH MASTER CYLINDER	91
Removing	91
Checking	91
HANDBRAKE	91
Removing and installing	91
RATCHET	92
Replacing	92
HAND BRAKE CABLE	92
Removing and installing	92
Cars with drum rear brakes	92
SHOES	92
Removing and installing	92
EXPANDER	92
Removing and installing	92

BRAKE SYSTEM
Bleeding

The brake fluid must be renewed every year. The reason for this is that the brake fluid absorbs moisture through the vent hole in the reservoir. This moisture gradually reduces the boiling point of the brake fluid from 240°C to 160–180°C. If this precaution is not taken, heavy use of the brakes can lead to steam formation and failure of the brake system. Never allow brake fluid to contact the car's paintwork. The brake fluid will damage the paintwork immediately. Connect the bleed device to the brake system reservoir.

Remove front wheel. Push bleed hose with collection vessel on to bleed screw. Open bleed screw. When no further air bubbles emerge, close the bleed screw. On the 4-piston fixed caliper front brake all 3 bleed screws must be bled, or else air bubbles may be trapped in the brake caliper. Always bleed lower piston B before lower piston C.

82 BRAKES

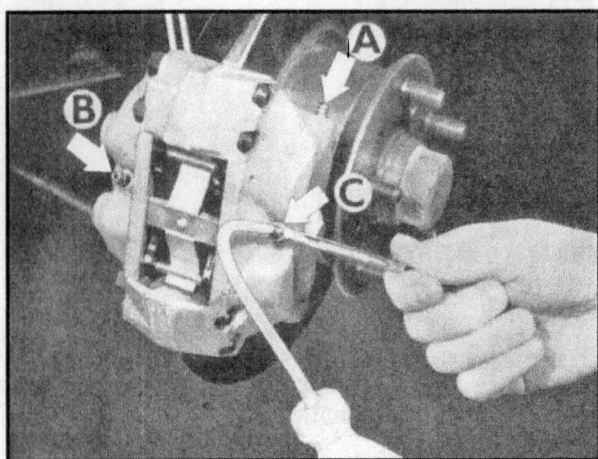

Bleed screws

HANDBRAKE
Adjusting
The handbrake should always be adjusted if the handbrake lever can be pulled up by more than 5 notches on the ratchet. Insert a screw driver through the 15 mm (0.6 in.) hole and turn the adjusting wheel until the brake disc can no longer be moved. Then back off the adjusting wheel by 2—3 teeth. Adjust the handbrake cables until the handbrake holds the vehicle securely before the fifth notch is reached.

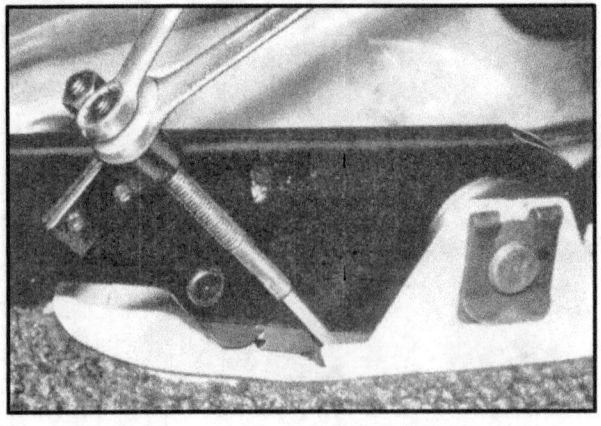

FRONT BRAKE PADS
Removing and installing
Remove front wheel. Drive out retaining pins. Take out spreader spring. Pull out the brake pads with extractor hook 3.9314-14002. Mark brake pads which have been bedded in. If the pad on one side is more severely worn, do not interchange the pads. Brake pads may be worn down until dimension 0.08 in.

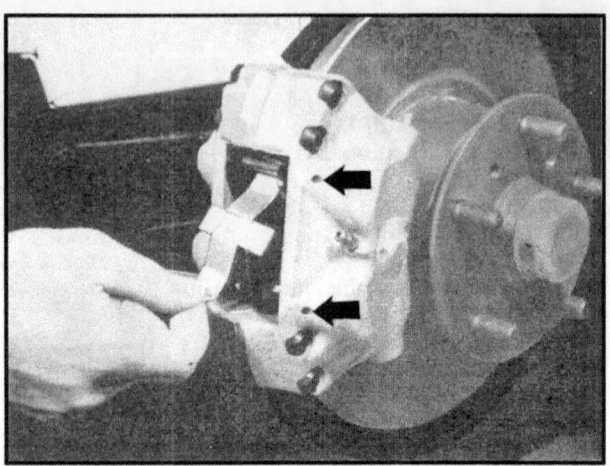

Replacing
Remove (install) front brake pads. All 4 front brake pads must be replaced at the same time. Use only genuine replacement brake pads. Use brake pads of the same make at both front and rear wheels. Clean out the fixed caliper with a narrow brush. When new, the brake pads must move easily inside the fixed caliper.

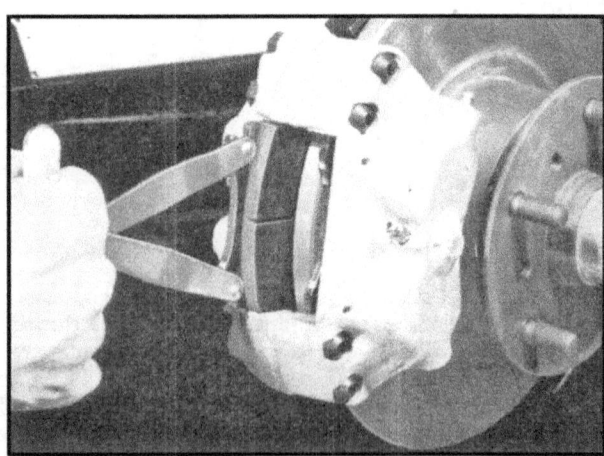

Using the special piston return pliers, push back the pistons into the fixed caliper as far as possible. When this is done, the brake fluid level in the reservoir will rise.

When installing: Depress the brake pedal several times until the brake pads are touching the brake disc.

Bed in new brake pads for 375 miles at normal driving speeds. Try to avoid emergency brake applications from high speeds. If these precautions are not observed, the brake pads will not attain their normal favorable wear and friction characterisitcs.

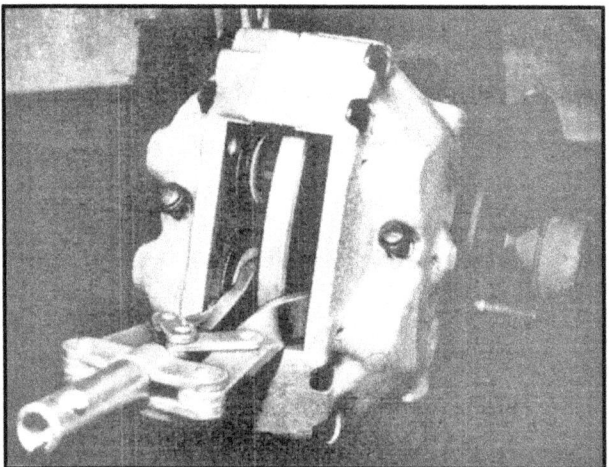

FRONT FIXED CALIPER
Removing and installing
Block the outlets from the fluid reservoir with two pointed wooden sticks. Remove front wheel and remove the caliper retaining bolts. Disconnect the brake lines.

When installing: Bleed the brake caliper.

When brake discs are removed, the brake lines need not be disconnected.

Replacing
Remove (install) front fixed caliper. Always replace brake pads for the other front wheel at the same time. Observe the procedure for bedding in new brake pads.

Overhauling
Remove (install) front fixed caliper. Remove brake pads. Extract clamp rings and rubber protecting caps. Hold one piston in place with the piston return pliers. Place a hardwood or felt pad between the caliper jaws. Press out the piston by applying a compressed air supply to the brake line connecting hole. Observe great care! A compressed air supply at 140 psi will develop a force of approximately 550 lbs. Carefully remove the sealing rings with a plastic rod.

When installing: Clean all parts with alcohol and coat with ATE brake cylinder paste before installing. Do not tilt the piston when inserting.

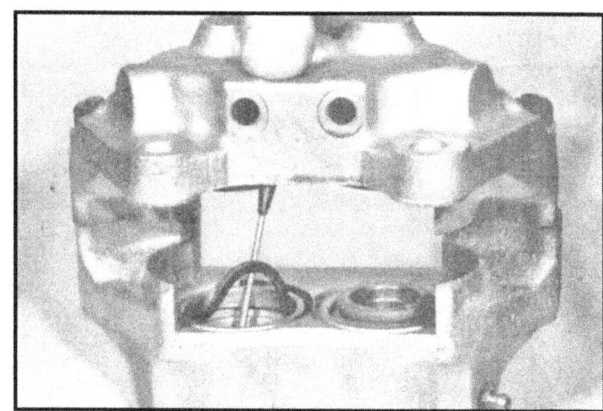

Use new sealing rings. Clean the sealing faces between the two halves of the caliper with alcohol. Do not separate the two halves of the caliper unless a leak is detected. Remove the expansion bolts.

When installing: Do not re-use the expansion bolts.

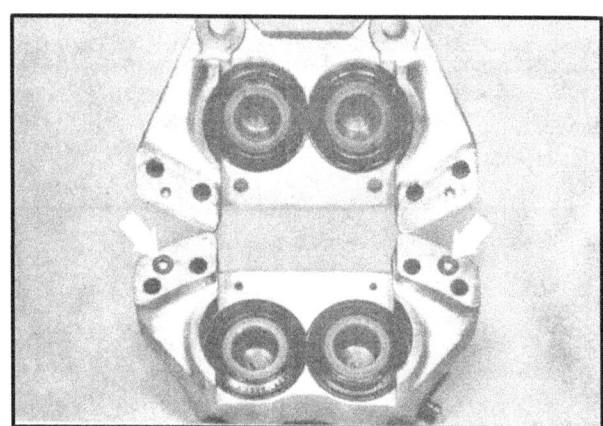

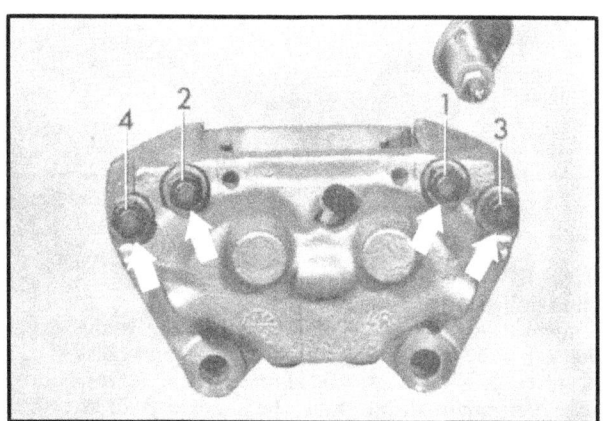

Tightening sequence 1 – 4

FRONT BRAKE DISC
Removing and installing
Remove (install) wheel hub. Detach brake disc from wheel hub. If the brake disc is rusted to the wheel hub, we recommend attaching the wheel hub to the wheel rim. The brake disc can then be turned backwards and forwards and pulled sharply upwards at the same time.

When installing: Repack wheel bearings with fresh grease.

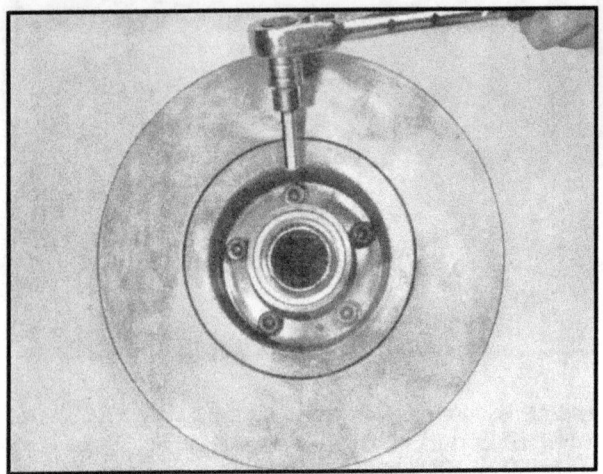

Checking runout and thickness variation
Remove brake pads. Attach dial gauge holder ATE 39314-13002 and measure lateral runout of brake disc. Check thickness variation by measuring with a micrometer at approximately 8 points within the friction area of the brake disc. The maximum tolerance must not be exceeded.

REAR BRAKE DRUM
Removing and installing
Remove the rear wheel and take off the brake drum. Check brake drum for ovality, scoring and cracks (acoustic test). The drum may be skimmed, but if this is done both rear brake drums must be machined to the same extent.

REAR BRAKE SHOES
Relining
When the brake shoe thickness is reduced to 0.12 in. the shoes must be relined. Always reline all four rear brake shoes at the same time. Remove the brake shoes. Drill out the rivets and remove the old linings.

When installing: The lining must seat correctly on the brake shoe and must not protrude at the sides. Insert the rivets. Use only brake linings of the same make on all shoes.

After the brake shoes have been relined the brakes must be readjusted. Release the handbrake. With special wrench 6038, turn the left wheel adjusting cam anti-clockwise and the right wheel cam clockwise until the brake shoes prevent the wheel from turning. Then back off the adjusting cams by about 1/8 turn of the screws until the wheel just turns freely.

Removing and installing
Remove brake drum and detach the brake shoes at the bottom. Detach the return spring at the bottom.

When installing: Note installed position of return spring.

Pull brake shoe ends out of wheel brake cylinder and detach thrust rod and handbrake cable.

When installing: The longer hooked end of the spring should be attached between the handbrake arm and the brake shoe.

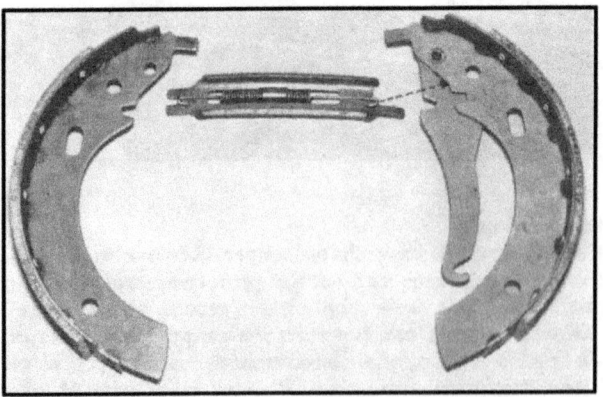

REAR WHEEL BRAKE CYLINDER
Removing and installing
Remove rear brake drum and fully unscrew both adjusting cams with 6038 wrench. Detach brake line and retaining screws from wheel brake cylinder.

When installing: Bleed the brake.

Press the wheel brake cylinder to the right and at the same time pull forward to remove.

Overhauling
Remove the wheel brake cylinder and dismantle the cylinder. Clean all parts with alcohol. Do not reuse the sleeves.

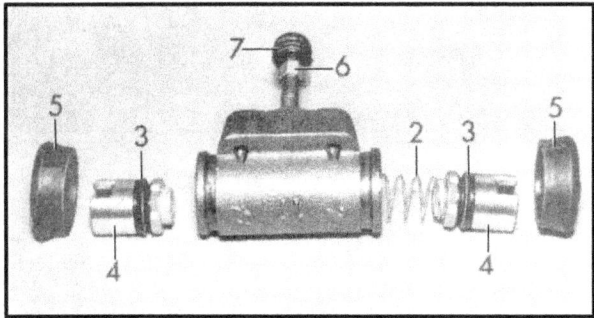

Components: wheel cylinder housing, coil spring (2), sleeves (3), piston (4), protecting caps (5), bleed valve (6), dust cap (7).

When installing: To simplify assembly and provide corrosion protection, coat the cylinder bore, piston rubbing surface and sleeves with a very thin layer of ATE cylinder paste. Re-adjust brake shoes with the adjusting cams, using 6038 special wrench.

REAR BRAKE PLATE
Replacing
Remove brake shoes and remove wheel brake cylinder. Remove rear axle shaft. Detach handbrake cable and unscrew and remove brake plate.

1. Wheel brake cylinder
2. Rear axle shaft

REAR BRAKE PADS
Replacing
Remove (install) rear brake pads. Always renew all 4 brake pads at the same time. Use only genuine replacement brake pads. Use brake linings of the same make on both front and rear axles. Clean out fixed caliper with a narrow brush. The new brake pads must move freely inside the fixed caliper.

Push the piston fully back into the fixed caliper with piston return pliers 3.9314-1800.2. When this is done, brake fluid level in the reservoir will rise. Check 20° angle setting of piston with piston gauge (3.9314-0600.1). The

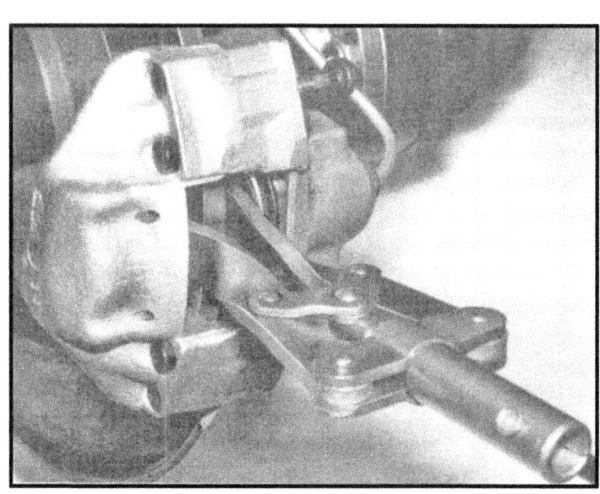

86　BRAKES

20° cutout on the piston must be adjacent to the point where the brake disc enters the fixed caliper. An incorrect piston setting will cause shake, squeaking, or incorrect contact between brake pad and disc. Repositioning of the piston to obtain the correct 20° setting is carried out with the piston rotating pliers (3.9314-1500.2).

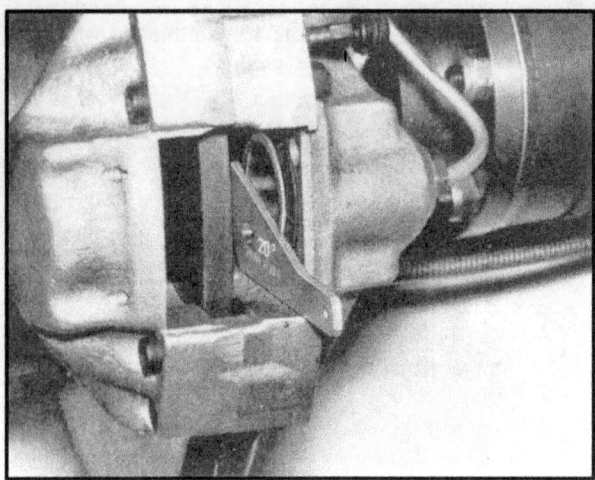

New brake pads should be bedded in for 375 miles under normal running conditions. Try to avoid emergency brake applications at high speed. If these precautions are not observed, the brake pads will not attain their most favorable wear and friction coefficients.

When installing: Depress the brake pedal several times until the brake pads are touching the brake disc.

Removing and installing
Remove rear wheel and drive out retaining pins. Remove spreader spring. Pull out brake pads with extractor hook 3.9314-14002. Mark brake pads which have been bedded in. If the brake pad on one side is more seriously worn, do not interchange the pads. Brake pads may be worn down to a thickness 0.08 in.

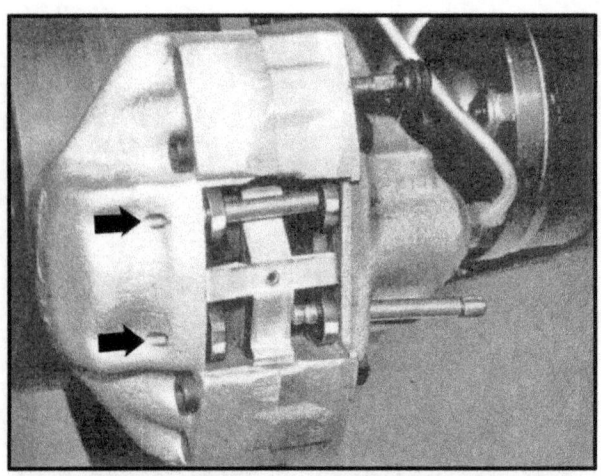

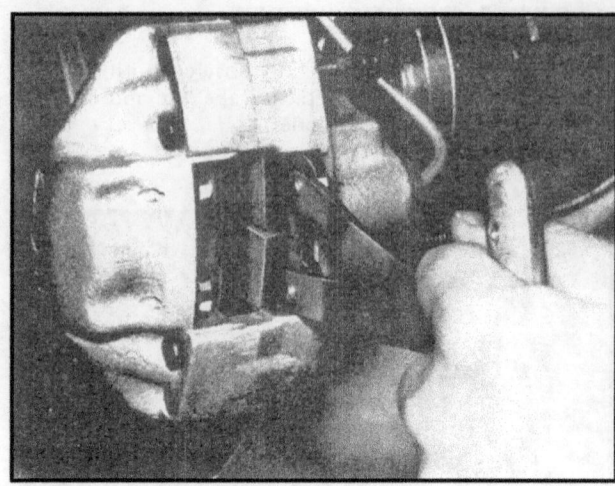

REAR FIXED CALIPER
Removing and installing
Block the fluid outlets from the reservoir with 2 pointed wooden sticks. Remove rear wheel and remove fixed caliper. Detach brake line.

When installing: Bleed brake caliper.

When the brake disc is removed, the brake line need not be disconnected. Pull the brake caliper rearwards.

Replacing
Remove (install) rear fixed brake caliper. Always replace brake pads on both sides of the vehicle at the same time. The brake pads should be bedded in in accordance with the usual procedure.

Overhauling
Remove (install) rear brake fixed caliper. Remove the brake pads and take out the clamp rings and rubber protecting caps. Insert a plug in the brake lining connecting hole and retain the piston in position with the piston return pliers (3.9314-1800.2). Insert a felt or hardwood pad between the caliper jaws. Apply a compressed air jet

to the bleed hole to press out the brake piston. Exercise great care! A compressed air supply at 142 psi will generate a force of approximately 550 lbs. Lift out the sealing rings with a plastic needle.

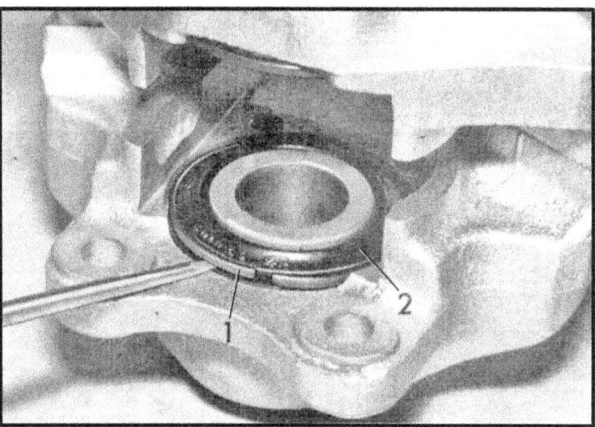

1. Clamp rings
2. Protecting caps

Components must be cleaned only with brake fluid or alcohol. Dry with a clean compressed air supply. Examine cylinder bores and pistons for damage. Always renew parts if damaged. To simplify assembly, apply a very thin layer of ATE brake cylinder paste to the cylinder and piston. This will also prevent corrosion. Insert the piston carefully into the cylinder bore without jamming. Using piston gauge 3.9314-0600.1, check the 20° position of the piston and if necessary turn the piston with the piston rotating pliers (3.9314-1500.2) to correct. The 20° cutout on the piston should be next to the point at which the brake disc enters the brake caliper.

Do not separate the two halves of the fixed caliper unless a sealing ring on one side has developed a leak. Clean the sealing faces of both caliper halves with alcohol.

When installing: Make sure that the sealing rings are correctly positioned.

The caliper halves are connected together by means of expansion bolts, which must not be reused after removal. Tighten the bolts.

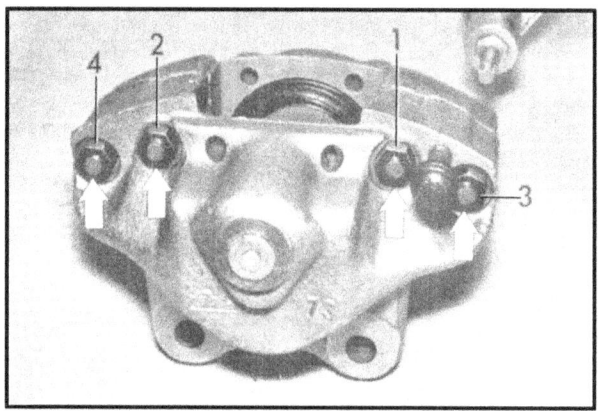

Tighten the bolts in the sequence 1 – 4.

REAR BRAKE DISC
Removing and installing
Remove (install) the rear fixed caliper. Separate the brake disc from the axle shaft.

When installing: Note the position of the holes on the brake disc and axle shaft flange.

REAR BRAKE DISC SHIELD PLATE
Removing and installing
Remove the rear axle shaft and the brake expander. Detach the handbrake cable reaction plate. Remove the front attachment screws. Pull away the shield plate. Detach the handbrake cable reaction plate.

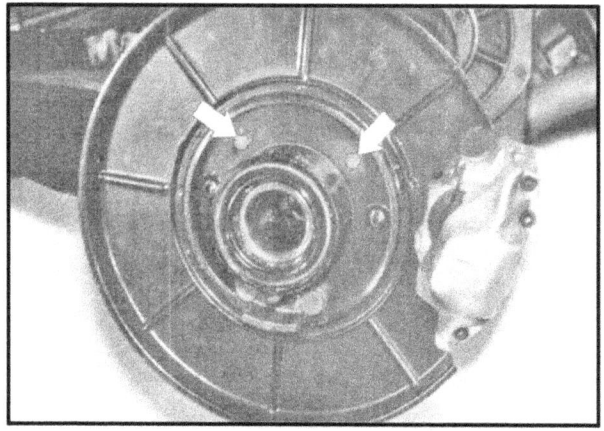

MASTER CYLINDER
Description
When the foot pedal is depressed the piston is moved forwards. The primary sleeve passes over the equalizing passage. This causes pressure to rise in chamber A, and to be exerted on the piston. As movement continues, the primary sleeve passes over the equalizing passage. The

pressure is now the same in Chambers A and B. Chamber A operates the front wheel brakes. Chamber B operates on both rear and front wheel brakes. If one brake circuit should fail, pedal travel will increase considerably. If the second brake circuit fails, pressure will rise in Chamber A and piston (1) will cause piston (4) in the pressureless Chamber B to be pressed against the dual master cylinder housing, thus operating the first brake circuit. If the front brake circuit should fail, piston (1) in the pressureless Chamber A will be pressed against the spring cap and the second brake circuit will be fully effective by way of Chamber B.

When installing: Check correct seating of sealing plugs in master cylinder and examine pipe bends for damage.

When installing: Check condition of rubber sealing ring. If the ring is defective no vacuum will be built up. When replacing the master cylinder, check clearance between thrust rod and master cylinder piston with plastigage and if necessary set to 0.02 in with a shim behind the plunger head. Bleed the brakes.

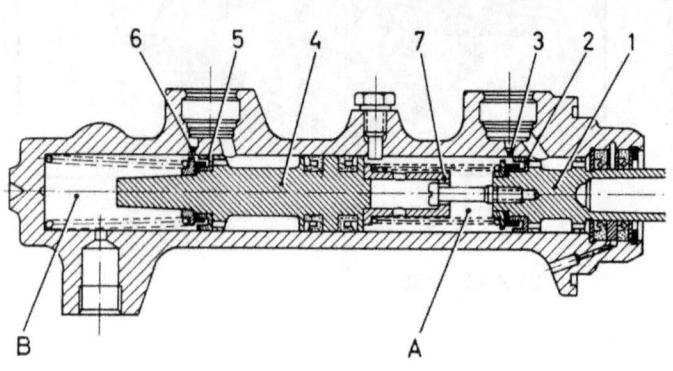

1. Piston
2. Primary sleeve
3. Equalizing passage
4. Piston
5. Primary sleeve
6. Equalizing passage
7. Spring cap
A & B Chambers

1. Sealing ring
2. Shim

Overhauling

Remove (install) master cylinder. Apply slight pressure to the piston and remove the stop screw.

When installing: Use a new copper gasket under the stop screw.

Lift out the Seeger circlip and exact the piston. Pull off the stop washer, secondary sleeve, intermediate ring, secondary sleeve, and stop washer.

When installing: Coat piston rod with silicone grease.

Removing

Block the outlets from the brake fluid reservoir with two pointed wooden sticks. Pull off the hoses at the master cylinder and raise the free ends above the fluid level. Do not tilt the pipe bend when removing, but pull off carefully while keeping vertical. If carelessly removed, the pipes may fracture at the bend. Detach the brake lines. Unscrew the master cylinder from the brake unit.

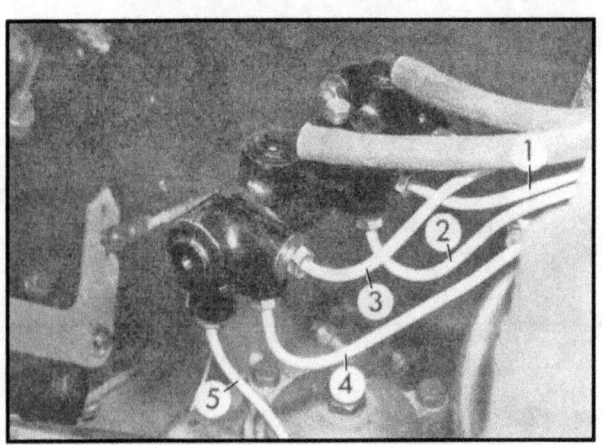

1. Front right } 2nd brake circuit
2. Front left
3. Front right } 1st brake circuit
4. Front left
5. Rear brakes

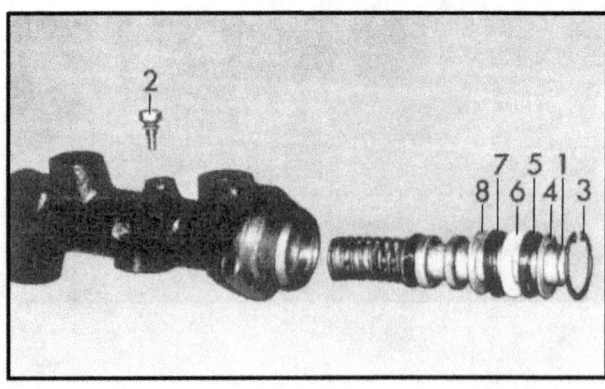

1. Piston
2. Stop screw
3. Seeger clip
4. Stop washer
5. Secondary sleeve
6. Intermediate ring
7. Secondary sleeve
8. Stop washer

To replace the primary sleeve, remove the special screw. Take off the spring cap, spring, spring cup, pressure plate and spacing washer. Carefully remove the piston by compressed air. Pull off the spring, spring cup, pressure plate, primary sleeve and spacing washer. Lift out the secondary sleeve and primary sleeve.

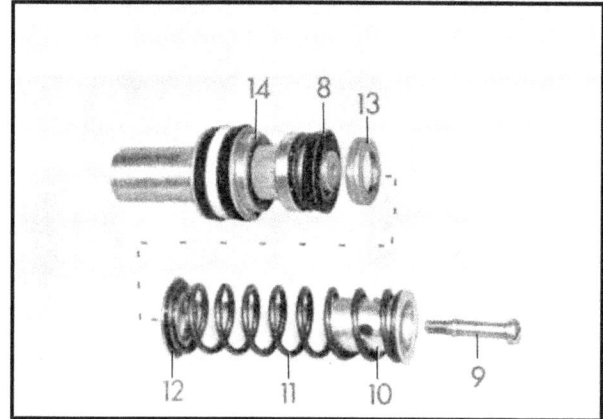

8. Primary sleeve
9. Special screw
10. Spring cap
11. Spring
12. Spring cup
13. Pressure plate
14. Spacing washer

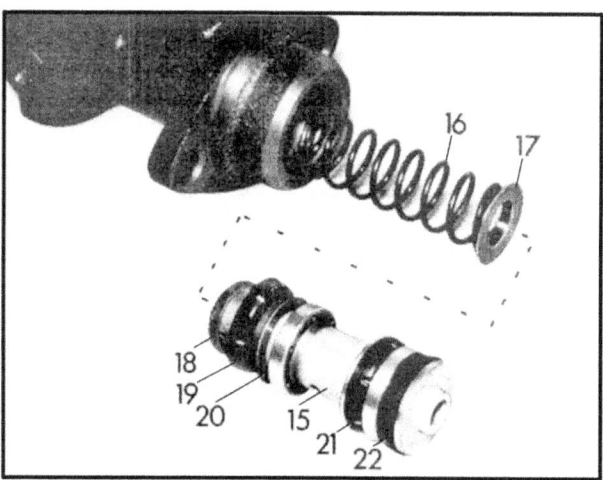

15. Piston
16. Spring
17. Spring cup
18. Pressure plate
19. Primary sleeve
20. Spacing washer
21. Secondary sleeve
22. Primary sleeve

Clean all parts with alcohol. Do not reinstall a master cylinder if the cylinder bore surface is damaged.

When installing: Apply ATE cylinder paste to new components. Clamp the master cylinder vertically into the vise to prevent the pressure plate from slipping during reassembly. Install piston with assembly sleeve 6063. Note installed position of piston and stop screw.

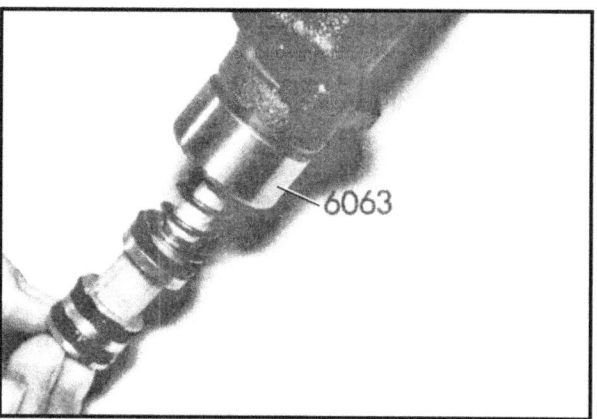

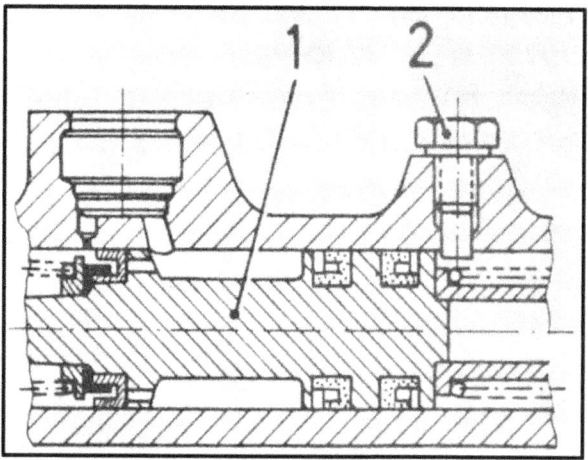

1. Piston
2. Stop screw

STOP LIGHT SWITCH
Replacing

Remove lower left instrument panel housing. Pull away rear fog warning light push button switch cable. Move the instrument panel housing over to the right.

When installing: + yellow/white
                   S grey/violet
                   31 brown

Pull off connections to stop light switch. Loosen locknut and unscrew the stop light switch.

When installing: Position the stop light switch so that 0.24–0.28 in. of the contact button are visible.

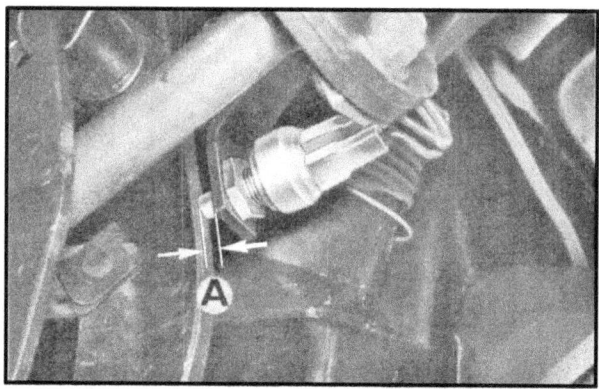

A. Contact button

90 BRAKES

BRAKE FLUID RESERVOIR
Replacing

Pull off the plug connections. Siphon brake fluid out of reservoir. Unscrew the reservoir and pull off the hoses. Do not tilt the pipe bends to remove but pull off vertically with great care. If carelessly removed, the pipes may fracture at the bend.

When installing: Add brake fluid to prescribed level.

To check the brake warning light system, fully release the handbrake. Remove the reservoir filler cap. Switch on the ignition. When the contact pin is pushed up, the warning light should not be illuminated. With the pin released, the warning light should burn. The warning light should be illuminated when the handbrake is applied or the brake fluid level is too low.

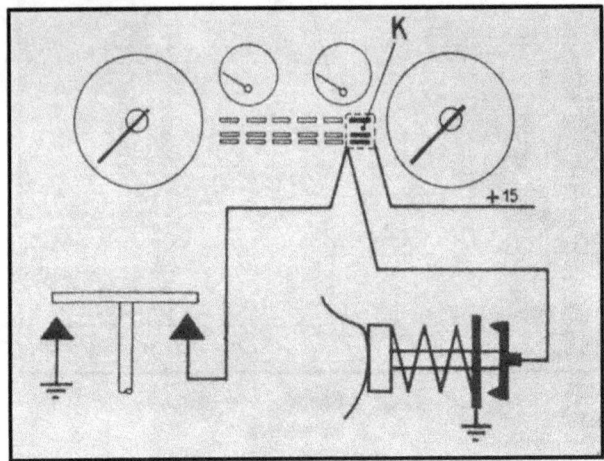

K – Warning Light

CONNECTING HOSE BETWEEN RESERVOIR AND MASTER CYLINDER
Replacing

Siphon off brake fluid from reservoir and detach the connecting hose from the reservoir and the master cylinder. Do not tilt the pipe bends when removing, but pull out carefully keeping vertical. If carelessly removed, the pipes may fracture at the bend.

When installing: Check correct seating of sealing plugs in master cylinder.

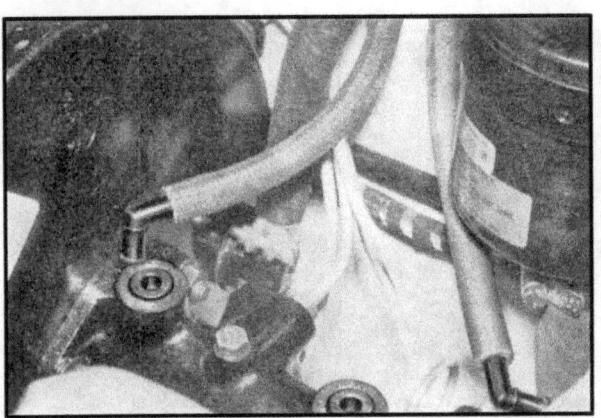

ONE FRONT BRAKE HOSE
Replacing

Block the reservoir outlets with two pointed wooden sticks. Unscrew the brake hose from the master cylinder and brake caliper brake lines. Detach the retaining spring.

When installing: Do not distort the brake hose.

Bleed the brake.

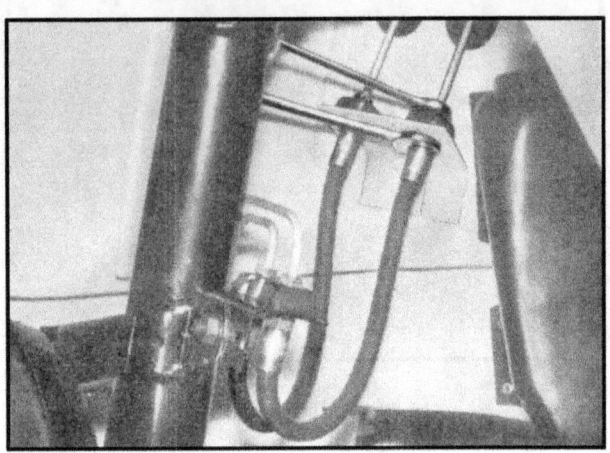

BRAKE PRESSURE LIMITER
Removing and installing

Block outlets from brake fluid reservoir with two pointed wooden sticks. Remove rear left brake hose. Unscrew brake lines from brake pressure limiter. Remove brake pressure limiter. Never attempt to alter the setting of the brake pressure limiter.

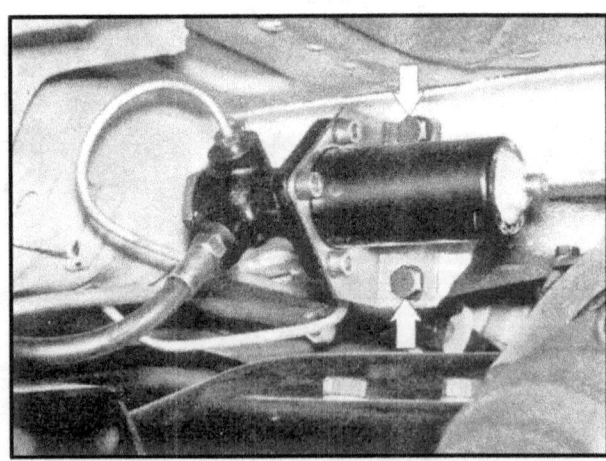

Checking

Connect a high pressure gauge to the front and rear axle brake circuit and a second gauge to the rear brake caliper. Depress the brake pedal and hold down with the pedal prop. Until a pressure of 285 psi is registered, both pressure gauges must indicate the same reading. From 285 psi upwards, the pressure at the rear fixed caliper should be correspondingly reduced.

BRAKES

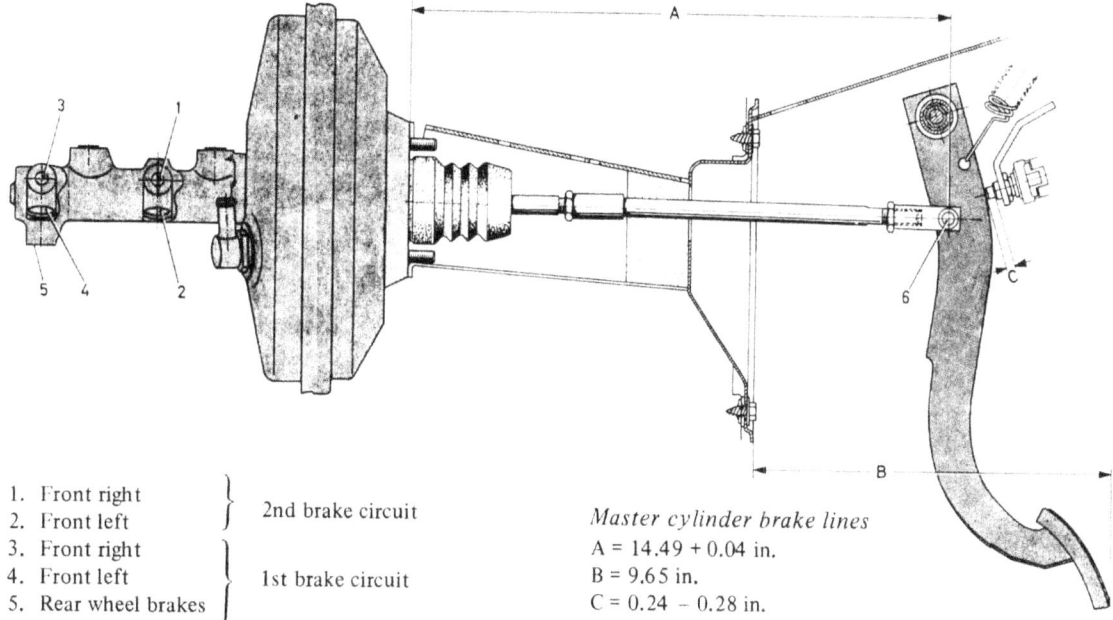

1. Front right
2. Front left } 2nd brake circuit
3. Front right
4. Front left
5. Rear wheel brakes } 1st brake circuit

Master cylinder brake lines
A = 14.49 + 0.04 in.
B = 9.65 in.
C = 0.24 – 0.28 in.

Remove the protecting cap, retaining ring, sound absorbing pad and ilter.

When installing: Clean the sound absorbing pad and filter.

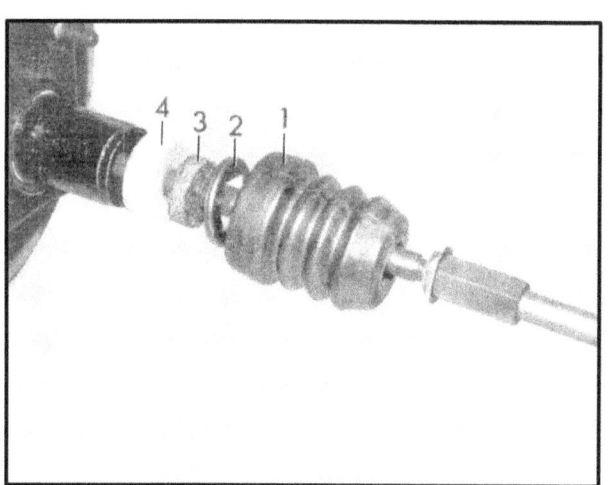

1. Protecting cap
2. Retaining ring
3. Sound absorbing pad
4. Filter

BRAKE UNIT WITH MASTER CYLINDER
Removing
Remove intake air cleaner. Remove battery, detach oil reservoir for hydraulic power steering and move to one side. Unscrew hose from radiator to coolant header tank at the tank and secure to one side. Block the brake reservoir outlets with two pointed wooden sticks and pull off the connecting hoses to the master cylinder.

When installing: Check correct seating of sealing plugs in master cylinder.

Remove the lower left instrument panel housing and secure to one side. Remove pin on the foot brake pedal. Detach the vacuum hose from the intake manifold. Detach brake lines from master cylinder. Unscrew the brake unit from the support bracket and pull out to the front.

When installing: Adjust length of piston rod to 14.49 + 0.04 in. and prevent nuts from turning with keeper plate. Check distance of brake pedal from bulk head 9.65 in. Adjust exposed depth of stop light switch plunger to 0.24–0.28 in. On cars equipped with rear drum brakes, the master cylinder is provided with an initial pressure valve.

Checking
With the engine stopped, depress the brake pedal about 10 times. Keep the brake pedal held down and start the engine. If the brake pedal moves further down, the brake system is in good order. If the brake pedal does not move, either the non-return valve, the vacuum hose or the rubber ring between master cylinder and brake unit may be defective or else the filter element is completely blocked.

HANDBRAKE
Removing and installing
Pull off the protecting rubber cap. Detach the handbrake cables. Lift out the keeper plate and press out the pivot pin. When installing, adjust the handbrake so that the vehicle is held evenly at all wheels before the lever reaches the fifth notch.

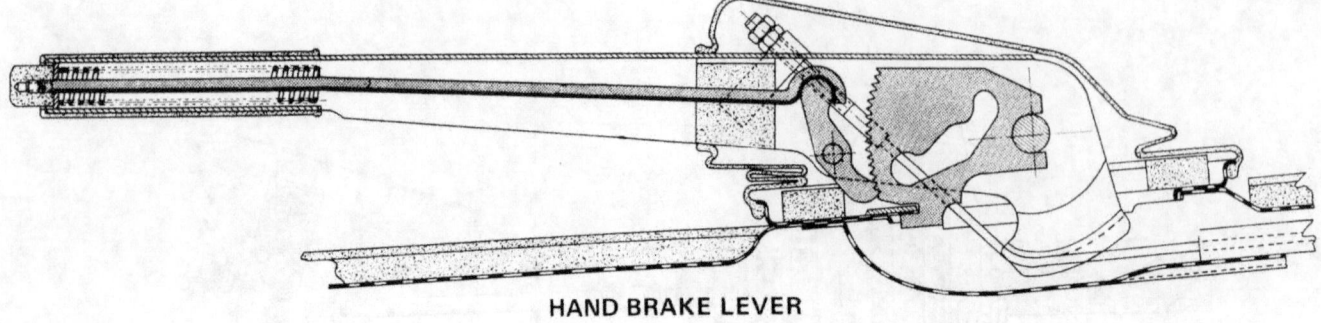

HAND BRAKE LEVER

RATCHET
Replacing
Remove the handbrake lever. Check condition of ratchet and replace if necessary. Warning: Note installed position of ratchet, pawl, and thrust rod.

HAND BRAKE CABLE
Removing and installing
Detach handbrake cable from handbrake lever.

When installing: Adjust handbrake so that the vehicle is firmly held at all wheels before the lever has reached the fifth notch.

Cars with drum rear brakes
Detach the brake shoes at the bottom. Detach the handbrake cable from the brake arm. Pull the handbrake cable out of the brake plate.

When installing: The shoulder on the handbrake cable must be pressed against the brake plate.

SHOES
Removing and installing
Remove rear brake disc. Detach lower return spring, using brake spring pliers. Turn the retaining springs through 90° with special key 7014, and detach. Pull the brake shoes apart at the bottom and lift away upwards.

Detach handbrake cable from trailing arm or unscrew. Pull the handbrake cable out of the protective tube.

When installing: The rubber sleeve must seal the end of the protective tube correctly.

Remove the expander mechanism. Detach the handbrake cable reaction plate. Pull out the handbrake cable.

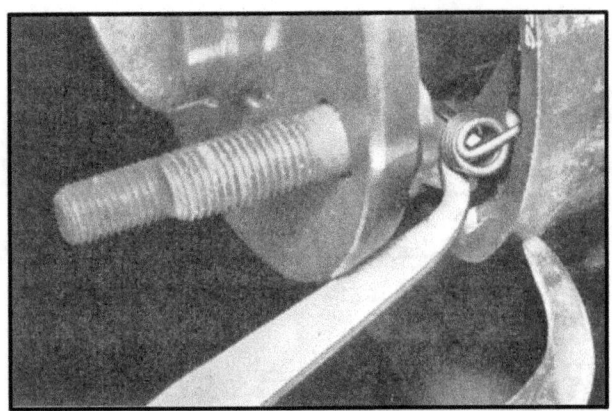

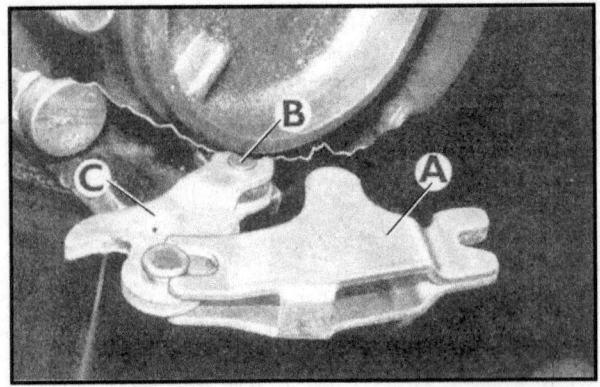

A – pull right, B – press out, C – pull left

EXPANDER
Removing and installing
Remove handbrake shoes. When installing, coat sliding surface with a thin layer of Molykote paste.

BRAKES

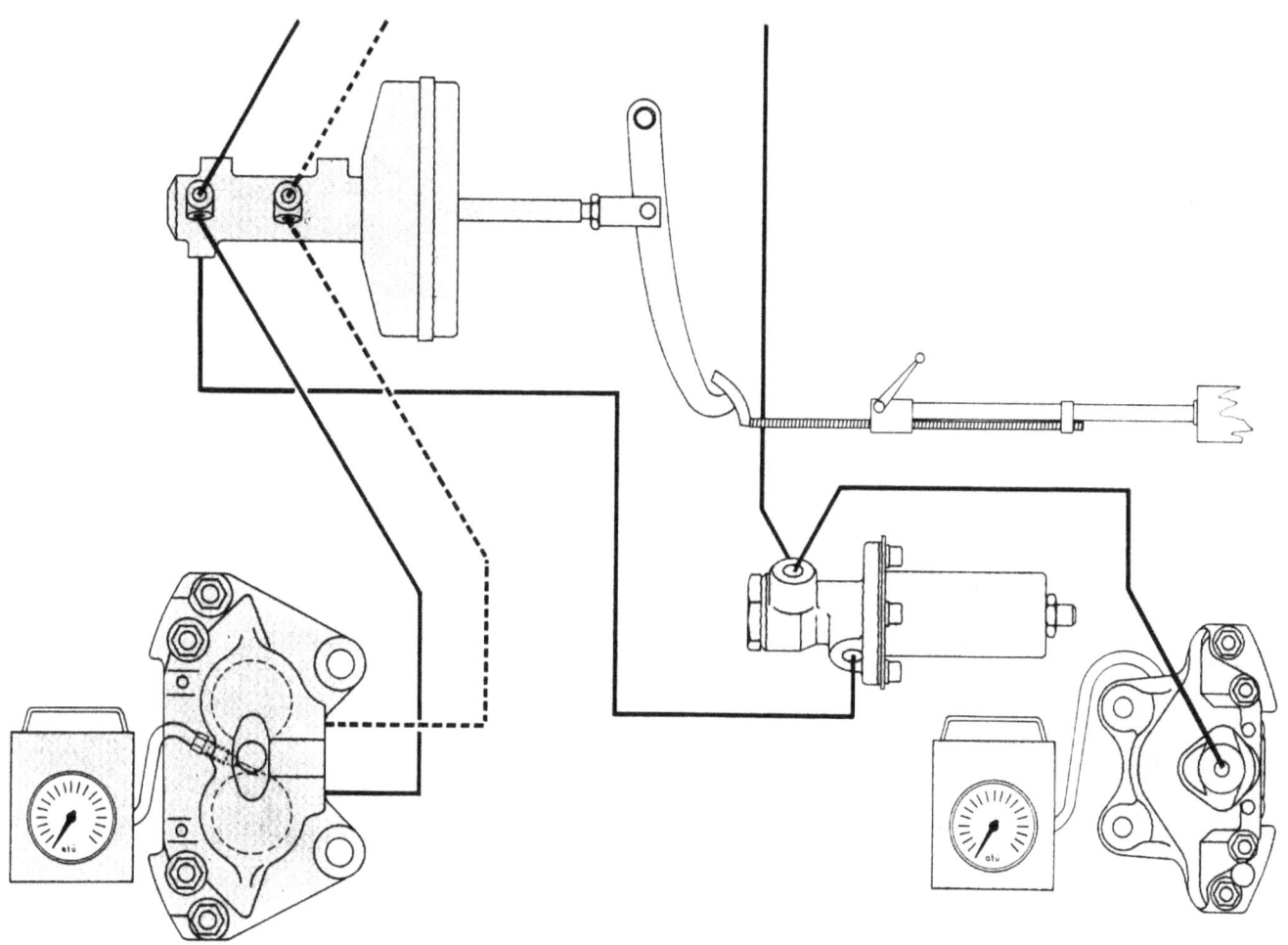

BRAKE PRESSURE LIMITER

NOTES

FRONT SUSPENSION

INDEX

	Page		Page
FRONT AXLE COMPLETE	95	TAPER ROLLER BEARING AND SHAFT SEALING RING	99
Removing and refitting	95	Replacing	99
Replacing	97	WHEEL STUD	99
CONTROL ARM GUIDE JOINT	98	Replacing	99
Removing and refitting	98	SUSPENSION STRUT/SHOCK ABSORBER COMPLETE	99
TIE BAR	98	Removing and installing	99
Removing and refitting	98	Replacing	100
RUBBER BEARING IN FRONT AXLE BRACKET	98	SHOCK ABSORBERS	100
Replacing	98	Replacing	100
RUBBER BEARING IN CONTROL ARM	98	SUSPENSION STRUT THRUST BEARING	100
Replacing	98	Removing and refitting	100
WHEEL BEARING PLAY	98	COIL SPRING	101
Adjusting	98	Removing and refitting	101
SEALING CAP	99	Replacing	101
Removing and refitting	99	SLEEVE	101
WHEEL HUB	99	Replacing	101
Removing and installing	99		

FRONT AXLE COMPLETE
Removing and refitting

Remove wheels. Undo brake stirrup. Remove angle piece from suspension strut/shock absorber. Brake lines should remain connected. Lift brake stirrup and tie in position. Slacken bolts. Push universal joint upwards to its fullest extent.

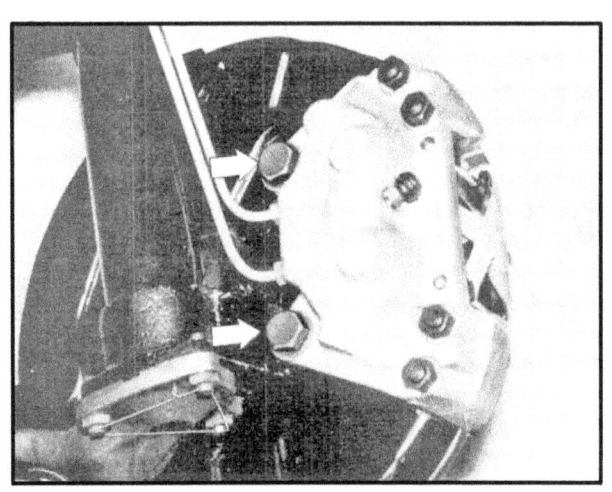

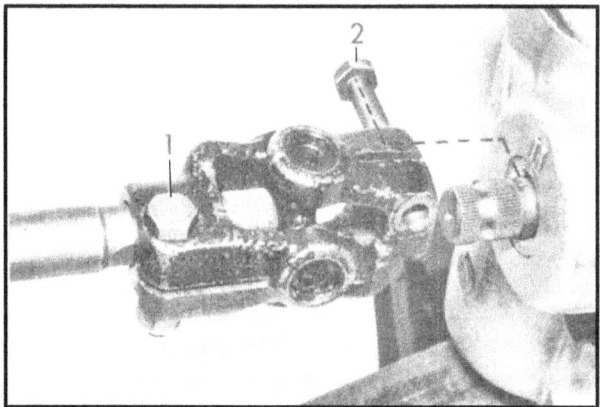

1 & 2. Bolts

When installing: Steering wheel and front wheels should be in straight ahead position. Markings on housing and steering shaft must line up. Fitting position bolt in locking groove.

Applicable only where hydraulic-assisted steering is fitted. Press off track rod from steering drop arm. Track rod pressing off tool 70009. Detach hydraulic-assisted steering from front axle bracket and tie to brake servo unit. Undo left-hand and right-hand engine supports. Detach suspension strut shock absorber bearings from wheel arch. Lower suspension strut shock absorbers outwards.

FRONT SUSPENSION

BMW 2500 — Front suspension
BMW 2800

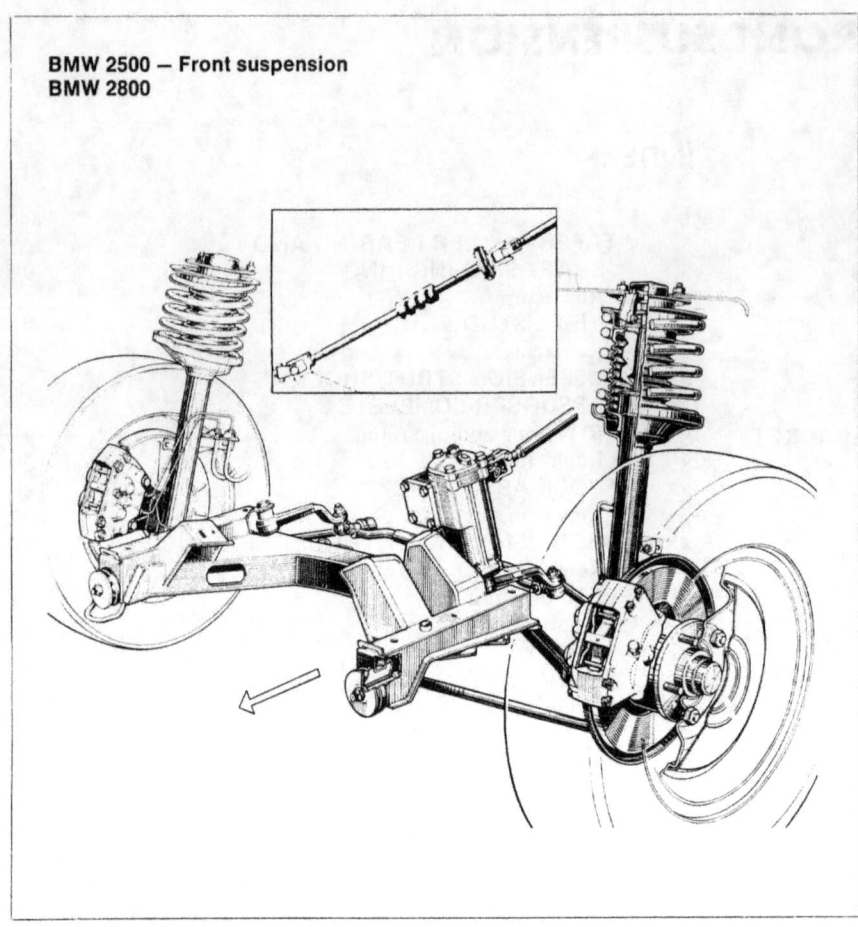

BMW 2800 CS - Front Suspension

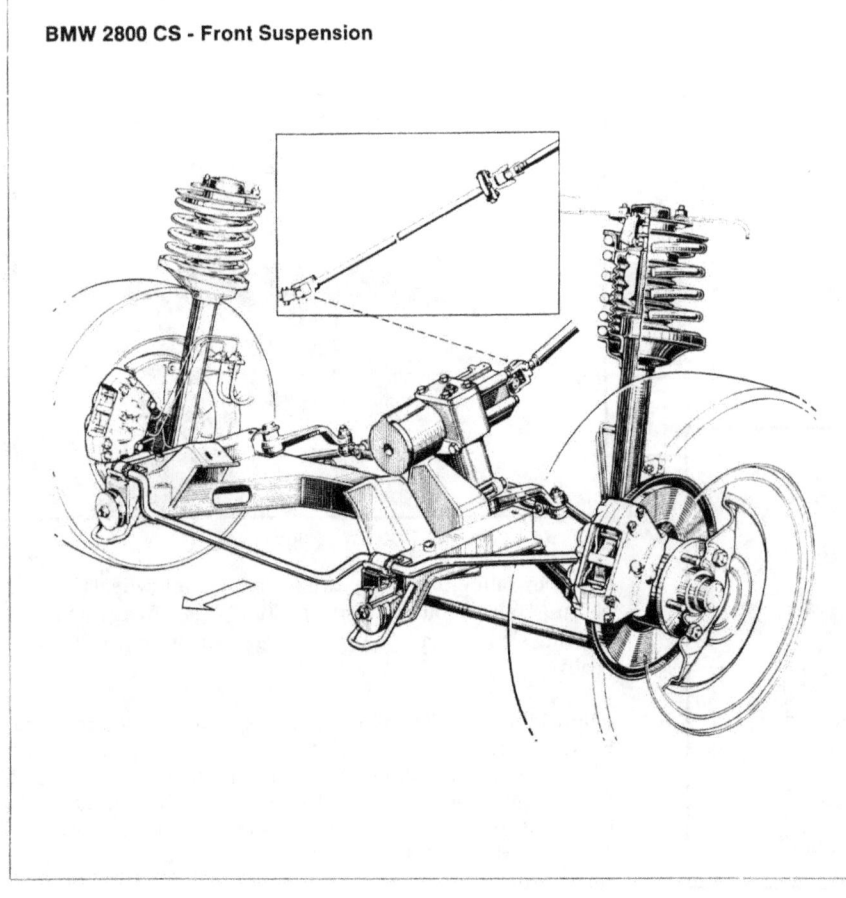

Front suspension
Independent, with lower wishbones, trailing links and spring/shock absorber struts; struts inclined rearwards at top, and incorporating double-acting hydraulic telescopic shock absorbers. Wishbones and trailing links pivoting in large-diameter rubber bushes; strut centre-line and wheel axis offset to provide the desired castor angle displacement; coil springs high mounted and offset in relation to strut axis; rubber auxiliary springs; total wheel travel 7.1" (180 mm).

FRONT SUSPENSION 97

Engage engine on hoist with lifting bar 7000. Support front axle brackets with jack and lifting rail. Do not jack up vehicle under front axle bracket cover plate. Release front axle bracket from frame member and lower.

Detach cross arm from front axle bracket.

When installing: Tighten locknut in normal position. Spacer ring should locate on front axle bracket.

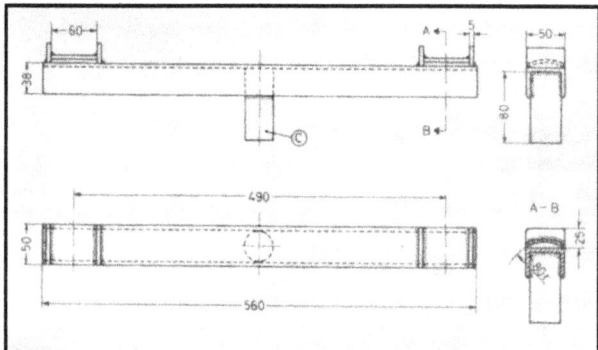

Sketch for manufacture of lifting rail
C will be determined by jack profile.

1. Spacer ring

Remove steering gearbox from front axle bracket and tie to brake servo unit. Remove steering guide arm.

When installing: Check Fluidbloc and replace if necessary.

Replacing
Remove wheels. Disconnect front strut.

When installing: Tighten castellated nut in normal position.

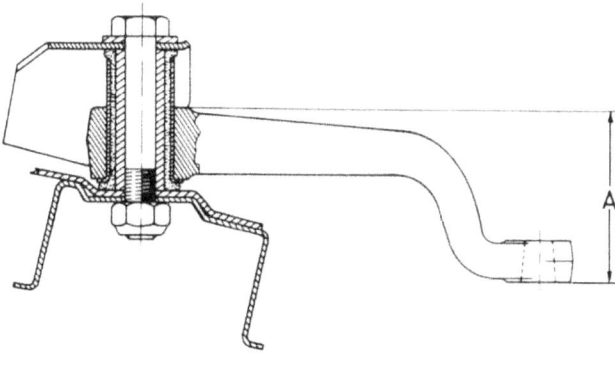

1.653 + 0.019"

98   FRONT SUSPENSION

Undo engine supports left and right. Engage engine on hoist with lifting bar 7000. Detach front axle bracket from frame member. Renew rubber bushes in front axle bracket.

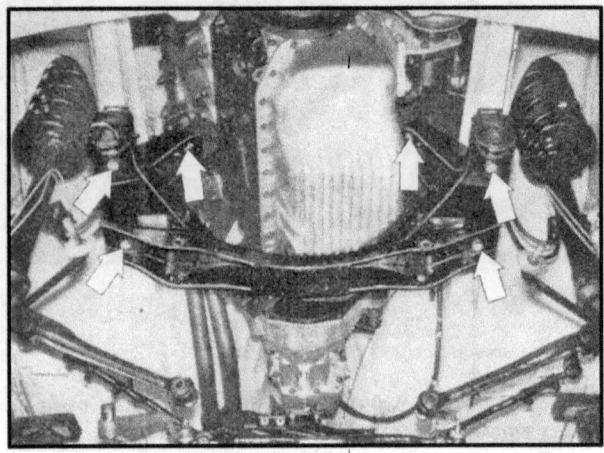

CONTROL ARM/GUIDE JOINT
Removing and refitting
Remove wheels and remove wire seal. Disconnect track rod arm from suspension strut shock absorber. Press guide joint out of track rod arm – Kukko pressing out tool. Remove tie bar. Detach control arm from front axle bracket.

When installing: Tighten locknut in normal position. Spacer ring should locate on front axle bracket.

TIE BAR
Removing and refitting
Detach control arm from front axle bracket.

When installing: Tighten locknut in normal position. Spacer ring should locate on front axle bracket.

Remove tie bar.

When installing: Tighten castellated nut in normal position. The dished outer radius of washers should face towards the rubber bearing.

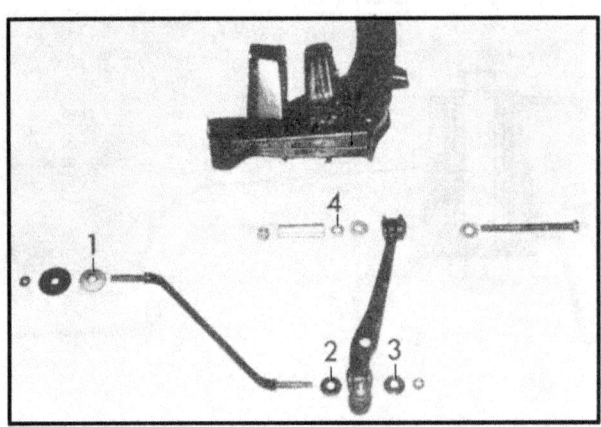

1-4.   Washers

RUBBER BEARING IN FRONT AXLE BRACKET
Replacing
Extract rubber bearing. The following tool will be of assistance: sleeve of inside diameter 2.677".

When installing: Smear rubber bearing with soft soap on front edge. The following tool will be of assistance: sleeve of inside diameter 2.362", wall thickness 0.034".

RUBBER BEARING IN CONTROL ARM
Replacing
The following tool will be of assistance: sleeve of inside diameter 1.378". Smear front edge of rubber bearing with soft soap.

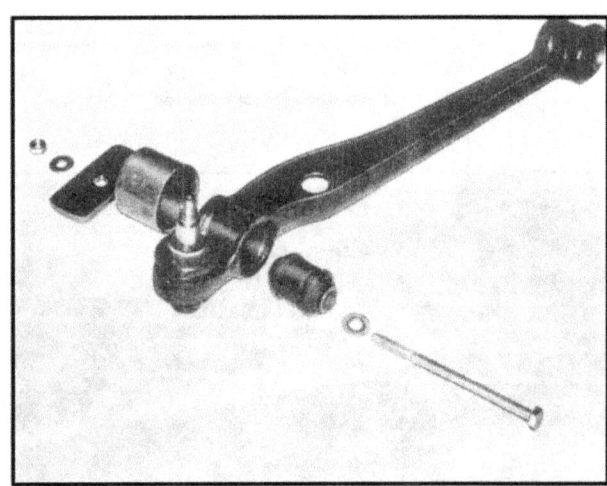

WHEEL BEARING PLAY
Adjusting
Remove and replace sealing cap on wheel hub. Remove wheel and remove split cotter from castellated nut. Tighten castellated nut using torque of 7.233 lb/ft turning the wheel hub continuously. This will ensure proper alignment of taper rollers and bearing inner races. At the same time the grease taking up play will be pressed out.

FRONT SUSPENSION

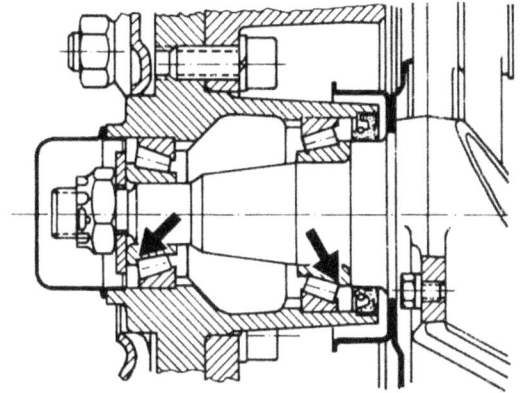

Slacken castellated nut approximately 1/4 turn. It must be possible to move the washer with lug to left and right. Fix dial gauge holder on wheel hub. Set dial gauge to 1 mm (0.039"). Push the wheel hub to and fro several times, at the same time reading off the wheel bearing play. Minimum wheel bearing play should be aimed at.

SEALING CAP
Removing and refitting
Remove hub cap. Pull off sealing cap with special pliers 6014.

When installing: Check grease packing in sealing cap.

WHEEL HUB
Removing and installing
Remove and refit sealing cap. Detach brake caliper. Disconnect angle piece from suspension strut/shock absorber. Remove split pin from castellated nut. Pull off washer with lug and wheel hub.

When installing: Adjust wheel bearing play. Check grease packing in wheel hub.

TAPER ROLLER BEARING AND SHAFT SEALING RING
Replacing
Lift out shaft sealing ring. Extract taper roller bearing. Drive out bearing outer races through cutouts in wheel hub.

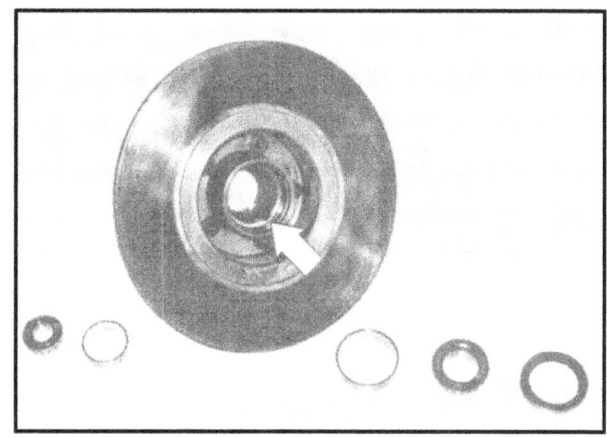

When installing: Press in bearing outer races with a suitable sleeve. Pack shaft sealing ring with graphite grease. Renew grease packing.

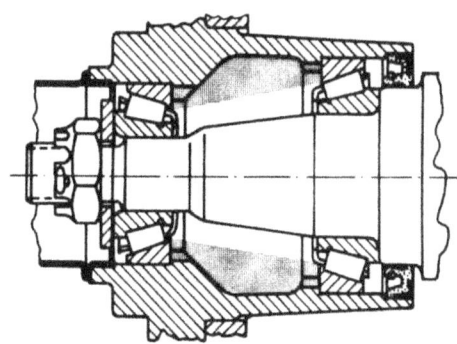

WHEEL STUD
Replacing
Mark relative position of brake disc and hub, then remove disc. Remove (install) the wheel stud.

SUSPENSION STRUT/SHOCK ABSORBER COMPLETE
Removing and installing
Remove wheel. Detach brake caliper – brake lines remain connected – and disconnect angle piece from suspension strut/shock absorber. Remove wire keeper. Detach track rod arm from suspension strut/shock absorber. Disconnect suspension strut thrust bearing from wheel arch.

FRONT SUSPENSION

SHOCK ABSORBERS
Replacing
Only replace shock absorbers in pairs. Remove coil spring. Pull off sleeve and helper spring. Release threaded ring with socket wrench 6016. Pull out shock absorber.

When installing: Before fitting shock abosrber, pour 50 cc of SAE 30 engine oil into the suspension strut tube. The oil is needed to conduct away heat.

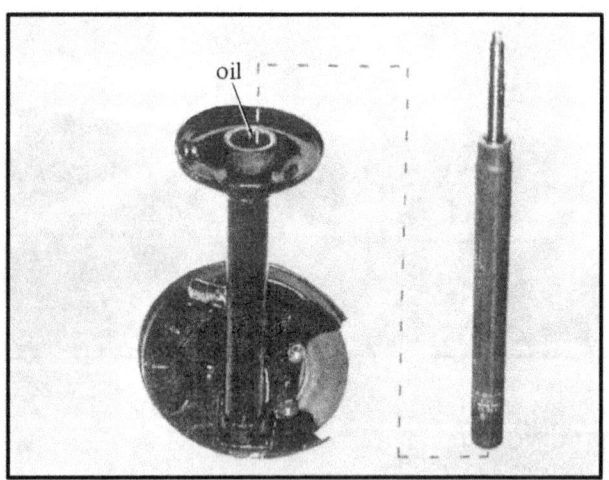

Replacing
Only replace suspension strut/shock absorbers in pairs. Remove coil spring. Pull off sleeve and auxiliary spring. Lift off spring base. Remove wheel hub. Remove shield plate.

SUSPENSION STRUT THRUST BEARING
Removing and refitting
Remove suspension strut/shock absorber complete. Compress coil spring — spring compressor 6035. Lift off sealing cap. Unscrew locknut. Lock piston rod. Remove suspension strut thrust bearing. Only replace suspension strut thrust bearing as a complete unit.

When installing: Internal dishing of sealing washer should face towards thrust bearing.

FRONT SUSPENSION

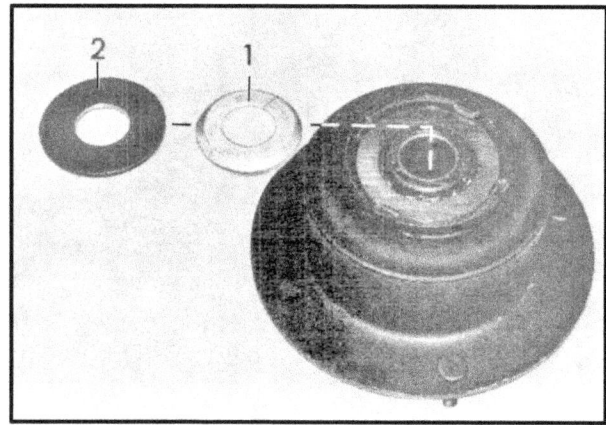

1. Sealing washer
2. Thrust bearing washer

COIL SPRING
Removing and refitting
Remove suspension strut/shock absorber complete. Remove suspension strut thrust bearing. Remove spring plate and compressed coil spring.

Replacing
Remove suspension strut thrust bearing. Spring length, spring thickness and coil spring strength must be uniform on left and right hand sides. Check spring bases. Wind spring ends into spring plates.

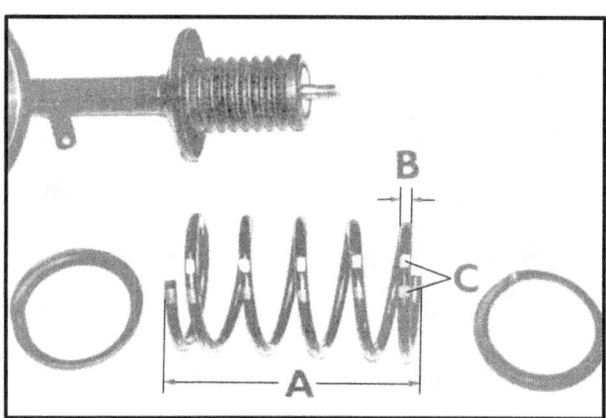

A. Spring length
B. Spring thickness
C. Coil spring length

SLEEVE
Replacing
Remove suspension strut thrust bearing. Remove spring plate and compress coil spring. Pull off sleeve with helper spring.

When installing: Refit bleeder plate.

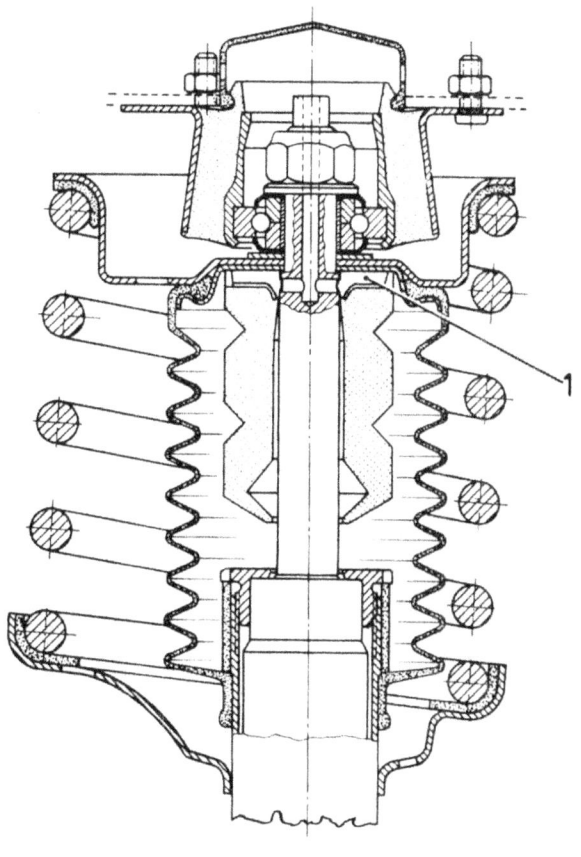

32 00 024 Front axle optical alignment

The following conditions must be fulfilled before wheel alignment can take place:

1. Good, even tire tread.
2. Correct specified tire pressure.
3. Rims in good condition.
4. Correct wheel bearing play.
5. Vehicle in normal load position:
   2 x 65 kg (143 lb.) on rear seats,
   1 x 65 kg (143 lb.) on front seats.
   30 kg (66 lb.) in luggage compartment at left, fuel tank full.

Measure actual values with the optical wheel alignment device.

Enter these values on the wheel alignment chart.

For nominal values, see technical data.

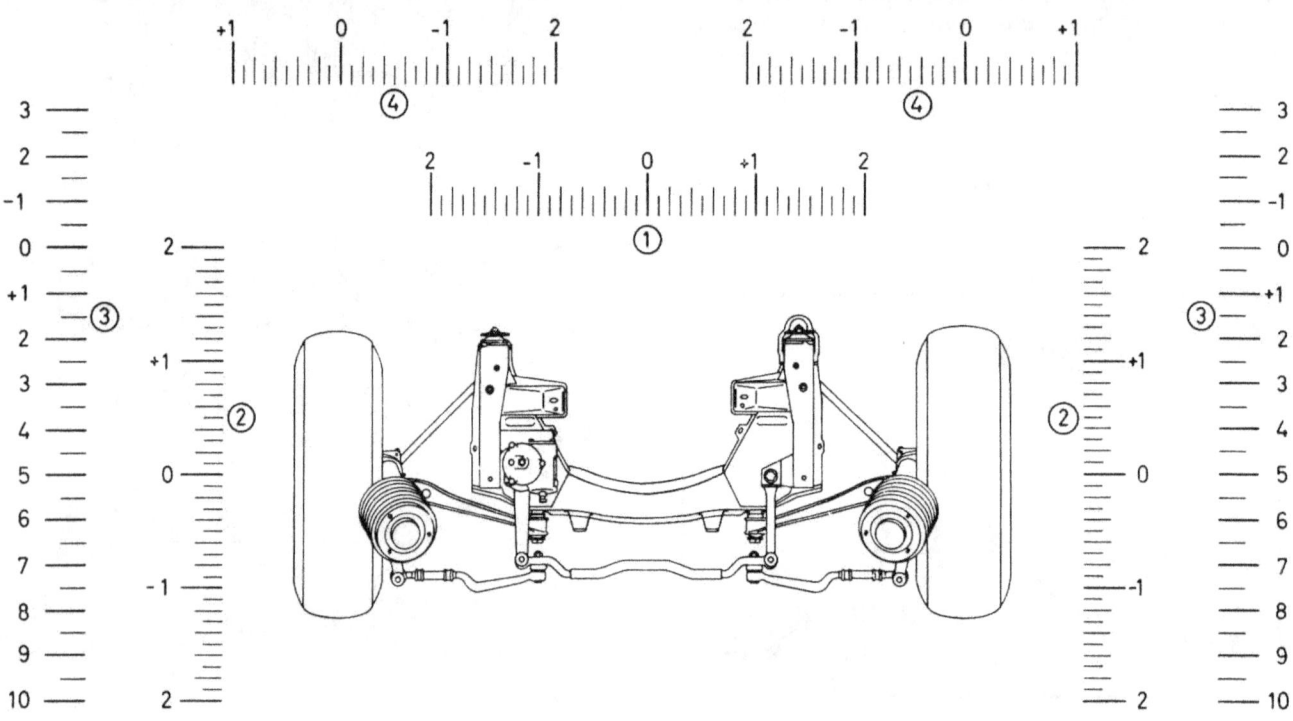

20° RIGHT LOCK
measured at left wheel

20° LEFT LOCK
measured at right wheel

Trouble shooting:

① Incorrect track
a) Track rod bent,
b) Track rod arm bent,
c) Track rod ball joint loose.

② Incorrect camber angle
a) Lower wishbone distorted,
b) Spring strut distorted,
c) Front axle beams distorted,
d) Wheel box distorted,
e) Guide joint loose,
f) Excessive wheel bearing play,
g) Excessive spring compression,
h) Floor panel assembly distorted.

③ Incorrect castor angle
a) Trailing link distorted,
b) Lower wishbone distorted,
c) Spring strut distorted,
d) Wheel box distorted,
e) Floor panel assembly distorted.

④ Incorrect toe-out on turns
assuming that camber and castor angles are correct
a) Track rods not adjusted to same length,
b) Track rod arm bent,
c) Steering drop arm incorrectly mounted.

STEERING

INDEX

	Page
STEERING BOX — (GEMMER STEERING)	103
Adjusting	103
Removing and installing	104
Dismantling and reassembling	104
SEALING RINGS FOR STEERING ROLLER SHAFT AND WORM	104
Replacing	104
STEERING ROLLER SHAFT AND WORM (STEERING BOX DISMANTLED)	104
Replacing	104
HYDRAULIC POWER STEERING	105
Bleeding	105
PRESSURE POINT	105
Adjusting	105
STEERING BOX — HYDRAULIC POWER STEERING	105
Removing and installing	105
Dismantling and reassembling	105
Steering drop arm	105
Cover-pressure point	106
Segment shaft	106
Valve housing	106
Intermediate cover	106
Teflon rings, worm head, piston	107
Total friction value of worm head	107
Checking and adjusting	107
Piston and worm	107
STEERING GUIDE ARM	110
Removing and installing	110
TRACK ROD ARM	110
Replacing	110
OUTER TRACK ROD	110
Replacing	110
CENTER TRACK ROD	110
Replacing	110
UPPER STEERING COLUMN HOUSING	110
Removing and installing	110
JOINT DISC	111
Replacing	111

	Page
LOWER STEERING COLUMN	111
Removing and installing	111
UPPER STEERING COLUMN	111
Removing and installing	111
CANCELING CAM	112
Replacing	112
UPPER STEERING COLUMN BEARING	112
Replacing	112
LOWER STEERING COLUMN BEARING	112
Replacing	112
UPPER UNIVERSAL JOINT	113
Replacing	113
LOWER UNIVERSAL JOINT	113
Replacing	113
STEERING LOCK	113
Removing and installing	113
STEERING LOCK BARREL	113
Replacing	113
STEERING WHEEL	114
Removing and installing	114
HORN PUSH IN STEERING WHEEL	114
Replacing	114
CARBON BRUSH ON SWITCH PLATE	114
Replacing	114
SLIP RINGS FOR CARBON BRUSH	114
Replacing	114
HIGH PRESSURE PUMP AND OPERATION OF POWER STEERING	114
Checking	114
Vane type pump	114
Hydraulic power steering	114
Mechanical play in steering (Pressure point correctly adjusted)	115
HIGH PRESSURE PUMP	115
Removing and installing	115
Dismantling and reassembling	115
FILTER IN OIL RESERVOIR	116
Replacing	116

STEERING BOX — (GEMMER STEERING)

Adjusting

Move the front wheels to the straight ahead position. Press the track rod away from the steering drop arm (7009 extractor). Remove the steering wheel center. Determine the straight ahead position by dividing the total number of turns at the steering wheel by 2. Turn the steering wheel about 1 complete turn to the left. Install the friction meter and turn the steering wheel to the right through the straight ahead position. Read off the friction value at this point. To adjust friction value, turn the steering wheel back approximately 1 turn to the left. In this position the worm cannot be pressed into its bearing at one side by the steering roller shaft, and this may create the impression that no play is present. Loosen the locknut. Turn the adjusting screw until the correct friction value is obtained when the steering wheel passes through the straight ahead position.

104 STEERING

Removing and installing
Loosen the screw and remove it. Press the universal joint upward as far as possible.

When installing: With the steering wheel and front wheels in the straight ahead position, the marks on the steering box and steering shaft must be aligned.

Note installed position of screw in the keeper groove. Unscrew the castellated nut. Press off the track rod with the 7009 extractor. Separate the steering box from the front axle beam and remove downwards.

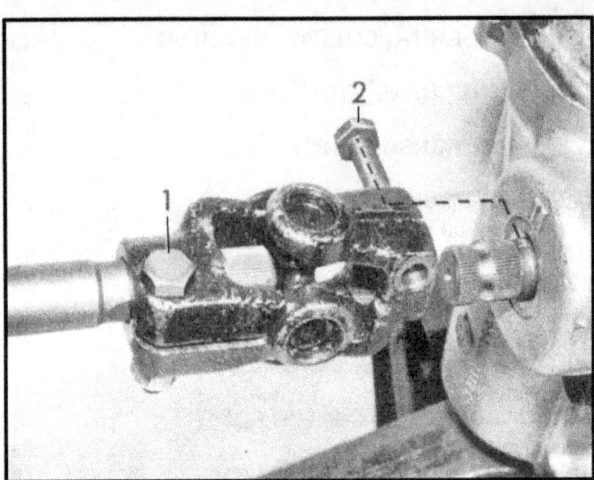

Adjusting screw

Dismantling and reassembling
Drain the oil. Open the tab washer. Unscrew the nut. Pull off the steering drop arm with Kukko 204-2 puller.

When installing: The arrow on the steering drop arm must be aligned with the mark on the steering roller shaft.

Check steering drop arm for distoriton. Remove the steering box cover with the steering roller shaft.

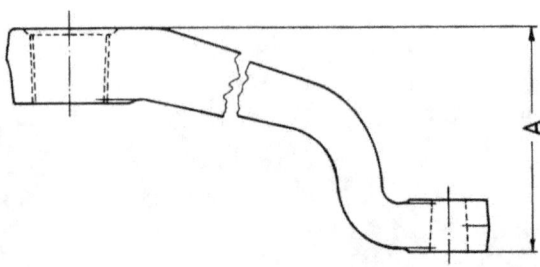

A=3.524 + 0.020 in.

When installing: Apply Atmosit to the steering box sealing face and screws.

Remove the end cover. Note shims. Drive out the worm shaft from the steering box with a plastic headed hammer.

When installing: Apply Atmosit to screws, end cover and shims.

Install the steering worm and roller shaft. Check friction value and adjust if necessary.

SEALING RINGS FOR STEERING ROLLER SHAFT AND WORM
Replacing
Drive in oil seal until it seats firmly and oil seal until flush with the steering box housing.

STEERING ROLLER SHAFT AND WORM – (STEERING BOX DISMANTLED)
Replacing
Examine condition of ball and needle roller bearings and replace if necessary. With a suitable Kukko extractor, remove the ball race from the housing.

When installing: Press in the ball race with a drift of precisely the correct size.

Remove both needle roller bearings from the steering box housing with a suitable Kukko extractor.

When installing: Press in the needle roller bearings with a drift of precisely the correct size.

A = 1 mm (0.039 in.)
B = 56 mm (2.205 in.)

Loosen the locknut. Unscrew and remove the adjusting screw from the steering box cover. Adjust play of steering roller shaft with locating washer. Install the steering worm. Secure device 7015 into position and tighten the housing cover screw while rotating the steering worm continuously. If the friction value is too high, increase thickness of shims. If the friction value is too low, reduce thickness of shims. Refill steering box with oil. Adjust the steering roller shaft to the prescribed friction value with the adjusting screw while turning through the straight ahead position.

STEERING

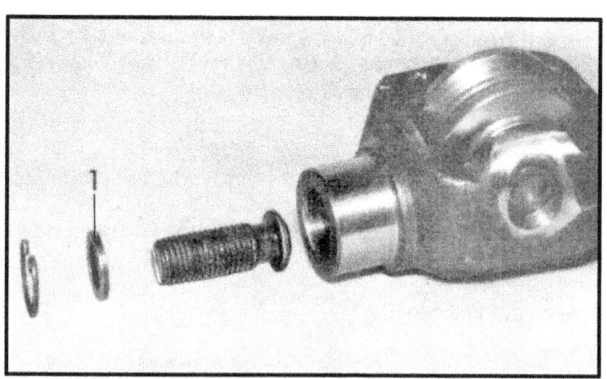

HYDRAULIC POWER STEERING
Bleeding

The hydraulic power steering must be bled whenever the hydraulic system is opened or the oil level falls so low that the vane type pump draws in air. Fill the reservoir up to the rim with oil. Turn the engine over with the starter and continue to add oil. When the oil level no longer falls, run the engine at idle speed. Turn the steering wheel rapidly from one full lock position to the other and back until no further air bubbles rise in the reservoir. During this operation and afterwards the oil level must always remain at the upper mark.

PRESSURE POINT
Adjusting

Move the front wheels to the straight ahead position. Press the track rod away from the steering drop arm with 7009 extractor. Take off the steering wheel center. Determine the straight ahead position by measuring the total number of turns at the steering wheel and dividing by 2. Turn the steering wheel approximately 1 turn to the left. Install the friction meter and turn the steering wheel to the right across the pressure point. Read off the friction value at this point.

Before adjusting, the steering wheel must again be turned approximately 1 turn to the left of the straight ahead position and loosen the locknut. Turn the adjusting screw until the prescribed friction value is obtained as the steering passes the pressure point.

STEERING BOX – (HYDRAULIC POWER STEERING)
Removing and installing

Turn the steering to full left lock. This will move the piston to the top of its travel. Drain the oil. Do not re-use oil drained from the steering.

When installing: Bleed the power steering.

Press the track rod away from the steering drop arm with 7009 extractor. Remove the lower screw from the universal joint. Loosen the upper screw. Drive the universal joint as far as possible on to the steering column.

When installing: With the steering in the straight ahead position, the marks on the steering box and the worm shaft must be aligned when the worm shaft is turned to the midpoint of its total range of movement.

Detach the oil hoses. Seal the hose connections with dust caps. Separate the steering box from the front axle beam and remove downwards.

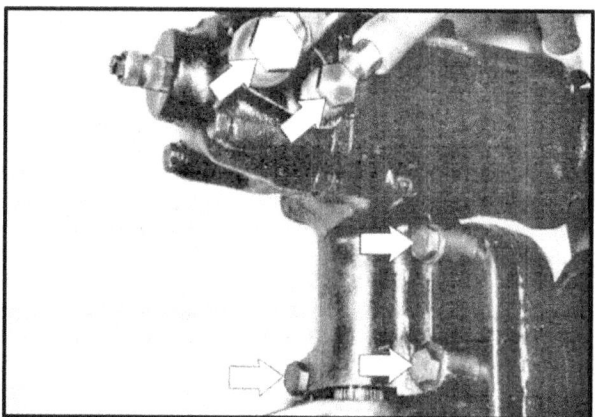

Dismantling and reassembling
Steering drop arm

Open the tab washer.

When installing: The longer of the two metal tabs should be on the right of the steering drop arm looking forward. Unscrew the nut.

Pull off the steering drop arm with Kukko 204-2 extractor.

When installing: The arrows on the steering drop arm and the marking on the segment shaft must be aligned.

106 STEERING

Cover – pressure point
Unscrew nut and remove the cover attachment screws. Raise the cover by turning the adjusting screw clockwise.

When installing: Check condition of O-ring in cover and replace if necessary.

Before tightening the cover screws, turn the adjusting screw until the cover is firmly seated.

When installing: Determine the mid-point of worm shaft movement by halving the total number of turns. Turn back the worm shaft 1 complete turn to the left. Using attachment 7015 and a friction meter, turn the shaft clockwise over the pressure point and read off the friction value. To adjust the friction value, first turn back the worm shaft 1 turn to the left. Turn the adjusting screw until the prescribed friction value is obtained as the pressure point is crossed.

Segment shaft
Pull out the segment shaft while in the central position.

When installing: Pack the splines with high temperature bearing grease. Insert the segment shaft carefully to avoid damaging ring seals.

Check axial play of adjusting screw and if necessary correct by installing a thicker washer. The adjusting screw must turn freely without sticking. Lift out the Seeger circlip and ring seal. Extract the needle roller bearing. Drive out needle roller bearing with thrust washer and ring seal. When installing the sealing lips on the ring seals must face the interior of the steering box.

Valve housing
Pull off the protecting cap and remove the valve housing.

When installing: To prevent damage to the ring seal, cover the splines with scotch tape.

Remove the ball bearing.

When installing: Check condition of ring seals and replace if necessary.

If the needle roller bearing is replaced, press off the bearing race. Slide off the double needle roller cage. Pull bearing race out of the valve housing with a Kukko extractor.

When installing: Fit bearing and needle roller cage without play. For this purpose the needle roller cages are available in 4 different sizes.

Adjust friction value with bearing disc.

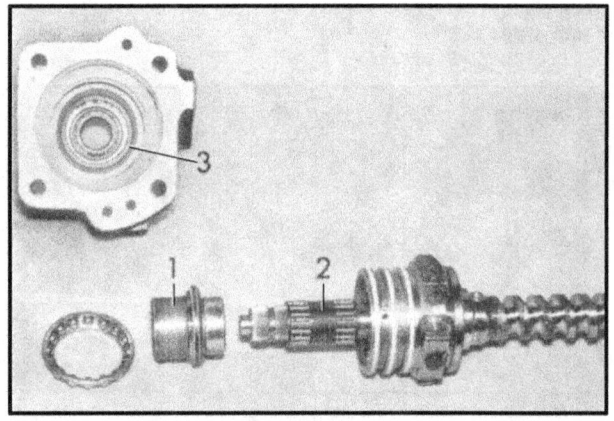

Intermediate cover
Extract the worm with the intermediate cover and piston from the steering box housing.

When installing: Check condition of sealing rings and replace if necessary.

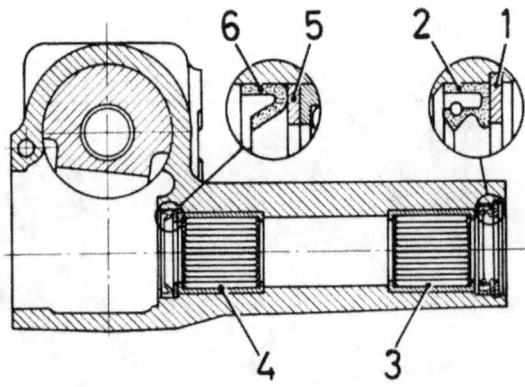

1. Seeger clip
2. Ring seal
3. Needle roller bearing
4. Needle roller bearing
5. Thrust washer
6. Ring seal

1-4. Sealing rings

Unscrew the worm from the piston. Do not allow balls to escape. Remove intermediate cover. Take off the recirculating tube. Check condition of needle roller cage, bearing washer, slotted ring, O-ring and sealing ring. The shim washer is needed for adjusting the position of the slotted ring.

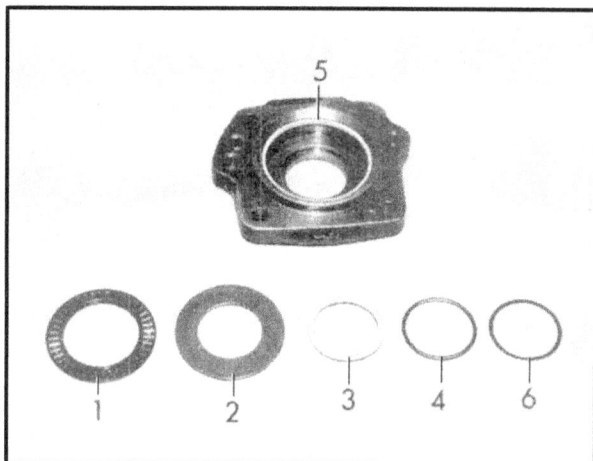

1. Needle roller cage
2. Bearing washer
3. Slotted ring
4. O-ring
5. Sealing ring
6. Shim washer

When installing: Attach the valve housing without ring seal, the worm head without the Teflon sealing rings, the intermediate cover without the O-ring and the slotted ring with ball bearing, needle roller cage and bearing washer to the valve housing.

Tighten the screws evenly to 25 lb/ft torque. Adjust friction value of worm bearing with bearing washers. Check preload of Teflon ring in intermediate cover. Place the bearing washer and needle roller cage into the intermediate cover. Insert the O-ring and Teflon ring into the slot. Install the worm shaft. With the 7015 attachment in position, measure the friction value with the assembly vertical. If the friction value is too low, install a thicker Teflon ring.

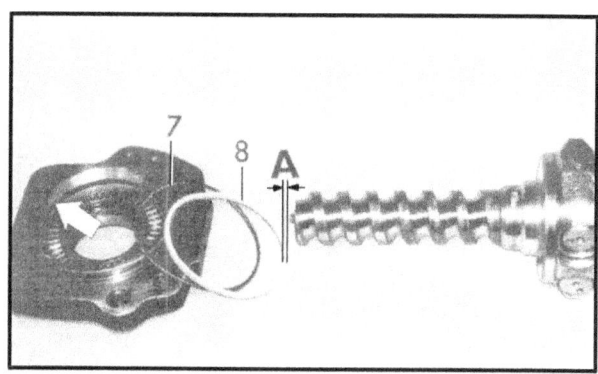

7. O-ring
8. Teflon ring
A = 0.07 in.

Teflon rings, worm head, piston

Using a feeler gauge, lift the Teflon rings away from the worm head and piston. Lift out the O-ring.

When installing: Do not re-install rings once removed.

Total friction value of worm head
Checking and adjusting

Install the Teflon rings in the worm head and the sealing ring in the valve housing. Install the Teflon rings in the intermediate cover and measure the friction value. Insert the O-ring and slotted rings seal (with sealing lips facing the piston together) with the same shims as were previously removed. Install the worm head in the valve housing. Attach the intermediate cover to the valve housing with 25.6 lb/ft torque. Measure the friction value. Using shims, adjust preload of the slotted ring seal until 0.07 lb/ft higher than the previously determined friction value in the intermediate cover.

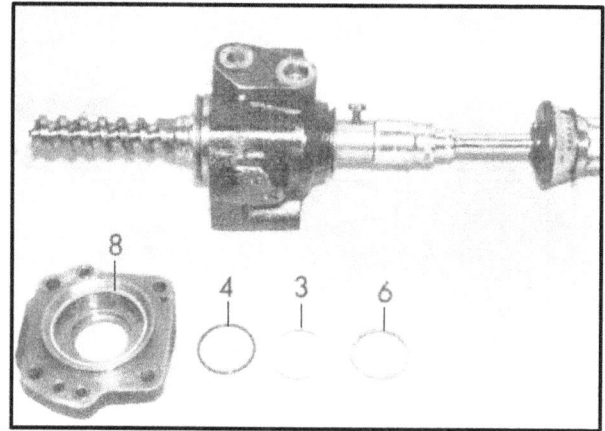

3. Slotted ring seal
4. O-ring
6. Shims
8. Teflon ring

Piston and worm

The valve piston must not be removed. If these pistons are removed, the hydraulic center line, which has been accurately adjusted by means of the steering column and torsion bar, will no longer be correct. The steering limit valve must open shortly before the full lock stop is reached. Adjust the stop screw so that the steering limit

STEERING

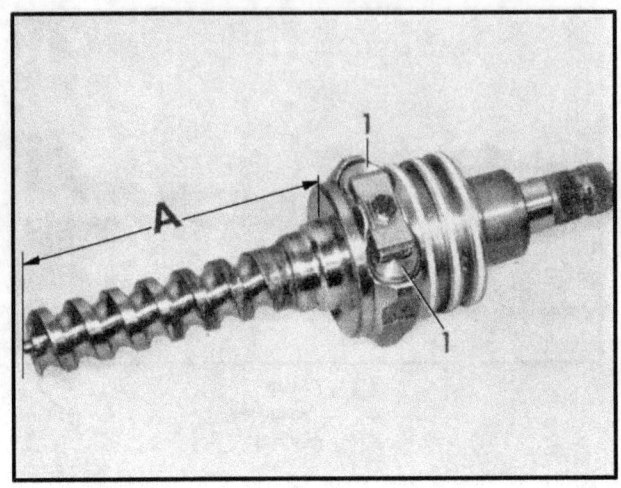

A 107-0.2 mm (4.213-.008 in.)

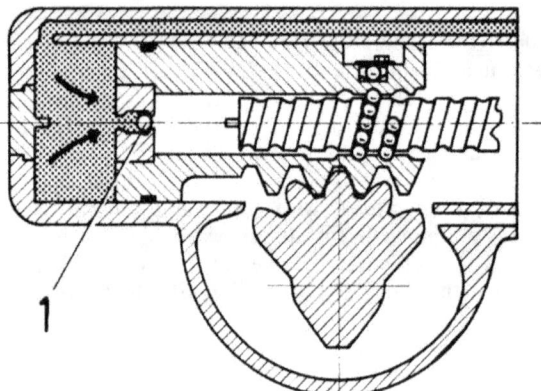

Steering limit valve (1) closed
Steering in neutral position

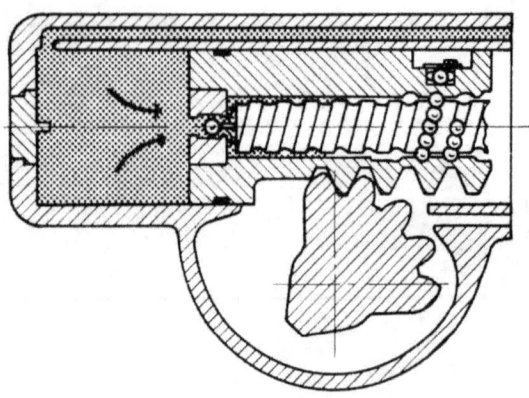

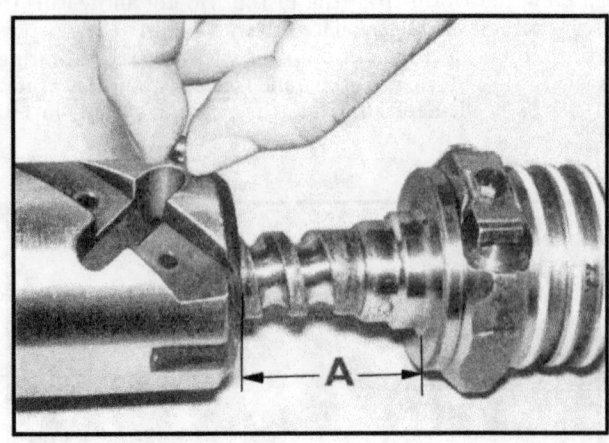

A = approx. 4 cm (1.6 in.)

valve opens 4.213-0.008 in. before the track rod arm stop makes contact. Insert worm into piston. Add 16 balls through the front recirculation hole. While adding balls, screw in the worm. Place 7 balls in the recirculating tube. Prevent the 2 outer balls from escaping by packing with grease. Attach the recirculating tube to the piston. Lock the screws by bending over the ends of the clips.

Unscrew the worm about 3½ turns. With attachment 7015 positioned horizontally, measure the friction value over a range of movement of at least 90°. The friction value is determined by the diameter of the balls. Use only balls of identical diameter (in the same tolerance group). After correctly adjusting friction value, remove the worm. Remove the intermediate cover and assemble the worm and piston. Never unscrew the worm by more than 3½ turns or the balls may fall into the piston barrel.

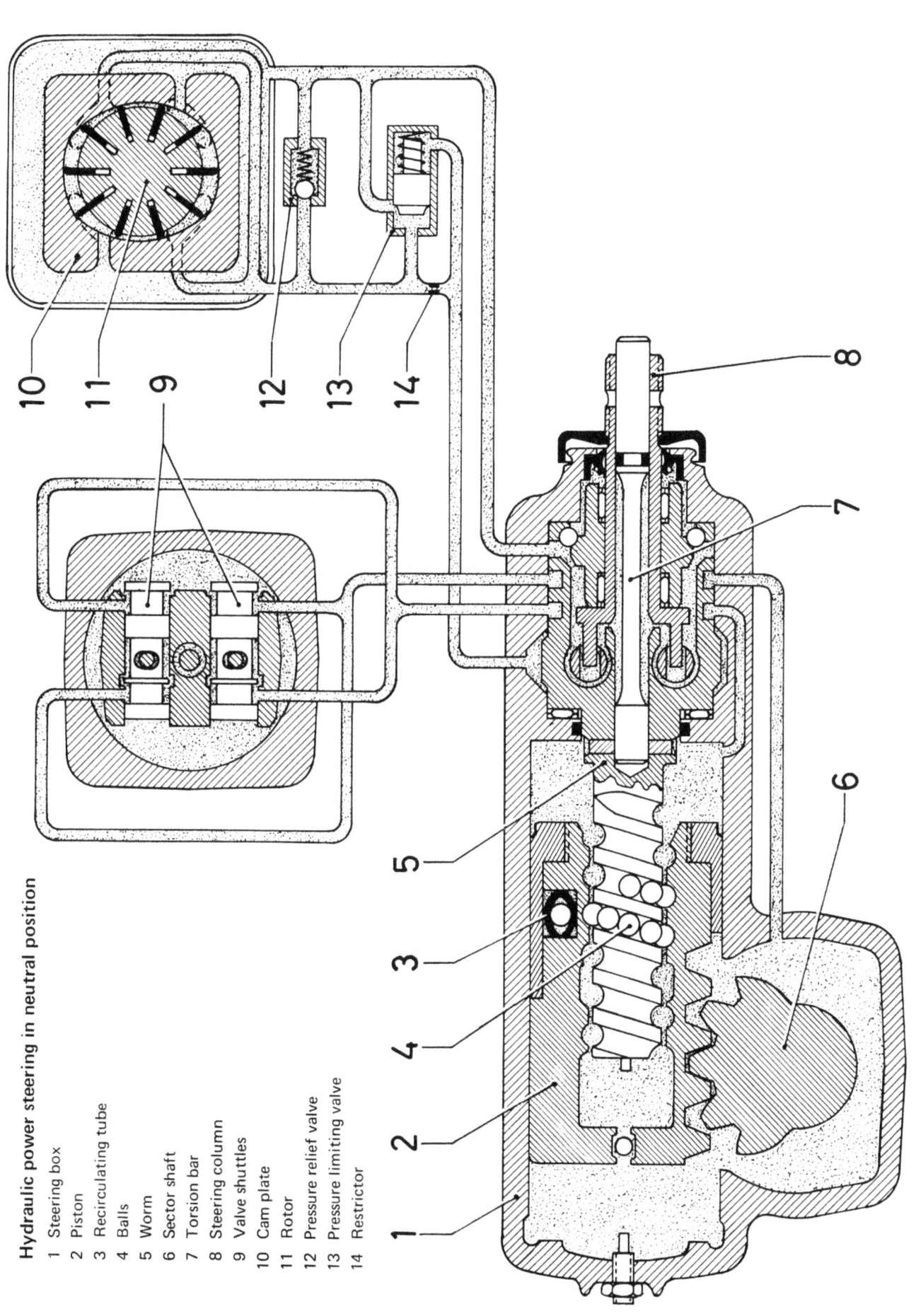

Hydraulic power steering in neutral position
1 Steering box
2 Piston
3 Recirculating tube
4 Balls
5 Worm
6 Sector shaft
7 Torsion bar
8 Steering column
9 Valve shuttles
10 Cam plate
11 Rotor
12 Pressure relief valve
13 Pressure limiting valve
14 Restrictor

110 STEERING

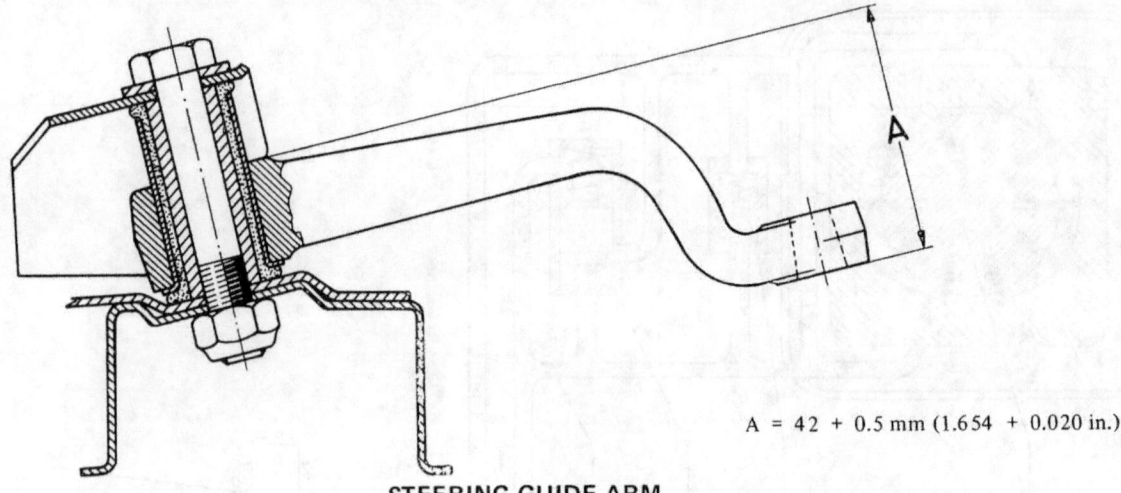

$A = 42 + 0.5$ mm $(1.654 + 0.020$ in.$)$

STEERING GUIDE ARM

STEERING GUIDE ARM
Removing and installing
Remove the castellated nut and press off the track rod with 7009 extractor. Separate the steering guide arm from the front axle beam.

When installing: Check condition of steering guide arm and Fluid-bloc bush, and replace if necessary.

TRACK ROD ARM
Replacing
Press off track rod from track rod arm with 6056 extractor. Remove the wire keeper. Separate track rod arm from spring strut. Unscrew the castellated nut. Press off track rod arm from lower wishbone with Kukko extractor.

When installing: Check condition of track rod arm. Distance from center of hole to spring strut thrust face in direction of steering drop arm is 2.11 in.

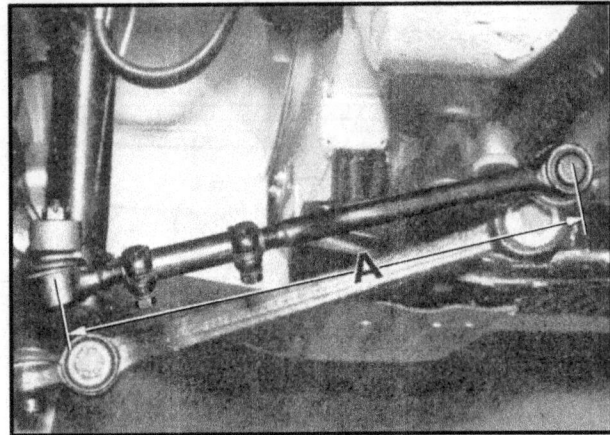

$A = 13$ in.

CENTER TRACK ROD
Replacing
Press off outer track rod from center track rod with 6056 extractor. Press off center track rod from steering drop arm and steering guide arm with 7009 extractor.

When installing: Soak Vulkollan ring with oil to prevent premature failure of the joint through ingress of water.

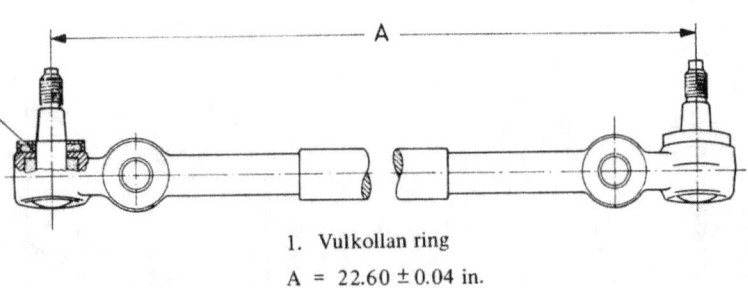

1. Vulkollan ring
$A = 22.60 \pm 0.04$ in.

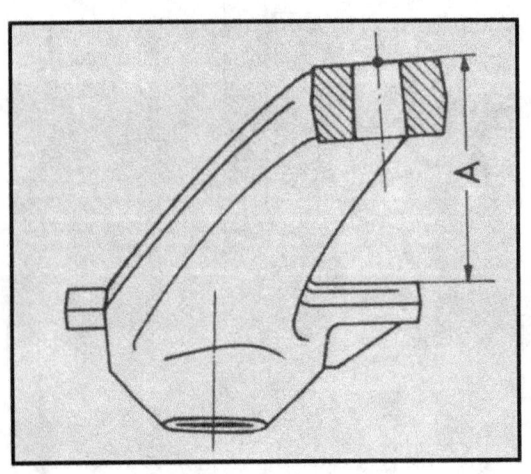

$A = 2.11$ in.

OUTER TRACK ROD
Replacing
Press off track rod from track rod arm with 6056 extractor. Press off track rod from center track rod with 6056 extractor. Basis length of track rod 13 in. Measure front axle with optical alignment device. Loosen clamp screw and adjust track.

UPPER STEERING COLUMN HOUSING
Removing and installing
Remove steering wheel. Remove lower section of housing. Remove housing. Detach cable from rear fog warning light switch, and swing down the housing panel.

STEERING

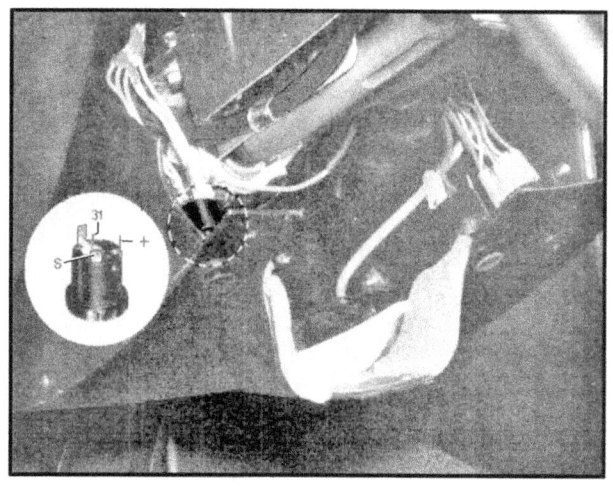

LOWER STEERING COLUMN
Removing and installing

Loosen screw on universal joint. Mark the installed position of steering column and universal joint in the straight ahead position of the steering (with chalk or similar) and remove the housing. Pull off the cable to the rear fog warning light switch and swing the housing panel to the right.

Unscrew the stop nuts. Detach the upper section of the housing from the pedal pivot bracket. Pull away the joint disc from the lower steering column. Pull the lower steering column out of the universal joint. Check condition of plastic bush.

When installing: + yellow/white, S grey/violet, 31 brown

Remove screw from universal joint. Remove turn indicator and dip switch from switch plate.

When installing: See Canceling cam – replacing.

Detach cable from carbon brush. Remove bulb for control lever illumination. Detach cable clips. Loosen grub screw. Pull out the ignition/starter switch. Detach upper section of housing from pedal pivot bracket and pull away from the universal joint together with the steering column.

JOINT DISC
Replacing

Detach the housing panel. Pull off the cable to the rear fog warning light switch and swing the housing panel to the right.

1. Plastic bush

When installing: Check the condition of gaiter.

UPPER STEERING COLUMN
Removing and installing

Remove the steering wheel and the lower section of housing. Detach housing. Pull off cable to rear fog warning light switch and swing the housing to the right.

When installing: + yellow/white, S grey/violet, 31 brown

Pull off the canceling cam and collar.

(See Canceling cam – replacing.)

Detach joint disc from both halves of the steering column.

When installing: Note position of earth (ground) strap. Detach upper section of housing from pedal pivot bracket. Take off the joint disc.

Lift out the circlip. Recess in collar locates over circlip. Take off the washer, coil spring and ring. The ring shank faces the steering column bearing. Remove screw. Detach upper section of housing from pedal pivot bracket. Pull steering column out of universal joint. Drive steering column with lower steering column bearing out of the upper section of the housing.

112 STEERING

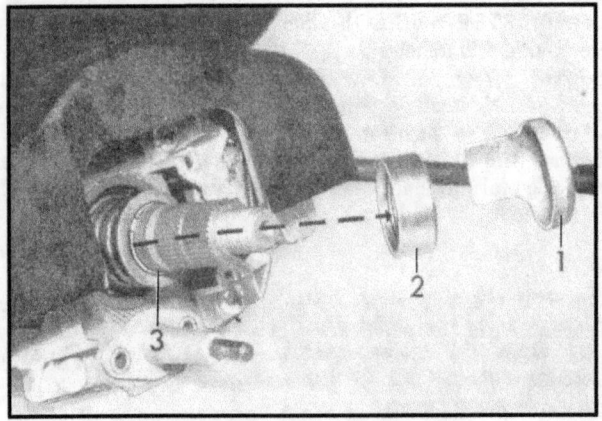

1. Canceling cam
2. Collar
3. Circlip

When installing: Press the circlip into the groove on the steering column using the collar the wrong way up.

CANCELING CAM
Replacing
Remove steering wheel and pull off the canceling cam.

When installing: Place the steering in straight ahead position. Turn the indicator switch in central position with the driving peg facing center of canceling cam. Clearance approximately 0.012 in. Adjust at turn indicator switch.

UPPER STEERING COLUMN BEARING
Replacing
Remove steering wheel. Detach the lower section of housing and pull off the canceling cam and collar.

When installing: See Canceling cam – replacing.

Lift out circlip When installing, recess in collar locates over circlip. Take off the washer, coil spring and ring. Drive out steering column bearing from the upper section of the housing.

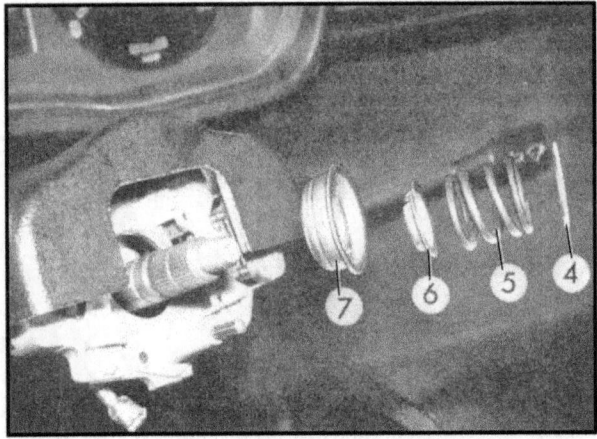

4. Washer
5. Coil spring
6. Ring
7. Steering column bearing

When installing: The ring shank faces the steering column bearing.

Press the circlip into the groove on the steering column using the collar the wrong way up.

3. Circlip

LOWER STEERING COLUMN BEARING
Replacing
Detach the housing. Pull off the cable from the rear fog warning light switch and swing the housing to the right.

Loosen the clamp bolt on the upper universal joint. Detach the upper section of the housing from the instrument panel. Pull the steering column upwards out of the universal joint. Attach the upper section of the housing loosely with 2 screws. Using the steering wheel, press the steering column downward and at the same time lift out the circlip. Take off the collar and drive out the steering column bearing.

When installing: The ring shank faces the steering column bearing.

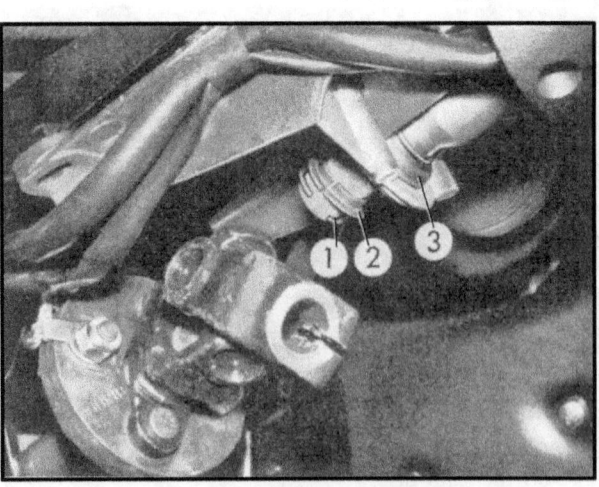

STEERING

UPPER UNIVERSAL JOINT
Replacing
Detach the housing. Pull off the cable from the rear fog warning light switch and swing the housing to the right.

When installing: + yellow/white, S grey/violet
31 brown

Remove the clamp screw and unscrew the stop nuts. Detach the upper section of the housing from the pedal pivot bracket. Pull the universal joint away from the steering column and out of the joint disc.

When installing: Check condition of plastic bush.

LOWER UNIVERSAL JOINT
Replacing
Remove the housing. Pull off the cable from the rear fog warning light switch and swing the housing to the right.

When installing: + yellow/white, S grey/violet
31 brown

Detach the upper section of the housing from the pedal pivot bracket. Loosen the clamp screw. Pull the steering column out of the universal joint. Remove the clamp screw. Pull the universal joint away from the steering box.

When installing: The steering wheel and front wheels must be in the straight ahead position. The marks on the steering box and steering shaft must be aligned. Note installed position of clamp screw in keeper groove. The longer yoke of the universal joint faces the steering column.

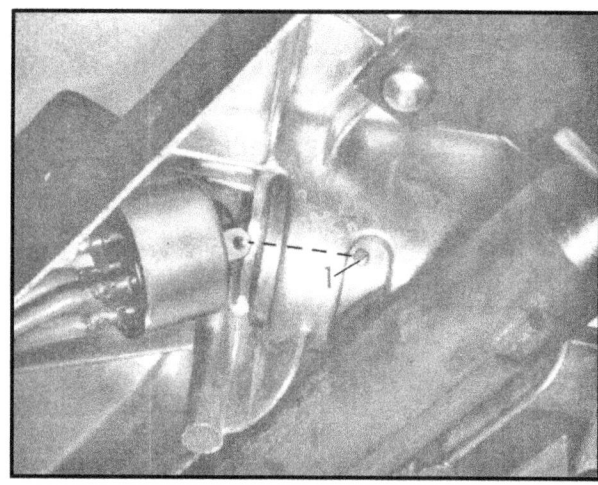
1. Grub screw

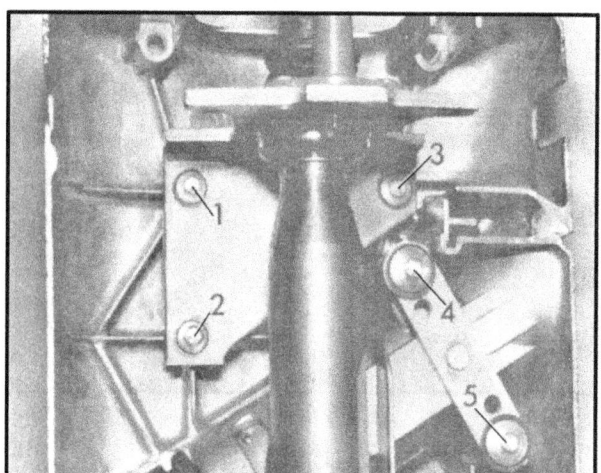
1-5. Shear bolts

STEERING LOCK
Removing and installing
Remove lower section of housing and remove the control lever light. Unscrew the grub screw. Pull out the ignition/starter switch. Loosen the shear bolts for the steering lock plate with a center punch or chisel and unscrew. Unscrew shear bolts only if the steering lock cannot be pulled out of the steering column despite being turned slightly in both directions. Take off the steering lock plate. Push in and turn the steering column until a milled groove is directly under the steering lock. Turn the steering column backward and forward while pulling out the steering lock, which should be in the "Fahrt" (Drive) position.

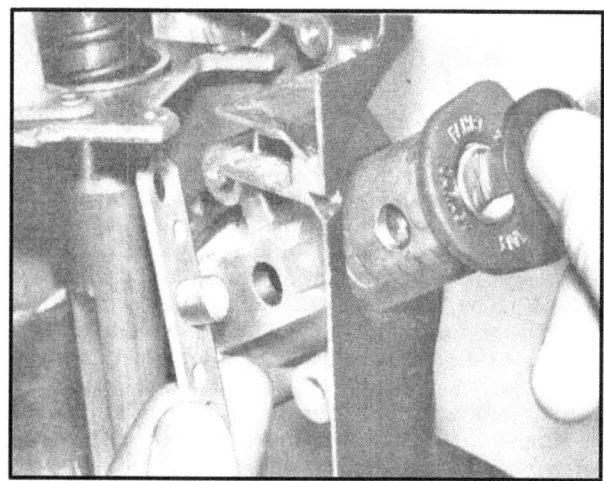

STEERING LOCK BARREL
Replacing
Remove steering lock and press the locking spring down. Pull out the lock barrel.

114 STEERING

STEERING WHEEL
Removing and installing
Remove the steering wheel center. Remove and install the steering wheel only in the straight ahead position.

HORN PUSH IN STEERING WHEEL
Replacing
Remove the steering wheel center. Detach the horn push from the steering wheel. Disconnect and reconnect the cable.

CARBON BRUSH ON SWITCH PLATE
Replacing
Remove steering wheel. Detach lower section of housing. Pull out cable. Drill out rivets.

When installing: Attach carbon brush with screws.

1,2.   Stop valve
A,B.   Pressure line

1.   Cable

SLIP RINGS FOR CARBON BRUSH
Replacing
Separate the plug connection. Remove the slip ring.

HIGH PRESSURE PUMP AND OPERATION OF POWER STEERING
Checking
Check operation of the power steering every 40,000 miles.

Vane type pump
If the power steering develops a fault, always check first the supply pressure from the high pressure pump. Detach pressure line from the high pressure pump and connect to pressure gauge 7017. Connect pressure line to the high pressure pump. Close the stop valve. Open stop valve – lever must be horizontal – and bleed the hydraulic system with the engine at idle speed. The engine must first reach normal operating temperature. After bleeding is complete, close stop valve for maximum 10 seconds – lever vertical – and read off the pressure on the gauge. Pressure should not be more than 10% below the value stated on the maker's plate of the high pressure pump. If the correct pressure is not reached, check the V-belt tension also. Examine valve piston for dirt, and replace if necessary. Install only a valve piston of the same tolerance group as before. The threaded section of the valve piston should face the coil spring. If the maximum pressure is still not reached, replace the pump rotor, vanes and cam disc as a unit.

Hydraulic power steering
Raise the vehicle. Block the steering with the steering wheel ½ to 3/4 of a turn before the full lock position (using a socket head or similar object). Pull the steering wheel for approximately 5 seconds towards the end stop with a force of 22 lb. Read off pressure on pressure gauge 7017. Repeat the measurement at the opposite lock position. If the pressures thus recorded are below the maximum pump pressure, the cause may be the high

pressure pump is delivering too little oil, the steering is losing oil through leakage, the steering box seals are damaged, the valve piston is contaminated, the valve piston is not closing correctly or the steering limit valve is not closing.

Mechanical play in steering
(Pressure point correctly adjusted)
Lock the steering drop arm in the straight ahead position of the wheels with 7016 locking device.

Connect pressure gauge 7017 with a dial calibrated 15–150 psi to the pressure line from the high pressure pump. Open the stop valve. Close valve. Run the engine at normal operating temperature and idle speed. Open valve.

Attach strips of paper to the steering wheel hub and the upper section of the housing. Carefully turn the steering wheel to the left until the pressure gauge indicates a rise of 14.2 psi over the normal supply pressure. Mark this position of the steering wheel. Carefully turn the steering wheel to the right until the pressure gauge again shows a rise of 14.2 psi over the normal supply pressure. Mark this position of the steering hub.

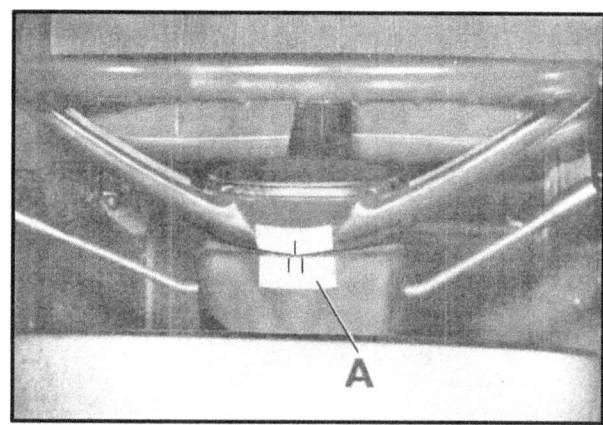

The total distance between the two markings must not exceed 0.276 in. If this distance is exceeded, check joint disc and universal joints. If these components are found to be serviceable, the steering box must be taken down. Remove pressure gauge 7017, add oil to the hydraulic system and bleed.

HIGH PRESSURE PUMP
Removing and installing
Disconnect the hoses from the high pressure pump. Do not re-use automatic transmission fluid escaping from the pump and hoses. Detach the high pressure pump from the rear mounting.

When installing: Secure the high pressure hose in such a way as to prevent friction against the engine mounting.

Detach the high pressure pump at the front.

When installing: It should be possible to press in the V-belt by 0.2–0.4 in. with the thumb. Bleed the hydraulic system.

Dismantling and reassembling
Force down the cover in a press and lift out the circlip. Extract the cover, coil spring and O-ring. Extract the end plate.

1. Circlip
2. Cover
3. Coil spring
4. O-ring

STEERING

When installing: Insert the pin in one of the small holes on the end plate.

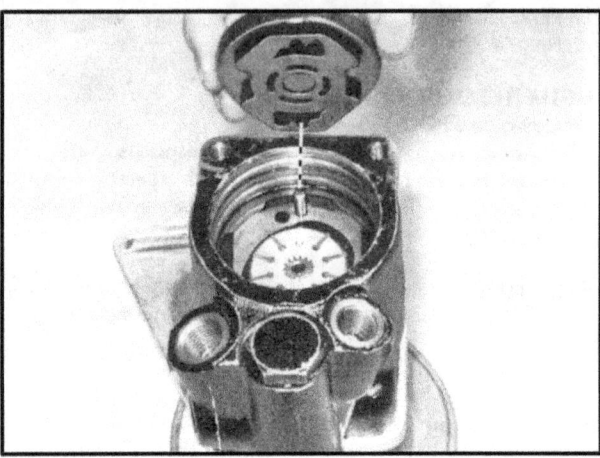

Extract the O-ring. Tilt the housing until the cam ring and rotor can be removed.

When installing: The side of the rotor with the recessed hole faces the drive shaft.

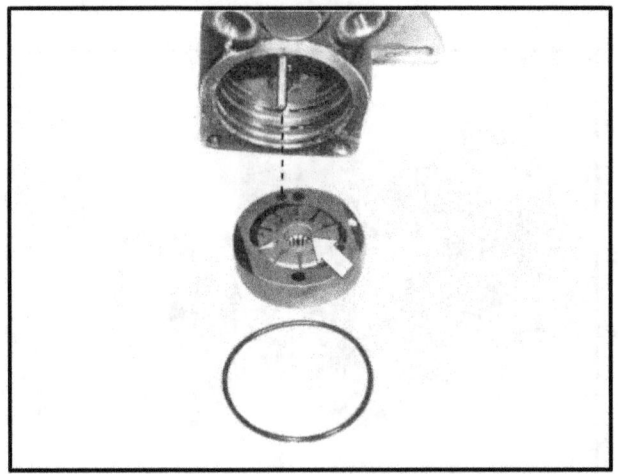

The rounded off side of the rotor faces the cam ring. The cast-in half arrow indicates the direction of rotation of the rotor. Extract the end plate. Use a new O-ring in the housing and in the end plate neck. Do not remove the drive shaft unless the cam ring cannot be moved. Take off the belt pulley. Extract the circlip. Force out the drive shaft. Check condition of ring seal and needle roller bearing and replace if necessary. Extract the circlip. Press off the ball bearing.

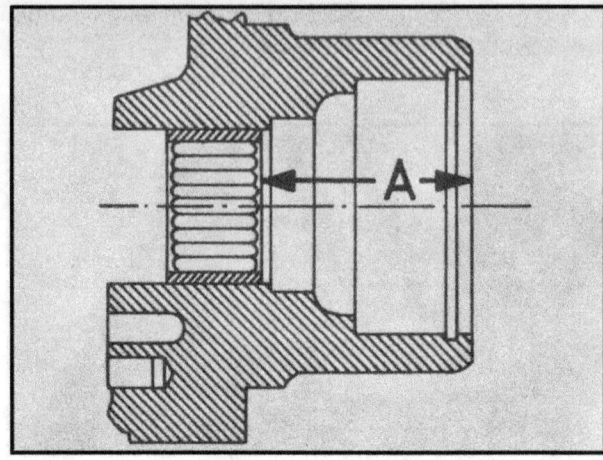

A = 1.457 + 0.008 in.

When installing: Do not alter the length of the coil spring or the thickness of the ring seal.

Remove the valve piston.

When installing: The threaded section on the valve piston faces the coil spring.

Clean the restrictor insert. The pressure valve is located inside the valve piston (flow limit valve). When taking down the valve piston do not clamp across the sliding surfaces. The thickness of the washers determines the cut-in range of the pressure valve.

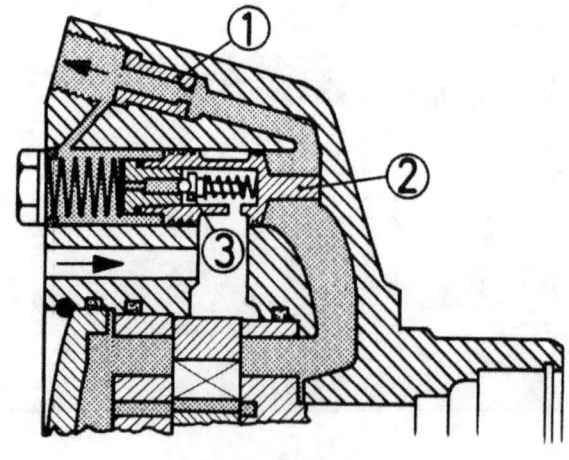

1. Restrictor insert
2. Valve piston
3. Pressure valve

FILTER IN OIL RESERVOIR
Replacing
Remove the end cap. Extract the filter cover. Replace the filter element.

ELECTRICAL

INDEX

	Page
FRONT CABLE HARNESS	118
Replacing	118
REAR CABLE HARNESS	118
Replacing	118
SWITCHES	118
HEADLIGHT DIP SWITCH	118
Removing and installing	118
TURN INDICATOR SWITCH	118
Removing and installing	118
STEERING LOCK/IGNITION–STARTER SWITCH	119
Removing and installing	119
MAIN LIGHT SWITCH	119
Removing and installing	119
WIPER SWITCH	119
Removing and installing	119
SWITCH FOR HEATED REAR WINDOW	119
Removing and installing	119
SWITCH FOR HAZARD WARNING FLASHERS	119
Removing and installing	119
SWITCH FOR REAR FOG WARNING LIGHT	119
Removing and installing	119
SIDE WINDOW LIFT ROCKER SWITCH	120
Removing and installing	120
SIDE WINDOW LIFT ROCKER SWITCH IN ARMREST	120
Removing and installing	120
TRANSMISSION SWITCH	120
Removing and installing	120
FLASHER UNIT	120
Removing and installing	120
STARTER LOCK RELAY	120
Removing and installing	120
HEADLIGHT HIGH BEAM RELAY	120
Removing and installing	120
HORN RELAY	120
Removing and installing	120
DELAYING RELAY FOR WINDSHIELD WASHER	120
Removing and installing	120
INTERMITTENT RELAY FOR WIPERS	121
Removing and installing	121
LOAD-SHEDDING RELAY FOR HEADLIGHTS AND HEATER BLOWER	121
Removing and installing	121
Checking condition of relay	121
SOCKET FOR CIGAR LIGHTER	121
Removing and installing	121
BOTH WIPER PIVOT BEARINGS	121
Replacing	121
WIPER MOTOR	122
Removing and installing	122
INSTRUMENTS	122
COMBINED INSTRUMENTS	122
Removing and installing	122
COOLANT THERMOMETER	122
Removing and installing	122
FUEL GUAGE	122
Removing and installing	122
PRINTED CIRCUIT BOARD	123
Replacing	123
SPEEDOMETER	123
Removing and installing	123
SPEEDOMETER SHAFT	123
Removing and installing	123
REVOLUTION COUNTER	124
Removing and installing	124

	Page
CLOCK	124
Removing and installing	124
BULB FOR CONTROL ILLUMINATION	124
Replacing	124
TRANSMISSION SELECTOR LEVER POSITION INDICATOR	124
Removing and installing	124
FUEL GUAGE TANK FLOAT UNIT	125
Removing and installing	125
COOLANT THERMOMETER CONTACT	125
Removing and installing	125
COMPLETE INSTRUMENT PANEL	126
Removing and installing	126
BULB FOR CLOCK ILLUMINATION	126
Replacing	126
BULBS IN INSTRUMENT PANEL	126
Replacing	126
BULB FOR HAZARD WARNING FLASHER SWITCH	127
Replacing	127
BULBS IN TRANSMISSION SELECTOR LEVER POSITION INDICATOR	127
Replacing	127
HEADLIGHTS	127
Beam alignment	127
MAIN AND DIPPED BEAM HEADLIGHTS	127
Removing and installing	127
TURN INDICATOR BULB HOLDER	127
Replacing	127
REAR LIGHT LENS	127
Removing and installing	127
REAR LIGHT COVER PLATE	128
Removing and installing	128
LICENSE PLATE LIGHT	128
Removing and installing	128
INTERIOR LIGHT COMPLETE	128
Removing and installing	128
FRONT PARKING LIGHT BULB	128
Replacing	128
BULB(S) IN REAR LIGHT CLUSTER	128
Replacing	128
ALTERNATOR AND REGULATOR	128
Checking with engine tester	128
Rapid checking	129
ALTERNATOR	129
Removing and refitting	129
Overhauling	129
Positive diodes	130
Exciter diodes	130
Negative diodes	130
Stater winding – removing and checking	130
Claw pole rotor – checking	131
VOLTAGE REGULATOR	131
Removing and installing	131
STARTER IN VEHICLE	131
Checking with engine tester	131
Removing and refitting	131
Dismantling and reassembling	131
Overhauling	132
CARBON BRUSHES	132
Replacing	132
STARTER STRIPPED	132
Replacing exciter winding	132
ELECTRICAL DIAGRAMS	133

118 ELECTRICAL

FRONT CABLE HARNESS
Replacing

Remove the battery. Take off the air cleaner housing. Detach the sealing and sound deadening material from the heater bulkhead. Detach the coolant reservoir from both its mountings. Detach the bracket holding the brake unit and, if installed, the power steering oil tank from the wheel box. Remove both front side grills. Remove lower center left instrument panel trim. Detach fuse box and remove plug board from engine bulkhead. Detach cable harness at all connections and remove from vehicle. When installing check function of electrical system. On Coupe remove the battery. Take off the air cleaner body. Detach the coolant reservoir from both its mountings. Detach the bracket holding the brake unit and the power steering oil tank from the bulkhead. Remove both headlight casing covers and both horns. Remove both front side grills and both front turn indicators. Detach the steering wheel. Remove the lower left center instrument panel trim. Remove the glove box complete with hinge strap and detach the fuse box. Separate the speedometer drive shaft from the speedometer. Detach the combined instrument and the speedometer from the instrument panel. Detach the cable harness at all connection points and remove from the vehicle. When installing, check functions of electrical system.

REAR CABLE HARNESS
Replacing

Detach the negative lead from the battery. Remove the steering wheel. Remove the lower left center instrument panel trim. Remove the left glove box complete with hinge strap. Loosen the front lid control pivot mounting. Remove the lower center right instrument panel trim. Remove the instrument panel. Remove the fuse box and the main light switch. Remove the wiper switch. Remove the fitted carpet for the luggage compartment, the rear panel trim and the two luggage compartment floor trims. Remove both license plate lights, detach both rear light cluster cover plates, remove the rear left wheel arch edge protection and partly loosen the left wheel arch trim in the luggage compartment. Remove the rear seat and seat back. Remove both door operated courtesy light switches, partly loosen the left fitted carpet. Disconnect the cable harness at all connection points and remove. Detach the cables to the handbrake light contact, reversing light switch and interior light from the main cable run, install plug-in terminals and re-connect. When installing check function of electrical system.

On Coupe detach negative cable from battery and remove steering wheel. Remove lower center left instrument panel trim. Remove left glove box complete with hinge strap. Loosen front lid control pivot mounting and remove main light switch, glove box light and right glove box complete with hinge strap. Remove stowage compartment. Partly loosen both door sill rails. Remove both front wheel box trims, both door switches for courtesy lights and both rear seats. Detach rocker switches for electric side window lifts from both armrests and disconnect cables. Remove both armrests, rear side panel trim and insulating board. Remove (install) fitted carpet for luggage compartment floor, both luggage compartment floor trims, luggage compartment light and luggage compartment front bulkhead trim, detach lens for rear fog warning light, both license plate lights and housings for both rear light clusters. Remove rear wheel arch edge protection, rear panel support and stop bracket. Partly loosen left inner luggage compartment wheel box trim. Partly loosen fitted carpets, carpets on door sills, carpet on transmission tunnel and "Acella" sheet on both wheel boxes at front. Detach combined instrument and speedometer from instrument panel. Disconnect cable harness at all connection points and remove. Separate the cables for the heated rear window and interior roof light at the main harness, install plug-in connectors and re-connect. When installing, check function of electrical system.

SWITCHES
HEADLIGHT DIP SWITCH
Removing and installing

Remove lower section of steering column housing. Remove lower center left instrument panel trim. Take off steering wheel. Unscrew the headlight dip switch.

When installing: Position in the middle of the slots. Pull off the cable to the horn push carbon brush.

Extract the cable harness from the retaining clips. Detach the flasher unit and place on one side. Pull out the multi-pin plug.

TURN INDICATOR SWITCH
Removing and installing

Remove lower section of steering column housing. Remove lower center left instrument panel trim. Remove steering wheel. Unscrew the turn indicator switch.

When installing: Steering must be in straight-ahead position. Turn indicator must be in central (cancelled) position. Actuating peg should point to center of cancelling cam. Set clearance to approximately 0.012 in. with the turn indicator switch.

A = 0.012 in.

Extract the cable harness from the retaining clips. Pull out the control lever light, detach the flat plug and separate the cable connection. Pull off the black multi-pin plug and the grey-blue cable.

ELECTRICAL

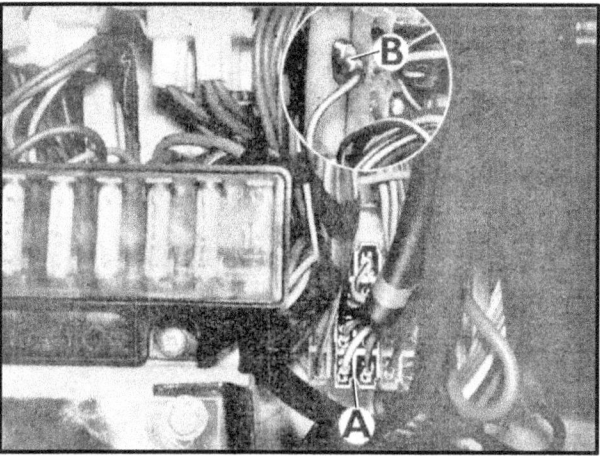

A. Black multi-pin plug
B. Grey–blue cable

STEERING LOCK/IGNITION-STARTER SWITCH
Removing and installing
Remove the negative cable from the battery. Remove the lower section of the steering column housing. Remove the lower center left instrument panel trim. Remove the grub screw. Pull out the switch. Separate the plug connection in the grey cable. Detach the cable harness from the fuse box and the plug board.

1. Grub screw
2. Plug connection in grey cable

When installing: Green – fuse 7, violet – fuse 10, and red – plug board.

MAIN LIGHT SWITCH
Removing and installing
Unscrew knob of main light switch. Unscrew collar securing main light switch with double pin screwdriver. Pull the light switch out forward. Pull off the multi-pin plug.

WIPER SWITCH
Removing and installing
Remove lower center left instrument panel trim. On the Coupe, remove bracket in stowage compartment. Loosen switch collar and remove the switch. Pull off cable.

When installing: Black-yellow 53a, black-grey 53b, black-violet 53.

SWITCH FOR HEATED REAR WINDOW
Removing and installing
Remove lower left center instrument panel trim. Pull off cables.

When installing: brown –, black-red +, green-blue S. Unscrew the switch.

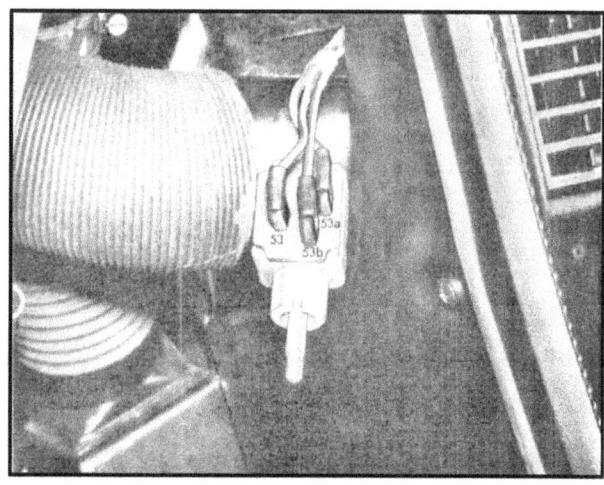

53a black–yellow
53b black–grey
53 black–violet

SWITCH FOR HAZARD WARNING FLASHERS
Removing and installing
Remove lower center left instrument panel trim. Pull off the multi-pin plug. Red – 30, green-white – 15, red-blue – L, green-yellow – 49a, green-violet – 49, blue-black – R. Unscrew the switch.

SWITCH FOR REAR FOG WARNING LIGHT
Removing and installing
Remove center left instrument panel trim. Pull off the cables.

When installing: brown –, violet +, grey-violet S. Unscrew the switch.

120 ELECTRICAL

SIDE WINDOW LIFT ROCKER SWITCH
Removing and installing
Lift out the rocker switch. Pull off the cable.

When installing: Green-blue – 30, green-yellow – 33, black-red – 32.

SIDE WINDOW LIFT ROCKER SWITCH IN ARMREST
Removing and installing
Lift out the rocker switch. Pull off the cable.

When installing: Green-blue – 30, green-yellow – 33, black-red – 32.

TRANSMISSION SWITCH
Removing and installing
Loosen the multi-pin plug. Unscrew the retaining plate. Pull the cable away from the retaining clips. Disconnect the linkage. Loosen the screw. Pull off reversing light cable.

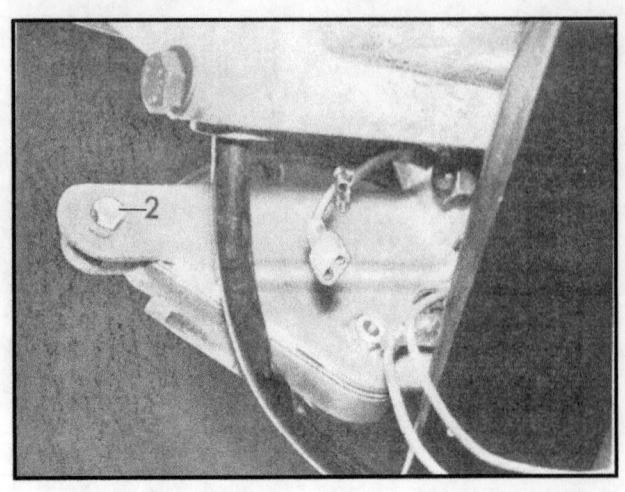

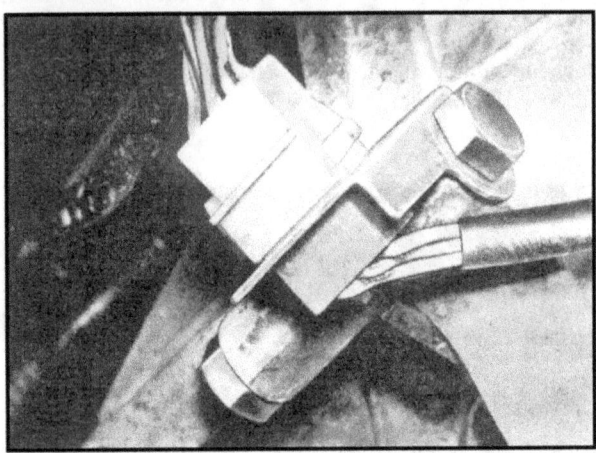

When installing: After loosening screws adjust position of transmission switch until the correct light is illuminated on the scale in the instrument housing when the selector lever is fully engaged.

Supply lines to transmission switch are electrically live. Transmission switch is on positive (+) side of circuit.

FLASHER UNIT
Removing and installing
Open the left glove box. Detach the flasher unit. Pull off the multi-pin plug.

STARTER LOCK RELAY
Removing and installing
Unscrew the relay from its bracket. Pull off the cables.

When installing:
red		30/51
brown-black		86
black 1.5mm dia		85
black 2.5mm diz.		87

HEADLIGHT HIGH BEAM RELAY
Removing and installing
Pull the relay case out of the multi-pin socket.

HORN RELAY
Removing and installing
Pull the relay case out of the multi-pin socket.

DELAYING RELAY FOR WINDSHIELD WASHER
Removing and installing
Open left glove box. Pull relay out of multi-pin socket.

ELECTRICAL

INTERMITTENT RELAY FOR WIPERS
Removing and installing
Open the left glove box. Pull the relay out of the multi-pin socket.

LOAD-SHEDDING RELAY FOR HEADLIGHTS AND HEATER BLOWER
Removing and installing
Open the left glove box. Pull the relay out of the multi-pin socket.

Checking condition of relay
Test connections in multi-pin base one after the other. If necessary, pull the multi-pin plug out of its retainer. If the supply lead (terminal 30/51) or the control lead are under power, the relay is defective. Pull the relay out of the multi-pin plug base and apply a 12 volt supply to pins 85 and 86. The relay should cut in — audible as a clicking sound.

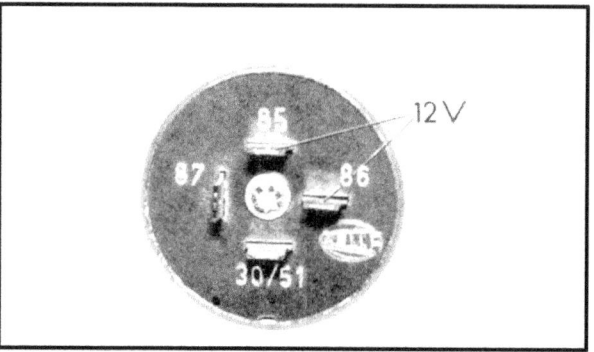

SOCKET FOR CIGAR LIGHTER
Removing and installing
Remove lower center right instrument panel trim. On Coupe, remove bracket in stowage compartment. Pull off cables.

When installing: Red +, brown –. Unscrew the element socket.

BOTH WIPER PIVOT BEARINGS
Replacing
Remove cover plate for heater unit.

When installing: Place a Terostat strip between the cover plate and the water drain gutter and pull off the wiper arms. When installing, push on the wiper arms so that the distance of the blades to the rubber front windshield surround in the parked position is approximately 0.4 – 0.8 in.

A. Terostat strip

Loosen the left and right wiper pivot bearings. Swing out the wiper motor with complete linkage. Pull the multi-pin plug away from the plug board and remove complete with rubber grommet. Press off the connecting link and the drive rod. Unscrew the wiper pivot bearings.

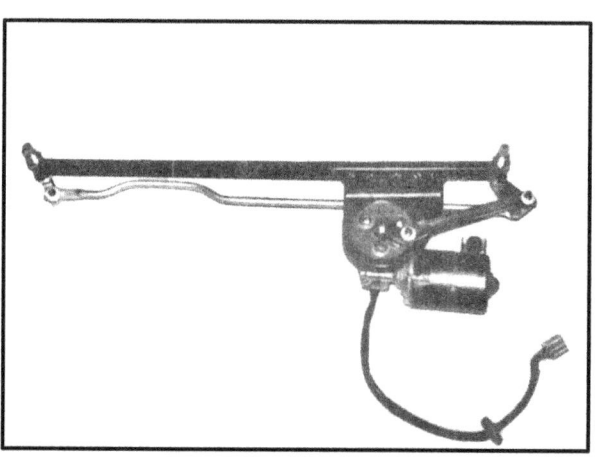

122 ELECTRICAL

WIPER MOTOR
Removing and installing
Unscrew the cover plate for the heater unit (not coupe). Unscrew the drive crank.

When installing: Set to correct limit position.

Unscrew the wiper motor and tilt down to remove. Pull the multi-pin plug away from the plug board and remove complete with rubber grommet. Check condition of wiper motor. Unscrew motor from bracket. Loosen motor crank and pull motor to front, but do not detach multi-pin plug. Using a test lamp or voltmeter at terminal 53 (black-yellow and green cables) or 53b (black-white and red cables), check if power is reaching the wiper motor. If the cables are live, the wiper motor itself must be defective. If the cables are dead, the fault must be traced in the electrical system.

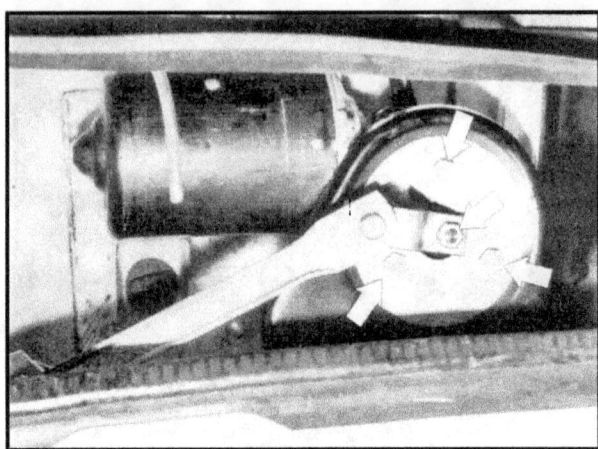

INSTRUMENTS
COMBINED INSTRUMENTS
Removing and installing
Remove the complete instrument panel carrier. Pull out all bulb holders.

When installing: Note color of wires to each bulb holder: grey-blue – Instrument lighting, blue – warning lamp for alternator L, brown-green – warning lamp for oil pressure O, brown-black – warning lamp for fuel level T, white – warning lamp for headlight high beam F.

Pull away the plug connections.

When installing: Note color coding of plug connections: green-white +, brown –, brown-white – Coolant thermometer sensor G, brown-yellow – Fuel tank float G.

Unscrew the combined instrument.

COOLANT THERMOMETER
Removing and installing
Remove revolution counter and speedometer. Unscrew printed circuit board. Unscrew the coolant thermometer and carefully lever away from the printed circuit board.

On Coupe model, (complete instrument panel removed), pull off bulb holder and plug connectors.

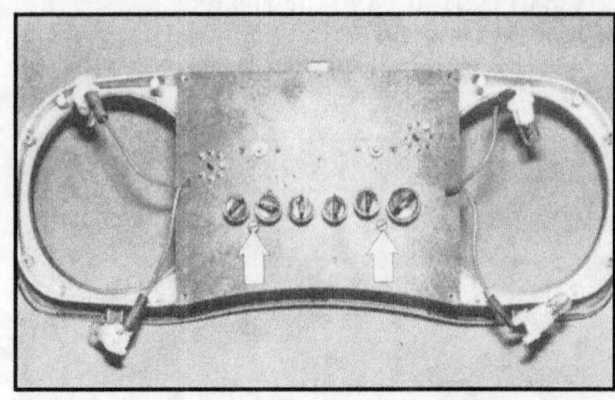

When installing: Green-white +, brown-white – G, brown –.

Remove screws and take off coolant thermometer. Check coolant thermometer. Detach wire from coolant thermometer sensor and connect to earth (ground). Switch on ignition momentarily. The coolant thermometer needle should be deflected fully into the red zone.

FUEL GAUGE
Removing and installing
Remove speedometer and revolution counter. Unscrew printed circuit board. Unscrew the fuel gauge from the printed circuit board and lift carefully away.

On Coupe model, pull out bulb holder and plug connectors.

When installing: Green-white +, brown-yellow – G.

Remove the screws and take off the fuel gauge. Check fuel gauge. Detach brown-yellow wire from fuel tank float and connect to earth (ground). Switch on the ignition momentarily. The fuel gauge needle should be deflected right over to the full position.

ELECTRICAL

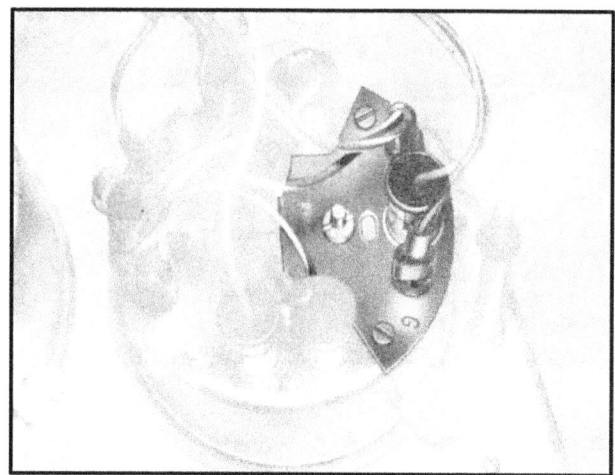

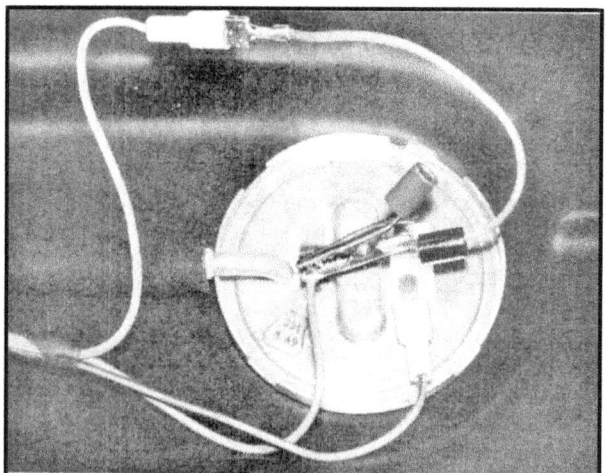

PRINTED CIRCUIT BOARD
Replacing

Remove speedometer and revolution counter. Unscrew printed circuit board. Remove coolant thermometer and fuel gauge from board. Remove all bulb holders from the printed circuit board. Pull the valve-base lamps for instrument illumination out of their holders.

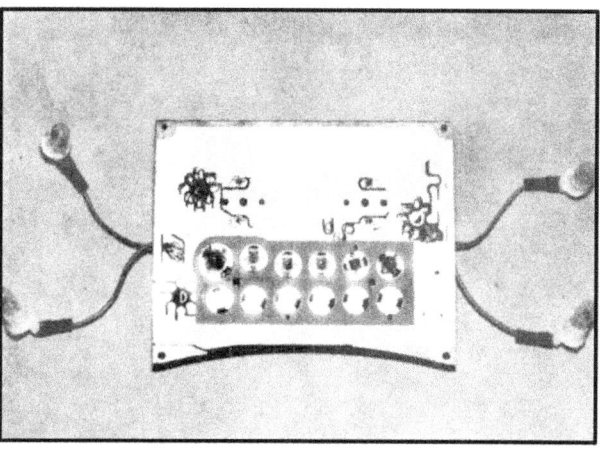

SPEEDOMETER
Removing and installing

Remove complete instrument panel. Pull out bulb holders. Unscrew the speedometer. When replacing the speedometer, note the correct gear ratio (W): BMW 2500 – w = 0.75. BMW 2800 – w = 0.70.

On coupe model, remove complete instrument panel. Pull out bulb holders and cable connector. Unscrew the speedometer. When replacing the speedometer, note the correct gear ratio (W): BMW 2800 CS – w = 0.69.

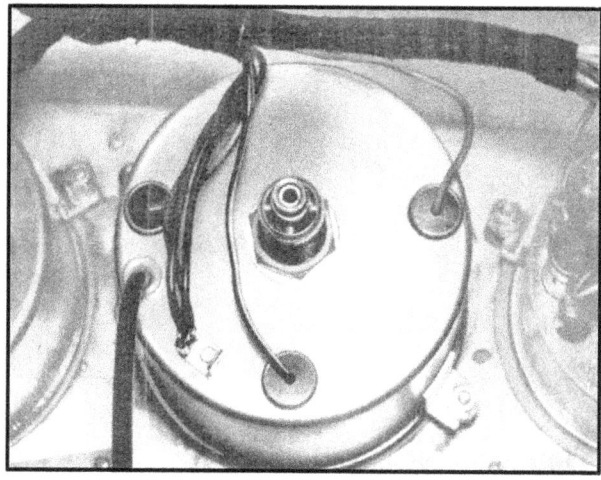

SPEEDOMETER SHAFT
Removing and installing

Detach speedometer shaft from gearbox. Pull the speedometer shaft away from the retaining clips. Open the left glovebox. Unscrew the speedometer shaft from the speedometer. Detach the hazard warning flasher relay and place on one side. Pull out the speedometer shaft with the rubber grommet.

ELECTRICAL

REVOLUTION COUNTER
Removing and installing

Remove complete instrument panel. Pull out bulb holders. Detach plug connector from printed circuit board. Unscrew revolution counter.

A = Plug connector

On coupe model, remove complete instrument panel. Detach bulb holders and cable connector.

When installing: Green-white +12, black 1, brown −.

Unscrew revolution counter.

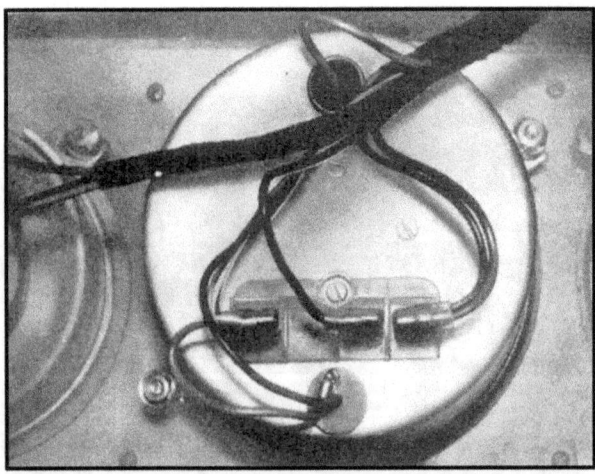

CLOCK
Removing and installing

Remove lower center right instrument panel housing. Take off the air hose angle pieces and place beneath. Unscrew the threaded knobs for the trim panel. Unscrew the threaded knobs holding the clock. Pull out the clock forward. Detach the cables.

When installing: Brown −, red +.

On Coupe models remove complete instrument panel. Pull off bulb holder and cable connectors.

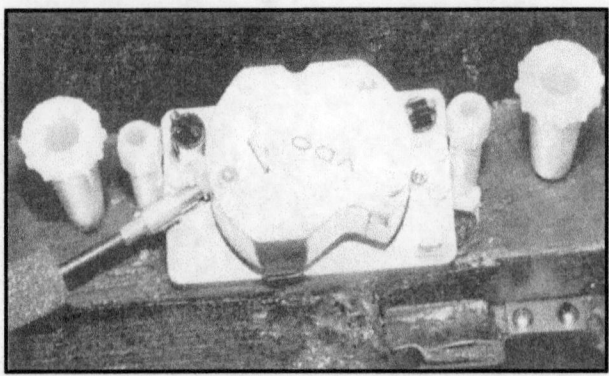

When installing: Red-white +, brown −.

Unscrew the clock.

BULB FOR CONTROL ILLUMINATION
Replacing

Remove lower section of steering column housing. Pull out the light. Detach the connecting wire.

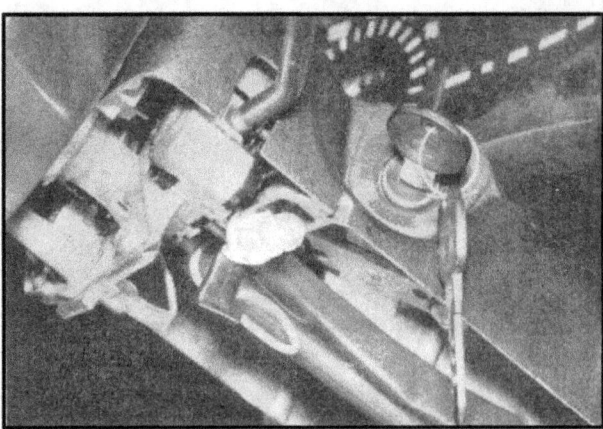

TRANSMISSION SELECTOR LEVER POSITION INDICATOR
Removing and installing

Remove the lower section of the steering column housing. Remove the lower center left instrument panel housing. Remove the two screws. Pull away the multi-pin plug for the selector lever position indicator. Press together the pins in the multi-pin plug and pull out to the rear.

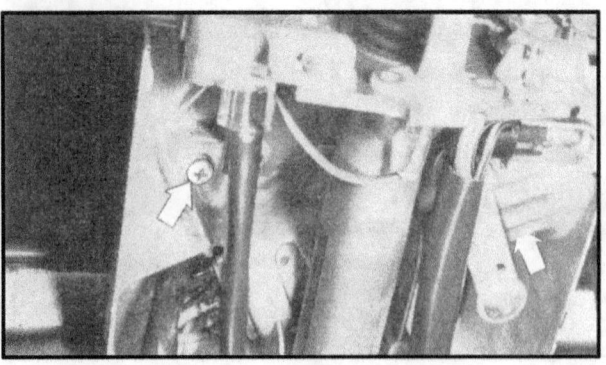

ELECTRICAL

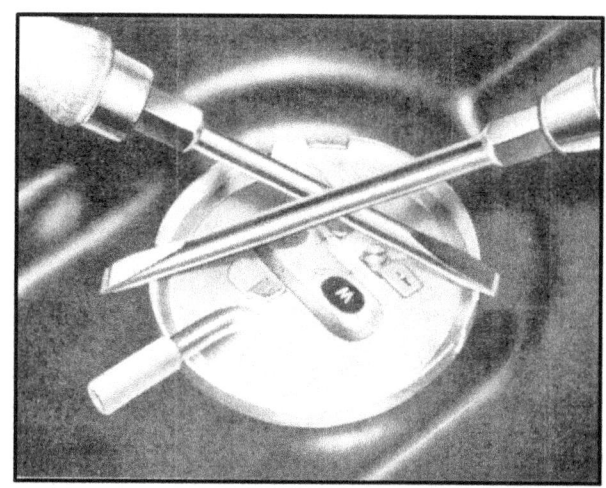

When installing: Cable color: Blue-grey — A, grey-yellow — P, blue-black — 2, blue-white — R, grey-red — 1, blue-red — O.

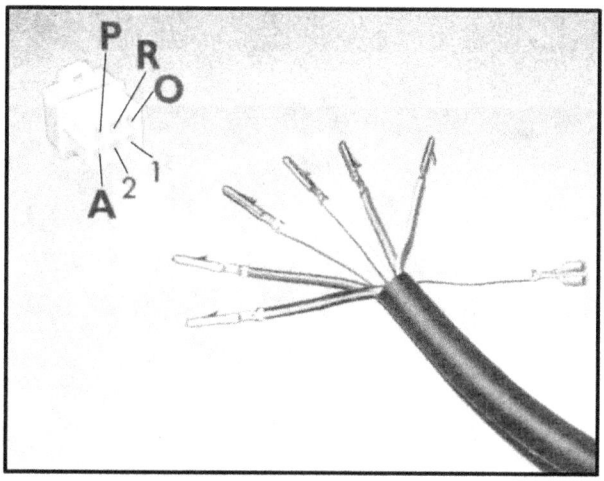

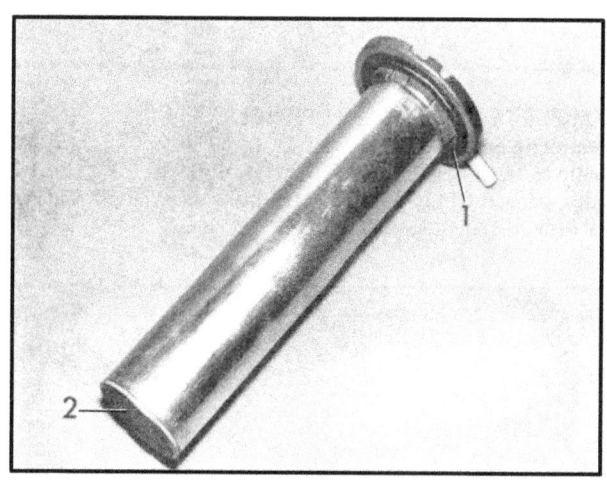

1. Ring seal
2. Mesh strainer

FUEL GAUGE TANK FLOAT UNIT
Removing and installing
Remove luggage compartment right side trim panel and right side floor panel. Detach fuel hose and wire from float unit.

When installing: Cable color: brown —, Brown-yellow — G, brown-black — W.

Unscrew the float unit anti-clockwise, using two crossed screwdrivers. The ring seal swells in contact with the fuel to provide a perfect seal. Previously installed ring seals do not regain their original shape until approximately 48 hours have elapsed. Always insert the ring seal by packing with Vaseline. Clean the fine mesh strainer. If the fuel gauge does not give a reading when the tank is completely or partly filled, test as follows: Remove the float unit. Connect on ohmmeter to terminals G and —. Tilt the float unit away from the horizontal until the float reaches the upper or lower end position. The ohm reading should be between 3.2 and 73.7 ohms. Do not take down the float unit.

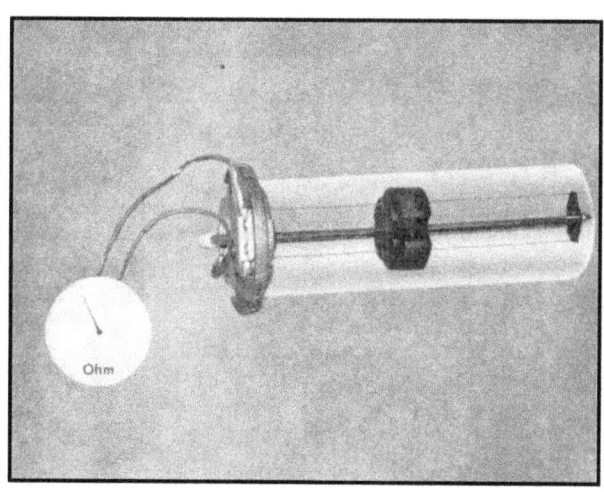

COOLANT THERMOMETER CONTACT
Removing and installing
Partly drain the coolant.

126 ELECTRICAL

When installing: Bleed the cooling system.

Detach the cable connector Unscrew the contact. An aluminum sealing ring is placed between the contact and the thermostat housing.

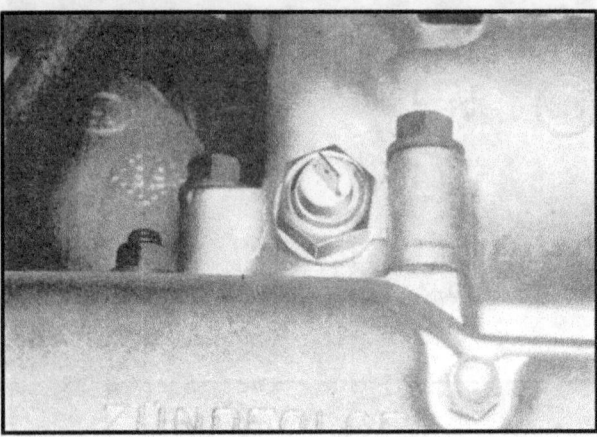

COMPLETE INSTRUMENT PANEL
Removing and installing
Remove the instrument panel hood. Pull out both central plugs. Unscrew the speedometer drive shaft. Pull out the instrument panel.

On Coupe models remove the steering wheel. Remove the heater control cover panel. Do not separate the cover panel and the switch plate. Remove screws. Unscrew the

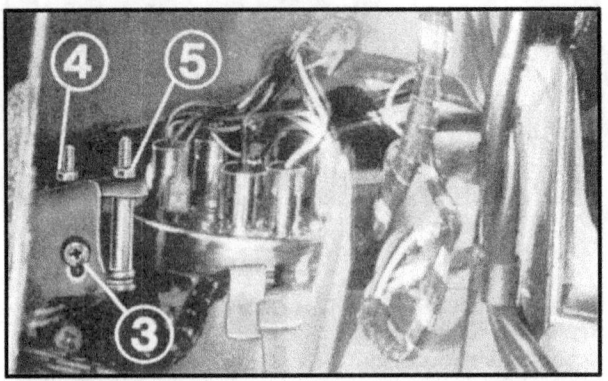

speedometer drive shaft at the speedometer. Gently press the instrument panel hood upward. Pull out the instrument panel. Press together the safety catches. Pull out the multi-pin plugs.

BULB FOR CLOCK ILLUMINATION
Replacing
Remove clock. Pull out bulb holder. Replace bulb.

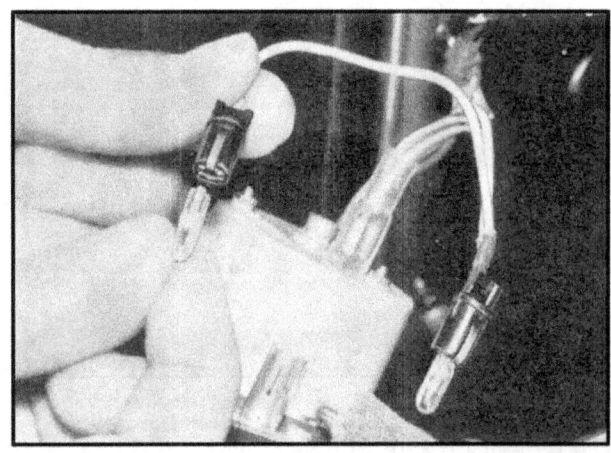

BULBS IN INSTRUMENT PANEL
Replacing
Remove instrument panel. Turn bulb holders to remove. Replace bulbs.

ELECTRICAL

On Coupe models: To replace bulbs in combined instrument open left glovebox. Pull out bulb holders. Replace bulbs. To replace bulbs in speedometer, revolution counter and clock: Remove lower center left instrument panel housing. Pull out bulb holders. Replace bulbs.

BULB FOR HAZARD WARNING FLASHER SWITCH
Replacing

Disconnect battery leads. Switch on hazard warning flasher system. Loosen pushbutton knob by turning anti-clockwise with pliers. To prevent scratching, insert a cloth between the pliers and the pushbutton. Unscrew pushbutton. A spring is compressed between the pushbutton and the bulb.

When installing: The wider end of the spring should be pressed into the pushbutton.

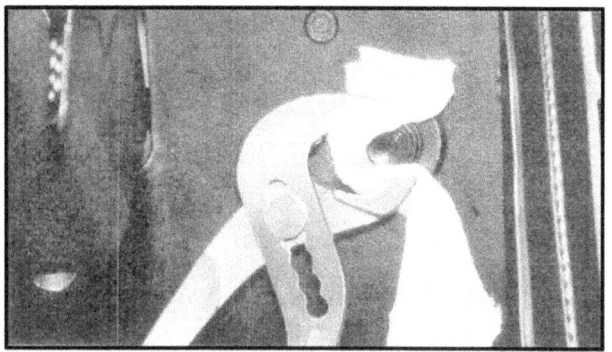

BULBS IN TRANSMISSION SELECTOR LEVER POSITION INDICATOR
Replacing

Remove screws at left and right of indicator box. Take off the cover. Replace the bulbs.

HEADLIGHTS
Beam alignment

Check tire pressures and correct if necessary. Place the car on a level surface and load the rear seat in the center with 70 kg (155 lbs) or the weight of one person. Open the front lid. On the Coupe unscrew the cover. Align the main and dipped headlight beams with an optical beam setting device, used in accordance with its manufacturer's instructions. Adjusting headlight beams, turn the knurled plastic knobs as required.

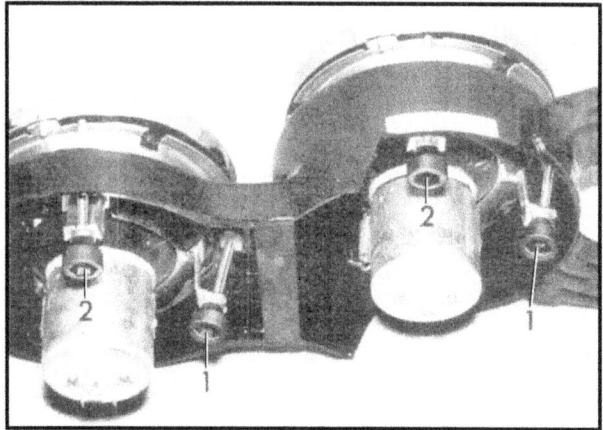

1. Horizontal adjustment
2. Vertical adjustment

MAIN AND DIPPED BEAM HEADLIGHTS
Removing and installing

Remove the front grill. Unscrew the headlight unit. Pull off the plug.

When installing: Insert the headlight unit in the cutouts in the support frame.

TURN INDICATOR BULB HOLDER
Replacing

Take off the turn indicator lens. Unscrew the bulb. Push back the rubber sleeve.

When installing: Inspect the rubber sleeve and replace if required.

Pull off the cable connector. Unscrew the bulb holder from the side panel and pull out to remove. On the Coupe, take off the lens. Remove the lower light screw. Loosen the upper right screw but do not remove completely. Push the bulb holder to the rear and pull away from the side panel. Remove the bulb holder completely. Pull off the cable plug. Bend up the metal tag with pliers and disconnect the earth (ground) wire.

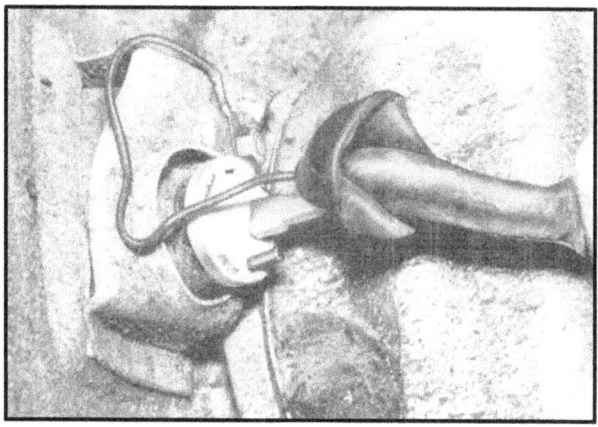

When installing: Insert the bulb holder, screw in upper screw, align retaining plate with a scriber or similar tool and insert the remaining screw.

REAR LIGHT LENS
Removing and installing

Remove cover panel from body tail panel. Unscrew the tail panel and remove. Loosen the screws and remove the

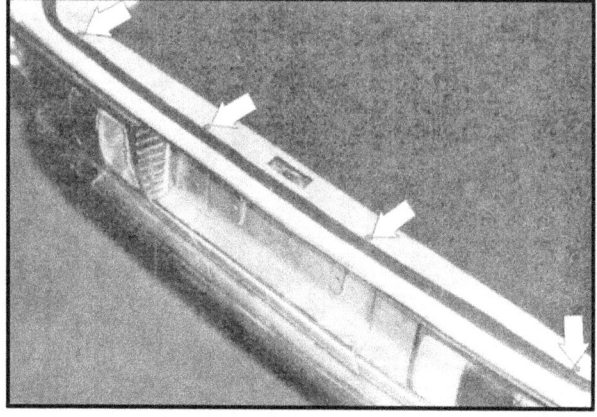

128 ELECTRICAL

complete lens unit. Next take off the plastic washers. Press off the decorative frame round the reflector and lens. Take off the sealing surround. On the Coupe, unscrew the housing. Detach the lens frame.

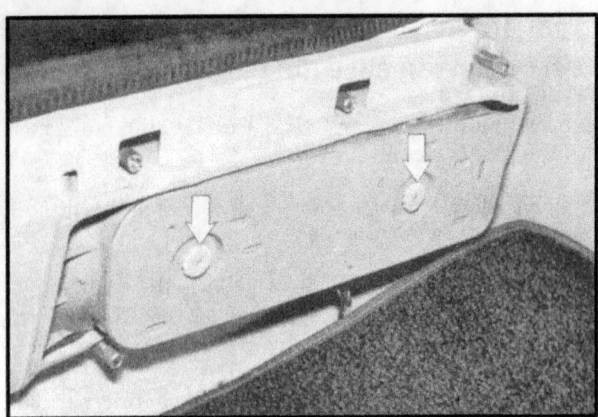

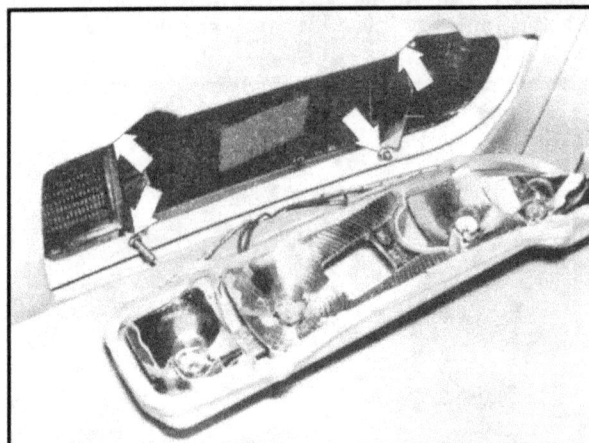

REAR LIGHT COVER PLATE
Removing and installing
Unscrew and pull out the cover plate. Pull off the multi-pin plug.

LICENSE PLATE LIGHT
Removing and installing
Remove the screws. Pull out the license plate light.

When installing: Replace the rubber underlay if porous.

INTERIOR LIGHT COMPLETE
Removing and installing
Unscrew the frame. Remove the lens. Unscrew the light housing. Disconnect the cables.

FRONT PARKING LIGHT BULB
Replacing
Open the engine compartment. On the Coupe unscrew the cover. Pull the cover cap away to the rear. Pull out the parking light bulb holder. Remove the bulb from its holder.

BULB(S) IN REAR LIGHT CLUSTER
Replacing
Unscrew and remove the cover plate. Remove the bulb(s).

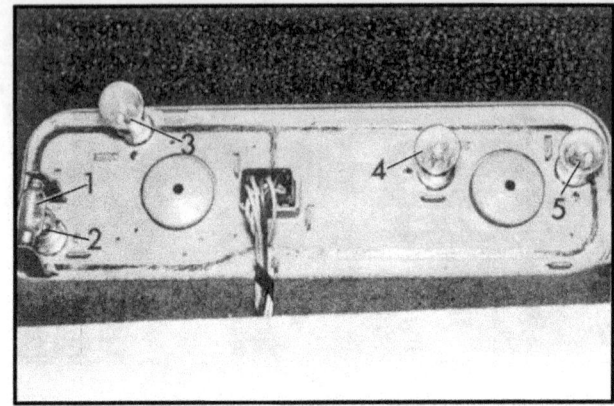

1. Rear fog warning bulb (if provided)
2. Rear light bulb
3. Turn indicator bulb
4. Brake light bulb
5. Reversing light bulb

ALTERNATOR AND REGULATOR
Checking with engine tester
Separate the leads between battery, alternator and regulator only with the engine stationary. If the battery is charged in position on the vehicle with a battery charger, both positive and negative leads should be disconnected from the battery. When arc welding, connect the earth clip of the welding unit direct to the vehicle section to be welded. If in exceptional cases the vehicle has to be used without its battery, D+, DF and D− should be connected to each other at the alternator or regulator terminal. The alternator will then develop no charge. The charge telltale warning light acts as a pre-exciter for the alternator. To check the regulator, disconnect B+ (red lead) at the alternator with the engine stationary. Connect voltmeter to B+ and D−. Start the engine. Shortly after the regulator begins to take effect, the voltage should be 13.5–14.2 volts.

If this value is exceeded or not attained, check the voltage under the same conditions of operation at D+/61 and D− (for ease of access use the terminal at the regulator [blue lead] instead of D+/61). With a voltmeter having a range of approximately 3 volt, the voltage differential between D+ and B+ can be measured directly. Up to 0.5 volts difference: defective regulator. 1.5 −4 volts difference: defective alternator.

To check charging current, connect ammeter A (measuring range 60 Amps) into the B+ lead. Connect a load resistance permitting a loading of up to 60 Amps parallel to battery B. Connect voltmeter V to terminals D+ and D− on the alternator. Run the engine at approximately 3000 rpm. Set the sliding resistance to maximum current and read off the regulated voltage under load at the voltmeter.

If the warning light burns with the ignition switched off but goes out when the ignition is switched on, the battery is being discharged through a positive diode which is not longer blocking. You should immediately disconnect red lead B+ at the alternator and regulator by pulling out the connector. It is possible to drive on as long as the state of battery charge will permit.

Rapid checking
Only required if warning light stays on when engine is running.

Pull multiple plug away from regulator. With a wire bridge connect flat connector of the blue lead (D+/61) with flat connector of black lead (DF). Start engine and run at approximately 1000 rpm. If the generator warning light goes out immediately, the alternator is defective. If the generator warning light glows or continues to burn brightly, overhaul alternator.

ALTERNATOR
Removing and refitting
Disconnect negative lead at battery. Pull off multi-pin plug. Disconnect cable from generator. Brown = earth. Red = B+. Unscrew fixing bolts at clamp strap and mounting. Lift out alternator.

When installing: It must be possible to depress the V-belt by 5 – 10 mm (0.2 – 0.4").

Overhauling
To replace brushes loosen screws and remove rotor.

When installing: Diode bracket is located in top half. Place corrugated washer in front of grooved bearing. Check sliprings.

Remove diode bracket. Undo connecting cable and fixing bolts for carbon brush holder. Unsolder and resolder carbon brushes.

When installing: Do not let resin from solder run into the copper braid.

Push carbon brushes up and secure. Reassemble alternator. Push carbon brushes on to sliprings.

To renew ball bearings, hold fan plate in position and remove and lift out Woodruff key. Detach spacer ring and press out rotor. Unscrew the retaining plate. Press ball bearing out of the bearing plate.

When installing: Grease ball bearing with Ft 1 v 34. The open side of the bearing should face toward the rotor. Push flat piece over securing wire.

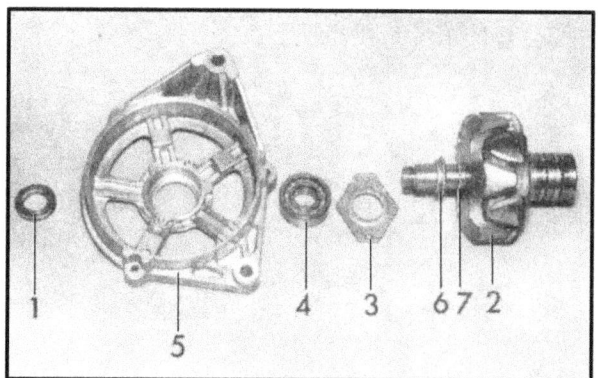

1. Spacer ring
2. Rotor
3. Retaining plate
4. Ball bearing
5. Bearing plate
6. Flat piece
7. Securing wire

Pull off ball bearing from rotor.

When installing: only use C3 bearings.

ELECTRICAL

Grease ball bearing with FT 1 v 34. The open side of the bearing should face toward the housing. Place corrugated washer in the housing in front of the ball bearing.

Positive diodes:
Undo diode bracket. Unsolder cable. Check diodes with maximum 24 volts. Test lamp should not light up if positive is touched on the housing.

When installing: Replace all three diodes together, complete with carrier.

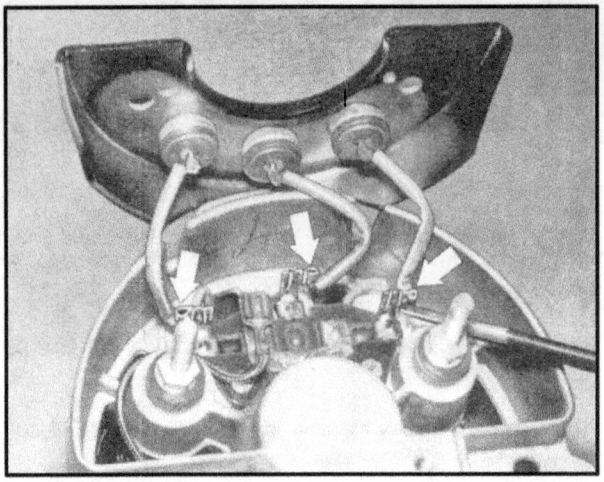

Stator winding — removing and checking
Remove the rotor. Unsolder stator cable at diode carrier. Remove the stator. Check stator winding with 40 volts AC for short to earth. Check resistance between phase outlets: 0.26 ohms + 10%.

Exciter diodes
Remove the rotor. Unsolder the positive and negative diodes and stator cables. Detach the diode carrier. Check diodes with maximum 24 volts. Test lamp should not light up if + is touched to plug connector. Replace all three diodes together complete with carrier.

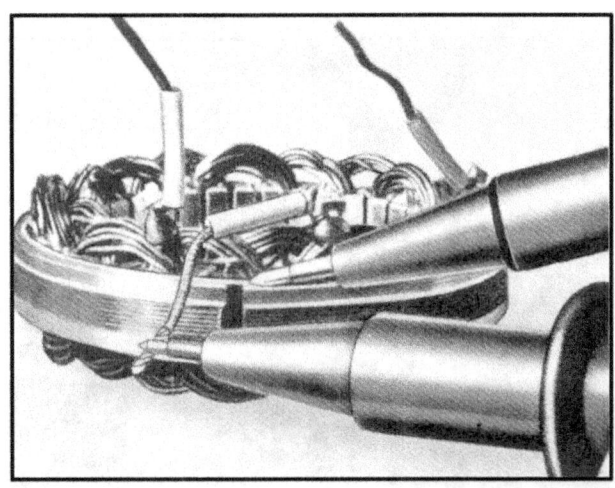

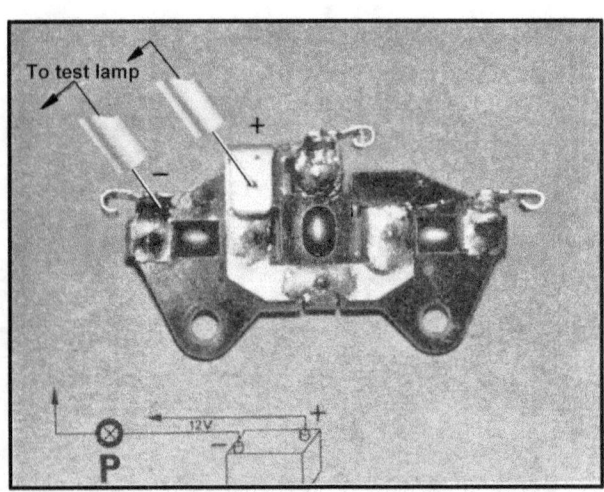

P. Test lamp

Negative diodes
Unsolder the stator cable and negative diodes. Pull off the flat plug. Detach the diode carrier. Remove the stator. Check diodes at maximum volts. The test lamp must light up when + is touched to the housing. Coat the diodes with OL 63 v 2 silicone oil and press into a sleeve of inside diameter 0.67 in. with die EFLJ 57.

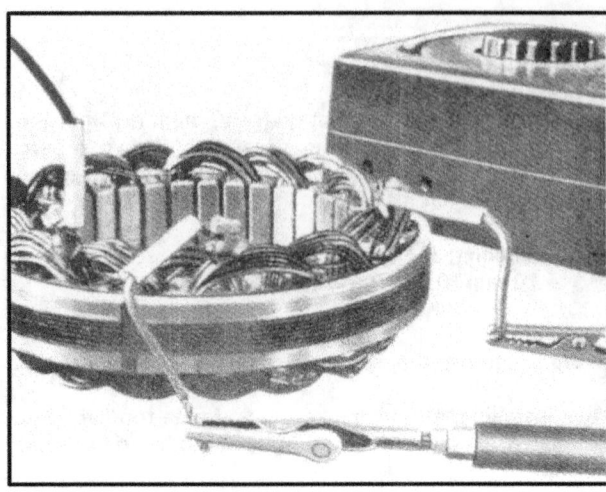

ELECTRICAL

Claw pole rotor — checking

Check the claw pole rotor after removal at 40 volts AC for short to earth (test probes EFAW 84). Check exciter winding (Ohmmeter). 14 volt generator = 4.0 Ohms + 10%. To skim sliprings, tailstock backrest EFAW 75 or GDF 85 R 3 must be used. Minimum slipring diameter 31.5 mm (1.24 in.). After skimming, check sliprings for concentricity. Maximum permissible runout 0.0012 in.

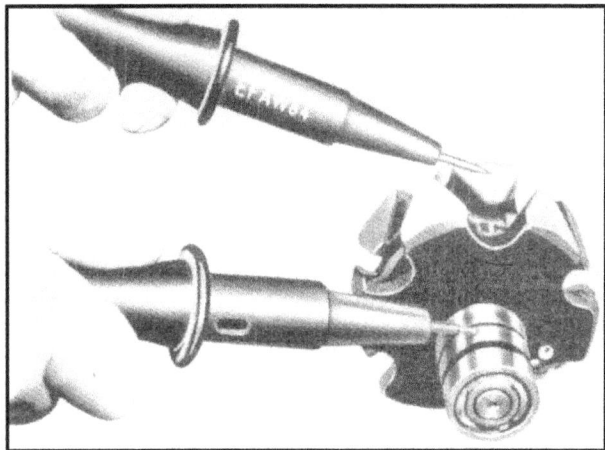

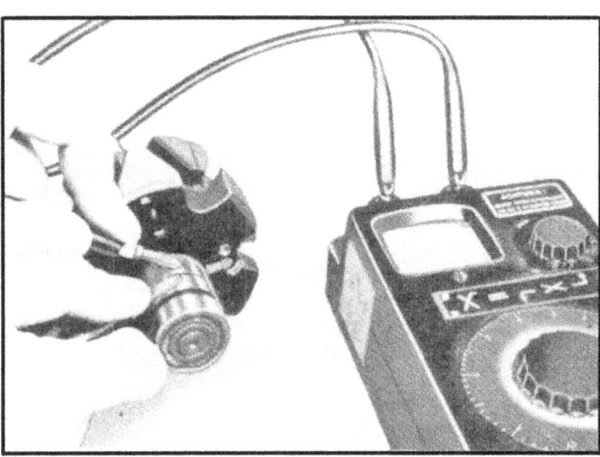

VOLTAGE REGULATOR
Removing and refitting

Pull off multi-pin plug. Undo screws.

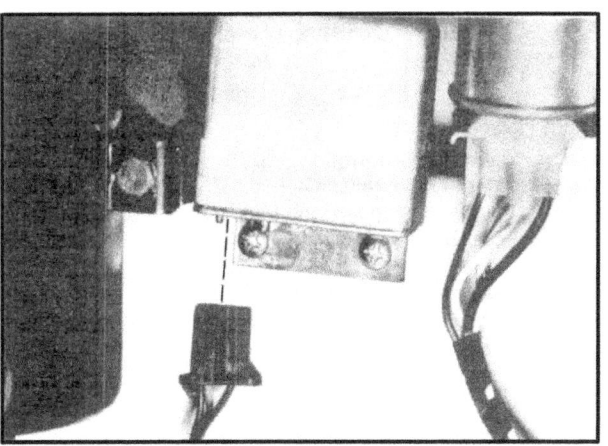

STARTER IN VEHICLE
Checking with engine tester

In the case of automatic transmission, checking can only be carried out on starter test rig. To check, engage 4th gear and depress foot brake. Operate starter for 2 – 3 seconds; starting voltage should not fall below 8 volts under load and must be equal when voltmeter connected as per 1 and 2; if this is not the case there is a faulty earth connection at motor or battery. At the same time read off current consumption on ammeter.

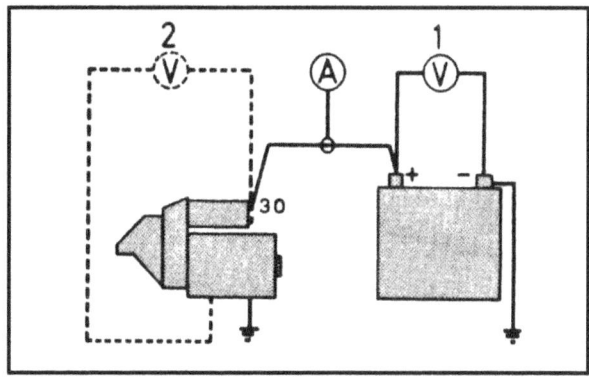

Removing and refitting

Disconnect negative lead from battery, plug connections and starter cable. Detach starter from flange.

Dismantling and reassembling

Unscrew cable to exciter winding. Disconnect solenoid. Disconnect engagement arm. Detach dust cap. Detach

ELECTRICAL

securing plate, shim and seal. Remove pole housing bolt. Pull off cap.

When installing: Shim armature axial play to 0.0039–0.0059".

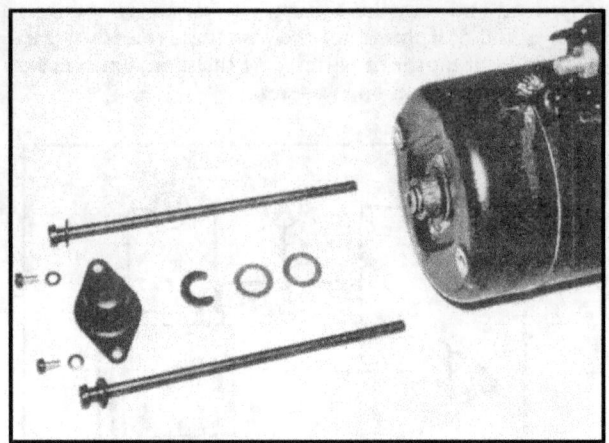

Check commutator bearing. Lift out positive brushes and detach brush retainer plate. Separate pole housing from drive bearing. Remove bearing screw on engagement lever. Pull out armature with engagement lever. Push back thrust ring. Lift out circlip. Pull off starter gear.

When installing: Smear starter thread and engagement ring with silicone grease Ft 2 v 3.

Pull thrust ring over circlip.

Overhauling
Check armature and field winding — 220 volt test lamp. Touch probes on commutator and laminated core. In the case of a short to earth the lamp will come on — exchange armature. Connect ammeter (measuring range 60 amps) in circuit and probe round the commutator briefly from segment to segment. Test voltage 2 – 4 volts. The deflection of the instrument should be the same with each of the individual segments. Wide variations indicate open circuit. An armature with any open circuits should be replaced. Check exciter winding for earthing. Visual check. Renew burnt or fouled windings.

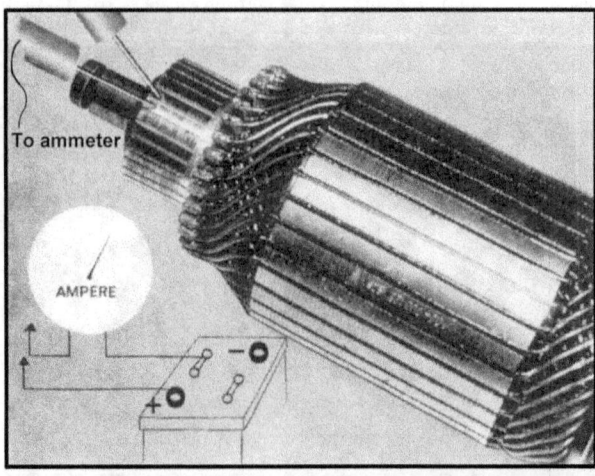

Precision skim the commutator. Commutator diameter should not be less than 1.3". Undercut commutator segments. Insulators should be 0.0197" below the level of the segments. Press out worn bush.

When installing: Before fitting a new bush soak for at least ½ hour in engine oil and press in until flush.

CARBON BRUSHES
Replacing
Unsolder and resolder carbon brushes at exciter winding and brush retainer plate.

1. Washer on armature
2. Insulating washer

STARTER STRIPPED
Replacing exciter winding
Mark pole shoes so that when reassembling they will be refitted in the same position. Unscrew 4 pole shoe bolts. Extract pole shoes and exciter winding from pole housing.

When installing: Before final tightening of pole screws, pole shoes should be lined up so that they are exactly parallel to the longitudinal axis.

Insert paper insulator strip(s) between exciter winding and pole housing.

NOTES

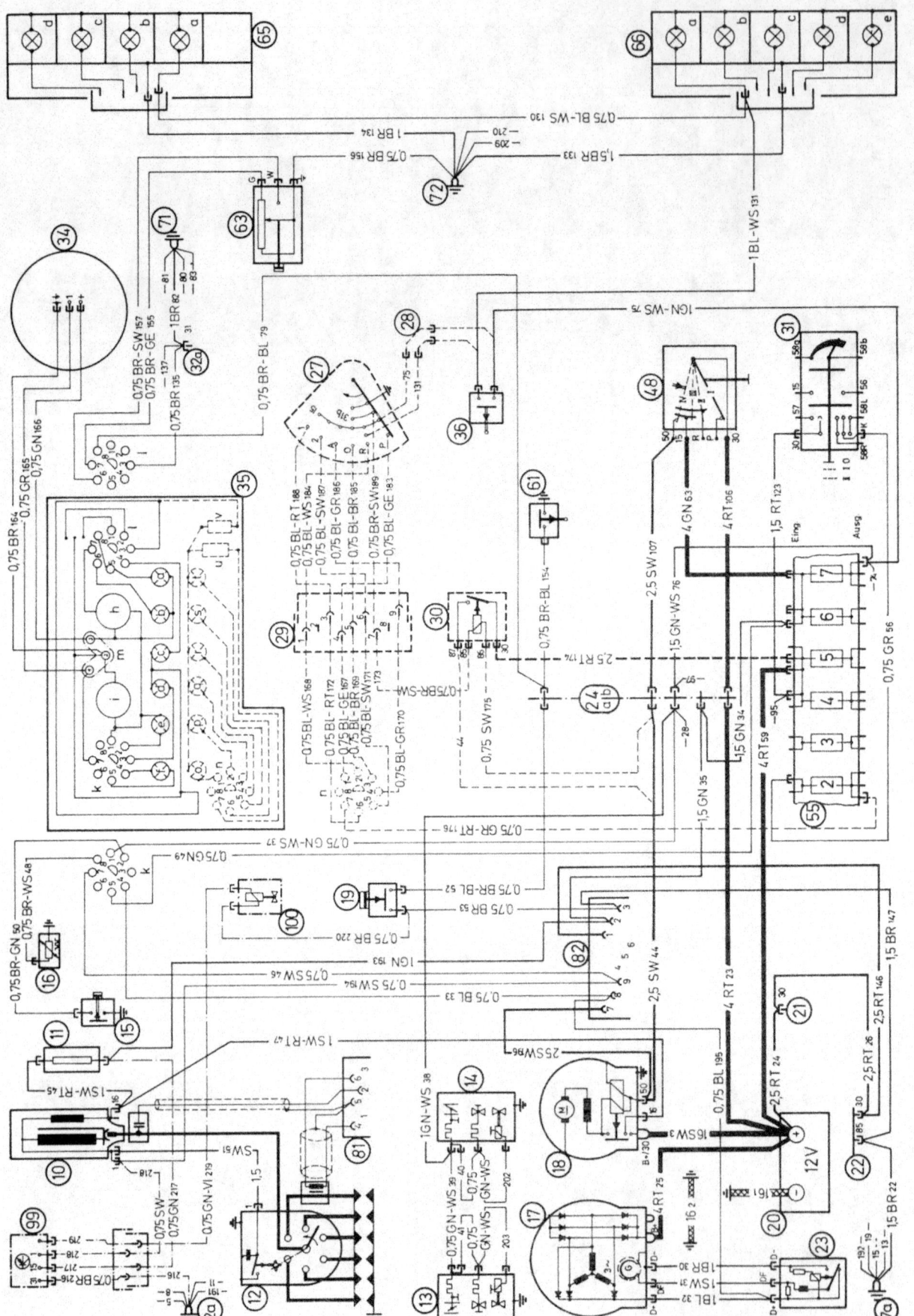

Wiring diagram, typical engine electrical system and controls

Key to wiring diagram: 1 Turn indicator, front right   2 Low beam headlight with sidelight, right   2a Earth for headlight, right   3 High beam headlight, right   4 Horn, right   5 Horn, left   6 High beam headlight, left   7 Low beam headlight with sidelight, left   7a Earth for headlight, left   8 Turn indicator, front left   9 Connection for engine compartment light   10 Coil   11 Primary resistance   12 Distributor   13 Electrical connection to automatic choke, front carburetter   14 Electrical connection to automatic choke, rear carburetter   15 Oil pressure switch   16 Remote coolant thermometer contact   17 Alternator   18 Starter   19 Brake fluid level control switch   20 Battery   21 Horn relay   22 Headlight high beam relay   23 Regulator   24a Plug board, engine side   24b Plug board, passenger side   25 Screenwasher pump   26 Screenwiper motor   27 Gearbox switch (automatic only)   28 Socket for gearbox switch (automatic only)   29 Plug for gearbox switch (automatic only)   30 Starter relay (automatic only)   31 Light switch   32 Switch for rear fog light   32a Connection for fog lamp switch

Instrument panel: 22 Speedometer   34 Revolution counter   35 Printed circuit panel: a Brake fluid and handbrake telltale (red)   b Fuel level telltale (white)   c Turn indicator telltale (green)   d Headlight main beam (blue)   e Oil pressure telltale (orange)   f Battery charge (red)   g Dial illumination   h Fuel gauge   i Coolant thermometer   k Plug for instrument panel   l Plug for instrument panel   m Plug for instrument panel

Automatic transmission only: n Plug for instrument panel   o Selector lever position indicator P (white)   p Selector lever position indicator R (red)   q Selector lever position indicator O (white)   r Selector lever position indicator A (green)   s Selector lever position indicator 2 (green)   t Selector lever position indicator 1 (green)   u Primary resistance   v Primary resistance

36 Reversing light switch (not automatic transmission)   37 Heater blower motor   38 Heater controls   39 Clock   40 Glove box illumination   41 Cigar lighter and socket   42 Wiper speed control   43 Hazard warning flasher switch   44 Hazard warning flasher unit   45 Switch for heated rear window   46 Horn push ring   47 Dip and flasher switch   48 Ignition/starter switch: I Halt   II O   III Fahrt (Drive)   IV Start   49 Switch illumination   50 Turn indicator switch   51 Stoplight switch   52 Load-shedding relay   53 Changeover relay   54 Delay relay   55 Fuse box   56 Door-operated switch, left   57 Switch for luggage compartment light   58 Luggage compartment light   59 Interior light   60 Heated rear window   61 Reversing light   62 Door-operated switch, right   63 Fuel gauge contact   64 Licence plate lighting   65 Rear light cluster, right: a Reversing light   b Stoplight   c Turn indicator   d Rear light   66 Rear light cluster, left: a Reversing light   b Stoplight   c Turn indicator   d Rear light   e Rear fog light   67 Connection for radio   68 Plug connector for radio   69 Plug connector for heated rear window   70 Plug connector for luggage compartment light   71 Earth   72 Earth   73 Plug connector for ignition/starter switch   74 Connection for fog light relay   75 Connection for electric sliding roof   76 Connection for electric fuel pump   77 Connection for motor-operated radio aerial   78 Connection for trailer turn indicators   79 Door-operated switch, rear right   81 Diagnostic plug, ignition system   82 Diagnostic plug   83 Connection for sidelight   84 Door-operated switch, rear left   85 Connection for reading light   90 Plug for warning buzzer (USA)   91 Warning buzzer   92 Warning buzzer contact (USA)   93 Plug for side marker light, rear left   94 Plug for side marker light, rear left   95 Side marker light, rear left   96 Side marker light, rear right   97 Plug for side marker light, rear right   98 Plug for side marker light, rear right   99 Engine speed governor switch (USA)   100 Magnetic valve (USA)

Wiring colour code: **BL** Blue   **BR** Brown   **GE** Yellow   **GN** Green   **GR** Grey   **RT** Red   **SW** Black   **WS** White
Where a cable has two colour codes, the first denotes the main colour, the second the colour of the tracer stripe. The figure preceding the colour code indicates the cross-sectional area of the wire in sq mm. The figure following the colour code is the individual cable number.

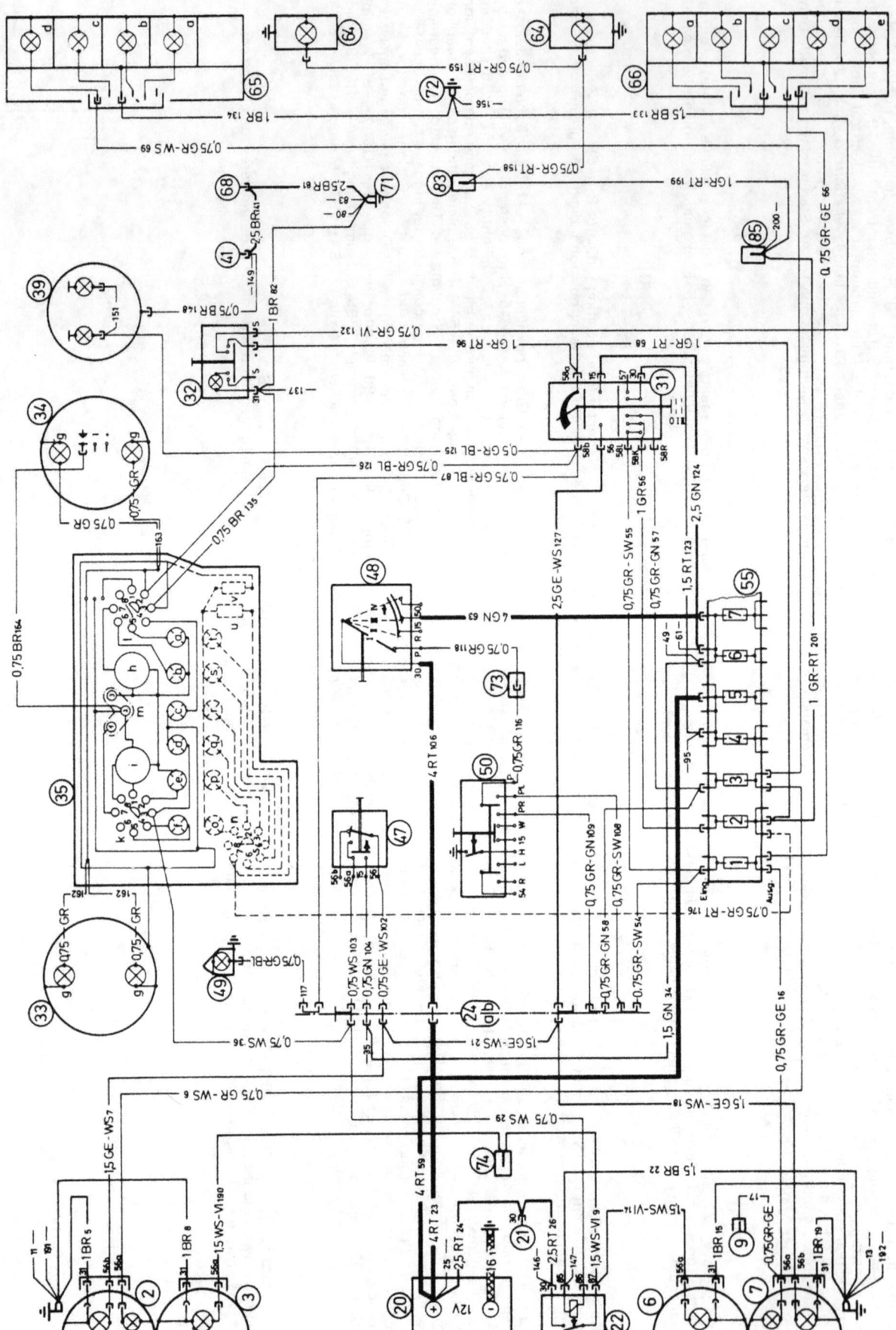

Wiring diagram, typical lighting system (Europe)

Key to wiring diagram: 1 Turn indicator, front right 2 Low beam headlight with sidelight, right 3 High beam headlight, right 4 Horn, right 5 Horn, left 6 High beam headlight, left 7 Low beam headlight with sidelight, left 7a Earth for headlight, left 8 Turn indicator, front left 9 Connection for engine compartment light 10 Coil 11 Primary resistance 12 Distributor 13 Electrical connection to automatic choke, front carburetter 14 Electrical connection to automatic choke, rear carburetter 15 Oil pressure switch 16 Remote coolant thermometer contact 17 Alternator 18 Starter 19 Brake fluid level control switch 20 Battery 21 Horn relay 22 Headlight high beam relay 23 Regulator 24a Plug board, engine side 24b Plug board, passenger side 25 Screenwasher pump 26 Screenwiper motor 27 Gearbox switch (automatic only) 28 Socket for gearbox switch (automatic only) 29 Plug for gearbox switch (automatic only) 30 Starter relay (automatic only) 31 Light switch 32 Switch for rear fog light 32a Connection for fog lamp switch

Instrument panel: 22 Speedometer 34 Revolution counter 35 Printed circuit panel : a Brake fluid and handbrake telltale (red) b Fuel level telltale (white) c Turn indicator telltale (green) d Headlight main beam (blue) e Oil pressure telltale (orange) f Battery charge (red) g Dial illumination h Fuel gauge i Coolant thermometer k Plug for instrument panel l Plug for instrument panel m Plug for instrument panel

Automatic transmission only: n Plug for instrument panel o Selector lever position indicator P (white) p Selector lever position indicator R (red) q Selector lever position indicator O (white) r Selector lever position indicator A (green) s Selector lever position indicator 2 (green) t Selector lever position indicator 1 (green) u Primary resistance v Primary resistance

36 Reversing light switch (not automatic transmission) 37 Heater blower motor 38 Heater controls 39 Clock 40 Glove box illumination 41 Cigar lighter and socket 42 Wiper speed control 43 Hazard warning flasher switch 44 Hazard warning flasher unit 45 Switch for heated rear window 46 Horn push ring 47 Dip and flasher switch 48 Ignition/starter switch: I Halt II O III Fahrt (Drive) IV Start 49 Switch illumination 50 Turn indicator switch 51 Stoplight switch 52 Load-shedding relay 53 Changeover relay 54 Delay relay 55 Fuse box 56 Door-operated switch, left 57 Switch for luggage compartment light 58 Luggage compartment light 59 Interior light 60 Heated rear window 61 Handbrake contact 62 Door-operated switch, right 63 Fuel gauge contact 64 Licence plate lighting 65 Rear light cluster, right: a Reversing light b Stoplight c Turn indicator d Rear light 66 Rear light cluster, left: a Reversing light b Stoplight c Turn indicator d Rear light e Rear fog light 67 Connection for radio 68 Plug connector for heater 69 Plug connector for heated rear window 70 Plug connector for luggage compartment light 71 Earth 72 Earth 73 Plug connector for ignition/starter switch 74 Connection for fog light relay 75 Connection for electric sliding roof 76 Connection for electric fuel pump 77 Connection for motor-operated radio aerial 78 Connection for trailer turn indicators 79 Door-operated switch, rear right 81 Diagnostic plug, ignition system 82 Diagnostic plug 83 Connection for sidelight 84 Door-operated switch, rear left 85 Connection for reading light 90 Plug for warning buzzer (USA) 91 Warning buzzer (USA) 92 Warning buzzer contact (USA) 93 Plug for side marker light, rear left 94 Plug for side marker light, rear left 95 Side marker light, rear left 96 Side marker light, rear right 97 Plug for side marker light, rear right 98 Plug for side marker light, rear right 99 Engine speed governor switch (USA) 100 Magnetic valve (USA)

Wiring colour code: **BL** Blue   **BR** Brown   **GE** Yellow   **GN** Green   **GR** Grey   **RT** Red   **SW** Black   **WS** White
Where a cable has two colour codes, the first denotes the main colour, the second the colour of the tracer stripe. The figure preceding the colour code indicates the cross-sectional area of the wire in sq mm. The figure following the colour code is the individual cable number.

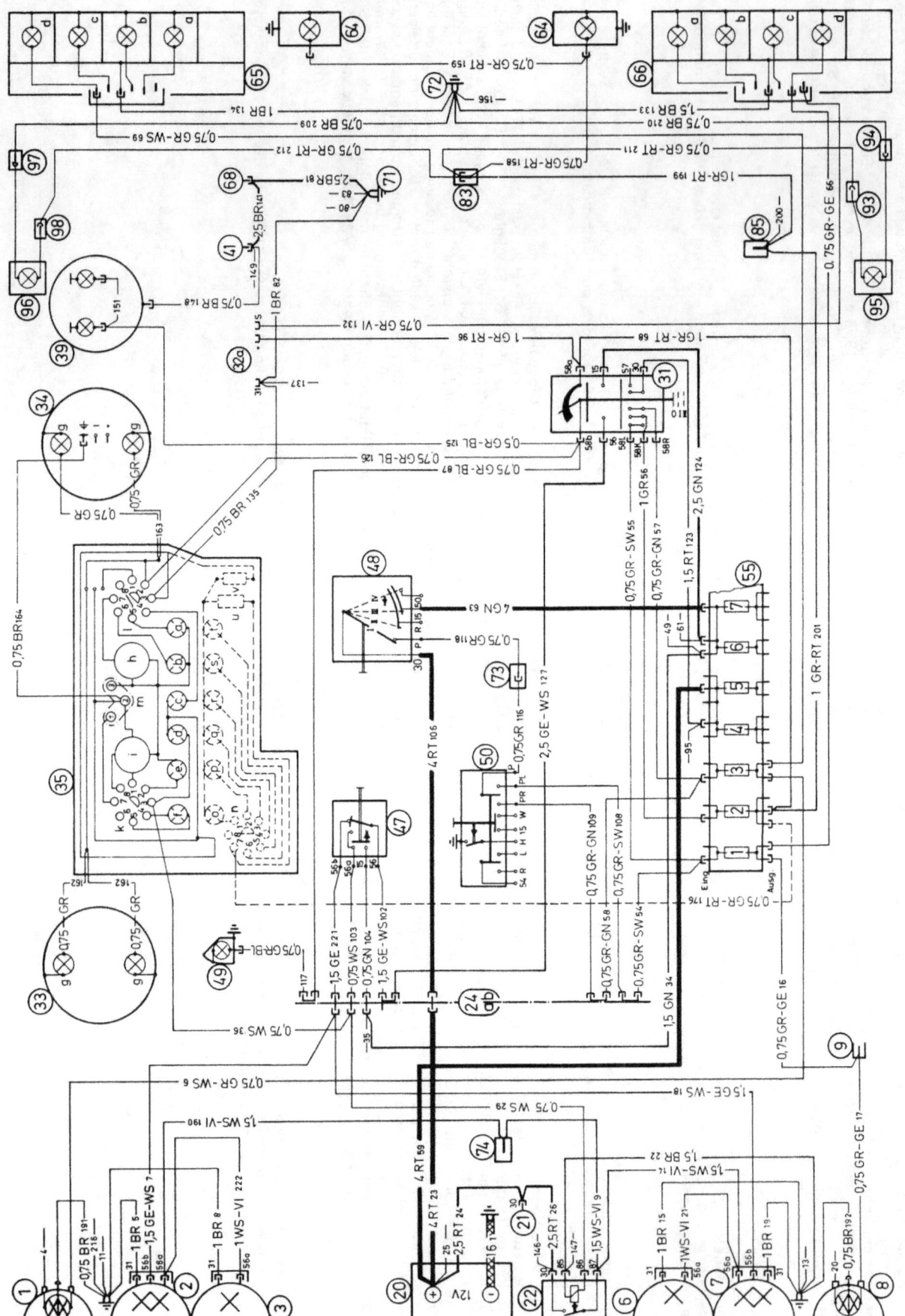

Wiring diagram, typical lighting system (USA)

Key to wiring diagram: 1 Turn indicator, front right 2 Low beam headlight with sidelight, right 2a Earth for headlight, right 3 High beam headlight, right 4 Horn, right 5 Horn, left 6 High beam headlight, left 7 Low beam headlight with sidelight, left 7a Earth for headlight, left 8 Turn indicator, front left 9 Connection for engine compartment light 10 Coil 11 Primary resistance 12 Distributor 13 Electrical connection to automatic choke, front carburetter 14 Electrical connection to automatic choke, rear carburetter 15 Oil pressure switch 16 Remote coolant thermometer contact 17 Alternator 18 Starter 19 Brake fluid level control switch 20 Battery 21 Horn relay 22 Headlight high beam relay 23 Regulator 24a Plug board, engine side 24b Plug board, passenger side 25 Screenwasher pump 26 Screenwiper motor 27 Gearbox switch (automatic only) 28 Socket for gearbox switch (automatic only) 29 Plug for gearbox switch (automatic only) 30 Starter relay (automatic only) 31 Light switch 32 Switch for rear fog light 32a Connection for fog lamp switch

Instrument panel: 22 Speedometer 34 Revolution counter 35 Printed circuit panel: a Brake fluid and handbrake telltale (red) b Fuel level telltale (white) c Turn indicator telltale (green) d Headlight main beam (blue) e Oil pressure telltale (orange) f Battery charge (red) g Dial illumination h Fuel gauge i Coolant thermometer k Plug for instrument panel l Plug for instrument panel m Plug for instrument panel

Automatic transmission only: n Plug for instrument panel o Selector lever position indicator P (white) p Selector lever position indicator R (red) q Selector lever position indicator O (white) r Selector lever position indicator A (green) s Selector lever position indicator 2 (green) t Selector lever position indicator 1 (green) u Primary resistance v Primary resistance

36 Reversing light switch (not automatic transmission) 37 Heater blower motor 38 Heater controls 39 Clock 40 Glove box illumination 41 Cigar lighter and socket 42 Wiper speed control 43 Hazard warning flasher switch 44 Hazard warning flasher unit 45 Switch for heated rear window 46 Horn push ring 47 Dip and flasher switch 48 Ignition/starter switch: I Halt II O III Fahrt (Drive) IV Start 49 Switch illumination 50 Turn indicator switch 51 Stoplight switch 52 Load-shedding relay 53 Changeover relay 54 Delay relay 55 Fuse box 56 Door-operated switch, left 57 Switch for luggage compartment light 58 Luggage compartment light 59 Interior light 60 Heated rear window 61 Handbrake contact 62 Door-operated switch, right 63 Fuel gauge contact 64 Licence plate lighting 65 Rear light cluster, right: a Reversing light b Stoplight c Turn indicator d Rear light 66 Rear light cluster, left: a Reversing light b Stoplight c Turn indicator d Rear light e Rear fog light 67 Connection for radio 68 Plug connector for radio 69 Plug connector for heater 70 Plug connector for luggage compartment light 71 Earth 72 Earth 73 Plug connector for ignition/starter switch 74 Connection for fog light relay 75 Connection for electric sliding roof 76 Connection for electric fuel pump 77 Connection for motor-operated radio aerial 78 Connection for trailer turn indicators 79 Door-operated switch, rear right 81 Diagnostic plug, ignition system 82 Diagnostic plug 83 Connection for sidelight 84 Door-operated switch, rear left 85 Connection for reading light 90 Plug for warning buzzer (USA) 91 Warning buzzer (USA) 92 Warning buzzer contact (USA) 93 Plug for side marker light, rear left 94 Plug for side marker light, rear left 95 Side marker light, rear left 96 Side marker light, rear right 97 Plug for side marker light, rear right 98 Plug for side marker light, rear right 99 Engine speed governor switch (USA) 100 Magnetic valve (USA)

Wiring colour code: **BL** Blue **BR** Brown **GE** Yellow **GN** Green **GR** Grey **RT** Red **SW** Black **WS** White Where a cable has two colour codes, the first denotes the main colour, the second the colour of the tracer stripe. The figure preceding the colour code indicates the cross-sectional area of the wire in sq mm. The figure following the colour code is the individual cable number.

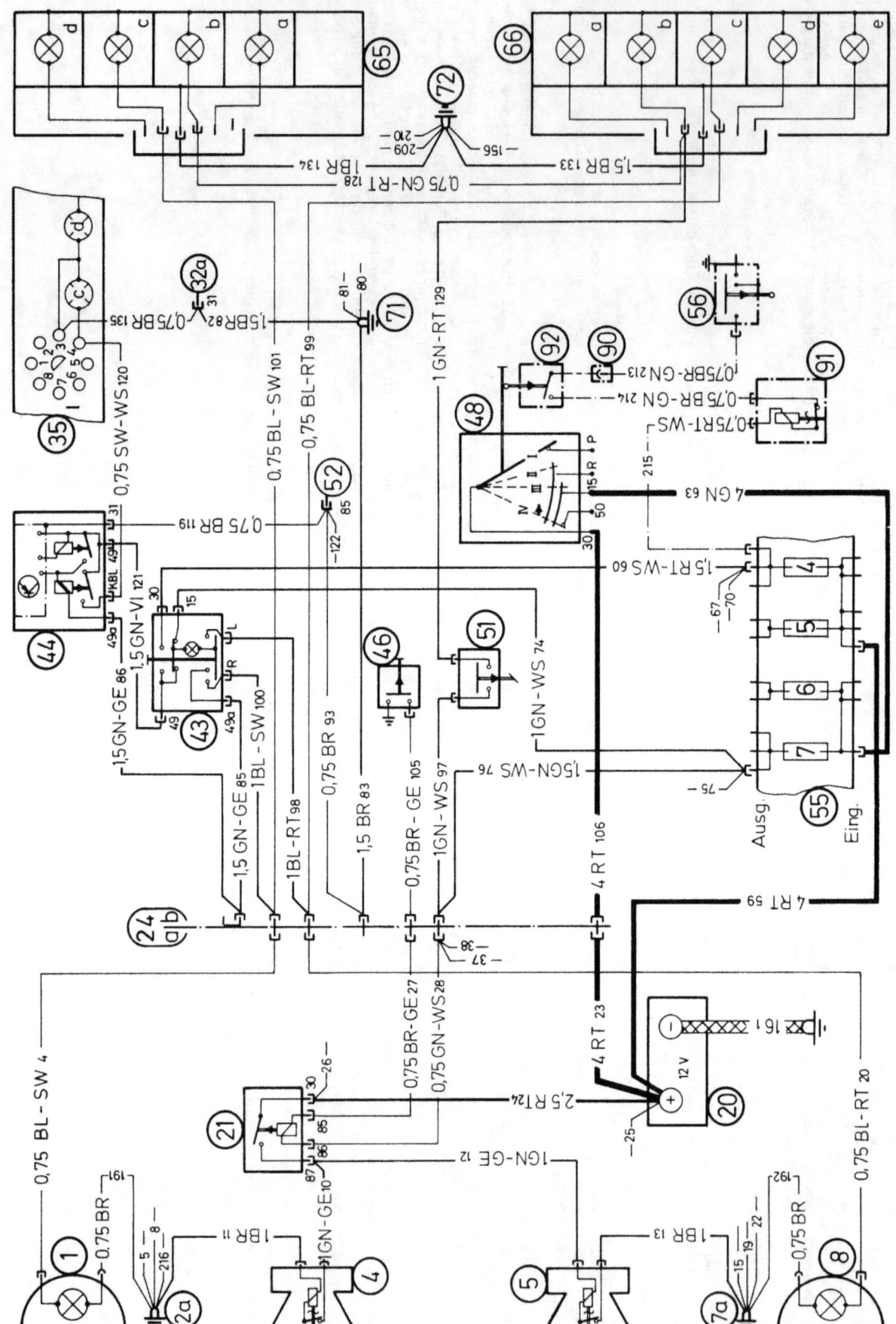

Wiring diagram, typical signalling system

Key to wiring diagram: 1 Turn indicator, front right 2 Low beam headlight, front right 3 High beam headlight, right 4 Horn, right 5 Horn, left 6 High beam headlight, left 7 Low beam headlight, left 7a Turn indicator, front left 8 Turn indicator, front left 9 Connection for engine compartment light 10 Coil 11 Primary resistance 12 Distributor 13 Electrical connection to automatic choke, front carburetter 14 Electrical connection to automatic choke, rear carburetter 15 Oil pressure switch 16 Remote coolant thermometer contact 17 Alternator 18 Starter 19 Brake fluid level control switch 20 Battery 21 Horn relay 22 Headlight high beam relay 23 Regulator 24a Plug board, engine side 24b Plug board, passenger side 25 Screenwasher pump 26 Screenwiper motor 27 Gearbox switch (automatic only) 28 Socket for gearbox switch (automatic only) 29 Plug for gearbox switch (automatic only) 30 Starter relay (automatic only) 31 Light switch 32 Switch for rear fog light 32a Connection for fog lamp switch

Instrument panel: 22 Speedometer 34 Revolution counter 35 Printed circuit panel: a Brake fluid and handbrake telltale (red) b Fuel level telltale (white) c Turn indicator telltale (green) d Headlight main beam (blue) e Oil pressure telltale (orange) f Battery charge (red) g Dial illumination h Fuel gauge i Coolant thermometer k Plug for instrument panel l Plug for instrument panel m Plug for instrument panel

Automatic transmission only: n Plug for instrument panel o Selector lever position indicator P (white) p Selector lever position indicator R (red) q Selector lever position indicator O (white) r Selector lever position indicator A (green) s Selector lever position indicator 2 (green) t Selector lever position indicator 1 (green) u Primary resistance v Primary resistance

36 Reversing light switch (not automatic transmission) 37 Heater blower motor 38 Heater controls 39 Clock 40 Glove box illumination 41 Cigar lighter and socket 42 Wiper speed control 43 Hazard warning flasher switch 44 Hazard warning flasher unit 45 Switch for heated rear window 46 Horn push ring 47 Dip and flasher switch 48 Ignition/starter switch: I Halt II O III Fahrt (Drive) IV Start 49 Switch illumination 50 Turn indicator switch 51 Stoplight switch 52 Load-shedding relay 53 Changeover relay 54 Delay relay 55 Fuse box 56 Door-operated switch, left 57 Switch for luggage compartment light 58 Luggage compartment light 59 Interior light 60 Heated rear window 61 Handbrake contact 62 Door-operated switch, right 63 Fuel gauge contact 64 Licence plate lighting 65 Rear light cluster, right: a Reversing light b Stoplight c Turn indicator d Rear light 66 Rear light cluster, left: a Reversing light b Stoplight c Turn indicator d Rear light e Rear fog light 67 Connection for radio 68 Plug connector for radio 69 Plug connector for heated rear window 70 Plug connector for luggage compartment light 71 Earth 72 Earth 73 Plug connector for ignition/starter switch 74 Connection for fog light relay 75 Connection for electric sliding roof 76 Connection for electric fuel pump 77 Connection for motor-operated radio aerial 78 Connection for trailer turn indicators 79 Door-operated switch, rear right 81 Diagnostic plug, ignition system 82 Diagnostic plug 83 Connection for sidelight 84 Door-operated switch, rear right 85 Connection for reading light 90 Plug for warning buzzer (USA) 91 Warning buzzer (USA) 92 Warning buzzer contact (USA) 93 Plug for side marker light, rear left 94 Plug for side marker light, rear right 95 Side marker light, rear left 96 Side marker light, rear right 97 Plug for side marker light, rear left 98 Plug for side marker light, rear right 99 Engine speed governor switch (USA) 100 Magnetic valve (USA)

Wiring colour code: BL Blue BR Brown GE Yellow GN Green GR Grey RT Red SW Black WS White
Where a cable has two colour codes, the first denotes the main colour, the second the colour of the tracer stripe. The figure preceding the colour code indicates the cross-sectional area of the wire in sq mm. The figure following the colour code is the individual cable number.

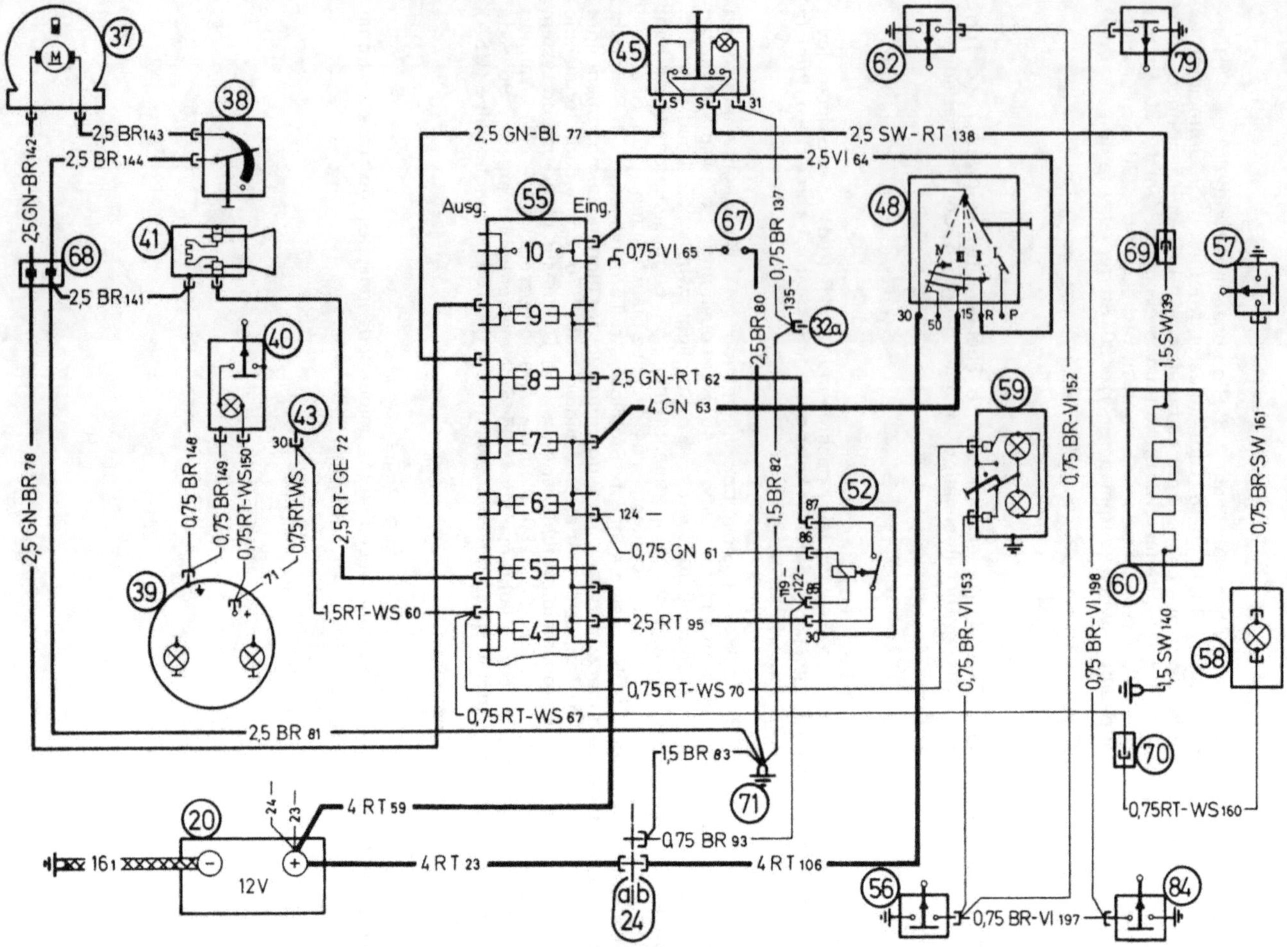

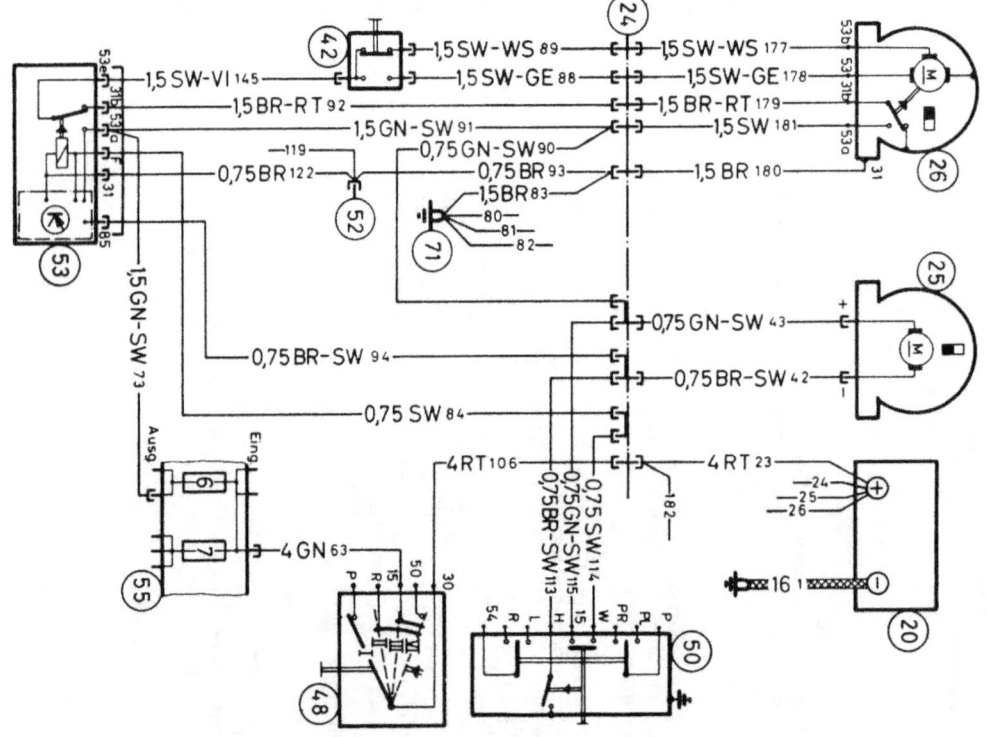

Wiring diagram, typical body electrical system

Wiring diagram, typical wiper and washer system

Wiring colour code: **BL** Blue **BR** Brown **GE** Yellow **GN** Green **GR** Grey **RT** Red **SW** Black **WS** White

Where a cable has two colour codes, the first denotes the main colour, the second the colour of the tracer stripe.
The figure preceding the colour code indicates the cross-sectional area of the wire in sq mm.
The figure following the colour code is the individual cable number.

HEATER-AIR CONDITIONING

INDEX

	Page
CABLES FOR HEATING AND VENTILATION	
CABLE FOR SHUT–OFF FLAP	145
Adjusting	145
CABLE FOR MIXTURE FLAP	145
Adjusting	145
CABLE FOR DEMISTER FLAPS	145
Adjusting	145
CABLE FOR FRESH AIR FLAPS	145
Adjusting	145
CABLE FOR SHUT–OFF FLAP	145
Replacing	145
CABLE FOR MIXTURE FLAP	146
Replacing	146
CABLE FOR DEMISTER FLAP	146
Replacing	146
CABLE FOR FRESH AIR FLAP	146
Replacing	146
HEATER	146
Removing and installing	146
HEATER BLOWER MOTOR	148
Removing and installing	148
COVER FOR HEATER CONTROLS	148
Removing and installing	148
FRESH AIR GRILLE COVER	148
Removing and installing	148
FRESH AIR GRILLE	148
Removing and installing	148
COMPLETE SWITCH PLATE FOR HEATER CONTROLS	148
Removing and installing	148
RESISTANCE ON SWITCH PLATE	148
Replacing	148
HEATER BODY – (HEATER REMOVED)	149
Replacing	149

	Page
HOT WATER HOSE (SUPPLY)	149
Replacing	149
HOT WATER HOSE (RETURN)	149
Replacing	149
AIR HOSE FOR LEFT DEMISTER OUTLET	150
Replacing	150
AIR HOSE FOR RIGHT DEMISTER OUTLET	150
Replacing	150
AIR HOSE FOR LEFT FRESH AIR OUTLET	150
Replacing	150
AIR HOSE FOR RIGHT FRESH AIR OUTLET	150
Replacing	150
LEFT DEMISTER OUTLET	150
Removing and installing	150
RIGHT DEMISTER OUTLET	152
Removing and installing	152
AIR CONDITIONING	152
Evacuating and refilling	152
EVAPORATOR BODY	154
Removing and installing	154
BLOWER	154
Removing and installing	154
EVAPORATOR	155
Removing and installing	155
COMPRESSOR	155
Removing and installing	155
OIL LEVEL IN COMPRESSOR	155
Checking	155
DEHUMIDIFIER	156
Removing and installing	156
CONDENSER	156
Removing and installing	156
AUXILIARY BLOWER	156
Removing and installing	156

144 HEATER/AIR CONDITIONING

Layout of flaps and control levers

1. Mixture flap
   a. cold
   b. warm
2. Shut-off flap – blower
   c. closed – off
   d. open – on
3. Heating – demisting
   e. heating
   f. demisting
4. Fresh air
   g. closed
   h. open

Correct length of connecting rod
A 120mm (4.72 in.)

HEATER/AIR CONDITIONING

CABLES FOR HEATING & VENTILATION
CABLE FOR SHUT-OFF FLAP
Adjusting

Remove lower center right instrument panel housing. Pull off the air hose end angle for the fresh air outlet. Loosen clamp screw and adjust cable so that the distance between the control lever and the stop on the switch plate is approximately 0.12 in. On coupe, open glovebox.

A. Clamp screw

CABLE FOR MIXTURE FLAP
Adjusting

Remove lower center right instrument panel housing. Detach the air hose to the right demister outlet. Before adjusting the cable, check length of connecting rod and

A = 4.72 in.

adjust if necessary. (4.72 in.) Loosen clamp screw and adjust cable so that the distance between the control lever and the stop on the switch plate is approximately 0.12 in.

CABLES FOR DEMISTER FLAPS
Adjusting

Remove lower center right instrument panel housing. Regulate the demister flaps so that they both open and close together. Loosen clamp screw and adjust cable so that the distance between the control lever and the stop on the switch plate is approximately 0.12 in.

CABLE FOR FRESH AIR FLAPS
Adjusting

Remove lower center right instrument panel housing. Detach the air hose end angle for the fresh air outlet. Loosen clamp screw and adjust the cable so that the control lever is slightly preloaded when located at the end stop position.

CABLE FOR SHUT-OFF FLAP
Replacing

Take off the fresh air grille cover. Pull away the air hose end angle for the right fresh air outlet. Allow the center section to hang from the left air hose. Detach clips and clamp screw. Remove the cable.

When installing: Adjust length of cable.

On Coupe only — remove cover for heater controls but do not unscrew the switch plate. Remove the air hose to the right demister outlet and proceed as above.

*1-7. Clips — A-D clamp screws

146 HEATER/AIR CONDITIONING

CABLE FOR MIXTURE FLAP
Replacing
Remove the heater. Detach clips, clamp screw and snap fastening on control lever. Remove the cable.

When installing: Adjust length of cable.

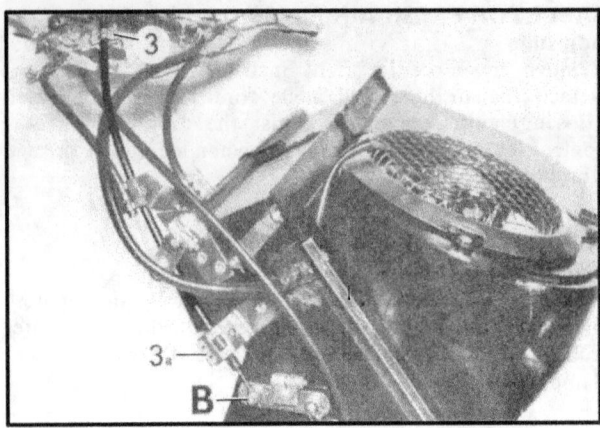

On Coupe only – remove cover for heater controls but do not detach switch plate and proceed.

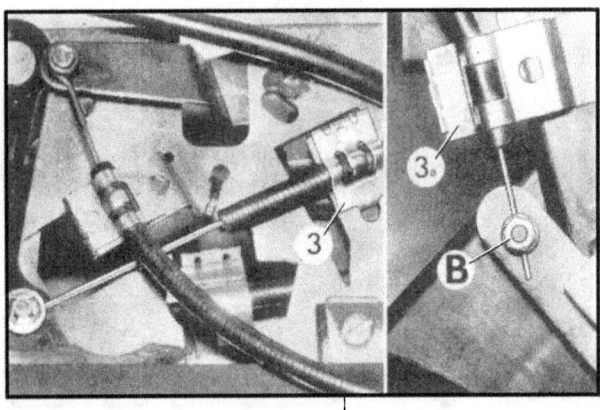

CABLE FOR DEMISTER FLAP
Replacing
Remove the heater. Detach clip. On Coupe only – remove cover for heater controls but do not detach switch plate. Detach clip and clamp screw. Remove the cable.

When installing: Adjust length of cable.

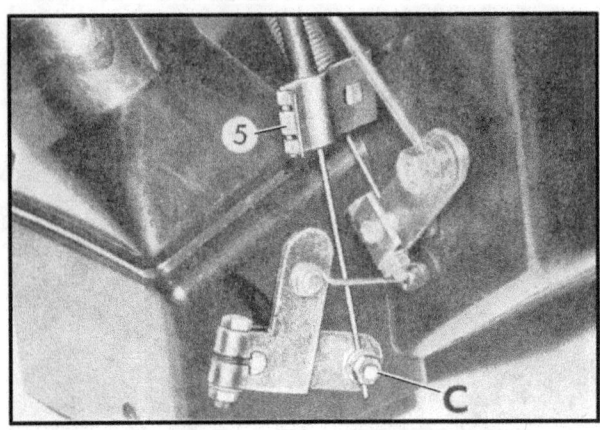

*1–7. Clips – A–D clamp screws

CABLE FOR FRESH AIR FLAP
Replacing
Remove the heater. Detach clip and clamp screw. Remove the cable.

When installing: Adjust length of cable.

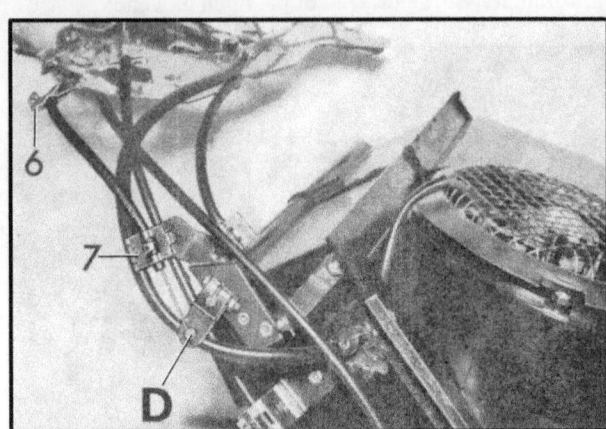

On Coupe only – remove cover for heater controls but do not detach switch plate and proceed.

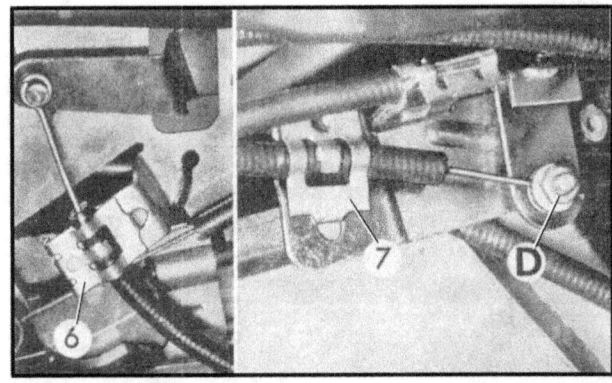

HEATER
Removing and installing
Partly drain the coolant.

When installing: Bleed the cooling system.

Detach the water hoses. Take off the screen and foam rubber seal.

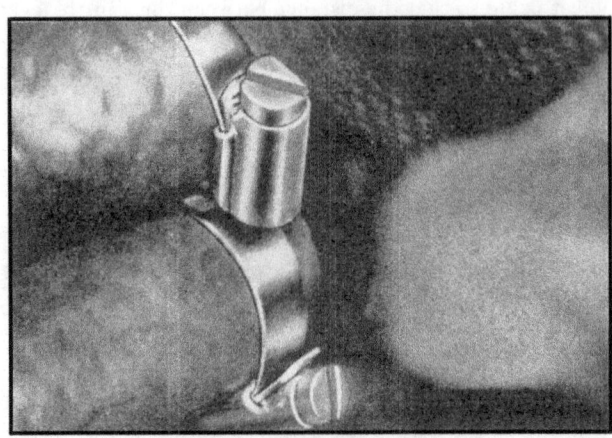

When installing: Place the foam rubber seal between the screen and the bulkhead and press the screen firmly against the bulkhead with the water hoses.

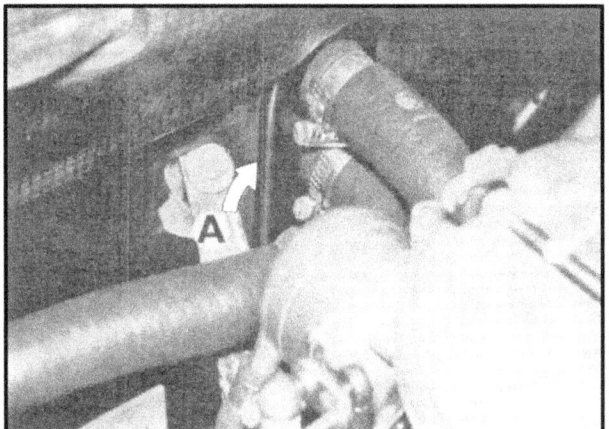

A. Foam rubber seal

Remove the fresh air grille cover. On Coupe models — remove the cover for the heater controls. Pull off the air hoses to the fresh air outlets. Remove the center section.

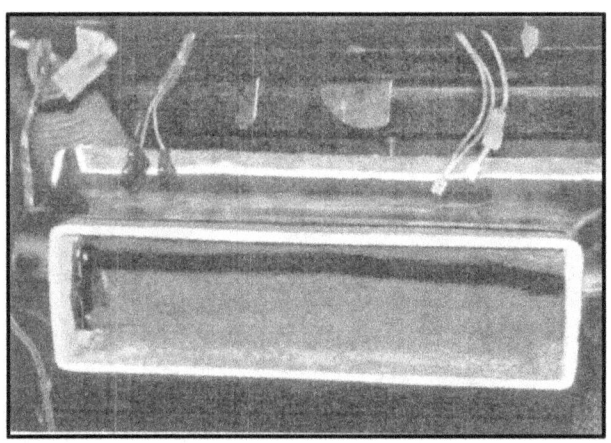

Detach the air hoses for the demister outlets from the heater. Gently press together and at the same time lift out the left air hose stub pipe. Pull off the heater control lever knobs. Remove the threaded knobs for the left instrument panel trim strip. Unscrew the rear switch plate.

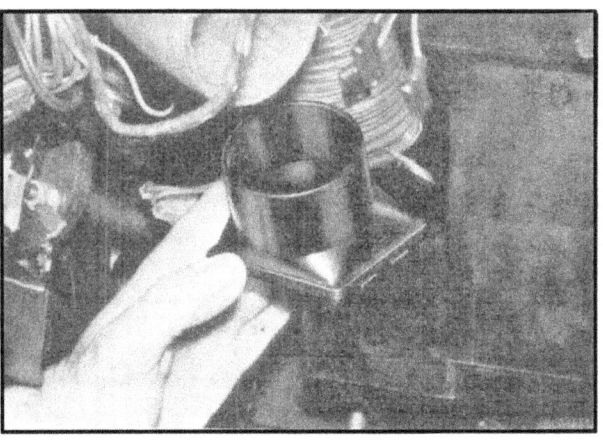

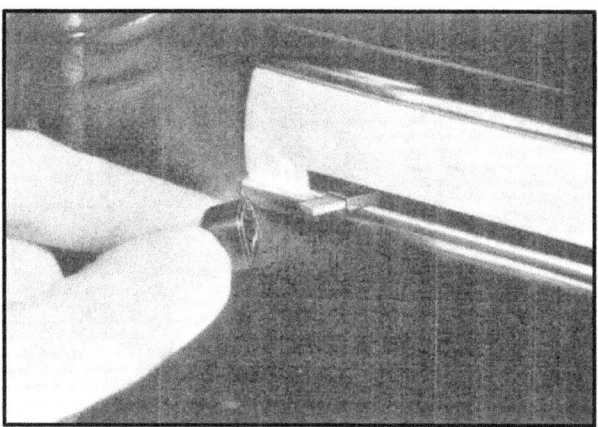

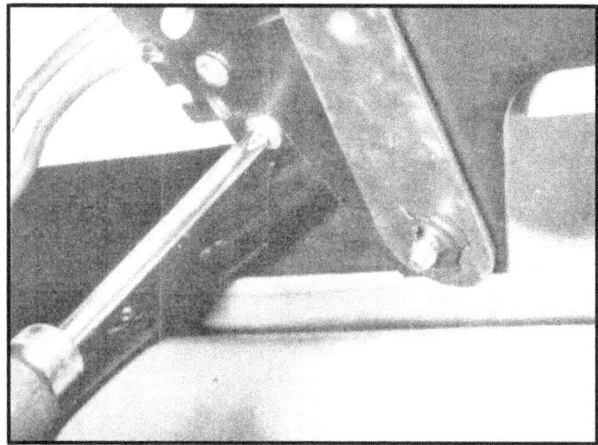

When installing: Install the switch plate so that the control levers do not scrape against the trim strip.

Unscrew the heater. Tilt the heater and switch plate inward to remove.

Unscrew the front switch plate.

When installing: First insert the switch plate into the instrument panel and screw lightly down, then insert the heater and tighten firmly. Check the foam rubber seal between the heater and the bulkhead and replace if necessary.

HEATER/AIR CONDITIONING

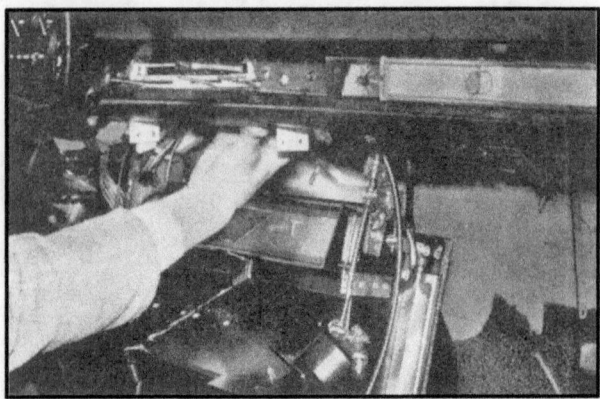

HEATER BLOWER MOTOR
Removing and installing
Unscrew the heater cover plate.

When installing: Place a Terostat sealing cord between the cover plate and the windshield surround.

Lift out the mesh grid over the blower. Pull off the cable connectors. Unscrew the motor mounting from the housing and pull out diagonally upwards. Release the retaining clips. Pull the motor away from its mounting.

When installing: The shorter end of the clip should be pressed over the motor mounting.

Do not pull the blower off the motor shaft as both components have been balanced together. Replace the motor only in unit with the blower.

COVER FOR HEATER CONTROLS
Removing and installing
Remove the center stowage compartment. Unscrew the left and right cover panels. Pull off heater control lever knobs. Unscrew the switch plate cover.

FRESH AIR GRILLE COVER
Removing and installing
Remove the center stowage compartment. Unscrew the left and right cover panels. Detach the cable connectors for the wiper switch and cigar lighter.

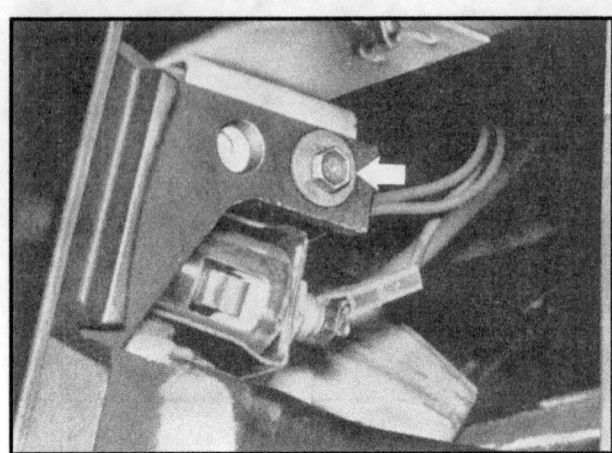

When installing: Cables to wiper switch – black-yellow – 53a, black-grey – 53b, black-violet – 53. Cables to cigar lighter – brown –, red +

FRESH AIR GRILLE
Removing and installing
Remove the fresh air grille cover. On Coupe models, remove cover for heater controls. Extract one pivot bearing. Take out the fresh air grille.

COMPLETE SWITCH PLATE FOR HEATER CONTROLS
Removing and installing
Remove the heater. On Coupe models, remove the cover for heater controls. Open the clips. Take off the cables.

When installing: Adjust length of cables.

RESISTANCE ON SWITCH PLATE
Replacing
Remove heater. On Coupe models, remove switch plate for heater controls. Remove the resistance.

When installing: Note the asbestos pads between the insulator and the switch plate.

HEATER/AIR CONDITIONING

HEATER BODY – (HEATER REMOVED)
Replacing

Detach the cable to the demister flap. Detach the retaining clips. Remove the seals. Pull the heater body out of the right housing half. Turn the heater body to remove from the housing.

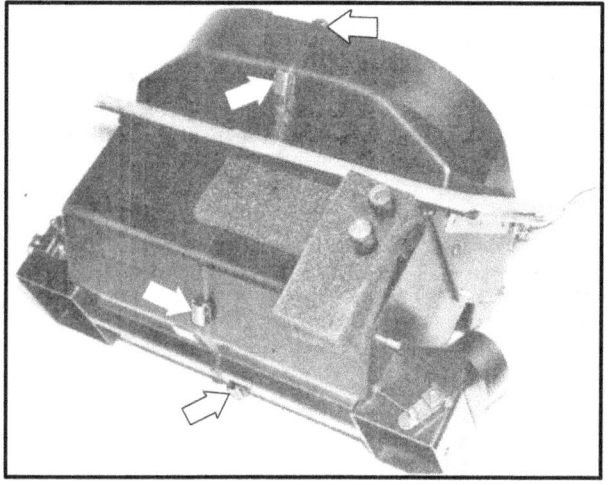

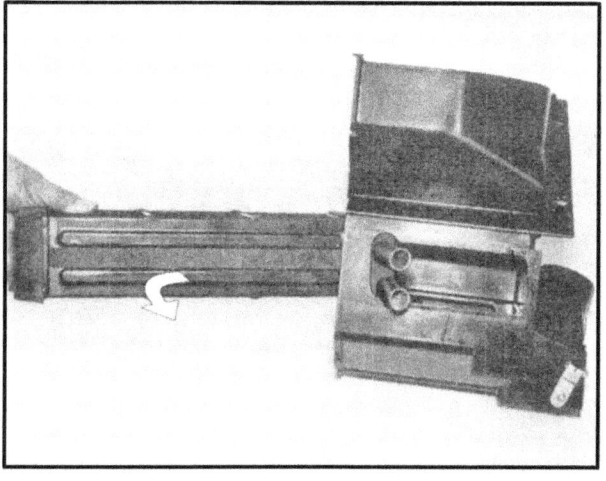

When installing: Note position of air guide section.

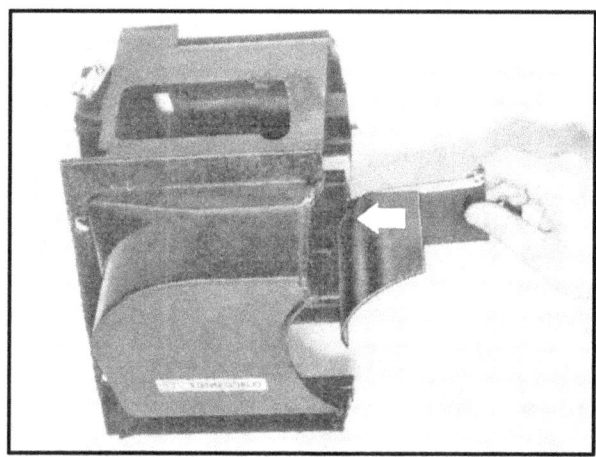

HOT WATER HOSE (SUPPLY)
Replacing

Remove the intake air filter housing. Detach hose clips.

When installing: Press the screen and foam rubber seal firmly against the bulkhead with the water hose.

Bleed the cooling system.

1 & 2   Hose clips

HOT WATER HOSE (RETURN)
Replacing

Remove the intake air filter housing. Detach hose clips.

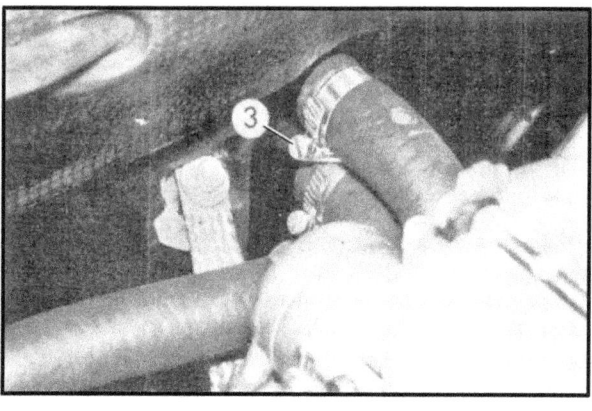

3. Hose clip

150 HEATER/AIR CONDITIONING

Pull off water hose. Detach hose clip for hot water hose and remove.

4 & 6. Hose clips
5. Water hose

When installing: Press the screen and foam rubber seal firmly against the bulkhead with the water hose.

Bleed the cooling system.

AIR HOSE FOR LEFT DEMISTER OUTLET
Replacing
Remove the lower center left instrument panel housing but leave cables connected. Pull off the air hose to the fresh air outlet from the center piece and press upwards. Detach the hose clip and pull off the air hose to the demister outlet.

When installing: Clamp the air hose and demister outlet firmly to the retaining bracket with the hose clip.

AIR HOSE FOR RIGHT DEMISTER OUTLET
Replacing
Remove lower center right instrument panel housing. On Coupe only, open glovebox, disconnect glovebox pivot joint and swing glovebox down. Pull off the air hose angle end for the fresh air outlet from the center section. Detach hose clip and pull off air hose for demister outlet.

When installing: Clamp the air hose and demister outlet firmly to retaining bracket with the hose clip.

AIR HOSE FOR LEFT FRESH AIR OUTLET
Replacing
Remove lower center left instrument panel housing but leave cables connected. Pull off the air hose from the fresh air outlet and center section. Pull the air hose out to the left.

AIR HOSE FOR RIGHT FRESH AIR OUTLET
Replacing
Remove lower center right instrument panel housing. Pull off air hose from fresh air outlet and angle end.

LEFT DEMISTER OUTLET
Removing and installing
Remove fresh air grille cover. Pull off air hoses to fresh air outlets. Pull off center section. Detach hose clip at demister outlet. Pull off air hose from demister outlet. Pull the demister outlet away to the right.

When installing: Insert the end of the demister outlet into the retaining clip. Clamp the air hose and demister outlet firmly to the retaining bracket with the hose clip.

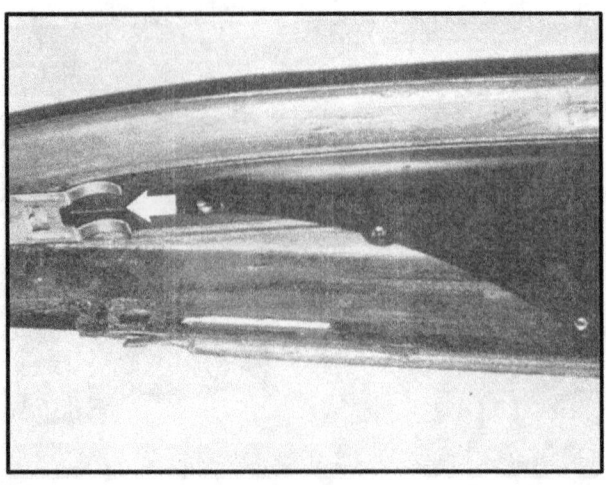

HEATER/AIR CONDITIONING

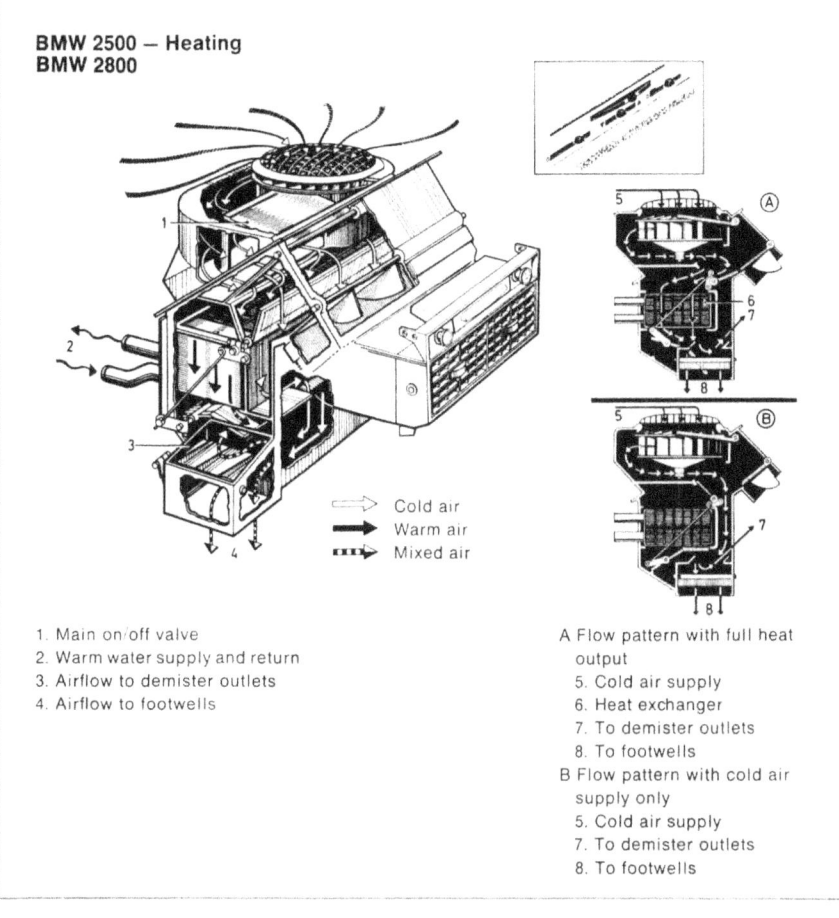

BMW 2500 — Heating
BMW 2800

⇒ Cold air
→ Warm air
⇢ Mixed air

1. Main on/off valve
2. Warm water supply and return
3. Airflow to demister outlets
4. Airflow to footwells

A Flow pattern with full heat output
5. Cold air supply
6. Heat exchanger
7. To demister outlets
8. To footwells

B Flow pattern with cold air supply only
5. Cold air supply
7. To demister outlets
8. To footwells

Heating and ventilation

Fresh-air heater with hot water heat exchanger permanently in circuit and three-speed radial blower (140 Watt); airflow 106, 159 or 212 cu. ft. per hour (3, 4.5 or 6 cu. m/hr). Instant temperature selection within fine limits by means of 4-lever control system. Total of 4 footwell and front screen demister outlets, with airflow to front side windows if required.

Independently of hot air supply, cold air can be supplied to swivelling outlets at either end of the facia and to an outlet grill in the centre of the facia, adjustable in any desired direction. This ensures stratified interior air temperatures for fatigue-free driving.

Stale extraction through slots above the rear window leading to ducts and outlets on the rear roof pillars, and apertures below the rear window communicating with staggered extractor slots in the space between rear compartment lid and bodyshell.

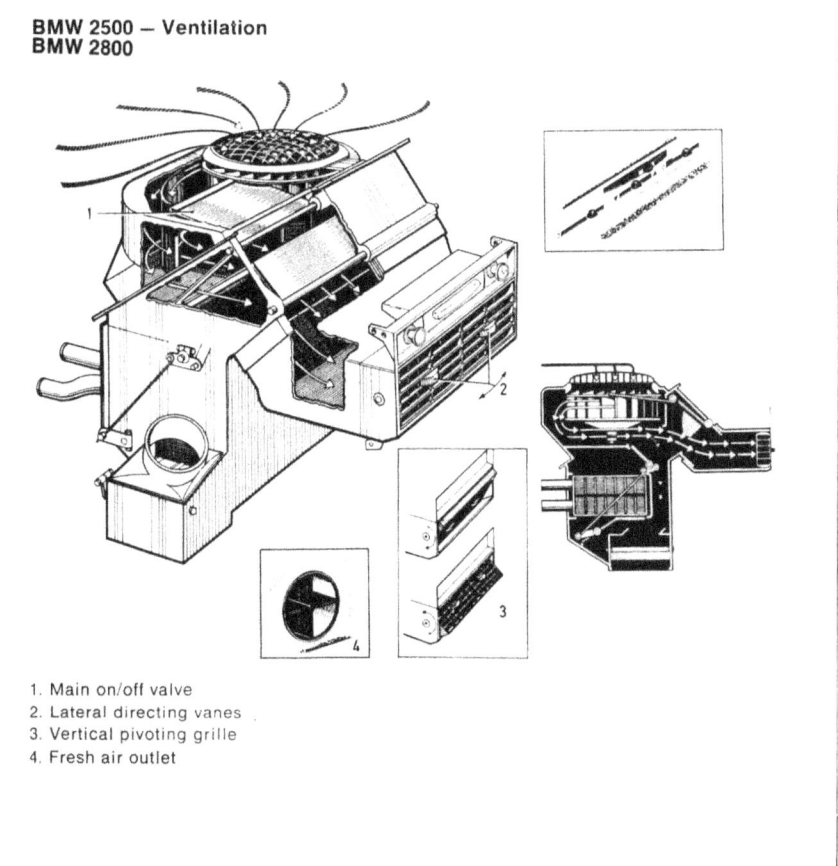

BMW 2500 — Ventilation
BMW 2800

1. Main on/off valve
2. Lateral directing vanes
3. Vertical pivoting grille
4. Fresh air outlet

152 HEATER/AIR CONDITIONING

RIGHT DEMISTER OUTLET
Removing and installing
Remove lower center right instrument panel housing. Detach hose clip. Pull away air hose from demister outlet. Pull the demister outlet away to the left.

When installing: Insert the end of the demister outlet into the retaining clip. Clamp the air hose and demister outlet firmly to the retaining bracket with the hose clip.

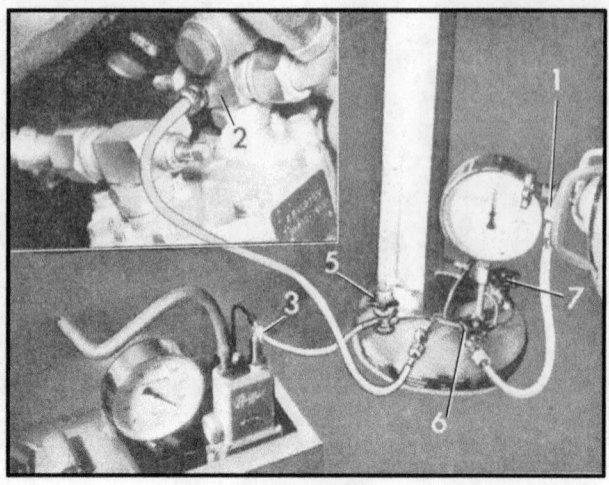

1. Coolant bottle
2. Suction valve
3. Vacuum pump
5-7. Filling column valves
8. Pressure valve

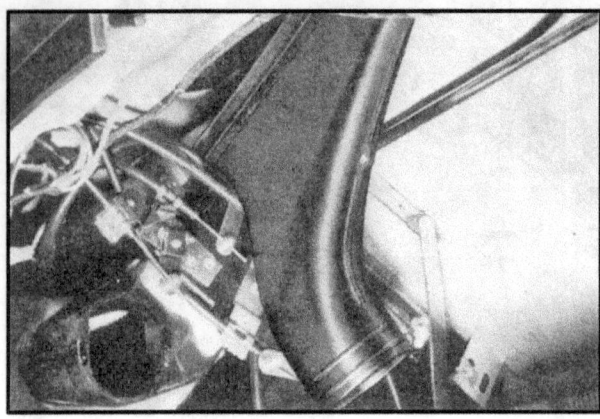

AIR CONDITIONING
Evacuating and refilling
Safety precautions, Frigen R 12 is not explosive or flammable, does not corrode, has no smell and is heavier than air. When working on the air conditioning equipment, wear protective goggles at all times. Frigen R 12 evaporates at normal temperatures so rapidly that anything coming into contact with it will freeze. If any of the coolant should get into the eyes, wash it out immediately with a few drops of mineral oil followed by a weak boracic acid solution. Visit the doctor or optician without delay even if no pain is felt. Do not work in pits – danger of suffocation. Before the air conditioning system is filled with Frigen R 12, a vacuum must be produced in the entire system. This is achieved by means of a vacuum pump connected to the suction side of the compressor by way of the filling column and a filter. Connect hoses between the coolant bottle, the suction valve and the vacuum pump. Open valves on the filling column.

2. Suction valve
8. Pressure valve

Open pressure valve fully then open suction valve half way. With the vacuum pump, develop a vacuum of max. -1 kp/cm^2. Close valves. Open valve on the coolant bottle. Open valve again on the filling column and fill the column with 1000 grams of Frigen R 12. Refer to scale R 12 when filling the column.

Turn the blower switch and the temperature selector fully to the right. Close the valve on the coolant bottle and the valve on the filling column. Open valve. Run the engine at approximately 1500 rpm until the coolant (Frigen R 12) has left the column. Fully open the suction valve and remove the connecting hose. With a suitable leak detector, check all hose and threaded connections. The coolant inspection window indicates the presence of sufficient coolant in the air conditioning system. Run the engine at 1500 rpm. No foam nor air bubbles should be visible. If this is not the case, add more coolant until the foam or air bubbles have disappeared.

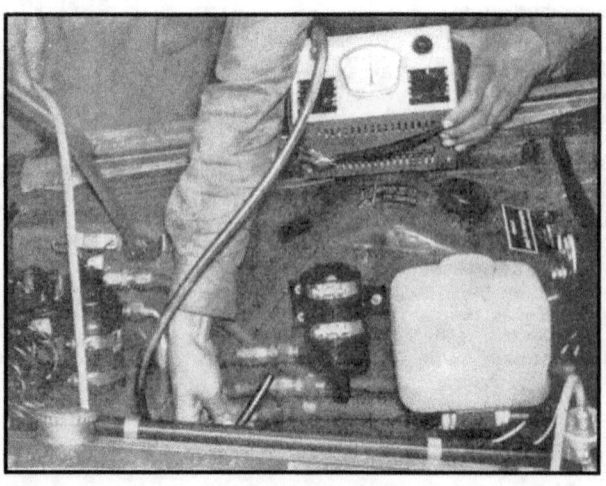

WIRING DIAGRAM – AIR CONDITIONING

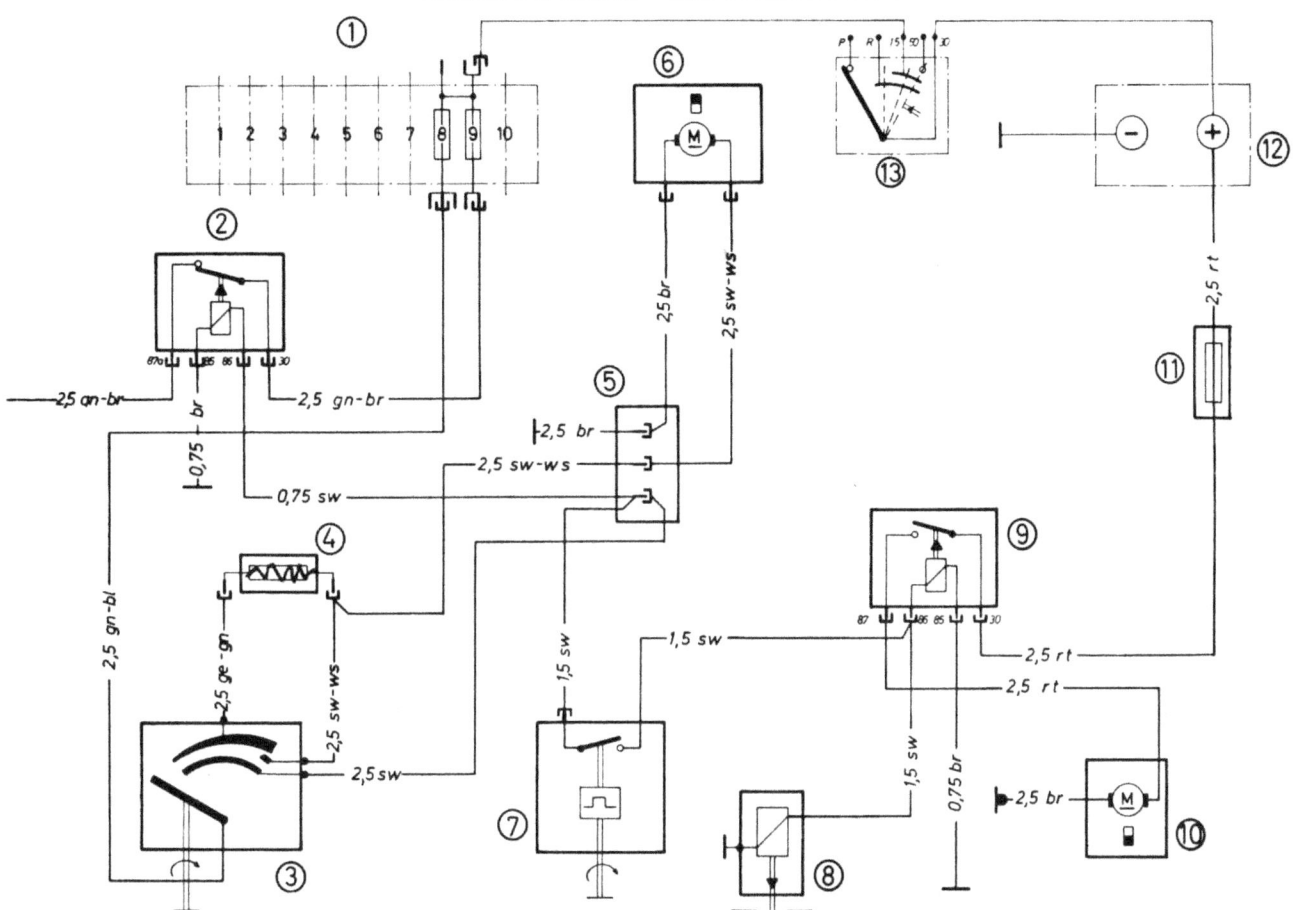

Wiring colour code: **BL** Blue **BR** Brown **GE** Yellow **GN** Green **GR** Grey **RT** Red **SW** Black **WS** White

Key to electrical wiring diagram:

1. Fuse box (standard)
2. Relay
3. Blower switch
4. Resistor
5. Plug connection (behind air conditioner cover plate)
6. Blower motor
7. Temperature sensitive switch
8. Magnetic clutch
9. Relay
10. Cooling fan motor
11. Flying fuse
12. Battery (standard)
13. Ignition starter switch (standard)

SPECIFICATION

Evaporator housing

Air distribution: the evaporator is integrated with the fresh air ventilating system. Air is thus distributed in the same way as on the standard vehicle. The fresh air outlet grill can be tilted through about 60° horizontally and its guide vanes through about 90° vertically. The deflecting slots in the fresh air outlet nozzles on the right and left of the dashboard can be tilted and rotated (provided on 2500 and 2800 models only).

Air circulation:	2 double flow radial impellers.
Airflow:	Approx. 7 cu.m (250 cu.ft.)/min.
Overload protection:	16 Amp. fuse in fuse box (2500/2800) 25 Amp. (2800 CS).
Lowest air outlet temperature at evaporator:	0–4° C (32–39° F)
Maximum cooling rate:	approx. 4500 Kcal/hr.

Compressor

Type:	York DA 210
No. of cylinders:	
Speed of rotation:	500–4500 rpm
Swept capacity:	160 cc (9.76 cu.in.)
Oil capacity (max.):	0.28 p (0.068 U.S. gal.)
Power consumption:	approx. 9 hp at maximum speed of rotation.

Clutch

Type:	Electromagnetic
Model:	Pitts 24 D – 05: 6 inch (6 return springs)

Condenser

Face area:	18.1 sq.dm (2500/2800/CS sq.in.)
Block depth:	40 mm (1.57")

Refrigerant

Grade:	Frigen 12 (difluor-dichlormethane, CF_2Cl_2)
Capacity:	1000 g (2.2 lb)

Vee belt

Narrow section:	12,5x850 DIN 7753

Drying bottle (Moisture trap)
Steel body with inspection window

Capacity:	0.54 cu.dm (3.36 cu.in.)

Auxiliary electric fan

In front of condenser, automatically switched on and off by magnetic clutch.

Manufacturer:	Bosch JPA 12 V
Type:	5 blade axial fan, 250 mm (9.8") diameter
Power consumption:	100 Watts at 13 V
Overload protection:	Flying fuse, 16 Amp.

Vibration damper

Steel housing:	approx. 0.54 cu.dm (3.36 cu.in.)

(In refrigerant circuit between compressor and condenser.)

154 HEATER/AIR CONDITIONING

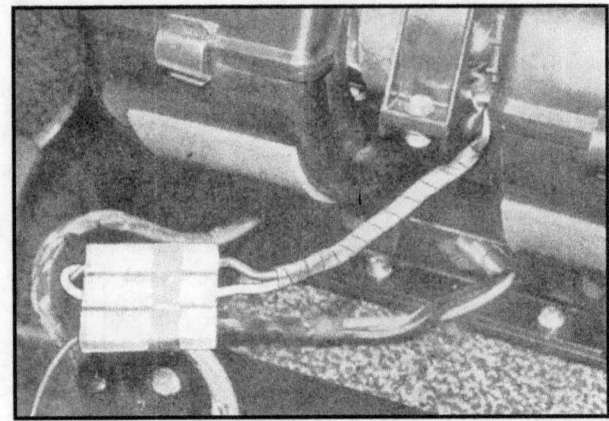

1. Multi-pin plug
2. Blower switch black cable
3. Cable harness black cable
4. Auxiliary blower black cable

EVAPORATOR BODY
Removing and installing

Open the pressure valve on the compressor (the front valve). Drain the coolant. Note safety precautions.

When installing: Evacuate (refill) the system and check oil level in compressor.

Remove lower center left, then right instrument panel trim. Unscrew blower cover at left and right. Remove screws holding side section. Take off the evaporator cover and carefully pull out the temperature sensor. On Automatic cars, remove the selector lever screen. Unscrew the fresh air grill cover. Pull off the cable connections.

When installing: Cables on wiper switch —
 black-yellow 53a
 black-grey 53b
 black-violet 53
 Cables on cigar lighter:
 brown —
 red +

Unscrew pipe union.

When installing: Do not re-use copper sealing rings. Apply low temperature oil to threads to prevent later seizure. Insulate the larger pipe union with No-Tape sealing strip to prevent condensate formation.

Unscrew and lift out the retaining bracket. Unscrew the evaporator at the rear. Remove evaporator complete with spacer. Disconnect the cables.

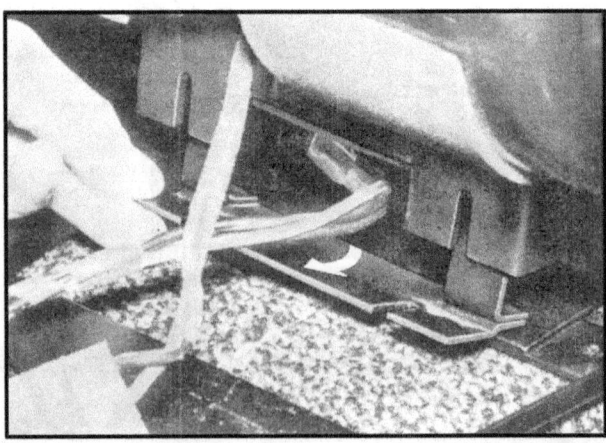

When installing: Pierce the hole for condensate drainage again, to remove any blockage.

BLOWER
Removing and installing

Remove the evaporator body. The coolant lines remain connected. Pull off the clips holding the two halves of the body. Loosen the screws and lift away the body. Lift out the motor. The motor and blower impellers are balanced as a single unit — do not separate.

HEATER/AIR CONDITIONING

Screws

EVAPORATOR
Removing and installing

Remove the evaporator body. Pull off the clips. Loosen both screws and lift away the body. Remove the evaporator.

COMPRESSOR
Removing and installing

Open the pressure valve on the compressor. Drain the coolant. Observe safety precautions.

When installing: Evacuate and refill the system.

Unscrew the coolant lines.

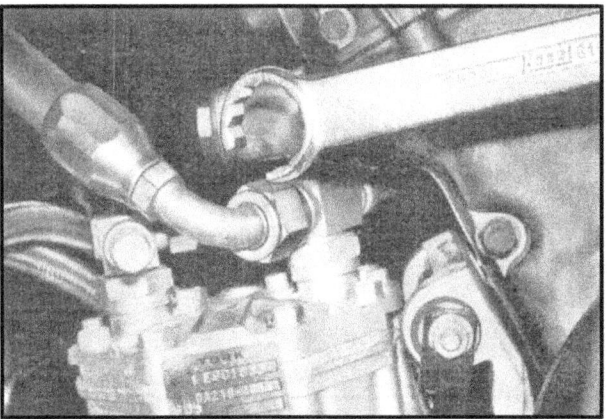

When installing: Coat threads with low temperature resistant oil. Do not re-use copper sealing rings.

Plug the coolant lines immediately after disconnecting, to prevent moisture from entering the dehumidifier and rendering it inoperative. Loosen the screws on the swivel plate. Take off the V-belt. Unscrew the compressor from the swivel plate. Break the electrical connections. Remove the compressor downward.

OIL LEVEL IN COMPRESSOR
Checking

Do not check oil level in the compressor unless a component in the air conditioning system has been exchanged, the coolant renewed or a leak repaired. Unscrew protective caps and connect pressure gauge to

1 & 2. Protective caps

suction valve. Turn the temperature selector and the blower switch fully to the right. Run the engine at 1200 – 1500 rpm for about 5 minutes. With the engine running at normal idle speed, turn the suction valve slowly to the right to close. The pressure gauge should read zero or below. Stop the engine. If the suction valve were to be closed suddenly, a large quantity of oil would be forced out of the crankcase. Close the pressure valve. The pressure gauge reading may rise to 0.5 kp/cm². Slowly open the level checking screw. Insert the oil dipstick as far as possible. The end of the handle section of the dipstick should be close to the compressor housing. The compressor shaft may need to be turned slightly. Check the oil level.

4. Pressure valve
5. Level checking screw

156 HEATER/AIR CONDITIONING

For subsequent filling, use only oils of the following grades: Shell Clavus 33; BP Energol LPT 100; Suniso No. 5; Texaco Capelle E. Draw off excess oil. Screw checking screw half way in. Disconnect the pressure gauge. Connect the reservoir of coolant to the suction valve and blow the compressor free from air with Frigen R 12 coolant. Allow the Frigen R 12 to overflow slowly, and at the same time close the level checking screw completely. Disconnect the filling line. Open the suction and pressure valves. Run the engine at idle speed and check the compressor for leaks.

S. Suction valve
5. Checking screw

DEHUMIDIFIER
Removing and installing

The dehumidifier contains an exceptionally hygroscopic 'gel,' which attracts and absorbs moisture. In normal conditions of humidity the dehumidifier will become unusable after only 20 minutes if left open. For this reason, always plug the dehumidifier immediately after disconnecting the coolant lines with suitable plugs. Open the pressure valve on the compressor and drain the coolant. Observe safety precautions.

When installing: Evacuate and refill the system.

Unscrew the coolant lines.

When installing: Coat threads with low temperature resistant oil. Do not re-use old copper sealing rings. Detach the dehumidifier.

CONDENSER
Removing and installing

Open the pressure valve on the compressor. Drain the coolant. Warning, observe the safety precautions. Remove all front grills. Remove the radiator. Remove the right headlights with support frame. Loosen screws at left. Loosen screws at right. Disconnect the coolant lines.

When installing: Do not re-use copper sealing rings. Coat threads with low temperature resistant oil to prevent seizure.

Plug the coolant lines immediately after disconnecting, to prevent moisture entering the dehumidifier. Detach the condenser.

AUXILIARY BLOWER
Removing and installing

Remove all front grills. Detach the auxiliary blower. Disconnect cable from relay. Remove auxiliary blower with cable harness. To replace carbon brushes, remove the auxiliary blower and take off the fan. Note left hand thread. Mark relative positions of bearing endplate and motor body. Loosen screws. Pull off armature and pole shoe housing. Unsolder the brushes.

HEATER/AIR CONDITIONING 157

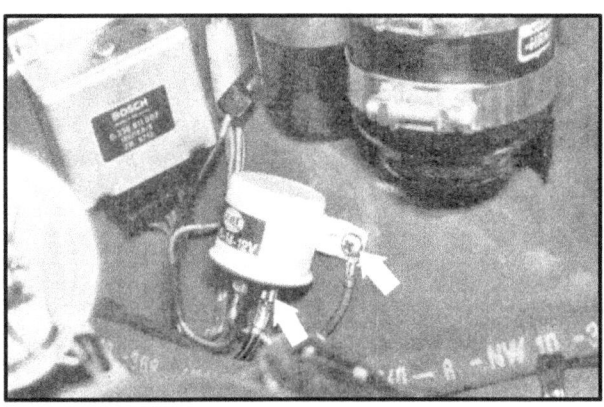
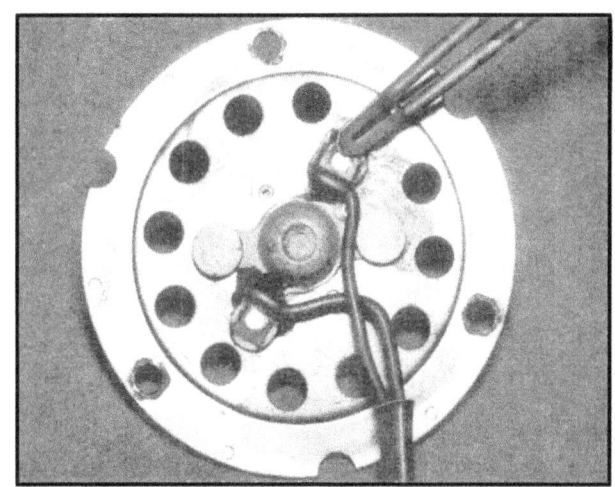

When installing: The new brushes must move easily in their guides.

Insulate the soldered joints with lacquer.

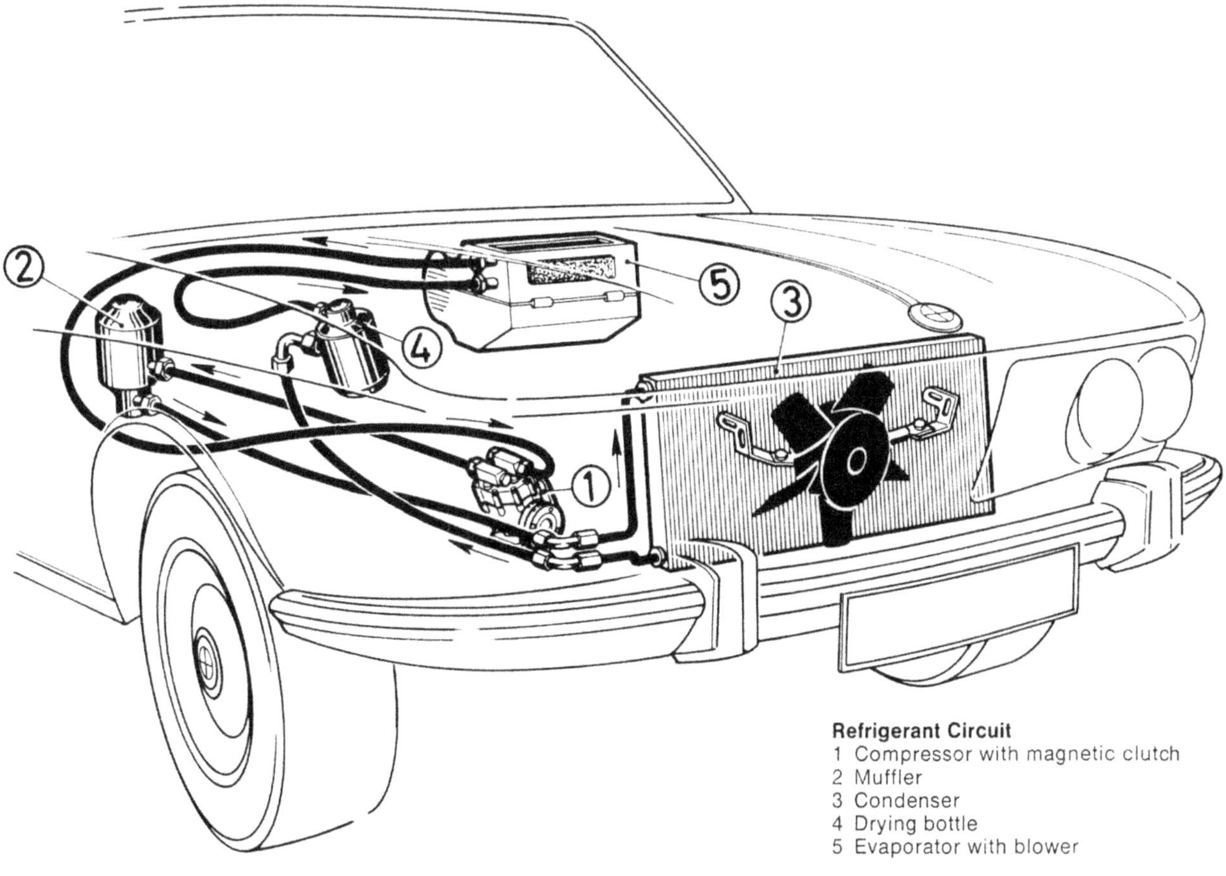

Refrigerant Circuit
1 Compressor with magnetic clutch
2 Muffler
3 Condenser
4 Drying bottle
5 Evaporator with blower

AIR CONDITIONING

NOTES

BODY

INDEX

	Page
FRONT DOOR	161
Aligning	161
Removing and installing	161
REAR DOOR	161
Aligning	161
Removing and installing	161
HOOD	162
Removing and refitting	162
CENTER STOWAGE COMPARTMENT	162
Removing and installing	162
SELECTOR LEVER SCREEN PLATE	163
Removing and installing	163
FRONT DOOR STRIKER PLATE	163
Replacing	163
FRONT DOOR LOCK	163
Removing and installing	163
FRONT DOOR LOCK BARREL COMPLETE	163
Removing and installing	163
FRONT OUTSIDE DOOR HANDLE AND LOCK OPERATING MECHANISM	164
Removing and installing	164
FRONT INSIDE HANDLE	164
Removing and installing	164
REAR DOOR STRIKER PLATE	164
Replacing	164
REAR DOOR LOCK	164
Removing and installing	164
CONNECTING ROD FOR LOCK MECHANISM	164
Removing and installing	164
FRONT WINDSHIELD	164
Removing and installing	164
REAR WINDOW	165
Removing and installing	165
FRONT WINDOW LIFT HANDLE	166
Removing and installing	166
FRONT DOOR WINDOW LIFT MECHANISM	166

	Page
Removing and installing	166
FRONT WINDOW LIFT RAIL HOLDER	166
Removing and installing	166
FRONT DOOR WINDOW	166
Adjusting	166
Removing and installing	166
FRONT DOOR WINDOW FRAME AND GLASS	166
Adjusting	166
REAR WINDOW LIFT HANDLE	167
Removing and installing	167
REAR DOOR WINDOW LIFT MECHANISM	167
Removing and installing	167
REAR DOOR WINDOW GLASS	167
Removing and installing	167
REAR DOOR WINDOW GUIDE RUBBER	167
Replacing	167
REAR DOOR WINDOW FRAME AND GLASS	167
Adjusting	167
UPPER SECTION OF INSTRUMENT PANEL	167
Removing and installing	167
UPPER SECTION OF INSTRUMENT PANEL HOUSING	168
Removing and installing	168
LOWER CENTER LEFT SECTION OF INSTRUMENT PANEL HOUSING	168
Removing and installing	168
LOWER CENTER RIGHT SECTION OF INSTRUMENT PANEL HOUSING	168
Removing and installing	168
SLIDING ROOF	169
Adjusting	169
SLIDING ROOF PANEL	169
Removing and installing	169
MOTOR AND GEARBOX FOR POWER SLIDING ROOF	169
Removing and installing	169

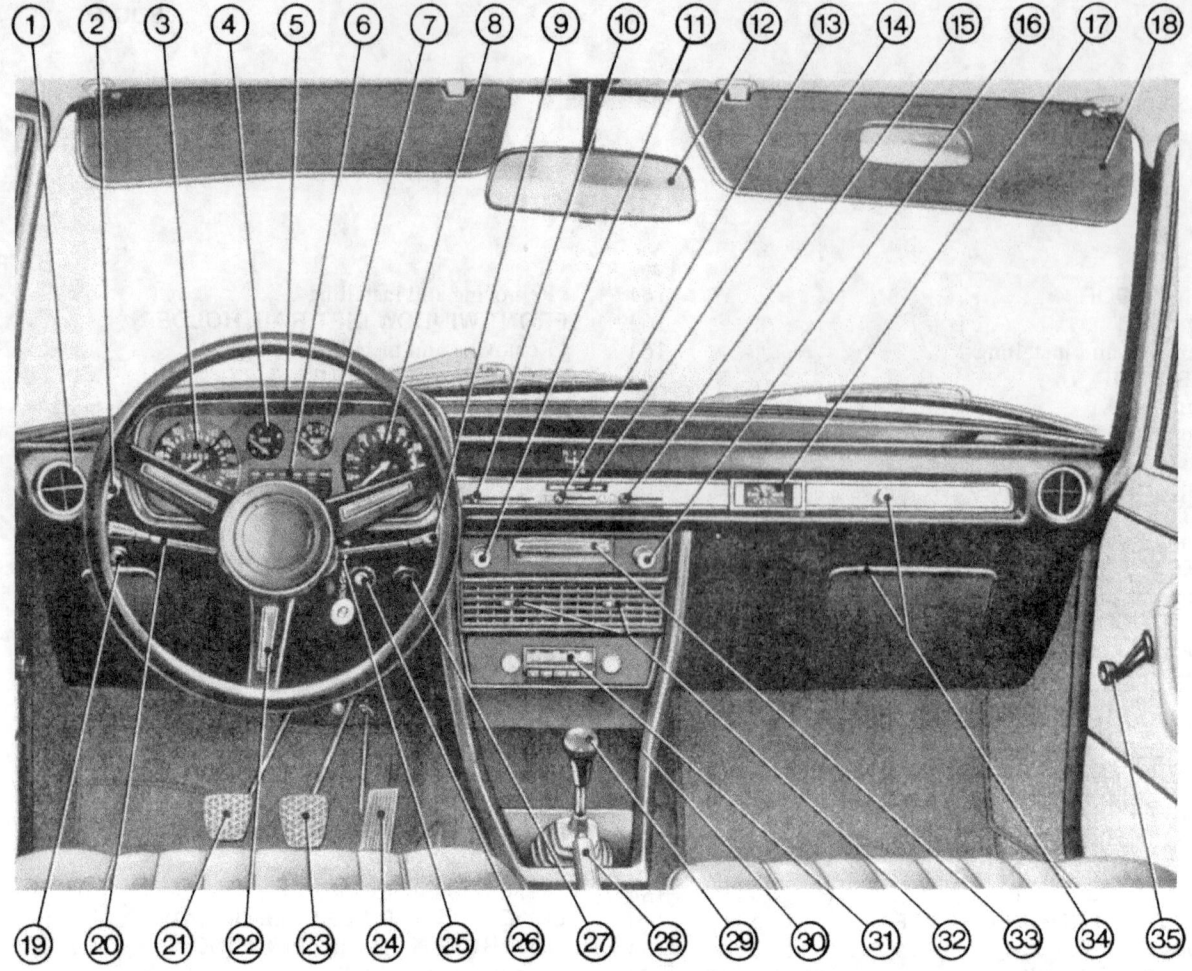

Controls and instruments

Note: figures in square brackets [ ] indicate pages on which items are described in detail.

1. Ventilation: fresh air inlet [21]
2. Headlamp and side lamp switch (2-position), with instrument and control lighting [8]
3. Speedometer with mileage and trip recorders [26]
4. Water temperature gauge [13]
5. Upper instrument panel hood with loudspeaker (optional) [37]
6. Telltale warning lamps [12] for:
   Battery charge (red)
   Oil pressure (orange)
   Headlamp main beam (blue)
   Turn indicators (green)
   Fuel level (white)
   Brake fluid level and handbrake (red)
   Selector lever position (on automatic model) [13]
   Positions: P (white)
             R (red)
             0 (white)
             A (green)
             2 (green)
             1 (green)
7. Fuel gauge [13]
8. Revolution counter with illuminated danger zone [26, 27]
9. Lever for turn indicators, parking lights, wipers and screenwasher [9]
10. Heater: main on/off lever [20]
11. Wiper speed control switch [9]
12. Interior rear view mirror [16]
13. Heater: air distribution lever [21]
14. Heater: temperature selector lever [20]
15. Ventilation: fresh air lever [21]
16. Cigar lighter with plug socket [19]
17. Clock [17]
18. Sun visors [16]
19. Stowage compartment with lid [10]
20. Headlamp dip and flasher lever [8]
21. Clutch pedal (not on automatic model)
22. Horn push [12]
23. Brake pedal
24. Accelerator pedal
25. Steering lock and ignition/starter switch [8]
26. Switch for heated rear window (optional) [12]
27. Switch for hazard warning flashers [12]
28. Handbrake lever [15]
29. Gear lever
    Selector lever (automatic model) [18]
30. Stowage space
31. Car radio (optional)
32. Ventilation: fresh air grille [20, 21]
33. Ashtray [19]
34. Glove box [17]
35. Window crank, right hand side

BODY

FRONT DOOR
Aligning
Remove front door trim panel. Loosen hinges slightly.

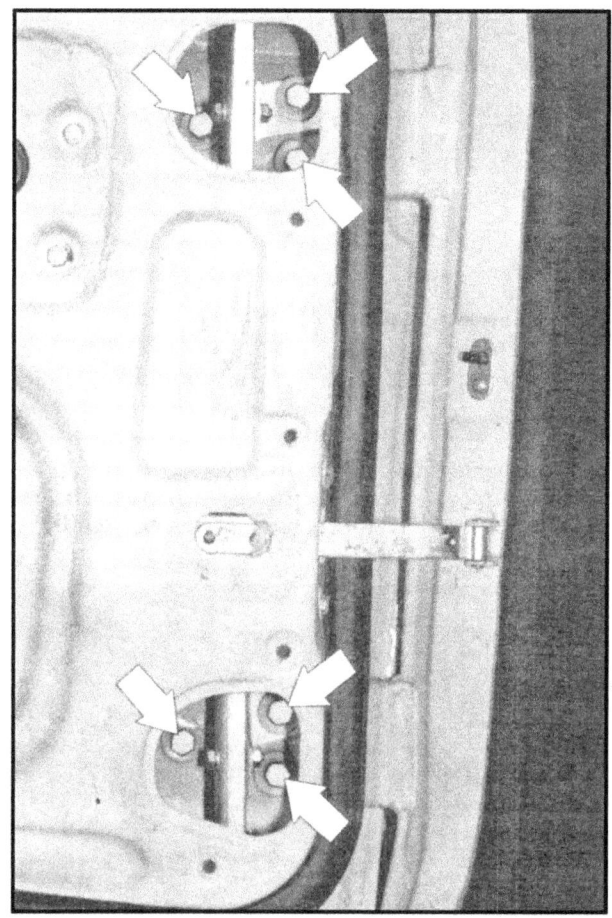

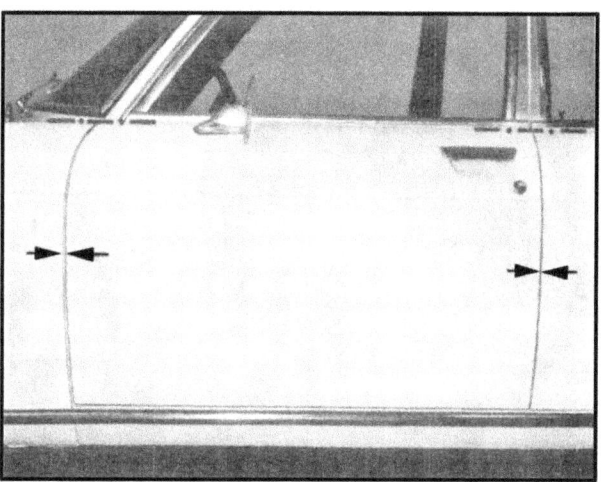

Insert a shim of the correct thickness in order to adjust the relative heights of door and side panel. Adjust gap between side panel and front door, front door and rear door, and top of door and window frame. Adjust door lock striker plate.

Removing and installing
Remove door trim panel. Drive out rivet for door stay. Half open door window. Remove door from hinge halves. Use correct shims.

When installing: Align front door.

REAR DOOR
Aligning
Remove door panel trim. Align relative heights of front and rear doors with shims. Loosen hinge attachment bolts and adjust gap between front and rear doors and rear door and rear side panel. Desired position: Rear door outer surface should be 0.04 in. lower than front door outer surface. Adjust height of door at joint between front and rear doors and between rear door and window frame where appropriate. Adjust lock striker plate.

Removing and installing
Remove door panel trim. Close door window. Drive out rivet holding door stay. Unscrew door from upper hinge half with ring spanner. Unscrew door from lower hinge half with a socket wrench.

When installing: Align rear door.

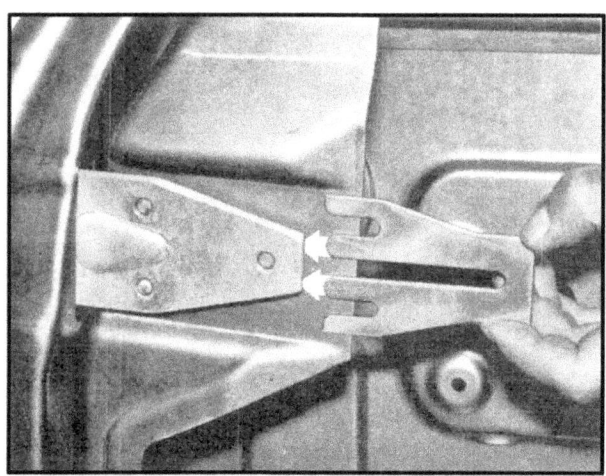

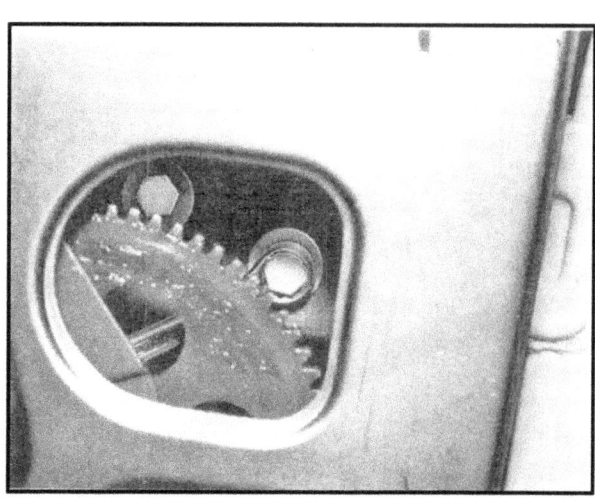

BODY

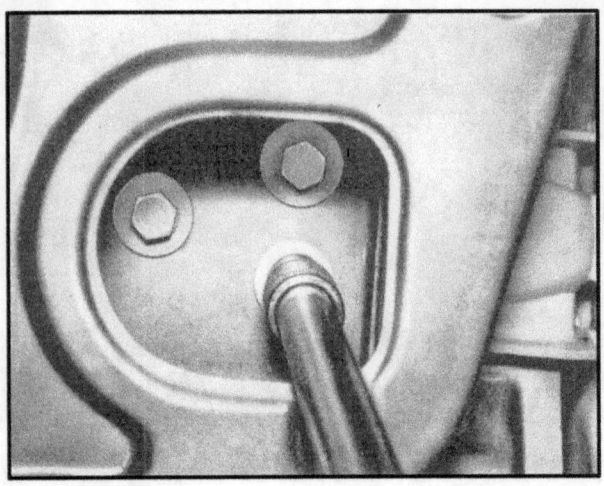

HOOD
Removing and refitting
Open retaining clips. Pull off cable from horn. Mark position of hinge. Unscrew two bolts. Slacken third bolt. Detach support arms. Remove third hinge bolt. Detach front lid.

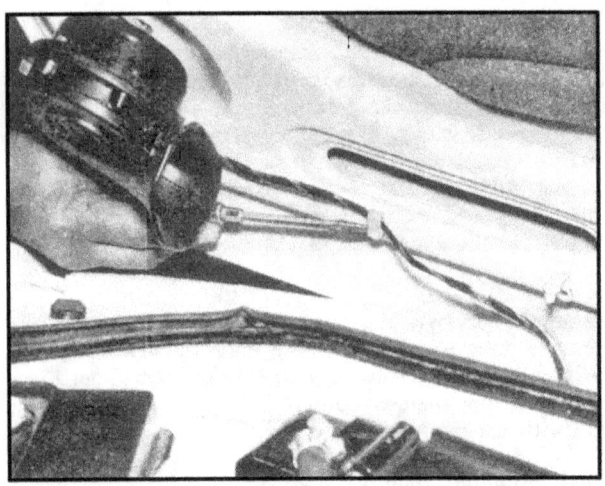

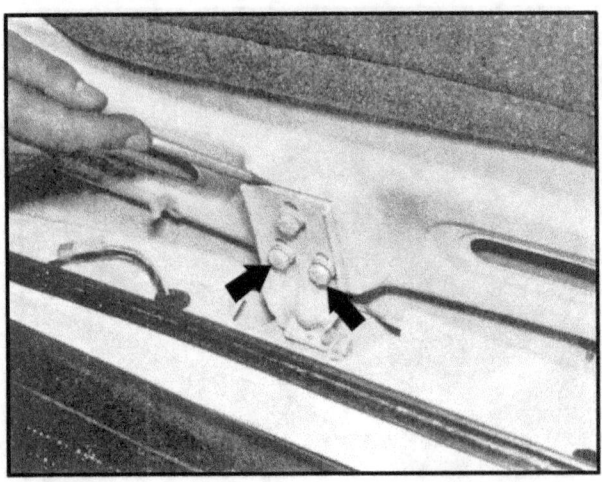

CENTER STOWAGE COMPARTMENT
Removing and installing
Remove housing for left side of instrument panel — do not disconnect cables. Remove screws. Remove housing

for instrument panel at right. Remove screws. If a radio is installed, remove it from the stowage compartment. Lift out the floor of the stowage compartment. Detach the

stowage compartment. Pull off the rubber gaiter. Select 2nd or 4th gear. Pull out stowage compartment to the rear. Coupe only: Open the zip fastener. Select 1st gear. Press out the tumbler switches for the electric window lift mechanisms from below. Remove the screws.

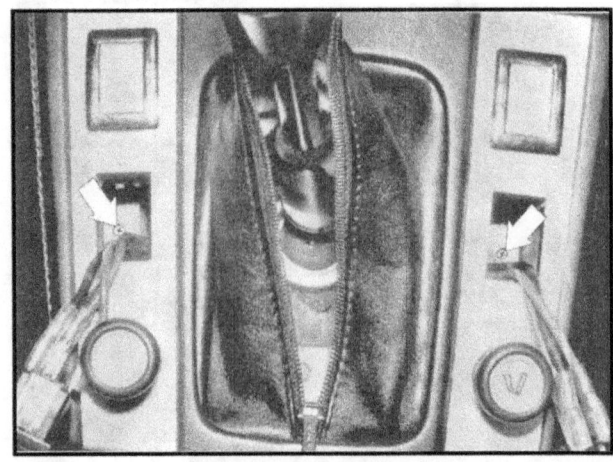

Pull the console upwards. Lift out the stowage compartment floor. Remove screws from transmission tunnel and stowage compartment. Remove pivot pin from glove box and swing down. Pull cables away from contact switch. Remove lower center left housing panel, but do not disconnect cables. Select 2nd or 4th gear. Pull away the stowage compartment.

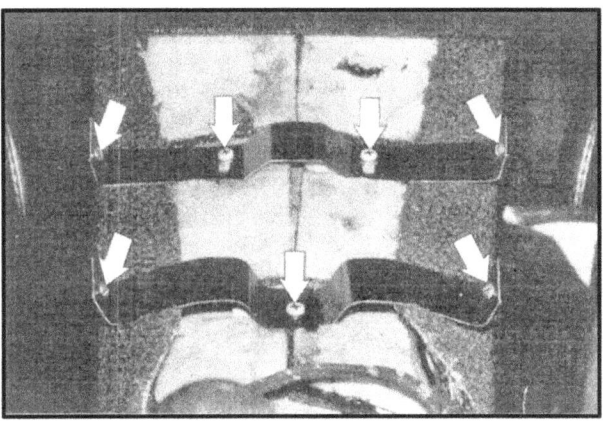

SELECTOR LEVER SCREEN PLATE
Removing and installing

Remove floor of stowage compartment. Pull off selector lever knob. Unscrew the screen plate.

FRONT DOOR STRIKER PLATE
Replacing

Press away the center door pillar lining. Remove all screws from door striker plate. Hold the threaded plate firmly by hand.

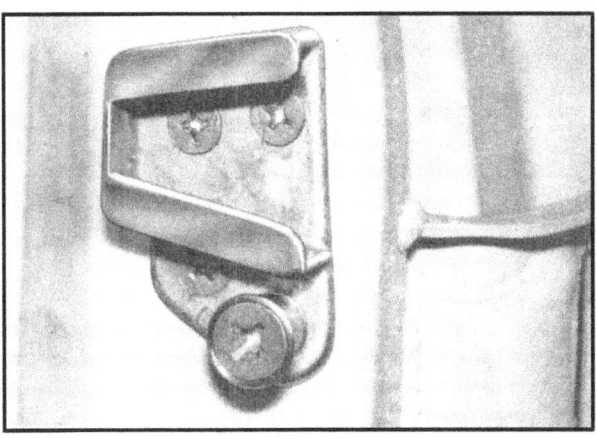

When installing: Screw the striker plate lightly into position and align with door lock. Adjust striker plate so that when the doors are closed the outer surface of the front door is 0.04 in. higher than the surface of the rear door. Tighten the striker plate firmly.

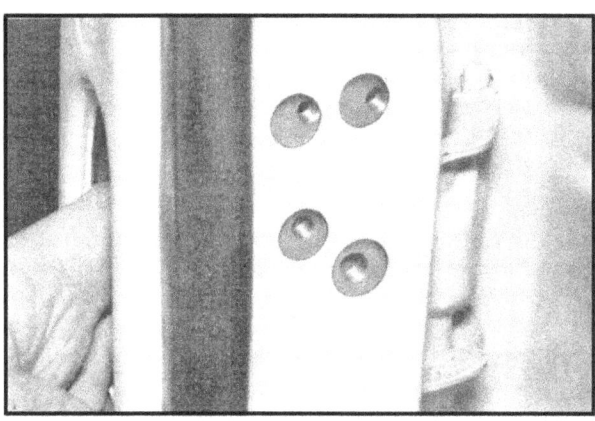

FRONT DOOR LOCK
Removing and installing

Remove the window frame. Unscrew and remove lock operating mechanism. Remove the guide buffer.

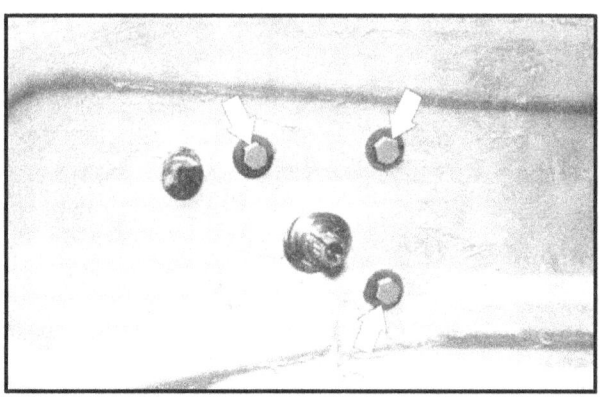

When installing: Insert spacing rollers into the guide buffer.

Remove screws holding lock. Remove lock in closed position complete with remote operating mechanism.

FRONT DOOR LOCK BARREL COMPLETE
Removing and installing

Remove inner door panel. Remove nut from inside of lock barrel. Extract the lock barrel towards the outside. Do not take down the lock barrel. When the lock barrel is removed, the key number can be seen. Replacement keys can only be delivered in pairs in accordance with the marking on the key head.

FRONT OUTSIDE DOOR HANDLE
Removing and installing

Detach outside door handle from lock operating levers.

When installing: In the closed position, the outside door handle must touch the rubber buffers.

FRONT OUTSIDE DOOR HANDLE AND LOCK OPERATING MECHANISM
Removing and installing
Take off the outside door handle. Remove the inside door panel. Remove all window frame attachment screws on the door lock side. Remove the lock operating mechanism. Lift the window frame and glass until the lock operating machanism can be removed.

When installing: Align the lock operating mechanism with the outside door handle.

FRONT INSIDE DOOR HANDLE
Removing and installing
Press the handle trim down at the rear and lift out at the front. Remove the screw and pull off the inside door handle with washer.

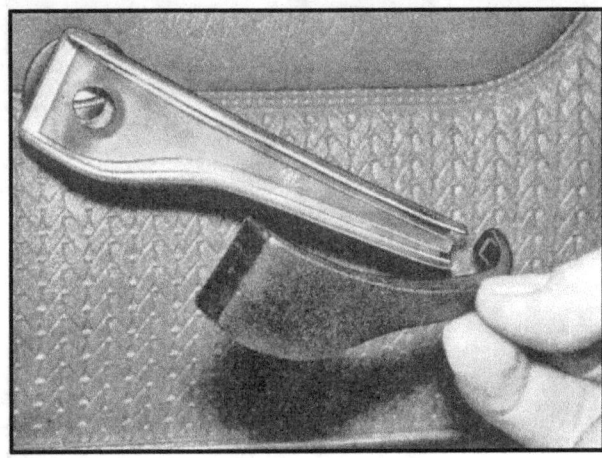

REAR DOOR STRIKER PLATE
Replacing
Unscrew (attach) the striker plate. Mark the installed position in pencil. (The threaded plate is attached to the door post.)

When installing: Screw on the striker plate lightly and align with the door lock. Adjust the striker plate so that the outer surface of the rear door is level with the rear side panel (fender) when closed. Then tighten the striker plate down firmly.

REAR DOOR LOCK
Removing and installing
Remove inner door trim panel. Remove remote lock operating mechanism. Detach the connecting rod at the door lock. Unscrew the front support bracket for the window frame and swing inwards. Take off the guide buffer.

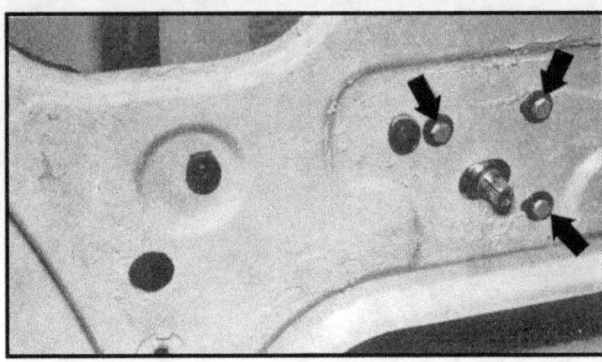

When installing: Insert the spacing roller into the guide buffer.

Remove the screws holding the lock. Remove the lock complete with remote operating mechanism in the closed position.

When installing: The child-proof lock mechanism lever should be in the upper (open) position.

CONNECTING ROD FOR LOCK MECHANISM
Removing and installing
Remove door trim panel. Detach bearing mounting. Detach the connecting rod at the door lock.

FRONT WINDSHIELD
Removing and installing
Pull off wiper arms. Carefully separate rubber surround from body, using a lip-type puller. Press out windshield with the feet, beginning in a top corner. Remove old sealing compound.

BODY

When installing: Replace rubber surround if porous. To prevent scratching the glass, use a soft support for the windshield. Pull on the rubber surround. Beginning at one corner, press the trim strip into the rubber surround.

Insert a cord or wire of approximately 0.12 in. diameter into the rubber surround. Overlap the ends by 12 in. Lip (A) should contain the cord or wire. Lip (B) should be evenly packed all around with Teroson 2322.

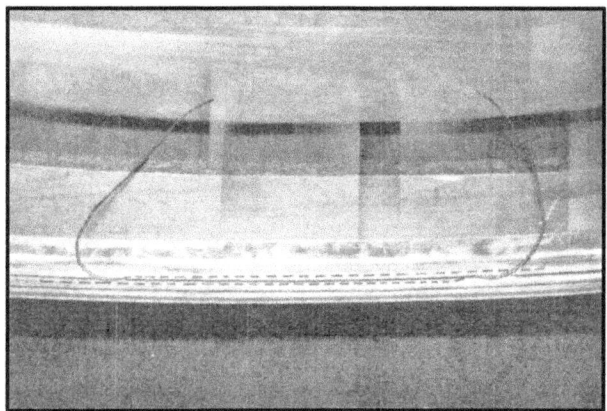

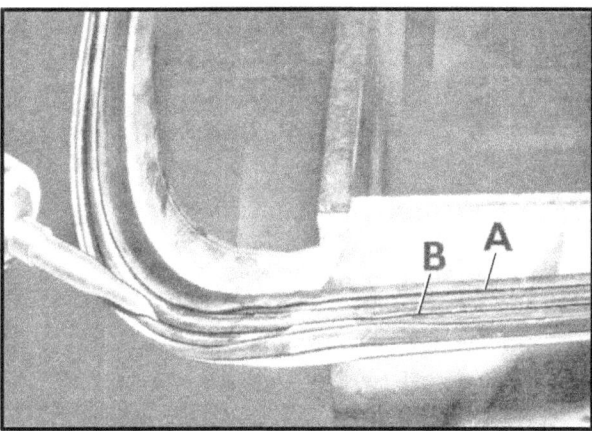

Place the windshield in this state of assembly against the window cutout and prevent from slipping sideways. Pull out the cord and force the rubber surround over the edge of the cutout in the body. As this installation process continues, force the windshield into its correct installed position by evenly distributed blows with a soft pad or the flat of the hand.

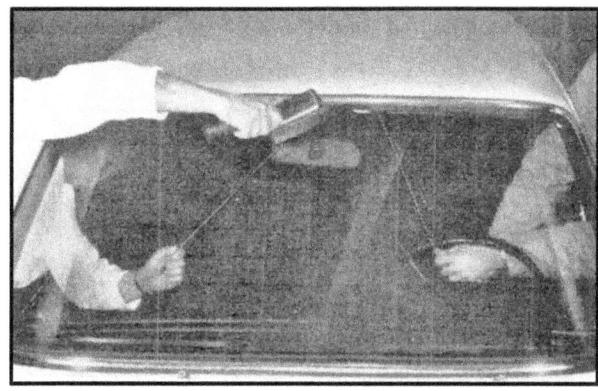

REAR WINDOW
Removing and installing

Pull off the connections to the electrically heated rear window.

When installing: Check correct operation of heating elements.

Beginning at one corner, force out the rear window by pressing with the feet.

When installing: For insertion of trim strip cut the rubber surround only if a Sigla laminated window is installed.

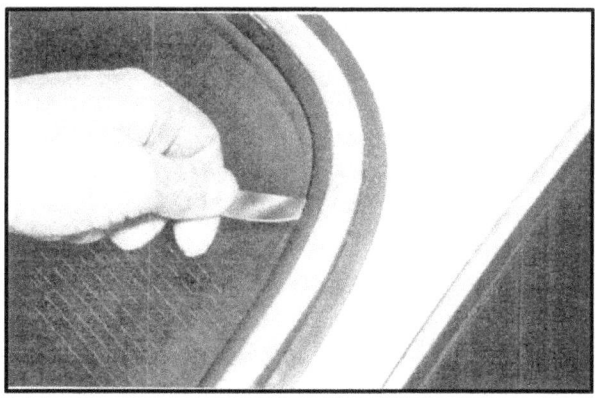

On 2800 CS/CS Automatic, remove rear seat. Unscrew the armrest at the top. Lift out the rear parcels shelf at one corner and disconnect the cable.

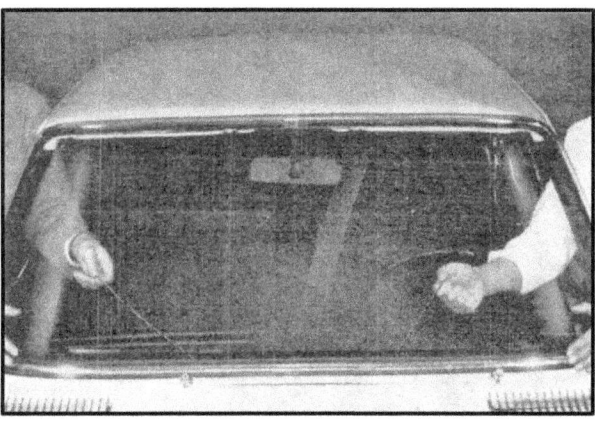

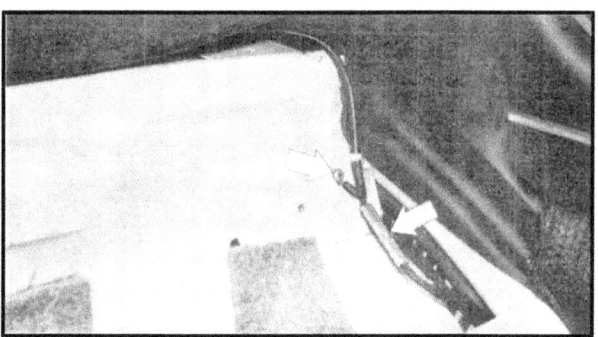

166 BODY

FRONT WINDOW LIFT HANDLE
Removing and installing

Pull away the insert trim. Remove the screw. Take off the handle with thrust washer.

When installing: With the window closed, the knob must point downwards.

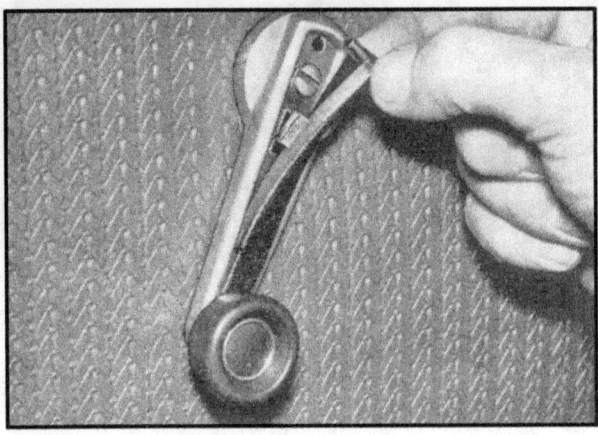

FRONT DOOR WINDOW LIFT MECHANISM
Removing and installing

Remove door trim panel. Take off plastic sheet. With the window closed, detach the window lift mechanism from the door. Hold the glass firmly at the top. Detach the lift arm from the lift rail.

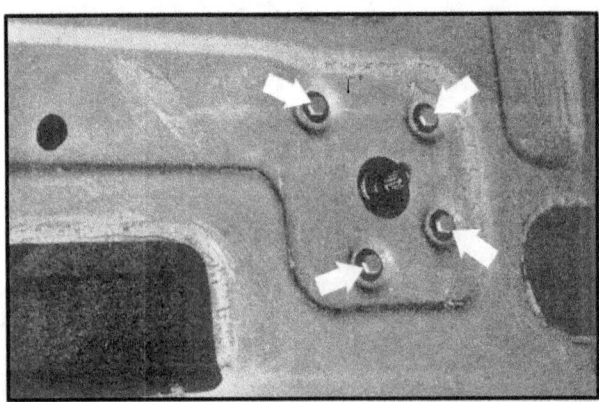

When installing: The lift rail must run between the two plastic washers. Apply a branded multi-purpose grease to the geared segment of the lift mechanism.

FRONT WINDOW LIFT RAIL HOLDER
Removing and installing

Remove door trim panel. Detach holder from lift rail.

When installing: Press the holder upwards, thus forcing both guide rollers against the guide rail.

FRONT DOOR WINDOW
Adjusting

Move the guide rail to align the door window with the window frame. Loosen the glass holder on the lift rail.

When installing: Press the holder upwards. Thus force both guide rollers against the guide rail.

Removing and installing

Take off the outer window aperture trim strip. Remove the window lift rail holder. Open the window by approximately 7 in., tilt forward and detach lift arm from lift rail.

When installing: The lift rail must run between the two plastic washers.

FRONT DOOR WINDOW FRAME AND GLASS
Adjusting

Remove the inner door trim. Partly remove the front and rear rubber door seal at the upper bolt holes.

When installing: Attach rubber door seal with Terakol 2444.

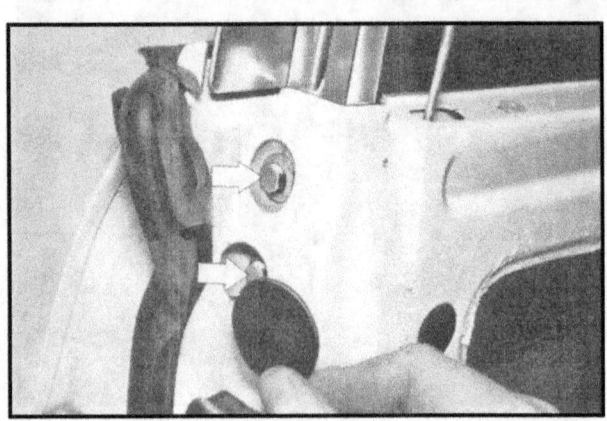

Loosen the bolts. Remove the upper and lower window frame retaining screws. Align window frame with body cutout. Tighten screws.

When installing: If necessary align door window glass with window frame.

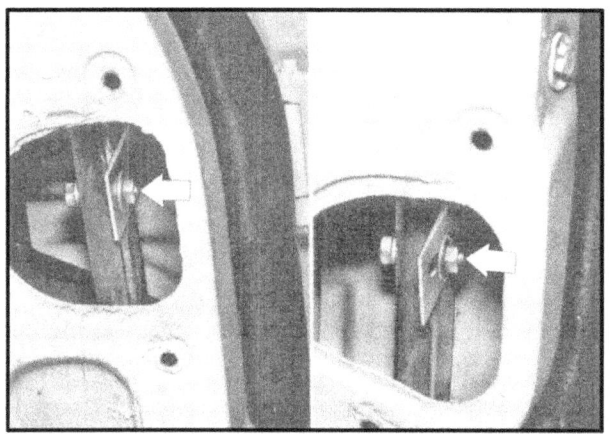

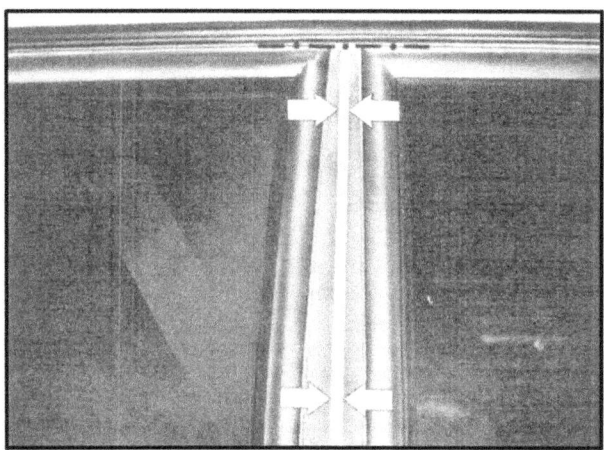

REAR WINDOW LIFT HANDLE
Removing and installing

Take off the insert trim. Unscrew the handle and take off complete with thrust washer.

REAR DOOR WINDOW LIFT MECHANISM
Removing and installing

Remove the inner door trim. Open the window by approximately 7 cm (2.75 in.) and detach the lift mechanism. Detach the lift arm from the lift rail.

When installing: The lift rail must run between the plastic washers.

REAR DOOR WINDOW GLASS
Removing and installing

Remove the window frame. Detach the glass from the lift arm and pull out upwards.

When installing: The lift rail must run between the plastic washers.

When installing: Adjust window frame position with the window lowered.

REAR DOOR WINDOW GUIDE RUBBER
Replacing

Remove window frame. Replace guide rubber.

When installing: Front and top guide rubbers with long face inside, rear guide rubber has both faces equal.

REAR DOOR WINDOW FRAME AND GLASS
Adjusting

Remove door trim panel. Remove screws holding window frame. Align window frame with body cutout. Push window frame towards body until the door sealing rubber is firmly pressed against the body.

When installing: Adjust window frame position with window open.

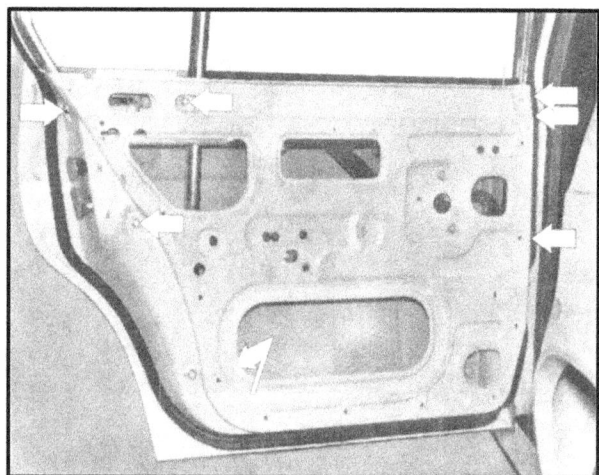

UPPER SECTION OF INSTRUMENT PANEL
Removing and installing

Remove (install) upper section of instrument panel housing. Pull out both central plugs. Unscrew speedometer drive shaft. Take off instrument carrier. Pull off control lever knobs. Partly loosen the right trim panel.

Remove the trim strip. Remove the clock. Remove screws. Remove screw, extreme left on bottom edge. Unscrew switch knob. Remove push-pull light switch. Remove screws.

BODY

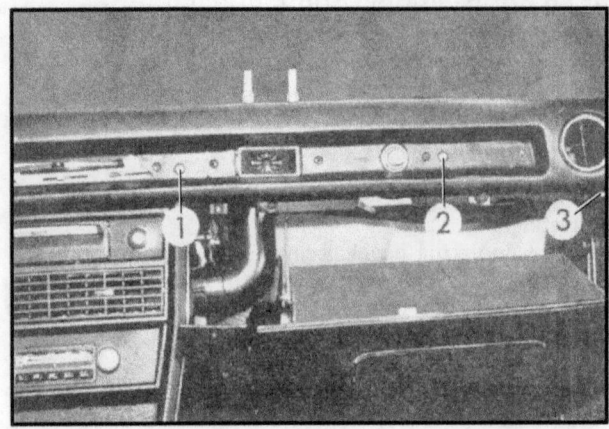

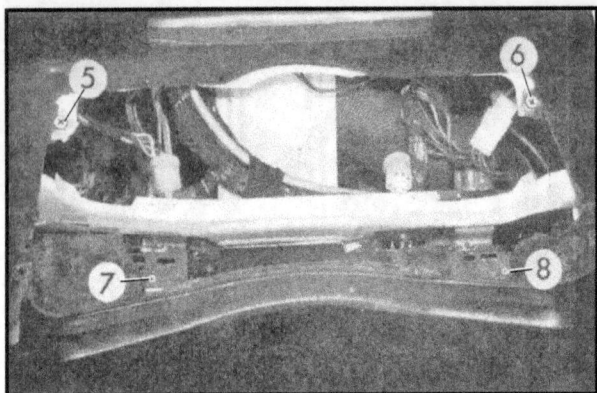

Detach instrument panel from support brackets. Pull away hoses from demister outlets. Remove 4 screws on top edge. Press down the inner ends of the demister slots and pull away the top cover forwards.

When installing: Push the outer demister slots under the metal clips.

UPPER SECTION OF INSTRUMENT PANEL HOUSING
Removing and installing
Remove screw at left. Remove screw at right. Pull away upper section of housing at front from instrument panel. Detach wires from loudspeaker.

LOWER CENTER LEFT SECTION OF INSTRUMENT PANEL HOUSING
Removing and installing
Open glove box at left. Remove screw. Take off the housing. Disconnect cables.

When installing: Connections to rear fog warning light switch: Yellow – white +, Grey – violet S, Brown –. Connections to heated rear window switch: Green – blue S, Black – red +, Brown –.

LOWER CENTER RIGHT SECTION OF INSTRUMENT PANEL HOUSING
Removing and installing
Open glove box at right. Remove keepers and press out pivot pins. Swing down the glove box. Remove screws and take off housing panel.

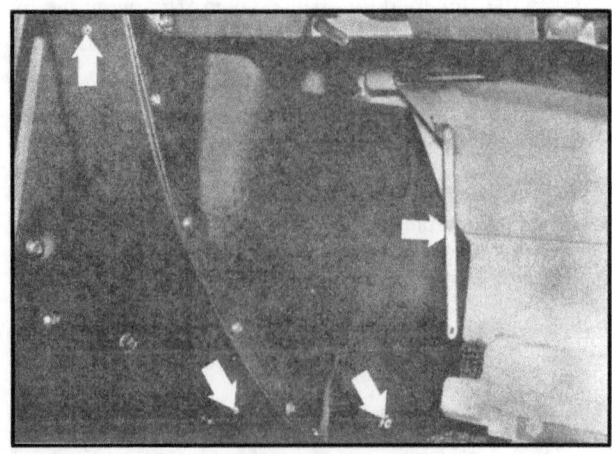

SLIDING ROOF
Adjusting
Remove the escutcheon, turn fully clockwise, then turn back 2 turns. Press the sliding roof panel evenly towards

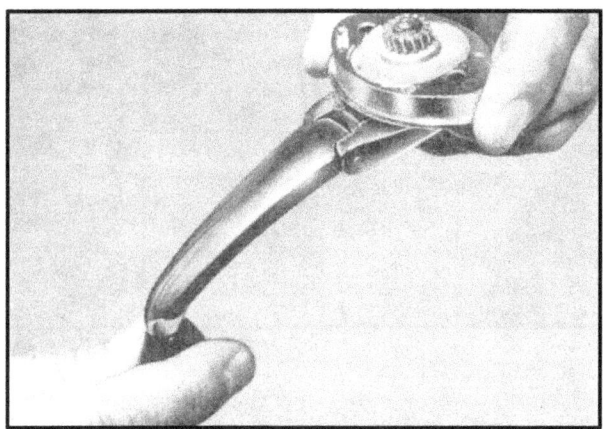

the front edge of the roof in order to align the guides. Install the escutcheon and close the roof several times. Keeping the roof closed, remove the escutcheon, turn fully clockwise, install and secure the handle in the center of the recess. The ideal sliding roof panel position is 0.04 in. deeper than the roof at the front and 0.04 in. higher at the back. Adjust after loosening screw. The guide piece has splines for height adjustment. For basic adjustment, mount the guide with the flat forked end on the guide rail. Fine adjustment is by turning the knurled nuts. If the cranked end is mounted on the guide rail, the sliding roof panel will be deeper at the front.

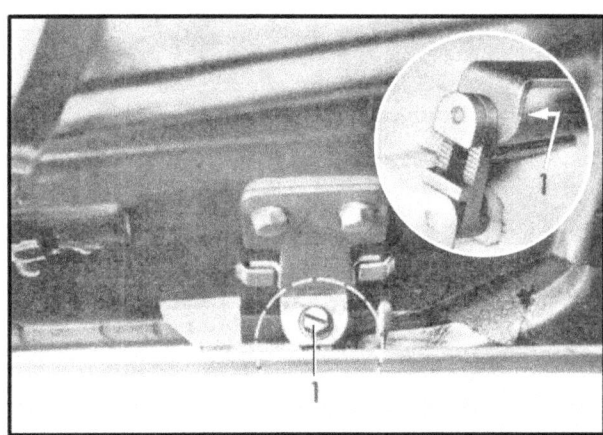

SLIDING ROOF PANEL
Removing and installing
Open sliding roof by about 20 cm (8 in.). Press away the front panel lining with a smooth, flat lever. Close the sliding roof. Push back the lining. Turn back the retaining spring. Remove the guide. Pull the keeper plate away from the guide. Remove the keeper plate and guide. Before removing, mark installed position of guide. Remove guide on the opposite side in the same sequence of operations. Lift out the sliding roof panel.

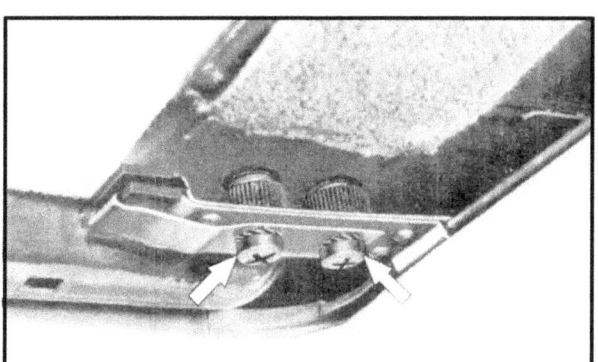

MOTOR AND GEARBOX FOR POWER SLIDING ROOF
Removing and installing
Open sliding roof by approximately 8 in. Open zip fastener. Remove screws for center cover plates. Remove screws for left and right cover plates. Remove sun visors and brackets. Pull out tumbler switch. Detach cables. Pull away tumbler switch surround. Remove the cover plate. Unscrew the engine with flexible drive shaft. Detach the cable connections. Unscrew and remove the center cover

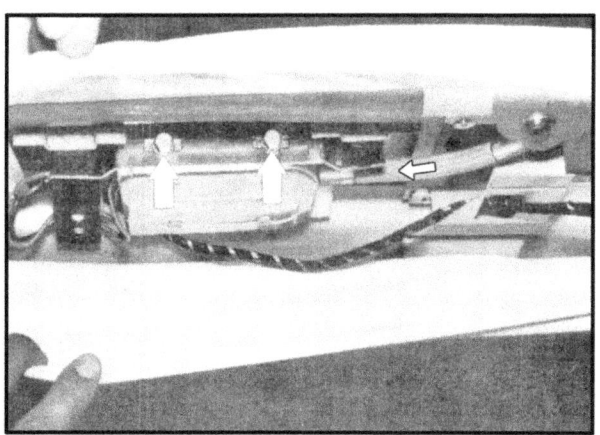

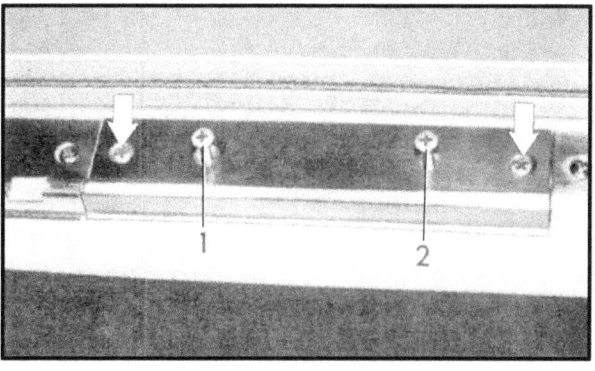

170 BODY

strip. The escutcheon is bolted to the drive plate with screws. Pull down the escutcheon and drive plate and remove. If the motor or electrical system develops a fault, the power sliding roof can be closed by hand. Open the zip fastener. Partly pull away the foam rubber sheet. Take off the plastic cap. Remove the screw. Shims underneath screwhead.

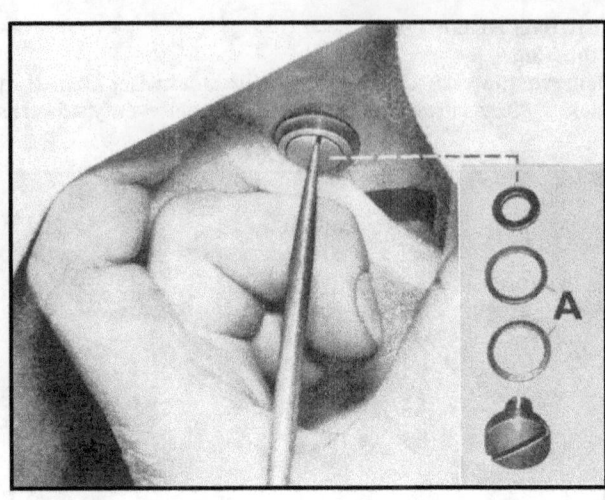

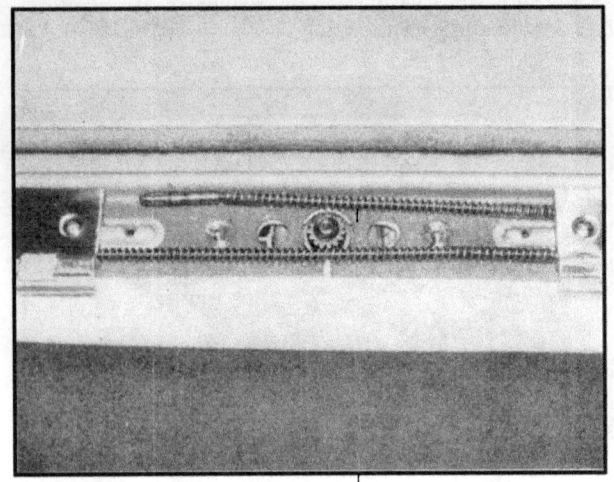

When installing: The shims are needed to adjust the slipping clutch. If the roof does not move when the motor is started, insert a shim. To close roof by hand, insert the handcrank into the threaded hole. Turn to close roof.

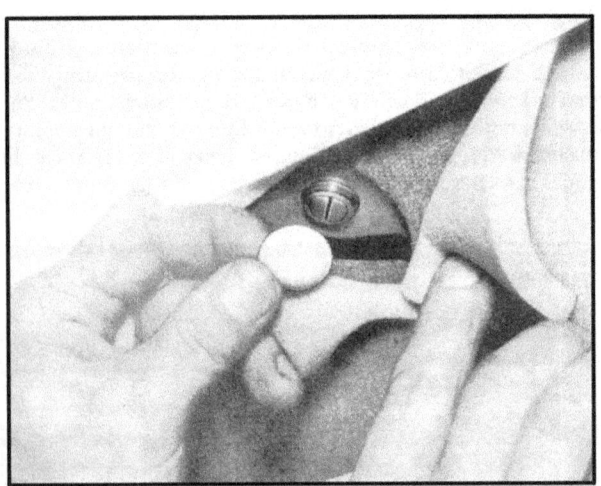

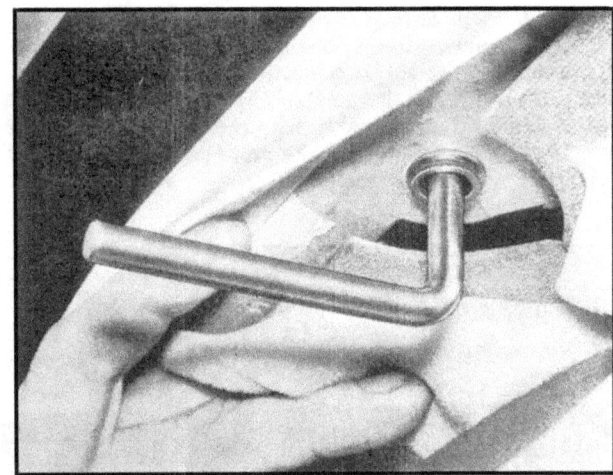

[Note: Specifications for 3.0 models same as 2800 models except as noted.]

Engine — Technical data

Type	2500	2500 Automatic	2800	2800 Automatic	2800 CS	2800 CS Automatic
Engine type reference (stamped next to engine number)	4310 Saloon 4311 USA sedan 4320 RHD saloon	4330 Saloon 4331 USA sedan 4340 RHD saloon	4410 Saloon 4411 USA sedan 4420 RHD saloon	4430 Saloon 4431 USA sedan 4440 RHD saloon	3421 Coupé 3421 USA coupé	3422 Coupé 3426 USA coupé
Bore mm (in.)	86 (3.3858)				89 (3.50) 3.0 model	
Stroke mm (in.)	71.6 (2.8189)		80 (3.1496)			
Stroke/bore ratio	0.83		0.93 (2800)		0.90 3.0 model	
Capacity (fiscal) cc (c. in.)	2478 (151.22)		2769 (168.97) 2800		2985 (182.1) 3.0 model	
Capacity (effective)	2494 (152.19)		2788 (170.13)			
Compression ratio	9.0 : 1					
Max. service output bhp (DIN) at engine speed (rpm)	150/6000		176/6000		180/6000 3.0 model	
bhp (SAE) at engine speed (rpm)	170/6000		192/6000			
Max. permitted continuous engine speed rpm	6000					
Output per litre bhp (DIN)	60.2		61.0			
Max. torque mkp (lb./ft.) at engine speed rpm	21.5 (154.8)/3700		24 (173.6)/3700		26 (188)/4300 3.0 model	
Torque per litre mkp (lb./ft.)	8.62 (62.31)		8.6 (62.2)			
Torque/weight ratio unladen mkp/1000 kg (lb./ft. per ton)	16.5 (121.5)		17.9 (132.1)		18.0 (132.8)	
Torque availability curve above mkp (lb./ft.) rpm	19.0 (137.4) 1920 ÷ 5870		21.0 (151.9) 1820 ÷ 5900			
Power/weight ratio in road trim with full tank kg/bhp (bhp/ton)	8.67 (118)		7.88 (128)		7.8 (130)	
fully loaded with luggage kg/bhp (bhp/ton)	11.82 (85)		10.65 (95)		10.05 (101)	
Mean piston speed m/sec (ft/min) at engine speed rpm	14.32 (2819) 6000		16.0 (3149) 6000			
Mean effective pressure kp/cm² (psi) at engine speed rpm	10.9 (165) 3700					
Compression test	good above 11.0 atm (156 psi) normal 10.0—11.0 atm (142—156 psi) poor 10.0 atm (142 psi)					
Test procedure	1. Remove spark plugs 2. Measure with calibrated compression pressure gauge: battery fully charged, engine at normal operating temperature, throttle fully open, engine rotated at starting speed.					
Weight complete kp (lb.)	204.5 (450)	192 (423)	207 (456)	194.5 (428)	211 (465)	198.5 (437)
Fuel consumption (DIN standard test method) litres per 100 km (mpg Imp./US)	10.9 (26/21.6)				10.5 (27/22.4)	
Specific fuel consumption g/bhp/hr at max. rated output rpm	242 6000		248 6000			

Engine lubrication:

System:	Pressure oil circulation, with pressure control valve in filtered oil circuit.
Oil filter	Full flow, with paper element and pressure relief valve
Opening pressure atm (psi)	2.5 ± 0.2 (25.6 ± 2.84)
Oil pump type	Rotor (Eaton system)
Oil pressure low level telltale illuminated below atm (psi)	0.2—0.5 (2.84—7.11)
Oil capacity litres (Imp./US pints)	5 (8.8/10.6) + 1.5 (2.6/3.2) if filter is changed
Oil consumption litres per 100 km (mpg)	0.05—0.1 (2800—5500)
Oil grade	Branded HD 4-stroke petrol engine oil
Viscosity for temperatures above 10° C (50° F) for temperatures below 10° C (50° F)	SAE 30 / SAE 20 W 40 / SAE 20 W 50 SAE 20 / SAE 10 W 30
Initial filling above 10° C (50° F) below 20° C (50° F)	Running-in grade 20 W 20 Running-in grade 10 W 10

Oil pump:

Oil pressure at idling speed atm (psi)	1.8—2 (25.6—31.3)
at max. engine speed atm (psi)	approx. 5 (71)
Pressure relief valve opens atm (psi)	4—5 (57—71)
Delivery rate litres (gal. Imp/US)/hr	approx. 2100 (460/555)
Clearance between extl. rotor and pump housing mm (in.)	0.1 ± 0.025 (0.0039 ± 0.00098)
Rotor extl. dia. mm (in.)	57.1 - 0.025 (2.2480 – 0.00098)
Housing intl. dia. mm (in.)	57.2 + 0.025 (2.2520 + 0.00098)

[Note: Specifications for 3.0 models same as 2800 models except as noted.]

Type	2500	2500 Automatic	2800	2800 Automatic	2800 CS	2800 CS Automatic
Rotor depth mm (in.)		22−0.041 (0.8661−0.00161)				
Housing depth mm (in.)	22+0.050 (0.8661+0.00197)					
Clearance between rotor and housing mm (in.)	0.050–0.091 (0.00197–0.00358)					
Backlash between intl. and extl. rotor mm (in.)	0.12–0.30 (0.0047–0.0118)					
Recess in cover max. mm (in.)	0.05 (0.0020)					
Free length of pressure relief spring mm (in.)	68.0 (2.677)					
Distance between housing bulkhead and pinion contact surface at hub mm (in.)	44.3 (1.744)					
Valve clearances: Adjust with engine cold or at max. 35° C (95° F) Inlet and exhaust	0.25 ÷ 0.30 mm (0.010 ÷ 0.012")					
Valve clearance adjustment.	by eccentric rocker pivots					

Order of adjustment

TDC Cyl. No.	Valve Overlap Cyl. No.
1	6
5	2
3	4
6	1
2	5
4	3

Valve timing: with 0.5 mm (0.02") clearance between cam base circle and rocker pad

	2500 / 2500 Auto / 2800 / 2800 Auto		2800 CS / 2800 CS Auto	
Inlet opens BTDC	6°		6°	
Inlet closes ABDC	50°		54°	
Exhaust opens BBDC	50°	± 2.5°	54°	± 2.5°
Exhaust closes ATDC	6°		6°	
Inlet phase (CS)	236°		240°	
Exhaust phase (CS)	236°		240°	

with 0.37 mm (0.015") clearance between cam base circle and rocker pad

	2500 / 2500 Auto / 2800 / 2800 Auto	2800 CS / 2800 CS Auto
Inlet opens BTDC	18°	18°
Inlet closes ABDC	62°	66°
Exhaust opens BBDC	62°	66°
Exhaust closes ATDC	18°	18°
Inlet phase (CS)	260°	264°
Exhaust phase (CS)	260°	264°

Valve operation:	
Valve gear	Light alloy rockers with case hardened pads, single overhead camshaft
Camshaft drive	Duplex roller chain, automatic oil-damped tensioner with backlash reducer
Timing chain	3/8" x 7/32"
Roller diameter mm (in.)	6.35 (¼)
Number of links	94

Valves:	
Overall length Inlet mm (in.)	106.5 ± 0.2 (4.193 ± 0.0079)
Exhaust mm (in.)	107.2 ± 0.2 (4.221 ± 0.0079)
Head dia. Inlet mm (in.)	46 (1.811)
Exhaust mm (in.)	38 (1.496)
Shank dia. Inlet mm (in.)	$8^{-0.040}_{-0.025}$ ($0.3150^{-0.0157}_{-0.0098}$)
Exhaust mm (in.)	$8^{-0.040}_{-0.055}$ ($0.3150^{-0.0157}_{-0.0217}$)
Min. thickness at rim Inlet mm (in.)	1.5 ± 0.1 (0.0591 ± 0.0039)
Exhaust mm (in.)	2.2 ± 0.1 (0.0866 ± 0.0039)
Max. valve head runout mm (in.)	0.02 (0.0008)
Valve seat ring extl. dia. Inlet mm (in.)	$47.15^{-0.009}_{-0.025}$ ($1.8568^{-0.00035}_{-0.0098}$)
Exhaust mm (in.)	$40.15^{-0.009}_{-0.025}$ ($1.5807^{-0.00035}_{-0.0098}$)
Bore in cyl. head for valve seat Inlet mm (in.)	$47^{+0.025}_{0}$ ($1.8504^{+0.0098}_{0}$)
Exhaust mm (in.)	$40^{+0.025}_{0}$ ($1.5748^{+0.0098}_{0}$)
Shrink fit in cylinder head mm (in.)	0.10 ÷ 0.15 (0.0039 ÷ 0.0059)

[Note: Specifications for 3.0 models same as 2800 models except as noted.]

Type		2500	2500 Automatic	2800	2800 Automatic	2800 CS	2800 CS Automatic
Valve seat angle		45°					
Valve seat width:							
Inlet	mm (in.)			1.6—2.0	(0.063—0.079)		
Exhaust	mm (in.)			2.0—2.4	(0.079—0.095)		
Valve seat ring oversize	mm (in.)			0.2	(0.0079)		
Valve guide overall length	mm (in.)			52	(2.047)		
Extl. dia.	mm (in.)			$14 ^{+0.044}_{+0.033}$	$(0.5512 ^{+0.00173}_{+0.00130})$		
Intl. dia.	mm (in.)			$8 ^{+0.015}_{0}$	$(0.3150 ^{+0.00059}_{0})$		
Bore in cylinder head	mm (in.)			$14 ^{+0.018}_{0}$	$(0.5512 ^{+0.00071}_{0})$		
Projection in cylinder head	mm (in.)			15–0.5	(0.591–0.0197)		
Shrink fit in cylinder head	mm (in.)			0.044–0.015	(0.00173–0.00059)		
Temperature of cylinder head for fitting				220—250°C	(430—480°F)		
Oversize diameters	mm (in.)			14.1/14.2/14.3	(0.5551/0.5591/0.5630)		
Valve operating clearance:							
Inlet	mm (in.)			0.025—0.055	(0.00098—0.00217)		
Exhaust	mm (in.)			0.040—0.070	(0.00157—0.00276)		
Max. wear tolerance	mm (in.)			0.15	(0.006)		
Valve operation: drive mechanism		Light alloy rockers with case hardened pads; single overhead camshaft.					
Camshaft drive		Duplex roller chain with automatic oil damped tensioner and backlash reducer					
Timing chain		3/8" × 7/32"					
Roller dia.	mm (in.)			6.35	(0.25)		
No. of links		94					
Valve springs: Colour code		Green spot[1]					
Wire thickness	mm (in.)			4.25	(0.167)		
Extl. coil dia.	mm (in.)			31.9	(1.26)		
Free length	mm (in.)			43.5[2]	(1.713)		
Spring force/test length		29 kp/37.6 mm (64 lb./1.48")[3]			70 kp/28.5 mm (154 lb./1.12")[4]		
Rockers: Bore in rocker	mm (in.)			15.5 + 0.018	(0.610 + 0.0007)		
Bore in cylinder head	mm (in.)			15.5 + 0.027	(0.610 + 0.0011)		
Rocker shaft dia.	mm (in.)			$15.5 ^{-0.016}_{-0.034}$	$(0.610 ^{-0.00063}_{-0.00134})$		
Rockers shaft running clearance	mm (in.)			0.016 ÷ 0.061	(0.00063 ÷ 0.00240)		
Rocker running clearance	mm (in.)			0.016 ÷ 0.052	(0.00063 ÷ 0.00205)		
Camshaft: Bearing dia.	mm (in.)			$35 ÷ 44 ÷ 45 ÷ 46 ^{-0.025}_{-0.041}$	$(1.378 ÷ 1.732 ÷ 1.722 ÷ 1.811 ^{-0.00098}_{-0.00161})$		
Bore in cylinder head	mm (in.)			$35 ÷ 44 ÷ 45 ÷ 46 ^{+0.034}_{+0.009}$	$(1.378 ÷ 1.732 ÷ 1.722 ÷ 1.811 ^{+0.00134}_{+0.00035})$		
Running clearance	mm (in.)			0.034 ÷ 0.075	(0.00134 ÷ 0.00295)		
Axial play	mm (in.)			0.03 ÷ 0.18	(0.0012 ÷ 0.0071)		
Max. vertical runout of helical pinion (distributor drive)	mm (in.)			0.025	(0.00098)		
Cam base circle dia.	mm (in.)	26.5836	(1.0466)	26.587	(1.0467)		
Cam lift	mm (in.)	6.8471	(0.2696)	7.1161	(0.2802)		
Chain tensioner piston length	mm (in.)			57.4 ± 0.1	(2.260 ± 0.004)		
Free length of tensioner rail spring	mm (in.)			155.5	(6.122)		
Spring wire thickness	mm (in.)			1 ± 0.015	(0.0394 ± 0.0006)		
Crankshaft: Bearing bore in crankcase	red mm (in.)			$65 ^{+0}_{+0.01}$	$(2.5591 ^{+0}_{+0.0004})$		
	blue			$65 ^{+0.01}_{+0.019}$	$(2.5591 ^{+0.0004}_{+0.00075})$		
Bearing shell thickness: Standard	red mm (in.)			$2.5 ^{-0.01}_{-0.02}$	$(0.0984 ^{-0.0004}_{-0.0008})$		
	blue			$2.51 ^{-0.01}_{-0.02}$	$(0.0988 ^{-0.0004}_{-0.0008})$		

[Note: Specifications for 3.0 models same as 2800 models except as noted.]

Type			2500	2500 Automatic	2800	2800 Automatic	2800 CS	2800 CS Automatic
1st Oversize	red	mm (in).			2.625 $^{-0.01}_{-0.02}$	(0.1033 $^{-0.0004}_{-0.0008}$)		
	blue				2.635 $^{-0.01}_{-0.02}$	(0.1037 $^{-0.0004}_{-0.0008}$)		
2nd Oversize	red	mm (in).			2.75 $^{-0.01}_{-0.02}$	(0.1083 $^{-0.0004}_{-0.0008}$)		
	blue				2.76 $^{-0.01}_{-0.02}$	(0.1087 $^{-0.0004}_{-0.0008}$)		
Bearing play, radial	red	mm (in).			0.030—0.700	(0.0012—0.0028)		
	blue				0.030—0.068	(0.0012—0.0027)		
Main bearing journal dia. Standard	red	mm (in).			60.0 $^{-0.01}_{-0.02}$	(2.3622 $^{-0.0004}_{-0.0008}$)		
	blue				60.0 $^{-0.02}_{-0.029}$	(2.3622 $^{-0.0008}_{-0.011}$)		
1st Oversize	red	mm (in).			59.75 $^{-0.01}_{-0.02}$	(2.3504 $^{-0.0004}_{-0.0008}$)		
	blue				59.75 $^{-0.02}_{-0.029}$	(2.3504 $^{-0.0008}_{-0.011}$)		
2nd Oversize	red	mm (in).			59.50 $^{-0.01}_{-0.02}$	(2.3425 $^{-0.0004}_{-0.0008}$)		
	blue				59.50 $^{-0.02}_{-0.029}$	(2.3425 $^{-0.0008}_{-0.0011}$)		
Big end bearing journal dia. Standard		mm (in).			48 $^{-0.009}_{-0.025}$	(1.8898 $^{-0.00035}_{-0.00098}$)		
1st Oversize		mm (in).			47.75 $^{-0.009}_{-0.025}$	(1.8781 $^{-0.00035}_{-0.00098}$)		
2nd Oversize		mm (in).			47.50 $^{-0.009}_{-0.025}$	(1.8701 $^{-0.00035}_{-0.00098}$)		
Guide bearing width Standard		mm (in.)			30 $^{+0.064}_{+0.025}$	(1.1811 $^{+0.00252}_{+0.00098}$)		
1st Oversize		mm (in.)			30.20 $^{+0.064}_{+0.025}$	(1.1890 $^{+0.00252}_{+0.00098}$)		
2nd Oversize		mm (in.)			30.40 $^{+0.064}_{+0.025}$	(1.1969 $^{+0.00252}_{+0.00098}$)		
Max. imbalance (dynamic) without flywheel		cmp			25			
Crankshaft axial play		mm (in.)			0.085 ÷ 0.174	(0.0034 ÷ 0.0069)		
Max. permitted runout at centre main bearing journal with crankshaft supported at outer main bearing journals		mm (in.)			0.03	(0.0012)		
Connecting rod: Overall length		mm (in.)			135	(5.315)		
Small end bore		mm (in.)			24 + 0.021	(0.9449 + 0.00083)		
Small end bush Extl. dia.		mm (in.)		Mfr. Vanderwell Mfr. Glyco	24.067 ÷ 24.092 24.073 ÷ 24.094	(0.9475 ÷ 0.9485) (0.9477 ÷ 0.9486)		
Big end bore		mm (in.)			52 + 0.01	(2.0472 + 0.0004)		
Big end bearing shell thickness Standard		mm (in.)			1.983 ÷ 1.993	(0.0791 ÷ 0.0795)		
1st undersize 0.025 mm (0.00098")		mm (in.)			1.995 ÷ 2.005	(0.0799 ÷ 0.0807)		
2nd undersize 0.25 mm (0.0098")		mm (in.)			2.108 ÷ 2.118	(0.0830 ÷ 0.0834)		
3rd undersize 0.5 mm (0.0197") (Mfr. Glyco)		mm (in.)			2.233 ÷ 2.243	(0.0879 ÷ 0.0883)		
Bearing play radial		mm (in.)			0.033 ÷ 0.069	(0.0013 ÷ 0.0027)		
Max. deviation from parallel in big end bores with bearing shells at 150 mm (5.9") spacing		mm (in.)			0.04	(0.0016)		
Max. weight variation of 6 connecting rods in a single engine		g (oz.)			± 4	(± 0.14)		
Cylinders: Bore Standard		mm (in.)			86 $^{+0.022}_{+0}$	(3.3858 $^{+0.00087}_{+0}$)		
1st rebore		mm (in.)			86.25 $^{+0.022}_{+0}$	(3.3956 $^{+0.00087}_{+0}$)		
2nd rebore		mm (in.)			86.50 $^{+0.022}_{+0}$	(3.4055 $^{+0.00087}_{+0}$)		
Surface roughness					3—4μ			
Max. out of roundness		mm (in.)			0.01	(0.0004)		
Max. cylinder bore concentricity		mm (in.)			0.01	(0.0004)		

[Note: Specifications for 3.0 models same as 2800 models except as noted.]

Type		2500	2500 Automatic	2800	2800 Automatic	2800 CS	2800 CS Automatic
Max. deviation of cylinder centre line from vertical related to bearing bore mm (in.)				0.05 (0.0197)			
Max. cumulative wear tolerance at piston and cylinder mm (in.)				0.10—0.15 (0.0039—0.0059)			
Piston: Piston type				raised oval crown			
Weight classification				stamped + or —			
Gudgeon pin class				stamped W or S			
Piston diameter (standard) mm (in.)	A			85.960 (3.3843)			
	B			85.970 (3.3847)			
	C			85.980 (3.3851)			
1st oversize + 0.25 mm (0.0098") mm (in.)	A			86.210 (3.3941)			
	B			86.220 (3.3945)			
	C			86.230 (3.3949)			
2nd oversize + 0.50 mm (0.0197") mm (in.)	A			86.460 (3.4039)			
	B			86.470 (3.4043)			
	C			86.480 (3.4047)			
Fan clutch: Cut-in temperature °C (°F) of air passing through radiator				55 (131) - 2.5[1])			
Max. imbalance cmp				4			
Vibration damper: Max. imbalance at 1000 rpm cmp				8			
Max. radial runout mm (in.)				0.2 (0.0079)			
Max. axial runout at 210 mm (8.27 in) dia. mm (in.)				0.4 (0.016)			
Flywheel: Max. imbalance (dynamic) cmp				2.5			
Max. axial runout mm (in.)				0.1 (0.004)			
Minimum thickness at friction surface mm (in.)				13.5 (0.53)			
Max. skimming depth of friction surface mm (in.)				0.4 0.1 (0.016 0.004)			
Starter ring - fitting temperature °C (°F)				200-230 (390 - 445)			
Piston installed clearance Mfr. Mahle mm (in.)				0.04 (0.0016)			
Max. weight variation between complete pistons of a single engine g (oz.)				9—10 (0.317—0.3542)			
Assembled piston weights Mfr. Mahle g (oz.)		−695—705 (−24.52—24.87) +705—715 (−24.87—25.22)		−672—682 (−23.70—24.06) +682—692 (+24.06—24.41)			
Piston rings: 1st groove (rectangular)[1]) Height mm (in.)				$1.75^{-0.01}_{-0.02}$ $(0.0689^{-0.0004}_{-0.0008})$			
End gap mm (in.)				0.30—0.45 (0.0118—0.0177)			
Flank clearance mm (in.)				0.015—0.029 (0.00059—0.00114)			
2nd groove (cut back)[1]) Height mm (in.)				$2.0^{-0.01}_{-0.022}$ $(0.0787^{-0.0004}_{-0.0009})$			
End gap mm (in.)				0.30—0.45 (0.0118—0.0177)			
Flank clearance mm (in.)				0.012—0.022 (0.00047—0.00087)			
3rd groove (equal chamfer)[1]) Height mm (in.)				$4.0^{-0.01}_{-0.022}$ $(0.1575^{-0.0004}_{-0.0009})$			
End gap mm (in.)				0.25—0.40 (0.0098—0.0157)			
Flank clearance mm (in.)				0.011—0.025 (0.00098)			
Gudgeon pins: Offset from piston centre line mm (in.)				1.5 (0.0591)			
Gudgeon pin dia. mm (in.) Colour code white				$22^{-0}_{-0.003}$ $(0.8661^{-0}_{-0.00012})$			
Colour code black				$22^{-0.003}_{-0.006}$ $(0.8661^{-0.00012}_{-0.00024})$			
Gudgeon pin bush intl. dia. mm (in.) Colour code white or stamped "W" on pin				22.003—22.005 (0.86622—0.86630)			
Colour code black or stamped "S" on pin				22.001—22.003 (0.86614—0.86622)			

[Note: Specifications for 3.0 models same as 2800 models except as noted.]

Type	2500	2500 Automatic	2800	2800 Automatic	2800 CS	2800 CS Automatic
Gudgeon pin clearance [1] in piston mm (in.)			0.001—0.005 (0.00012—0.00020)			
Gudgeon pin clearance in small end bush mm (in.) Colour code white			0.005—0.013 (0.00020—0.00051)			
Colour code black			0.008—0.016 (0.00031—0.00063)			
Thermostat: Opening commences			at 80° C (176° F) – equivalent temperature at engine outlet approx. 85° C (185° F)			
Water pump: Clearance between housing and impeller mm (in.)			0.9 ± 0.2 (0.0354 ± 0.0079)			
Delivery rate at engine speed 5700 rpm with thermostat open litres (gal. Imp./US)/hr.			approx. 9315 (2050/2460)			
Engine – electrical system						
Battery: Voltage			12			
Capacity Amp/hr			55			
Earth (ground)			Negative			
Minimum starting voltage			8.5			
Starter: Type (Bosch)			GF 12 V			
Starting short circuit current Amp.			approx. 380			
Starter output hp			1			
Torque mkp (lb/ft)			1.75 (12.5)			
Alternator: Type (Bosch)			K 1 14 V 45 A 20 [1]			
Max. output Watts			630 [2]			
Max. current Amp.			45 [3]			
Charging commences rpm (Alternator)			approx. 1000			
Max. speed of rotation rpm			12000			
Voltage regulator: Type (Bosch)			ADN 1/14 V			
Regulated voltage off load V			13.5—14.2			
on load V			13.9—14.8			
Coil: Type (Bosch)			KW 12 V			
Starting spark length			10 mm (0.4") at 300 sparks/min. and 6 V			
Service spark length			15 mm (0.6") at 3600 sparks/min.			
Ignition voltage under load V			16000—20000			
Spark plugs: Thread			M 14 × 1.25			
Bosch			W 175 T 2			
Beru			175/14/3			
Electrode gap mm (in.)			0.6 + 0.1 (0.024 + 0.004)			
Distributor: Type (Bosch)			0 231 116 053			
Contact breaker points gap mm (in.)			0.3—0.4 (0.012—0.016)			
Contact breaker spring pressure g (oz.)			500—630 (17.6—22.2)			
Dwell angle			35°—41°			
Firing order			1–5–3–6–2–4			
Condenser capacity µF			0.15—0.20			
Condenser insulation resistance			above 200 000 Ohm			
Condenser series resistance			below 0.01 Ohm			
Distributor rotor resistance			5000 Ohm			
Ignition point (static) for engine assembly			T. D. C.			
Ignition point [1] (dynamic) Engine at normal operating temperature vacuum advance hose disconnected			22° at 1700 rpm			
Max. centrifugal advance			$33° \pm 2°$ at crankshaft			

[Note: Specifications for 3.0 models same as 2800 models except as noted.]

Type	2500	2500 Automatic	2800	2800 Automatic	2800 CS	2800 CS Automatic
Max. vacuum advance	14° at crankshaft					
Ignition timing:	Measure only with dwell angle tester while engine is at normal operating temperature; illuminate the T.D.C. (O.T.) mark with a light pistol. Remove vacuum advance hose.					
at 1000 rpm	8° ÷ 12°					
1500 rpm	18° ÷ 22°					
1700 rpm	22°					
2000 rpm	22° ÷ 26°					
2500 rpm	26° ÷ 30°					
3000 rpm	30° ÷ 34°					
3500 rpm	31° ÷ 35°					
Vacuum advance Begins mm (in.) Hg	80 (3.150)					
Ends mm (in.) Hg	325 (12.795)					
Adjustment range	14°					
Ignition timing:	On distributor tester; measure at distributor shaft					
at 500 rpm	0° ÷ 5°					
750 rpm	6° ÷ 9,5°					
1000 rpm	9,5° ÷ 12°					
1200 rpm	10° ÷ 13°					
1500 rpm	11.5 ÷ 14.5°					

Cooling system

Coolant capacity including heater litres (pints Imp./US)	12 (21.1/25.4)
Filler cap: Blow-off pressure atm (psi)	$1^{+1.15}_{-0.10}$ $(14.2^{+2.1}_{-1.4})$
Vacuum atm (psi)	0.1 (1.4)
Leak-off rate at 1 atm (14.2 psi) litres (pints Imp./US) hr.	15 (26.4/31.7)
Antifreeze	Long-life branded antifreeze (renew every 2 years)
Radiator test pressure atm (psi)	1.5 (21.3)
Transmission cooler test pressure atm (psi)	5^{+1} $(71.1^{+14.2})$

Clutch

Type	2500	2800	2800 CS
Clutch pattern:	Single dry plate with torsional vibration damper		
Maker's reference	F & S MF 240 k Sph		
Contact pressure kp (lb.)	500 ÷ 570 (1100 ÷ 1255)	550 ÷ 620 (1210 ÷ 1365)	
Colour code	blue	yellow	
Extl. dia of driving plate mm (in.)	240 ± 1 (9.45 ± 0.04)		
Intl. dia of driving plate mm (in.)	155 ± 1 (6.10 ± 0.04)		
Lining: engine side gearbox side	T 50 s/17		
Total thickness (removed) mm (in.)	10.3 ± 0.3 (0.406 ± 0.012)		
(under 600 kg/1323 lb. pressure) mm (in.)	9.3 ± 0.3 (0.366 ± 0.012)		
Minimum thickness (removed) mm (in.)	7.8 (0.307)		
(under 600 kg/1323 lb. pressure) mm (in.)	6.8 (0.268)		
Max. disc runout at periphery (238 mm/9.37" dia.) mm (in.)	0.6 (0.024)		
Max. imbalance cm	20		
Withdrawal arm bush intl. dia. mm (in.)	$38^{+0.112}_{-0.050}$ $(1.4961^{+0.00441}_{-0.00197})$		
Withdrawal arm bush depth mm (in.)	42 ± 0.4 (1.6535 ± 0.0158)		
Guide sleeve on gearbox mm (in.)	$38^{+0.050}_{-0.075}$ $(1.4961^{+0.00197}_{-0.00295})$		
Clutch play at withdrawal arm	none — automatic compensation		
Play at clutch pedal mm (in.)	approx. 5 (0.2)		
Master cylinder bore mm (in.)	19.05 (0.75)		
stroke mm (in.)	max. 30 (1.181)		
Slave cylinder bore mm (in.)	22.2 (0.874)		
stroke mm (in.)	max. 23 (0.906)		
Clutch pedal travel mm (in.)	160 (6.299)		

[Note: Specifications for 3.0 models same as 2800 models except as noted.]

Type	2500	2800	2800 CS
Max. runout from plane of diaphragm spring ends mm (in.)	0.6 (0.024)		
Clutch pattern:	Single dry plate with torsional vibration damper		
Maker's reference	F & S MF 240 k Sph		
Contact pressure kg (lb)	500—570 (1100—1255)	550—620 (1210—1365)	
Colour code	blue	yellow	
Extl. dia. of driving disc mm (in.)	240 ± 1 (9.45 ± 0.04)		
Intl. dia. of driving disc mm (in.)	155 ± 1 (6.10 ± 0.04)		
Lining engine side / gearbox side	T 50 s/17		
Total thickness (removed) mm (in.)	10.3 ± 0.3 (0.406 ± 0.012)		
(under 600 kg/1323 lb pressure) mm (in.)	9.3 ± 0.3 (0.366 ± 0.012)		
Minimum thickness (removed) mm (in.)	7.8 (0.307)		
(under 600 kg/1323 lb pressure) mm (in.)	6.8 (0.268)		
Max. disc runout at periphery (238 mm/9.37" dia.) mm (in.)	0.6 (0.024)		
Max. imbalance cmg	20		
Withdrawal arm bush intl. dia. mm (in.)	38 +0.112/−0.050 (1.4961 +0.00441/−0.00197)		
Withdrawal arm bush depth mm (in.)	42 ± 0.4 (1.6535 ± 0.0158)		
Guide sleeve on gearbox mm (in.)	38 +0.050/−0.075 (1.4961 +0.00197/−0.00295)		
Clutch play at withdrawal arm	none - automatic compensation		
Play at clutch pedal mm (in.)	approx. 5 (0.2)		
Master cylinder bore mm (in.)	19.05 (0.75)		
stroke mm (in.)	max. 30 (1.181)		
Slave cylinder bore mm (in.)	22.2 (0.874)		
stroke mm (in.)	max. 23 (0.906)		
Clutch pedal travel mm (in.)	160 (6.299)		
Brakes: front	ATE 4-piston fixed caliper disc brakes with automatic pad wear compensation		
rear	ATE 2-piston fixed caliper disc brakes with automatic pad wear compensation		Internal expanding drums with leading and trailing shoes
Hand brake	Duo-servo drums		on rear wheels only
Pedal pressure approx. kg (lb.)	30 (66)		
Max. permitted free travel at brake pedal	²/₃ of total travel for 80% retardation; vehicle fully loaded		
Test pressure (ATE specification)	100 atm (1425 psi); not to fall by more than 10% in one minute		
Equalizing reservoir	on wheel arch, with warning device		
Brake unit	T 51/920 [1]		
Duplex master cylinder: Piston dia. mm (in.)	23.81 (9.4)		
Front wheel brake cylinders: Piston dia. mm (in.)	40 mm (1.575") 2 M 4 - 40 K		
Rear wheel brake cylinders: Piston dia. mm (in.)	42 mm (1.654") L 42 K		22.2 mm (0.874")
Brake disc dia. front mm (in.)	272.2 ± 0.2 (10.717 ± 0.0079)		
rear	272.2 ± 0.2 (10.717 ± 0.0079)		—
Max. lateral runout of brake discs (removed) mm (in.)	0.05 (0.002)		
Max. permissible thickness variation over rubbed area of brake disc mm (in.)	0.02 (0.0008)		
Min. brake disc thickness front mm (in.)	11.7 (0.461)		
rear mm (in.)	8.5 (0.33)		—

Brakes

Type	2500	2500 Automatic	2800	2800 Automatic	2800 CS	2800 CS Automatic
Max. imbalance of brake disc cmp	50					
Front brake pad material	Textar V - 1431 FF[1] (green-yellow-green) or Necto 244 FG[1] (white-green-white)					
Rear brake pad or lining material	Textar V - 1431 FF[1] (green-yellow-green) or Necto 244 FG[1] (white-green-white)				Bremsit 5710 or Energit 217	
Min. brake pad thickness mm (in.)	7.0 (0.28)					
Min. brake pad lining thickness mm (in.)	2.0 (0.079)					
Brake drum dia. mm (in.)	—				250 (9.84)	

[Note: Specifications for 3.0 models same as 2800 models except as noted.]

Type	2500	2500 Automatic	2800	2800 Automatic	2800 CS	2800 CS Automatic
1st skimming mm (in.)	—	—	—	—	250+0.5 (9.84+0.0197)	250+0.5 (9.84+0.0197)
2nd skimming mm (in.)	—	—	—	—	250+1.0 (9.84+0.0394)	250+1.0 (9.84+0.0394)
Max. ovality mm (in.)	—	—	—	—	0.1 (0.0039)	0.1 (0.0039)
Brake shoe width mm (in.)	—	—	—	—	40 (1.575)	40 (1.575)
Min. brake lining thickness mm (in.)	—	—	—	—	3.0 (0.118)	3.0 (0.118)
Handbrake: drum dia. mm (in.)	160.0 (6.30)	160.0 (6.30)	160.0 (6.30)	160.0 (6.30)	—	—
shoe width mm (in.)	25 (0.98)	25 (0.98)	25 (0.98)	25 (0.98)	—	—
lining material	Energit 338	Energit 338	Energit 338	Energit 338	—	—
Brake pressure limiter: cut-in pressure atm (psi)	20 (285)	20 (285)	20 (285)	20 (285)	—	—

Fuel supply

Carburetors: Type	Zenith 2-stage 35/40 INAT with exhaust emission control system					
Main jet Stage 1	X 115					
Stage 2	X 140	X 140	X 135	X 135	X 135	X 135
Air correction jet Stage 1	80					
Stage 2	120	120	100	100	100	100
Venturi Stage 1	24					
Stage 2	30					
Idling jet	40					
Idling air passage	1.5					
Fuel jet for heat-sensitive choke valve	60					
Mixture tube Stage 1	6 S fixed					
Stage 2	4 N					
Control passage Stage 1	0.8					
Stage 2	0.8					
Outlet passage in pre-atomizer Stages 1 & 2	3.1					
Float valve gasket mm (in.)	1.0 (0.04)					
Pump injection tube	0.5					
Pump piston with bore	0.3					
Volume injected per stroke cc	0.6 ÷ 0.9					
Float needle valve	2.0					
Float weight g (oz.)	8.5 (0.3)					
Throttle butterfly gap Stage 2 mm (in.)	0.05 (0.002) (air gap) (equal to main jet 130 ± 10)					
By-pass passage in throttle butterfly section for heat-sensitive choke valve Stage 2	70					
Air-boost cover Stage 2	130					
Choke butterfly opening	2.8 ± 0.1	2.8 ± 0.1	3.0 ± 0.1	3.0 ± 0.1	3.0 ± 0.1	3.0 ± 0.1
Heater filament (automatic choke)	14.6 Volt / 0.45 Amp.					
Heat-sensitive choke valve	20 Ohm					
CO mixture at approx. 1000 rpm	1.5 ÷ 2.5%					
Increased idle speed rpm with vacuum hose removed from closure damper	approx. 1800					

Carburettors: Type	Zenith two-stage 35/40 INAT					
Main jet Stage 1	X 117.5					
Stage 2	X 140					
Air correction jet Stage 1	80					
Stage 2	120	120	100	100	100	100
Venturi Stage 1	24					
Stage 2	30					
Idling jet	45					
Idling air passage	1.5					
Fuel jet for heat-sensitive choke valve	—	60	—	60	—	60
Mixture tube Stage 1	4 S	4 S	6 S	6 S	6 S	6 S
Stage 2	4 N					
Control passage Stage 1	0.8					
Stage 2	0.8					
Outlet passage in pre-atomizer Stage 1 and 2	3.1					
Float valve gasket mm (in.)	1.0 (0.04)					
Pump injection tube	0.5					
Pump piston with bore	0.3					
Volume injected per stroke cc	0.6 ÷ 0.9					

[Note: Specifications for 3.0 models same as 2800 models except as noted.]

Type	2500	2500 Automatic	2800	2800 Automatic	2800 CS	2800 CS Automatic
Float needle valve	2.0					
Float weight g (oz.)	8.5 (0.3)					
Throttle butterfly gap Stage 2 mm (in.)	0.05 (0.002) air gap (Equal to main jet 130 ± 10)					
Bypass passages	0.8 / 1.0					
Intermediate jet in throttle butterfly section Stage 2	—	70	—	70	—	70
Air boost cover Stage 2	—	130	—	130	—	130
Choke butterfly opening mm	2.8 ± 0.1		3.0 ± 0.1			
Heater filament (automatic choke)	14.6 Volt / 0.45 Amp.					
Heat-sensitive choke valve	—	20 Ohm	—	20 Ohm	—	20 Ohm

Gearbox

Type	2500	2800	2800 CS
ZF gearbox: S 4–18/3	4 speed mechanical gearbox with ZF-B synchromesh on all forward gears; 1 reverse gear		
Gear lever	Central, floor mounted		
Ratios: 1st	3.85 : 1		
2nd	2.08 : 1		
3rd	1.375 : 1		
4th	1.0 : 1		
Reverse	4.13 : 1		
Speedometer drive	2.5 : 1		
Oil grade	Branded gearbox oil, SAE 80, or HD 30 engine oil		
Capacity litres (pints Imp./US)	1.2 (2.1/2.5)		
Max. torque rating mkp (lb/ft)	25 (180)		
Mainshafts: Axial play mm (in.)	max. 1.5 (0.0591)		
Layshaft: Axial play mm (in.)	0.1—0.2 (0.004—0.008) with bearing slack taken up		
Press removal force 3rd/4th speed pinion kg (lb)	5000 (11000)		
Fitting temperature 3rd/4th speed pinion °C (°F)	150—180 (300—355)		
Output journal runout on output shaft mm (in.)	0.03 (0.0012)		
Output flange: Radial runout mm (in.)	0.07 (0.0028)		
Face runout mm (in.)	0.07 (0.0028)		

Automatic transmission

Type	2500 Automatic	2800/2800 CS Automatic
Manufacturer	Zahnradfabrik Friedrichshafen AG	
Coding on cover	001	003
Number of ratios	3 forward, 1 reverse	
Mechanical reduction ratios 1st	2.50	
2nd	1.50	
3rd	1.00	
Reverse	2.00	
Torque converter dia. mm (in.)	260 (10.24)	280 (11.02)
Converter reference mark	blue spot	yellow spot
Lock-up speed	2010 ± 50 rpm at 18 mkp (130.2 lb./ft.) torque	2020 ± 50 rpm at 20.2 mkp (146.1 lb./ft.) torque
Starting conversion ratio	2.0	2.05
Permitted imbalance g (oz.)	30 (1.06)	
Max. plane runout of welded tabs mm (in.)	0.3 (0.012)	
Initial oil filling litres (US quarts/Imp. pints)	8 (8.45/14.1)	8.3 (8.77/14.6)

[Note: Specifications for 3.0 models same as 2800 models except as noted.]

Type	2500 Automatic			2800/2800 CS Automatic	
Oil change	with engine running and at normal operating temperature, selector lever in position P				
Oil filling (refills) litres (US quarts/Imp. pints)	approx. 1.8 (1.9/3.16)				
Quantity of oil between upper and lower marks on dipstick litres (US quarts/Imp. pints)	approx. 0.6 (0.63/1.06)				
Shift points[1]) Selector lever position A	1st/2nd gear				
Accelerator pedal position	1/4	1/2	3/4	Full throttle	Kickdown
Shift speeds kph (mph) upward	15 (9.5)	15 (9.5)	36 (22.4)	42 (26)	66 (41)
downward	13 (8.2)	13 (8.2)	29 (18)	35 (21.8)	61 (38)
Selector lever position A	2nd/3rd gear				
Shift speeds kph (mph) upward	27 (16.8)	27 (16.8)	101 (63)	106 (66)	117 (73)
downward	25 (15.5)	25 (15.5)	64 (40)	70 (43.5)	111 (69)
Selector lever movement	from A to 2 (3rd to 2nd gear)				
Downward shift point[2]) at kph (mph)	130 (81)				
Selector lever movement	from 2 to 1 (2nd to 1st gear)				
Downward shift point[2]) at kph (mph)	79 (49)				
Primary pressure Throttle cable detached at position: Idle atm (psi)	13 ÷ 14.5 (185 ÷ 205)				
Kickdown atm (psi)	18 ÷ 19.5 (255 ÷ 277)				
Clutch A Throttle cable detached at position: Idle atm (psi)	5.9 ÷ 6.5 (84 ÷ 92)				
Kickdown atm (psi)	8.0 ÷ 8.6 (114 ÷ 122)				
Converter pressure Throttle cable detached at position: Idle atm (psi)	3.5 ÷ 4.5 (50 ÷ 64)				
Kickdown atm (psi)	5.0 ÷ 6.5 (71 ÷ 92)				
Shift restrictor valve pressure Throttle cable detached at position: Idle atm (psi)	1.5 ÷ 1.6 (21.3 ÷ 22.8)				
Kickdown atm (psi)	3.6 ÷ 3.9 (51 ÷ 55.5)				
Governor pressure in atm (psi) at 50 kph (31 mph) road speed	1.4 ÷ 1.6 (20 ÷ 22.8)				
Towing away distances up to	50 km (31 miles)				
max. speed kph (mph)	50 (31)				
above 50 km (31 miles) or 50 kph (31 mph)	Detach propeller shaft from final drive and tie up				
Gap between control unit housing and pressure restrictor piston mm (in.)	2.6 (1.02)				
Axial clearance between ball bearing outer race and transmission cover mm (in.)	0.05 ÷ 0.1 (0.002 ÷ 0.004)				
Axial clearance between clutch bodies A/B mm (in.)	0.15 ÷ 0.25 (0.006 ÷ 0.01)				
Axial clearance between centering plate and circlip mm (in.)	0.15 (0.006)				
Installed depth of needle roller bearing in pump wheel mm (in.)	1.7 (0.067)				
Radial clearance between output wheel and housing mm (in.)	0.072 ÷ 0.19 (0.0028 ÷ 0.0075)				
Axial clearance between pump wheels and housing mm (in.)	(0.03 ÷ 0.05 (0.0012 ÷ 0.002)				
Basic length of thrust rod mm (in.)	275 (10.83)				

Approved oil grades: **Initial or subsequent filling**

BP	AUTRAN DX	B-10 511
Chevron	Automatic Transmission Fluid DEXRON	B-10 122
Esso	Automatic Transmission Fluid DEXRON	B-10 103
Quaker State	DEXRON, Quadromatic ATF	B-10 128
Shell	Automatic Transmission Fluid DEXRON	B-10 709
Valvoline	Valvomatic ATF, Type B	B-10 312

[Note: Specifications for 3.0 models same as 2800 models except as noted.]

Type		2500 Automatic		2800/2800 CS Automatic	
Subsequent filling					
Aral	ATF DEXRON gearbox oil	B-10 373	Gasolin — DEXRON gearbox oil		B-10 547
Aral	ATF 546 DEXRON gearbox oil	B-10 546	Gulf — Automatic Transmission Fluid DEXRON		B-10 486
Aseol	Aseol DEXRON 16—712	B-10 669	Labomatic — DEXRON		B-10 647
Castrol	TQ DEXRON	B-10 658	Mobil — ATF 220 DEXRON		B-10 104
Castrol	TQ DEXRON	B-10 476	Mobil — ATF 220 DEXRON		B-10 467
Castrol	TQ DEXRON	B-10 578	Orvematic — ATF-DEXRON Fluid		B-10 588
Exactol	HFL B 492	B-10 492	Rhein. Mineralöl Amoco ATF DEXRON		B-10 595
Fina	DEXRON-ATF	B-10 572	Shell — Automatic Transmission Fluid DEXRON		B-10 492
Frisia	DEXRON-ATF	B-10 492	Sunamatic — 128 DEXRON Automatic Transmission Fluid		B-10 107
Fuchs	Automatic TF 25 DEXRON	B-10 653	Texaco — Texamatic Fluid 6673		B-10 334
Gasolin	DEXRON gearbox oil	B-10 290	Total — DEXRON		B-10 631
			Veedol — ATF Special B 101 DEXRON		B-10 579

Propeller shaft

Type		2500	2500 Automatic	2800	2800 Automatic	2800 CS	2800 CS Automatic
Front section f	mm (in.)	603.5 (23.76)	466.5 (18.37)	603.5 (23.76)	466.5 (18.37)	519.5 (20.45)	382.5 (15.06)
Rear section g	mm (in.)	1051 (41.38)					

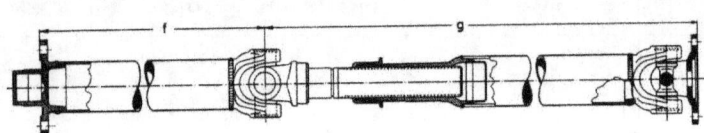

Rotary flank play at 60 mm (2.36") dia.	mm (in.)	0—0.03 (0—0.0012)
Universal joint radial play	mm (in.)	0.03 (0.0012)
Max. imbalance each side at test speed 3000 rpm	cmp	15
In centre, at test speed 3000 rpm	cmp	20
Permissible bending moment of steel joints	cmkp	3—7
Central bearing preload in direction of travel	mm (in.)	2 (0.079)

Front axle

		2500 / 2500 Automatic	2800 / 2800 Automatic / 2800 CS / 2800 CS Automatic
Track[1]	mm (in.)	1446 (56.93)	
Wheel travel (bump)	mm (in.)	90 (3.54)	
Wheel travel (rebound)	mm (in.)	90 (3.54)	
Coil spring:			
free length	mm (in.)	292^2 (11.5)	307.2 (12.09)
Wire thickness	mm (in.)	15 (0.591)	14.5 (0.571)
Coil extl. dia.	mm (in.)	166 ± 1.3 (6.535 ± 0.051)	165.5 ± 1.3 (6.516 ± 0.051)
Coil spring rating red white green	kg (lb.)	380–393 (838–866) 394–407 (869–897) 408–421 (899–928)	375–388 (827–855) 389–402 (858–866) 403–416 (888–917)
Auxiliary spring length	mm (in.)	85 (3.347)	
Anti-roll bar dia.	mm (in.)	—	17 (0.669)
Shock absorber type:		Spring strut, double tube telescopic	
Oil content between spring strut and shock absorber		Branded SAE 30 engine oil	
Capacity	cc	50	
Code letter		"A" = Manufacturer Boge / "B" = Manufacturer Fichtel & Sachs	"D"
Stroke	mm (in.)	177 (6.969)	
Shock absorber test:			
Test stroke	mm (in.)	25 (0.984)	25 (0.984)
Speed of rotation	rpm	100	100
Traction phase		85^{+7}_{-5} ($187^{+15.4}_{-11.0}$)	75 ± 5 (165 ± 11.0)
Compression phase	kg (lb.)	11^{+4}_{-3} ($24.2^{+8.8}_{-6.6}$)	10^{+2}_{-3} ($22.1^{+4.4}_{-6.6}$)

[Note: Specifications for 3.0 models same as 2800 models except as noted.]

Type	2500	2500 Automatic	2800	2800 Automatic	2800 CS	2800 CS Automatic
Wheel bearing lubrication: Packing between outer and inner bearings	50 g (1.8 oz.) Shell Retinax "A"					
Wheel hub cap	20 g (0.7 oz.) Shell Retinax "A"					
Friction rating of ball journal in guide joint Manufacturer						
Lemförder mkp (lb./ft.)	0.5 ÷ 0.7 (3.6 ÷ 4.9)					
Ehrenreich mkp (lb./ft.)	0.15 ÷ 0.5 (1.1 ÷ 3.6)					

Steering/wheel alignment

Front axle: Toe-in[1] mm (in.)	1 ± 1 (0.04 ± 0.04)					
Camber angle[1]	0° ± 30'					
Toe-out on turns[1] at 20° wheel lock (inner wheel)	1° 30'					
Kingpin inclination	6° 20'					
Castor	9° 30' ± 30'					
Rear axle: Toe-in[1] mm (in.)	1 ± 1 (0.04 ± 0.04)					
Toe-in unladen mm (in.)	2 ± 1 (0.08 ± 0.04)					
Camber angle[1]	2° ± 30' negativ					
Steering gear:	ZF-Gemmer				ZF hydraulic power-assisted	
Steering box ratio:	16.4 : 1				15.7 : 1	
No. of turns of steering wheel	4.4				4.1	
Splines on steering roller shaft	Taper, 1 1/8" X 36 ZGN 725					
Splines on worm	Parallel, 1 X 51 ZGM 715					
Straight-ahead position	Marked on steering box and worm splines					
Steered axle load kg (lb.)	800 (1764)				810 (1786)	
Max. wheel lock: Inner wheel	45°					
Outer wheel	35°					
Oil grade: Steering box	SAE 90 hypoid gear oil				See approved list on page 32-0/4	
Capacity cc	460				1200	
Friction rating for steering box in straight-ahead position cmkp	10–18				10–12	
Play in steering roller shaft mm (in.)	0.05 (0.002)				–	
Friction rating of worm bearing without oil seal cmkp	1 - 2.5				–	
Hydraulic power steering[2]: High pressure pump min. speed rpm	500					
max. speed rpm	6000					
Pressure atm (psi)	82 ± 7[3] (1170 ± 10)					
Friction rating for worm in piston cmkp	2 ÷ 4					
Friction rating for worm bearing in valve housing cmkp	1.5 ÷ 2.5					
Total friction rating of worm head cmkp	4 ÷ 6					
Friction rating of worm in intermediate cover cmkp	1 ÷ 2					

List of approved oils for hydraulic power steering

Initial or subsequent filling
Veedol   ATF Special 3433

Subsequent filling (max. ¼ litre/½ pint)
Aral   SGF AQ-ATF-1841 A gear oil
BP   Automatic Transmission Fluid Type A Suffix A AQ-ATF-2518 A
Castrol   TQ ATF AQ 737 A
Castrol   TQ ATF AQ 2418 A
DEA   DG 53 Type A AQ 1378 A
Duckham   Nolmatic-Fluid AQ 973 A
Esso   Automatic Transmission Fluid AQ-ATF-2974 A
Fina   Purfimatic Fluid AQ-ATF 2161 A
Fuchs   Fuchs Automatic TF AQ 837 A
Gasolin   Fluid AQ 1842 A gear oil
Labo   AQ-ATF-2660 A
Minera   Exaktol HFL 100 Automatic Transmission Fluid AQ 2415 A
Mobil   ATF 200 AQ 752 A
Quaker   State Quadromatic Fluid, Type A Suffix A AQ-ATF-899 A
Shell   Donax T6 AQ 2415 A
Stinnes-Fanal ATF Suffix A 67 AQ 2415 A gear oil
Sunoco   ATF AQ 737 A
Total   Fluide A AQ 1577 A
Valvoline Valvomatic ATF AQ 2694 A
Veedol   Automatic Transmission Fluid Type A Suffix A AQ 1407 A

Rear axle

Design:	Short neck			Short neck with limited slip differential		
Tooth contact pattern	Klingelnberg or Gleason			Klingelnberg		
No. of teeth	40 : 11			38 : 11		
Ratio	3.64 : 1			3.45 : 1		
Oil grade[2]	Branded running-in grade SAE 90[1] hypoid gear oil					
Capacity (initial filling) liters (pints Imp./US)	1.6 (2.8 / 3.4)					
(at oil change) liters (pints Imp./US)	1.5 (2.6 / 3.2)					
Tooth flank backlash between crown wheel and pinion mm (in.)	0.08–0.13 (0.0031–0.0051)					
Play between crown wheel/shim and differential bevel pinion mm (in.)	0.05–0.10 (0.0020–0.0039)					

[Note: Specifications for 3.0 models same as 2800 models except as noted.]

Type		2500	2500 Automatic	2800	2800 Automatic	2800 CS	2800 CS Automatic
Max. friction rating (differential bevel pinions)	mkp (lb/ft)	1.0 (7.2) at high spots on initial assembly, 2.0 (14.4)					
Friction rating (input pinion bearing without shaft sealing ring	cmkp	21–23					
with shaft sealing ring	cmkp	25–27					
Crown wheel bearing friction rating	cmkp	14–16					
Crown wheel assembly		cold					
Taper roller bearing assembly		cold					
Max. input pinion runout	mm (in.)	0.03 (0.0012)					
Height of input pinion head Klingelnberg	mm (in.)	37.0 (1.457)					
Gleason	mm (in.)	34.15 (1.345)					
Track[1]	mm (in.)	1464 (57.64)				1402 (55.30)[4]	
Wheel bearing play	mm (in.)	0.05 ÷ 0.1 (0.002 ÷ 0.004)					
Wheel bearing lubrication: per wheel		35 g (1.24 oz.) Shell Retinax "A"					
Wheel travel, bump	mm (in.)	90 (3.54)					
Wheel travel, rebound	mm (in.)	110 (4.33)					
Coil springs: Free length	mm (in.)	(306.2 (12.055))[2]		337.5 (13.287) (self-levelling)		344.8 (13.575)	
Coil spring rating red	kg (lb.)	354 ÷ 366 (780 ÷ 807)		255 ÷ 264 (562 ÷ 582)		397 ÷ 410 (875 ÷ 903)	
white		367 ÷ 378 (809 ÷ 833)		265 ÷ 273 (584 ÷ 602)		411 ÷ 425 (906 ÷ 937)	
green		379 ÷ 390 (836 ÷ 860)		273 ÷ 282 (602 ÷ 622)		426 ÷ 439 (939 ÷ 968)	
Wire thickness	mm (in.)	12.2 (0.480)		10.5 (0.413)		12.8 (0.504)	
Extl. coil dia.	mm (in.)	112.2 (4.417)		110.5 (4.350)		127.8 (5.032)	
Length of auxiliary cellular Vulkollan spring	mm (in.)	85 ± 1 (3.347 ± 0.04)				80 (3.150)	
Rubber disc thickness[3]	mm (in.)	approx. 15 (0.59)					
Anti-roll bar dia.	mm (in.)	18[a] (0.71) front, 8 (0.32) rear		16 (0.63) rear only		18 (0.709)	
Shock absorbers: type		spring strut, telescopic double tube		self-levelling spring/shock absorber strut		spring strut, telescopic double tube	
Colour code		black enamel					
Max. length	mm (in.)	550 ± 2.5 (21.654 ± 0.098)		552 ± 2.5 (21.732 ± 0.098)		550 ± 2.5 (21.654 ± 0.098)	
Min. length	mm (in.)	364 ± 2.5 (14.331 ± 0.098)		379 ± 2.5 (14.921 ± 0.098)		346 ± 2.5 (13.622 ± 0.098)	
Stroke limit		in traction phase				in traction and compression phases	
Shock absorber test: Test stroke	mm (in.)	25 (0.98)		50 (1.97)		25 (0.98)	
Speed of rotation	rpm	100		100		100	
Traction phase	kg (lb.)	35^{+5}_{-3}	$(77^{+11}_{-6.6})$	65 ± 8 (143 ± 17.6)		23 ± 4 (51 ± 8.8)	
Compression phase	kg (lb.)	10^{+4}_{-3}	$(22^{+8.8}_{-6.6})$	65 ± 8 (143 ± 17.6)		9 ± 3 (19.8 ± 6.6)	
Test stroke	mm (in.)	100 (3.94)		100 (3.94)		100 (3.94)	
Speed of rotation	rpm	100		100		100	
Traction phase	kg (lb.)	115^{+10}_{-5}	(254^{+22}_{-11})	135 ± 10 (298 ± 22)		105 ± 10 (231 ± 22)	
Compression phase	kg (lb.)	37^{+7}_{-2}	$(82^{+15.4}_{-44})$	135 ± 10 (298 ± 22)		39 ± 5 (86 ± 11)	
Halfshafts: Max. angular deflection		18°					
Axial displacement	mm (in.)	± 16 (0.63)					
Rotary backlash at 54 mm (2·13 in.) radius, max.	mm (in.)	0.1 (0.004)					
Joint assembly: force required	mkp (lb/ft)	100 - 500 (725 - 2170)					
Grease content per joint		120 g (4 oz.) Retinax AM					
Adhesive for flexible gaiter		Bostik 475					
Sealing compound for cover		Curil K					
Limited slip differential: Installed clearance of disc set with lozenge pattern	mm (in.)	0.1–0.2 (0.004–0.008)					
Installed clearance of disc set with spacer	mm (in.)	0.1–0.2 (0.004–0.008)					
Max. friction rating of differential pinions	cmkp (lb/ft)	50 (3.6)					
Wheels and tires							
Road wheels:		Disc					
Rim size (well base)		6 J x 14 steel disc or 6 J x 14 cast light alloy				6 J x 14 cast light alloy	
Max. vertical runout of rim	mm (in.)	1 (0.04)				0.3 (0.012)	
Max. lateral runout of rim	mm (in.)	1 (0.04)				0.3 (0.012)	
Wheel stud pitch circle	mm (in.)	120 (4.72)					
Approved suppliers		Kronprinz, Lemmerz, Südrad				Pedrini	
Tyres: Radial ply (tubed)		175 HR 14 or DR 70 HR 14		DR 70 HR14		195/70 HR x 14 3.0 model	

[Note: Specifications for 3.0 models same as 2800 models except as noted.]

Type	2500	2500 Automatic	2800	2800 Automatic	2800 CS	2800 CS Automatic
Max. tyre runout (vertical) mm (in.)		2 (0.08)				
Max. tyre runout (lateral) mm (in.)		2 (0.08)				
Tyre pressures: 175 HR 14		front				rear
Load up to: 4 persons atü (psi)		2.0 (28)				1.9 (27)
5 persons and luggage atü (psi)		2.1 (30)				2.2 (31)
DR 70 HR 14		front				rear
Load up to: 4 persons atü (psi)		1.9 (27)				1.8 (26)
5 persons and luggage atü (psi)		2.1 (30)				2.2 (31)
Winter or spiked tyres		no increase in pressure required				
Rolling circumference mm (in.)		1925 (75.79)				
Max. imbalance per wheel g (oz.)		10 (0.353)				
Road wheels:		Disc				
Rim size (well base)		6 J × 14 steel disc					6 J × 14 cast light alloy
Max. vertical runout of rim mm (in.)		1 (0.04)				
Max. lateral runout of rim mm (in.)		1 (0.04)				
Tyres: Radial ply (tubed)		175 HR DR 70 HR 14 or 195/70 HR 14				
Tyre pressures in atm (psi): 175 HR 14			front		rear	
Load up to: 4 persons			2.0 (28)		1.9 (27)	
5 persons and luggage			2.1 (30)		2.2 (31)	
DR 70 HR 14			front		rear	
Load up to: 4 persons			1.9 (27)		1.8 (26)	
5 persons and luggage			2.1 (30)		2.2 (31)	
Winter or spiked tyres		no increase in pressure required				
Rolling circumference mm (in.)		1925 (75.79)				
Max. imbalance per wheel g (oz.)		10 (0.353)				

Body

Length, overall mm (in.)		4700 (185.0)					4660 (183.5)
Width, overall mm (in.)		1750 (68.9)					1670 (65.7)
Height, overall (unladen) mm (in.)		1450 (57.1)					1370 (53.9)
Ground clearance (laden) mm (in.)		140 (5.5)				
Front overhang mm (in.)		865 (34.1)					955 (37.6)
Rear overhang mm (in.)		1143 (44.9)					1080 (42.5)
Luggage compartment dimensions: Width mm (in.)		1600 (63.0)					1500 (59.7)
Height mm (in.)		400 (15.7)					310 (12.2)
Depth mm (in.)		1150 (45.3)					1050 (41.3)
Capacity litres (cu.ft.)		approx. 650 (23)					approx. 450 (15.5)
Permissible trailer loads: unbraked kg (lb.)	650 (1433)	—	650 (1433)	—	650 (1433)	—
braked kg (lb.)		1300 (2866)				
Permissible load on roof kg (lb.)		75 (165)				

Air conditioning

Evaporator housing: Air distribution		Through standard fresh air grill - horizontal range of movement app. 60°, vertical app. 90°
Air circulation		Twin duct radial blower, speed continuously variable
Airflow cu.m (cu.ft)/min.		app. 7 (247)
Power consumption of blower motor Watts		132
Fuse Amps	16	25
Minimum outlet termperature at evaporator °C (°F)		0 - 4 (32 - 39)
Max. refrigerating capacity kcal (BTU)/hour		app. 4500 (17860)
Compressor: Type		York DA 210
Number of cylinders		2
Operating speed rpm		500 - 4500

[Note: Specifications for 3.0 models same as 2800 models except as noted.]

Type	2500	2500 Automatic	2800	2800 Automatic	2800 CS	2800 CS Automatic
Displacment per stroke cc	160					
Oil content cc	230 (min. 178 - max. 236)					
Oil grades	BP Energol LPT 100, Shell Clavus 33, Suniso No. 5, Texaco Capelle E					
Power consumption at max. speed HP	app. 9					
Clutch: Design	electromagnetic					
Type	Pitts 24 D - 05					
Condenser: Surface area sq. dm	18.1					
Block depth mm (in.)	40 (1.57)					
Refrigerant: Grade	Frigen R 12					
Capacity g (oz.)	1000 (35 oz.)					
V-belt:	Narrow section, 12.5 x 850 mm DIN 7753					
Dehumidifier: Capacity cu. dm	0.54					
Auxiliary electric blower: Position	In front of condenser, switched on and off together with electromagnetic clutch					
Manufacturer	Bosch JPA 12 V					
Design	5 bladed axial blower, 250 mm (9.8 in.) dia.					
Power consumption Watts	100					
Fuse Amps	16 (flying fuse)					
Vibration damper: Steel housing capacity app. cu.dm	0.54					

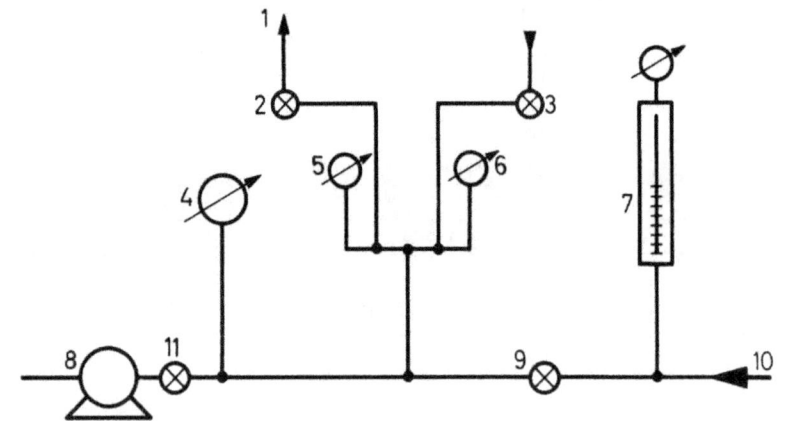

Fluid circuit
1 to compressor
2 Shutoff valve
3 Shutoff valve
4 Torr meter
5 Suction valve
6 Pressure valve
7 Filling column
8 Vacuum pump
9 Shutoff valve
10 to coolant reserve
11 Shutoff valve

Tightening torque values mkp (lb/ft)

Engine

Cylinder head bolts in 3 stages: 3 (22) - 7 (51) - 7 (51)	6.8 - 7.2 (49-52)	
Main bearing caps	5.8 - 6.3 (42-46)	
Big end bolts (12K)	5.2 - 5.7 (38-41)	
Flywheel to crankshaft[2)]	10.0 - 11.5 (72-84)	
Chain tensioner closure plug	3.0 - 4.0 (22-29)	
Flange on camshaft	14.0 (101)	
Clamp screw in rocker arm	0.9 - 1.1 (6.5-8.0)	
Plug for pressure relief valve on oil pump housing	2.5 - 3.0 (17-22)	
Oil drain plug	6.0 (43)	
Hollow bolt for camshaft oil feed	1.1 - 1.3 (8-9.5)	
Oil sump at crankcase and timing chest cover	0.8 - 1.1 (5.8-8)	
Vibration damper with hub on crankshaft	25.0 (180) with flat hex nut	
	35.0 (253) with shouldered hex nut	
Vibration damper to hub	2.2 0.2 (16 1.4)	

Engine – electrical system

| Alternator belt pulley | 3.5 ÷ 4.5 (25 ÷ 32.5) | Spark plugs | 2.3 ÷ 3 (17 ÷ 24) |
| Starter retaining bolts | 4.75 (34) | Oil pressure contact switch with cylindrical thread | 5 (36) |

Clutch

| Clutch to flywheel | $2.2^{+0.2}$ (16 + 1.5) |
| Thrust rod at clutch pedal | $3.2^{+0.3}$ (23 + 2.2) |

Brakes

Caliper to front steering knuckle	$8.0^{+1.5}$ (58 + 11)	Collar nut on brake pipe	$1.3^{-1.6}$ (9.4—11.6)
Caliper to rear axle	$6.0^{+0.7}$ (43 + 5.1)	Retaining bracket on brake unit rear	$2.2^{+0.2}$ (16 + 1.4)
Disc to wheel hub	$6.0^{+0.7}$ (43 + 5.1)	Brake unit bracket at wheel arch	$1.8^{+0.2}$ (13 + 1.4)
Hose to caliper	$1.3^{-1.6}$ (9.4—11.6)	Caliper halves: front	$4.2^{-0.5}$ (30—3.6)
		rear	2.2 (16)

[Note: Specifications for 3.0 models same as 2800 models except as noted.]

Type	2500	2500 Automatic	2800	2800 Automatic	2800 CS	2800 CS Automatic

Gearbox

Attachment to engine block M 8	2.5 (18)	Support bracket mounting	2—2.5 (14.5—18)	Centering flange	2—2.5(14.5—18)	
M 10	4.7 (34)	Output flange	14—16(100—116)	Gearbox casing	2—2.5(14.5—18)	

Exhaust system

Exhaust manifold to cylinder head	$2.2^{+0.2}$	(16+1.5)
Exhaust pipe to exhaust manifold	$4.3^{+0.5}$	(31+3.6)
Exhaust pipe triangular flange	$2.2^{+0.2}$	(16+1.5)

Automatic transmission

Transmission to engine M 8	2.5 (18)	Support shaft	1 (7)	
M 10	4.7 (34)	Primary pump	1 (7)	
Shoulder nut on output flange	10 ÷ 12 (72 ÷ 87)	Transmission extension	1.5 (11)	
Oil drain plug	3.5 (25)	Centrifugal governor	0.6 (4.3)	
End cap M 24 x 1.5	6 (43)	Converter dome	2.3 (17)	
M 18 x 1.5	3.5 (25)	Control unit	0.8 (5.8)	
Allen screws	1.5 (11)	Parking lock	1 (7)	
Converter dome to transmission extension	2.3 (17)	Notched cam sleeve	1.5 (11)	
Throttle cable	1.5 (11)			

Propeller shaft

Giubo joint	$6.0^{+0.7}$	(43+5)	Threaded bush	4.0 (2.9)
Centre bearing	$1.9^{+0.5}$	(14+3.6)	Propeller shaft to final drive	$6.0^{+0.7}$ (43+5)

Steering/wheel alignment

Steering wheel to steering column	$5.5+0.5$	(40+3.6)	Hoses on steering box	$4.5+0.5$	(32+3.6)
Joint disc	$1.9+0.5$	(14+3.6)	Hoses on hydraulic pump	$4.5+0.5$	(32+3.6)
Universal joint	$1.9+0.5$	(14+3.6)	Steering box to front axle beam	$4.0+0.7$	(29+5.1)
Steering drop arm at steering box	$12.0+2$	(87+14.5)	Guide lever to front axle beam	$8.0+2$	(58+14.5)
Hydraulic pump mounting on engine	$2.2+0.2$	(16+1.5)	Castellated nut on guide lever	8.0	(58)
Hydraulic pump to mounting	$2.2+0.2$	(16+1.5)	Track rod castellated nut	$3.5+0.5$	(25+3.6)
Adjusting screw locknut	3.0	(22)	Track rod clamp bolts	$1.2+0.3$	(8.7+2.2)

wheel

Wheel nuts	8^{+1}	(57+7.2)

Front axle

Spring/shock absorber strut at support bearing	$7.2+0.8$	(52+5.8)	Guide joint at track rod arm	$6.0+1$	(43+7.2)
Support bearing at wheel arch	$2.2+0.3$	(16+2.2)	Wishbone at front axle beam[1]	$15+2$	(108+14.4)
Spring/shock absorber strut threaded ring	$12.0+2$	(87+14.4)	Front axle beam to bodyshell	$7.3+0.8$	(53+5.8)
Track rod arm at steering knuckle	$2.2+0.3$	(16+2.2)	Trailing link to wishbone and front axle beam[1]	$6.2+2$	(45+14.4)

Rear axle

Housing cover	$2.0+0.5$	(14.5+3.6)	Hex bolt in drive flange	$9.0+1$	(65+7.2)
Crown wheel to differential housing (with loctite AVV)	$8.5+1$	(61+7.2)	Final drive to rear axle beam	$6.5+1$	(47+7.2)
Input pinion flange	15.0	(108)	Rubber mounting on body floor	$4.2+0.5$	(30+3.6)
Halfshaft to drive flange	$9.0+0.1$	(65+0.7)	Final drive to rubber mounting	$8.1+0.9$	(59+6.5)
Rear stub axle to drive flange	$25.0+5$	(180+36)	Crossmember at final drive	$6.0+0.7$	(43+5.1)
Halfshaft to final drive	$6.0+0.7$	(43+5.1)	Semi-trailing arm[1] at axle beam	$6.7+0.8$	(48+5.8)
Rear axle beam to body floor	$10.8+1.2$	(78+8.7)	Spring/shock absorber strut, lower end	$11.5+1.3$	(83+9.4)
Thrust links to body floor	$2.4+0.6$	(17.4+4.3)	Spring/shock absorber strut at wheel arch	$2.2+0.3$	(16+2.2)

LUBRICATION CHART 188

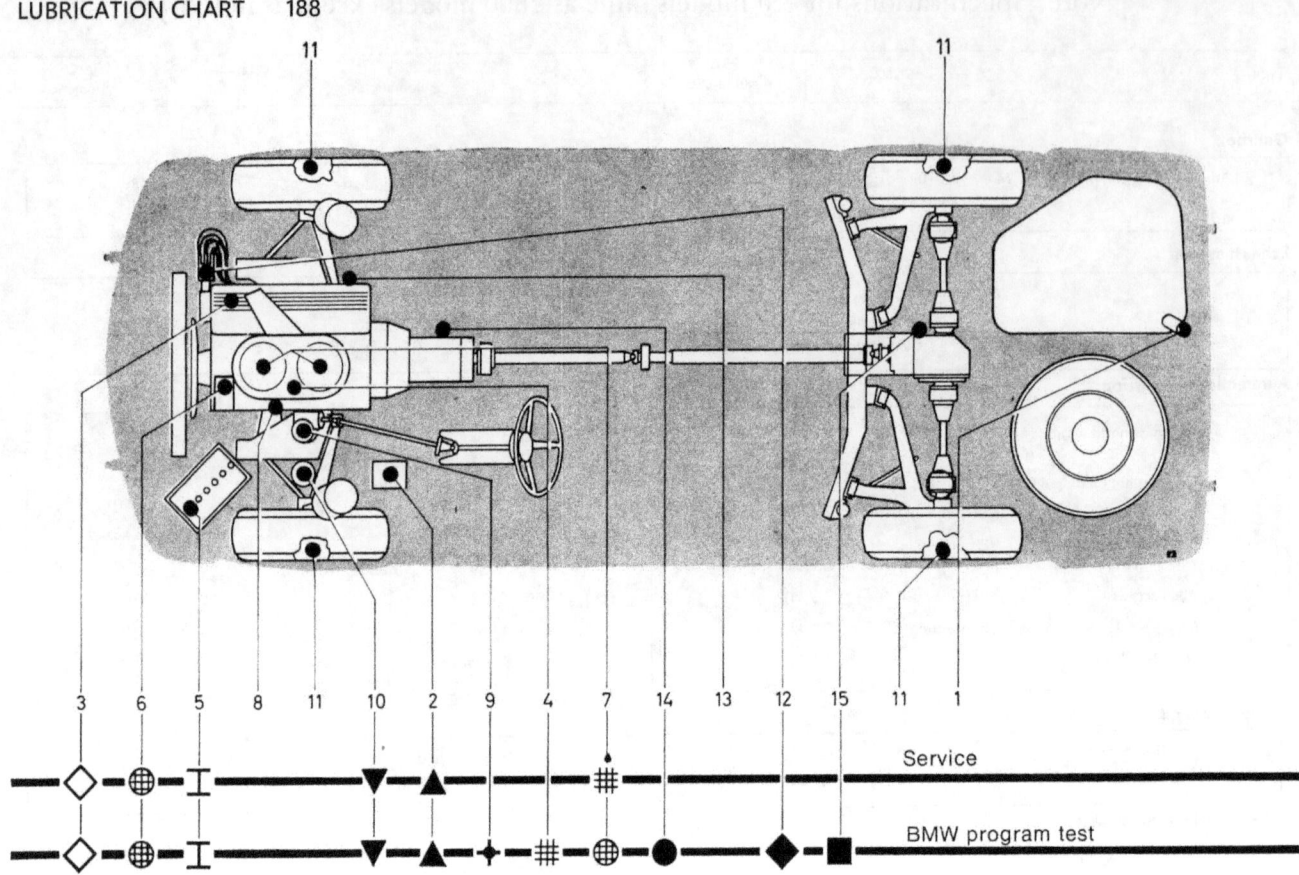

Key to lubrication chart

1.	Fuel filler	Branded super grade fuel
2.	Radiator filler cap on equalizing reservoir (Drain taps at lower right of radiator and rear right of engine block)	For details, see page 30 ▲ Check antifreeze concentration before and during the cold season
3.	Engine oil filler	Branded HD 4-stroke engine oil For grades, see page 45 ◇ indicates oil change
4.	Fuel pump mesh filter	⁑ indicates filter cleaning
5.	Battery	I Distilled water
6.	Engine oil filter	⊕ indicates filter renewal
7.	Intake air filter	⁑ indicates filter cleaning ⊕ indicates filter renewal
8.	Engine oil dipstick	Check oil level regularly
9.	Steering box (permanently filled) Power steering (optional) permanently filled	♦ Branded hypoid gear oil, SAE 90 ♦ Check oil level regularly (see page 47) For oil grades, see page 63
10.	Brake and clutch fluid reservoir	▼ ATE blue brake fluid; renew fluid in brake system once a year
11.	Wheel bearings (examine every 40 000 miles)	Shell Darina II grease, drip point 500° F (260° C) plus
12.	Distributor (for lubricating points, see page 48)	♦ Branded HD 4-stroke engine oil; Bosch Ft 1 v 4 grease
13.	Automatic transmission	Check oil level regularly
14.	Manual gearbox Automatic transmission	● Branded gear oil, SAE 80 (in an emergency, HD engine oil, SAE 30) For grades, see page 62 (change oil every 24 000 miles)
15.	Final drive	■ Branded running-in grade hypoid gear oil, SAE 90 (factory-approved grades can be recommended by a BMW dealer)

Important instruction for service shops

Lifting points for single-column car hoists with 4 pick-up pads:

Outer extremity of body, under the reinforced areas for the car's own jack.

Warning: If the car is hoisted up direct beneath the final drive, place a suitable piece of material between the jack pad and the housing to prevent damage to the final drive.

FUEL INJECTION SUPPLEMENT

Description

The Bosch D-Jetronic electronic fuel injection system is composed of 3 major subsystems: the air intake system, the fuel system, and the electronic control system. The D-Jetronic system uses constant fuel pressure and flow, so that only injection duration needs to be modified to control air/fuel mixture. The D-Jetronic system measures incoming airflow by monitoring intake manifold pressure. Engine speed, temperature, and other factors are monitored for the purpose of fine-tuning injection duration. An auxiliary air valve, cold start injector and thermotime switch aid in cold starting and operation.

Operation

Fuel system

An electrically driven fuel pump forces fuel through a filter, into the main system. Main system consists of one injector for each cylinder, a cold start injector and a pressure regulator, which maintains fuel pressure at 28 psi (2.0 kg/cm^2). A secondary system carries excess fuel from the pressure regulator back to fuel tank.

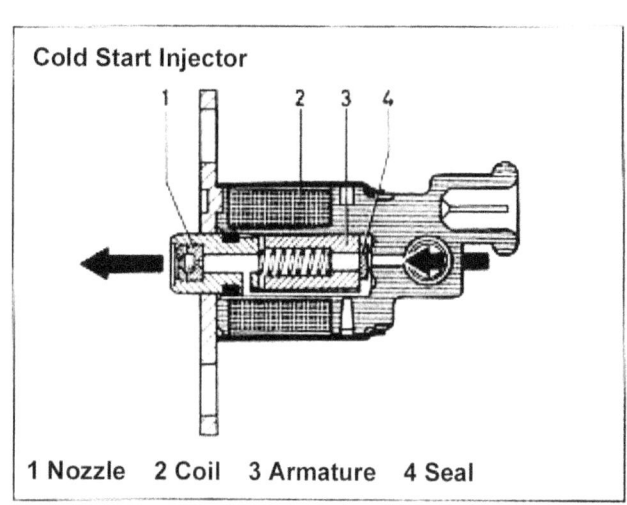

Cold Start Injector

1 Nozzle   2 Coil   3 Armature   4 Seal

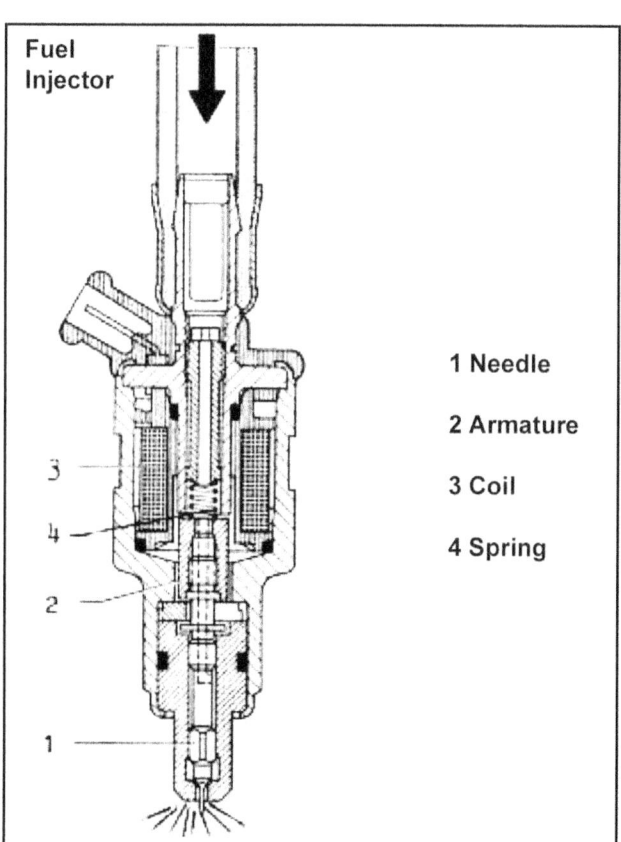

Fuel Injector

1 Needle
2 Armature
3 Coil
4 Spring

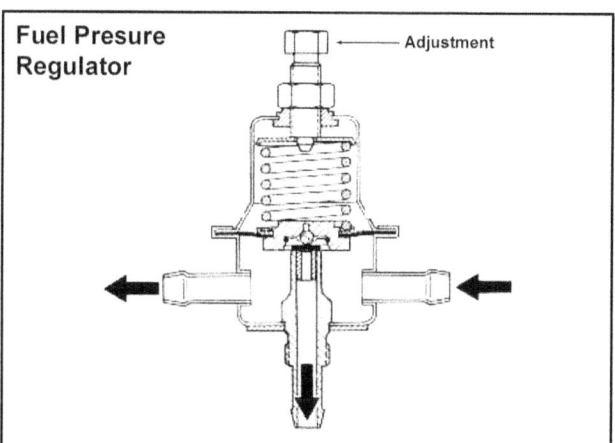

Fuel Presure Regulator

Air system

Intake manifold, connected to an intake air distributor, supplies the cylinders with air. A pressure sensor is connected to intake air distributor. The pressure sensor operates according to difference in manifold pressure and atmospheric pressure and signals control unit accordingly. A throttle valve, operated by accelerator pedal, is located at the mouth of the intake air distributor. The throttle valve and intake air distributor are connected to air cleaner by an air duct elbow. The idling air system is in the form of a by-pass system located between the air filter and air intake distributor. Its size can be varied with an idling air adjusting screw.

An auxiliary air line, from air cleaner (auxiliary air valve), to intake air distributor forms the warming-up air system. Its volume is varied, depending on engine temperature, by the auxiliary air valve.

FUEL INJECTION

Electronic control system

Electronic Control Unit

Control unit regulates the correct amount of fuel to be injected, depending on engine speed, intake pressure and engine temperature. When ignition is switched on, control unit receives its operating voltage directly from battery, via voltage supply relay. It also controls the fuel pump, which normally is provided with current from pump relay, only with engine running. A time switch, in control unit, allows fuel pump to run approximately 1 to 1.5 seconds after ignition is turned on. The control unit is connected to all sender units by a special wiring harness, coupled to a multiple plug. The control unit is usually located inside vehicle under the dash, under one of the seats or in the trunk.

Pressure Sensor

The pressure sensor is located in the engine compartment and is connected to the intake manifold by a vacuum hose. This sensor controls the basic amount of fuel to be injected, depending on pressure in the intake manifold and load on the engine.

Air Intake Temperature Sensor

The air temperature sensor provides control unit with information about air temperature, so that control unit can increase the injection quantity as necessary at low intake air temperature. This compensation ceases when intake air temperature is greater than 68° F (20° C).

Engine Temperature Sensor

The engine temperature sensor provides the control unit with information about coolant temperature (cylinder head temperature on VW). This enables control unit to adapt injection interval and determine how long the cold start injector should remain open during cold starting.

Triggering Contacts

The triggering contacts are located in the distributor. They provide signals which determine when and to which cylinder fuel is to be injected. The contacts also supply information concerning engine speed to determine the amount of fuel that needs to be injected into the engine.

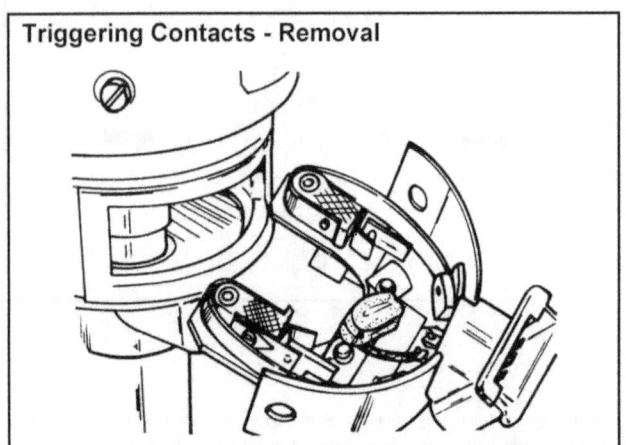

Triggering Contacts - Removal

Throttle Valve Switch

The throttle valve switch is mounted on the throttle housing. This switch signals the control unit of throttle position. During deceleration, above 1500 RPM, throttle switch cuts fuel supply off and below 900 RPM, fuel supply is turned on.

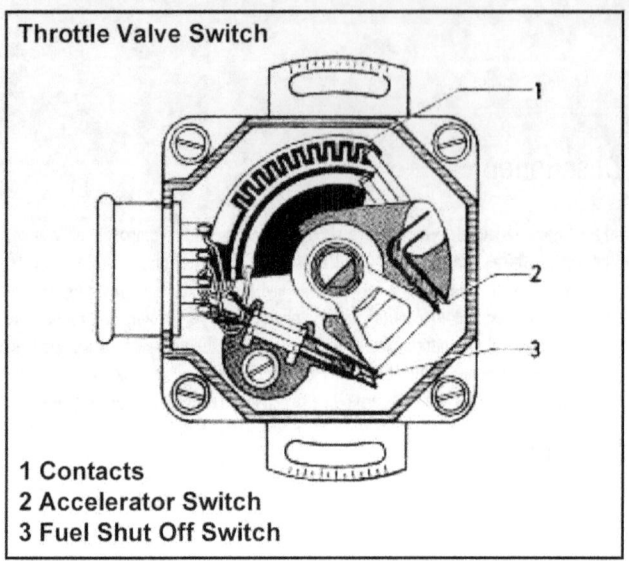

Throttle Valve Switch
1 Contacts
2 Accelerator Switch
3 Fuel Shut Off Switch

Auxiliary Air Valve

During cold starts, the auxiliary air valve opens to allow additional air into the inlet duct. As engine heats up, a bi-metallic element expands and closes valve. At approximately 140° F (80° C) the auxiliary air pipe is completely closed by the valve.

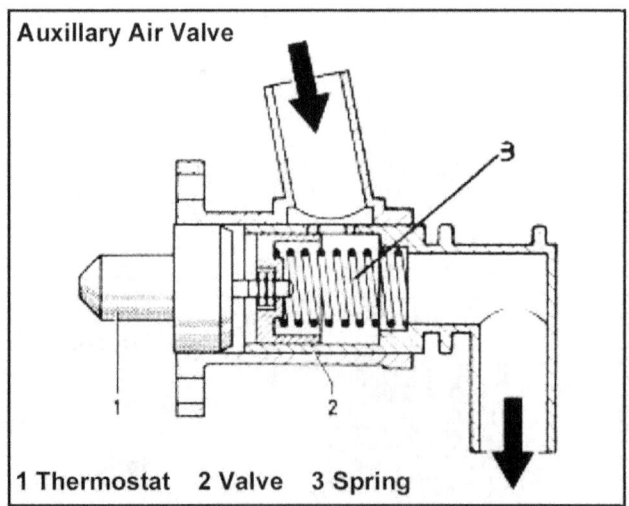

Auxillary Air Valve
1 Thermostat   2 Valve   3 Spring

BASIC ADJUSTMENT PROCEDURE

Description

3.0 Si, Si A, CSi, CSiA and 3.0 CSL models with 3.15 litre engines are equipped with electronically controlled fuel injection systems.

Fuel injection system

There are a number of control devices to ensure the correct timing and metering of this fuel injection charge, according to the ambient and engine temperature and the engine operating conditions at any moment. Apart from the items covered in this section, no attempts should be made to dismantle or adjust any part of the system. All such work should be carried out only by a BMW service station having the necessary special equipment and trained personnel.

Air cleaner:

The air filter element should be renewed at the intervals recommended in the manufacturer's service schedule. Between these periods, the filter element should occasionally be examined, and cleaned if necessary. To remove the element, release the spring clips and detach the air cleaner cover. Lift out the element. If renewal is necessary, discard the old element, wipe the inside of the air cleaner body and cover to remove dirt and grease, then reassemble using a new element. Note that the side of the element marked 'TOP' must be uppermost.

If the element is to be cleaned and refitted, blow out dirt using an air-line with pressure not more than 5 atmospheres (71lb/sq in). Apply the air jet from the bottom of the filter element only. Install the element as described previously.

To remove the air cleaner assembly complete, refer to **FIG 1**. Loosen the clamp on the throttle butterfly manifold and lift the air cleaner assembly from the guide rails. Detach the assembly by pulling the hose from the front panel. Refit in the reverse order of removal, releasing the catches securing the top cover before doing so. Relocate the catches on completion.

Slow-running adjustment:

Note that slow-running adjustments will only be effective if the sparking plugs, contact points and ignition system are in good order and the valve clearances correctly set. The injection system must also be operating correctly. Note that an accurate tachometer will be needed to check engine idle speed and suitable analytical equipment will be necessary to measure CO (carbon monoxide) content of the exhaust gas. If suitable equipment is not available for this purpose, the work should be carried out by a fully equipped service station.

It is most important that the engine is at normal operating temperature, with a coolant temperature of approximately 80°C (176°F) and an oil temperature of approximately 60°C (140°F). Make sure that the air cleaner element is in good condition as described previously.

Start the engine and adjust to an idle speed of 850 to 1000rev/min for European models, 900 to 950rev/min for USA models, using the idle air screw arrowed in **FIG 2**. Now adjust the fuel flow potentiometer arrowed in **FIG 3** to adjust the CO content of the exhaust gas. Turning anticlockwise will reduce emissions. CO content must be 1 to 2 per cent by volume for Europe, 1.5 to 2.0 per cent by volume for USA. Repeat the entire adjustment procedure if adjustment at the potentiometer alters engine idle speed beyond the stated limits. If the correct CO content cannot be obtained at the specified idle speed, the car should be taken to a service station for detailed checks to be made on the fuel injection system.

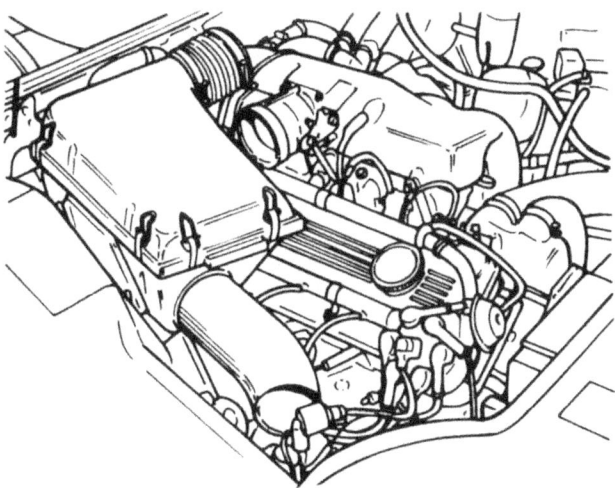

FIG 1 Air cleaner used with fuel injection system

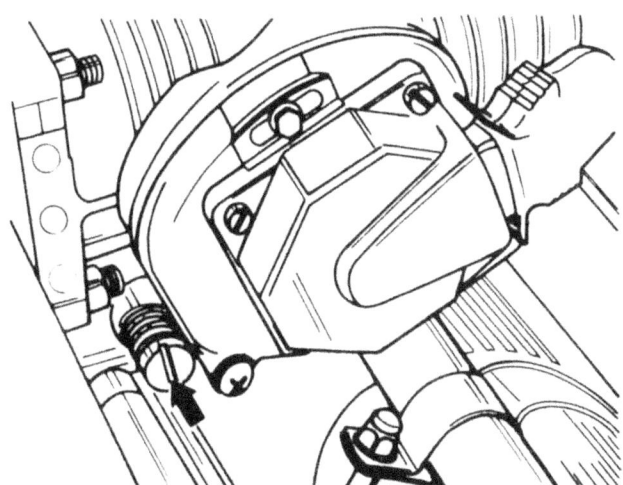

FIG 2 Idle air adjustment screw

FIG 3 Fuel flow potentiometer

FUEL INJECTION CURCIT

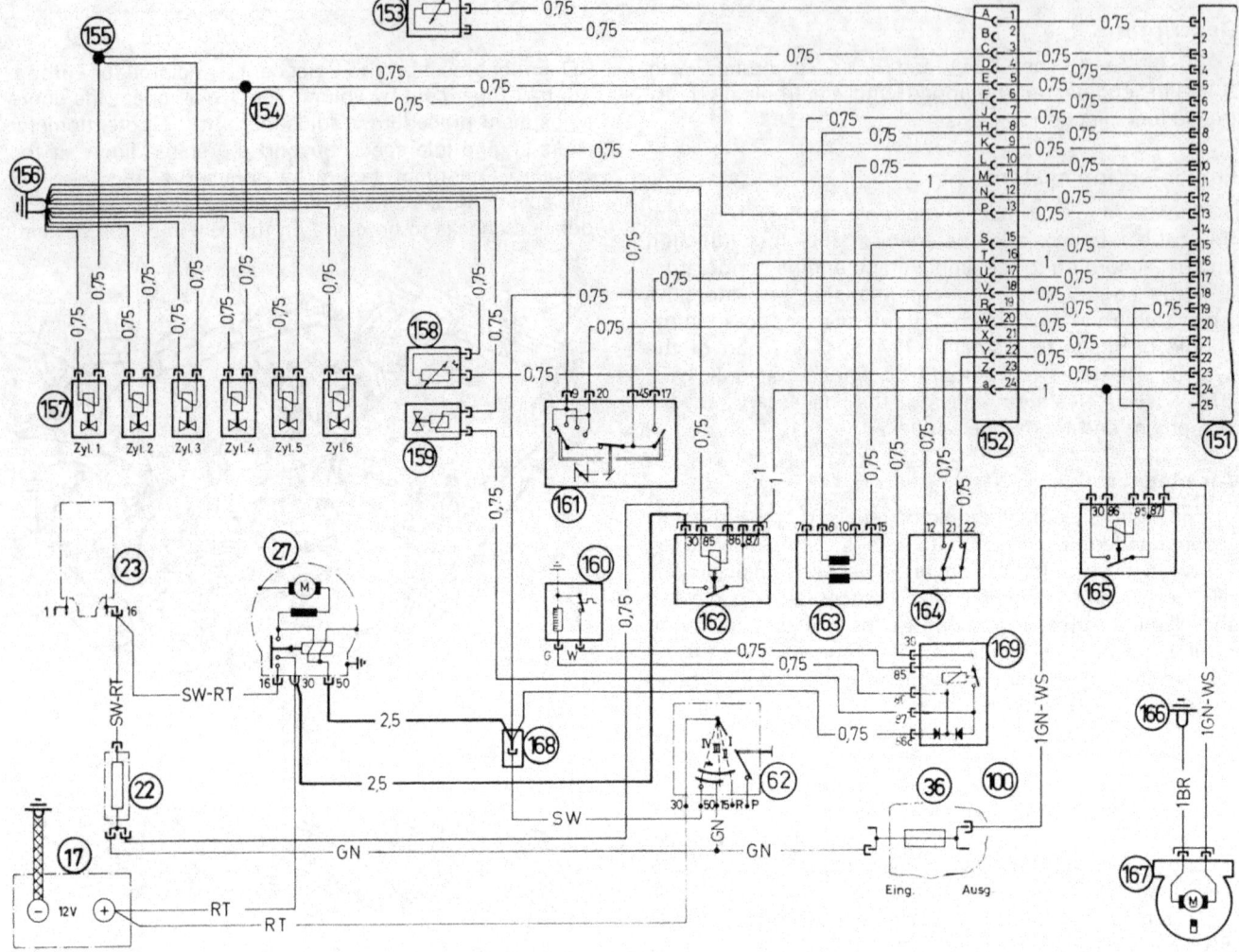

Key to fuel injection circuit: 151 Electronic control unit 152 Multiple plug 153 Temperature sensor, air 154 Soldered joint 155 Soldered joint 156 Earth 157 Injection valves 158 Temperature sensor, coolant 159 Starting valve 160 Thermo-switch, coolant 161 Throttle valve switch 162 Main relay 163 Vacuum sensor 164 Triggering device 165 Fuel pump relay 166 Earth 167 Fuel pump 168 Plug connector 169 Cold starting relay

17 Battery 22 Primary resistor 23 Ignition coil 27 Starter 36 Fuse box 62 Ignition/starter switch 100 Connection for electric fuel pump

Wiring colour code: **BL** Blue **BR** Brown **GE** Yellow **GN** Green **GR** Grey **RT** Red **SW** Black **WS** White

Where a cable has two colour codes, the first denotes the main colour, the second the colour of the tracer stripe.
The figure preceding the colour code indicates the cross-sectional area of the wire in sq mm.
The figure following the colour code is the individual cable number. Cables without code are black.

ADVANCED ADJUSTMENT PROCEDURE

NOTE: The ECU ground terminal, terminal No. 11, is used for electrical circuit testing. Ensure continuity exists between terminal No. 11 of the ECU and the vehicle chassis.

Voltage supply

1. Turn ignition on. Measure voltage between ECU terminals No. 16 and 11 of ECU connector. Measure voltage between ECU terminals No. 24 and 11 of ECU connector.

   See diagram above. If 11-12.5 volts are present, proceed to step 4). If no voltage is obtained, proceed to next step. If voltage is less than 11 volts, proceed to step 3).

2. If no voltage is present, check for open circuit in wire from main relay to ECU, defective main relay and/or ignition switch. Check for voltage at main relay terminals No. 86, 30/51 and 87. Replace relay as necessary.

3. If voltage is less than 11 volts, check for resistance in wires and/or connectors at ECU and main relay. Repair or replace as necessary.

4. If voltage supply to ECU and main relay is okay, check for voltage between terminal No. 50 on starter and ground. If 9-12 volts are present, system is okay. If no voltage but starter operates, repair open in wire from starter terminal No. 50 to ECU terminal No. 18. if less than 9 volts, check battery and resistance in wire from ignition switch to starter. If no voltage and starter is inoperative, replace ignition switch and/or repair open wire to starter.

Fuel pump

1. Connect pressure tester in fuel line between fuel pump and fuel supply lines. Remove injectors, fuel supply lines to intake manifold and cold start injector valve. Place pan beneath all injectors, to catch fuel being discharged. Connect remote starter switch to

ADVANCED ADJUSTMENT PROCEDURE - Contd.

terminal No. 50 on starter and to positive terminal of battery. Run starter and check that all injectors spray properly and evenly. If any one injector does not spray correctly, replace that injector.

2. Remove wire from terminal No. 33 of thermotime switch and ground the removed wire. if cold start injector does not spray, replace it. Operate starter and check fuel pressure. Pressure should be 3.0 psi (.21 kg/cm^2). If pressure is below specifications, crimp off fuel return line. Pressure should increase to 64.0 psi (4.5 kg/cm^2).

3. If pressure does not increase, or increase is not sufficient, check fuel filter, lines and/or pump. Remove crimp in fuel return line. if pressure is above initial specifications, adjust pressure regulator. If pressure does not decrease when crimped line is released, replace pressure regulator.

Manifold Pressure Control (MPC) sensor

1. Disconnect the harness connector at the MPC. Check the resistance at the MPC terminals. Terminal No. 11 is the ground circuit, there should be infinite resistance (open circuit) between terminal No. 11 and terminals No. 7, 8,10, and 15. Check primary resistance between terminals No. 7 and 15. Resistance should be about 90 ohms. Check secondary resistance between terminals No. 8 and 10. Resistance should be about 350 ohms. If resistance values are not to specifications or a short (continuity) exists between the ground circuit (terminal No. 11) and any of the other terminals, replace the sensor.

2. To check the harness, ensure MPC is disconnected and ignition is off. With the ECU connected ensure continuity exists between terminal No. 11, at the MPC connector, and vehicle chassis. If there is resistance in this circuit or an open exists, check ECU ground circuit. Disconnect the ECU connector. Check wiring continuity between the ECU and MPC connectors. If there is resistance (above 5 ohms) or an open, repair or replace wiring as necessary. With ECU and MPC disconnected there should not be continuity between harness terminals No. 1, 8, 10, or 15 and ground, if there is, repair short in wiring.

Injectors

1. Connect fuel pressure tester in line between fuel pump and fuel supply lines. Remove injectors and cold start injector valve. Place pan under all injectors, to catch fuel being discharged. Turn on ignition and operate a remote starter switch. Check spray of all injectors. If any one injector does not operate, replace it and recheck.

2. If all injectors of either group do not spray, check trigger contacts of distributor, trigger contact wiring to ECU and wires from ECU to injectors. If wires and connections check okay, replace ECU and recheck. If defect is still present, replace all injectors in that group and recheck. If recheck still shows defect, try another ECU.

3. If none of the injectors operate, disconnect MPC sensor electrical connector. Connect ohmmeter across terminals No. 15 and 7 of sensor. Reading should be 90 ohms. Connect ohmmeter across terminals No. 8 and 10. Reading should be 350 ohms. Reading between terminal No. 7 and ground should be infinite. If any of these readings are not within specifications, replace MPC sensor.

4. Sticking injectors can be detected with engine running. Connect tachometer, run engine and disconnect electrical connector to one injector at a time. Note RPM decrease. It RPM drop from one cylinder differs from that of all other cylinders, a faulty injector is indicated. Replace that injector and recheck. If same injector still show a defect, replace ECU and recheck.

NOTE: Do not overlook possibility of restriction in fuel line or connection to that injector.

Cold start injector

Perform pressure test. See step 1 under *Injectors* (see above). If cold start injector leaks during test it is defective and must be replaced. Remove connector at thermotime switch. and ground wire. Cold start injector should spray fuel during engine cranking. If fuel does not spray, temperature is either above 95°F (35°C) or injector is defective.

Air & engine temperature sensors

Disconnect electrical connectors of each temperature sensor. Use ohmmeter across terminals of sensor. If engine temperature is 68°F (20°C), air temperature sensor should have resistance of 260-340 ohms and engine temperature sensor should have resistance of 2100-3100 ohms. Each should have infinite resistance between terminals and ground.

Throttle valve switch

NOTE: If throttle terminal has voltage at all times, replace switch. If switch has no voltage, either before or after adjustment, replace switch.

1. Remove air cleaner. Loosen lock nut on throttle stop screw and turn out screw until it no longer touches throttle boss. Check that throttle is completely closed and throttle bore is clean. Screw in stop screw until it just touches boss, then turn it one additional full turn. Tighten lock nut.

2. Connect ohmmeter to terminals No. 9 and 12 of ECU connector. Depress accelerator slowly. Ohmmeter should fluctuate from zero to infinity. If zero reading only, replace switch.

3. Place accelerator at idle. Connect ohmmeter between terminals No. 12 and 17 of ECU connector. Ohmmeter should show continuity (zero ohm). If infinity reading is achieved, check throttle valve adjustment and/or check for open circuit. If infinity reading is still achieved, replace switch.

4. Slightly depress accelerator. Connect ohmmeter between terminals No. 12 and 17 of ECU connector. Ohmmeter should show infinity. If continuity (zero ohm) is achieved, check throttle valve adjustment and/or short in wires. Disconnect throttle valve switch and check ohmmeter reading. If continuity (zero ohm) is still achieved, and wires are okay, replace switch.

Auxiliary air valve

Remove hoses connected to each side of air valve. With cold engines (less than 95°F, 39°C), auxiliary air regulator should be at least partially open. To check valve, use a mirror and light and look through valve opening. Turn ignition on and make sure regulator valve closes within a few minutes.

Distributor trigger contacts

1. Attach one ohmmeter lead to terminal No. 12 on trigger connector. Alternately attach second lead to terminals No. 13, 14, 21 and 22 on trigger connector and note reading of each, while cranking engine without starting. See Fig. 10 or 11.

2. Ohmmeter should fluctuate between infinity and zero. If ohmmeter reading remains either infinity or zero, check each wire and connector terminal. If wires and terminals check okay, replace trigger contacts.

Electronic Control Unit

Without the use of special test equipment. the only way to check ECU operation is to substitute a known good ECU and test drive vehicle. Substituting a good ECU for a suspected defected ECU should only be done after all other components have been tested and repaired. Installing a good ECU while a problem still exists elsewhere in the system, could result in destroying the good ECU.

Adjustments

Pressure regulator

Remove hose at pressure regulator and connect pressure gauge to regulator. Operate fuel pump. Pressure should be 28 psi (2.0 kg/cm^2). Loosen lock nut on regulator and adjust as necessary. Replace regulator if specifications can not be achieved.

Throttle valve

1. Loosen lock nut on stop screw for throttle valve switch and turn out a couple of turns, so it does not touch stop on throttle valve spindle. Check to ensure switch is fully closed.

2. Screw in stop screw until it touches stop on switch spindle. Turn screw in 1 full turn and tighten lock nut. Check that throttle valve switch does not jam or seize in closed position.

Throttle valve switch

Remove air cleaner and place a .016" (.41 mm) feeler gauge between boss and stop screw. Connect voltmeter to terminal No. 17 on throttle valve switch and ground. Loosen switch retaining screws enough to move switch. Turn switch counterclockwise to its stop. Voltmeter reading should be zero volt. Now turn throttle switch clockwise and tighten retaining screws exactly at point a reading is noted on voltmeter.

Preliminary checks

Prior to trouble shooting the fuel injection system, check the following items:

- Battery condition.
- All electrical connections.
- Hoses or mating surfaces for vacuum leakage.
- Fuel lines for leakage.
- Ignition system.
- Idle speed and mixture.

Trouble shooting

Engine Will Not Start, Fuel Pump Inoperative

Check the following: Defective fuse, fuel pump. fuel pump relay, main relay or electrical circuit. Fuel pump relay should click when ignition is switched on and off. Should have voltage from main relay terminal No. 87 to fuel pump relay terminal No. 86. Fuel pump relay terminal No. 85 should have good ground from ECU.

> **NOTE:** Fuel pump operates approximately 1 to 2 seconds after switching ignition on. Relay is grounded from ECU. Ensure fuel pump operates during cranking.

Engine Will Not Start, Fuel Pump Operates

Check the following: Defective wire to starter terminal No. 50, Manifold Pressure Control (MPC) sensor and/or wiring, temperature sensors and/or wiring. Inadequate pressure in main fuel system, wire connector for distributor contacts disconnected and/or open circuit. Pressure should be 28 psi (2.0 kg/cm^2) with starter operating.

Engine Starts, Then Stalls When Cold

Check the following: Defective trigger contacts and/or wiring, MPC sensor or temperature sensors.

Engine Will Not Start Warm

Check the following: Defective thermotime switch, temperature sensors or high resistance at trigger contacts.

Engine Stalls And May Misfire

Check the following: Excessive resistance at trigger contacts, dirty trigger contacts, loose connector, temperature sensors or inadequate vehicle ground.

Engine Runs Rough, White Smoke Comes From Exhaust

Check the following: Injector sticking or connection to injector windings faulty.

Lack of Power

Check the following: Defective MPC sensor, fuel pressure too low, restricted air throttle valve or full-load contact does not close.

Excessive Fuel Consumption

Check the following: Defective sensors, ECU, MPC, improperly adjusted throttle switch or inadequate fuel pressure.

Engine Idles Erratically Between 1000 and 2000 RPM

Check the following: Hose between auxiliary air regulator and intake air distributor disconnected or cracked, throttle valve not closed at idle or idle speed too high.

High Idle, Unadjustable

Check the following: Vacuum leak, injector valve "0" ring leaking or throttle valve out of adjustment.

WIRING DIAGRAMS
SUPPLEMENT

This supplement includes comprehensive wiring diagrams for the following 1970 to 1976 models.

1970 & 1971 – 2500 & 2800	pgs. 196/197
1970 & 1971 – 2800 CS	pgs. 198/199
1972 Bavaria	pgs. 200/201
1972 & 1973 – 3.0 CS	pgs. 202/203
1974 – 3.0 Sedan & Bavaria	pgs. 204/205
1974 – 3.0 Coupe	pgs. 206/207
1975 – 3.0	pgs. 208/209
1976 – 3.0 Si	pgs. 210/211

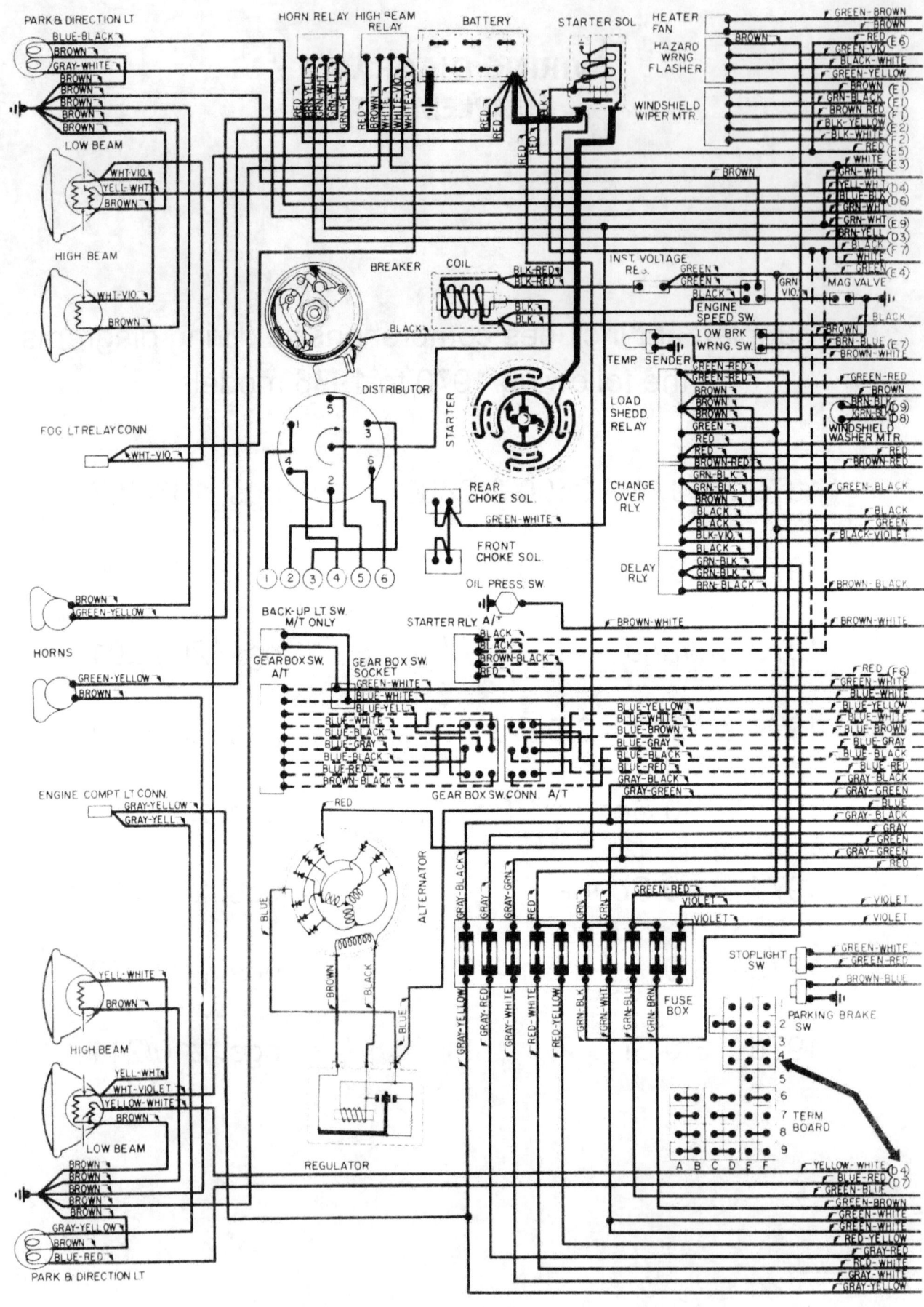

1970 & 1971 - 2500 & 2800

1970 & 1971 - 2500 & 2800

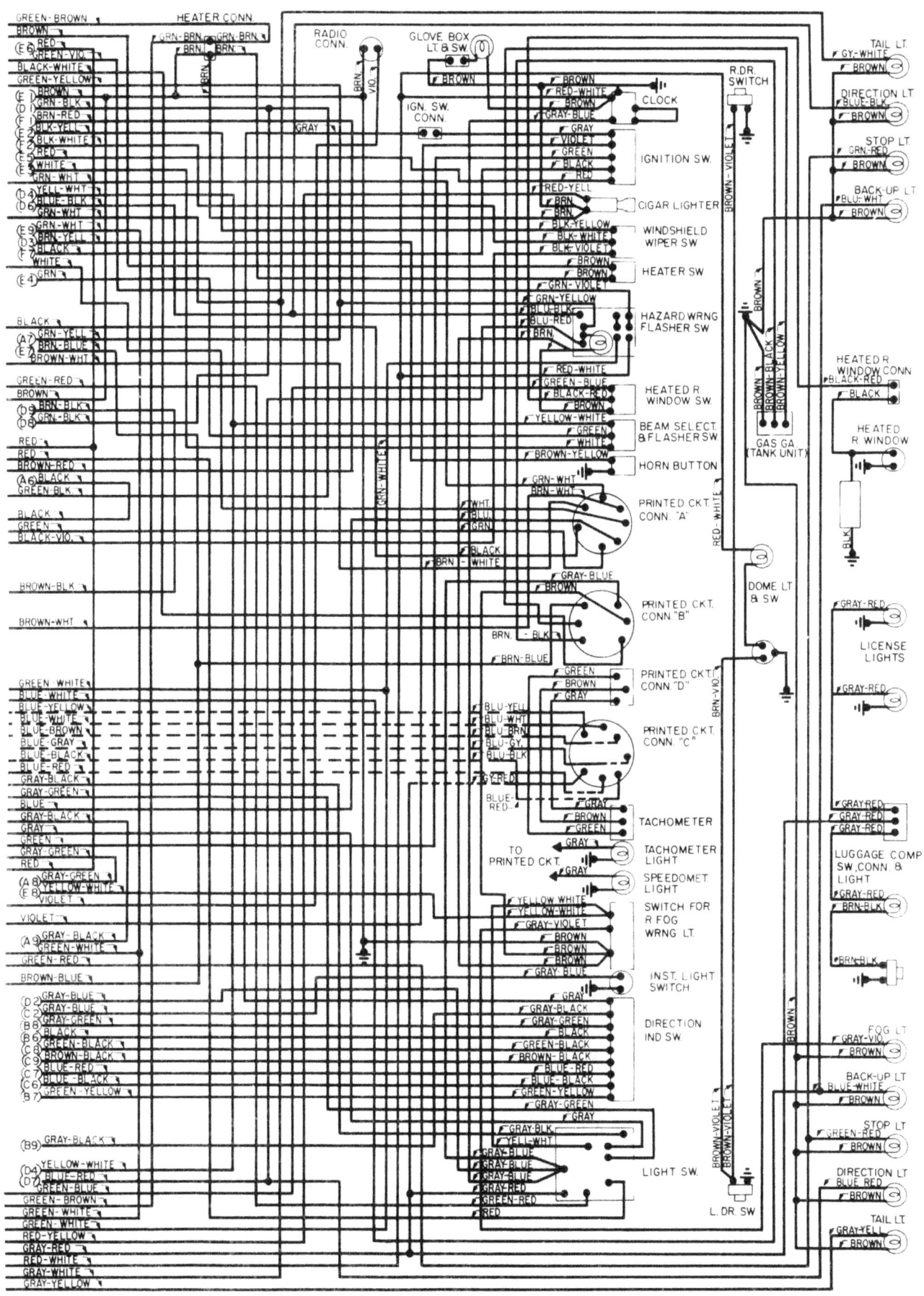

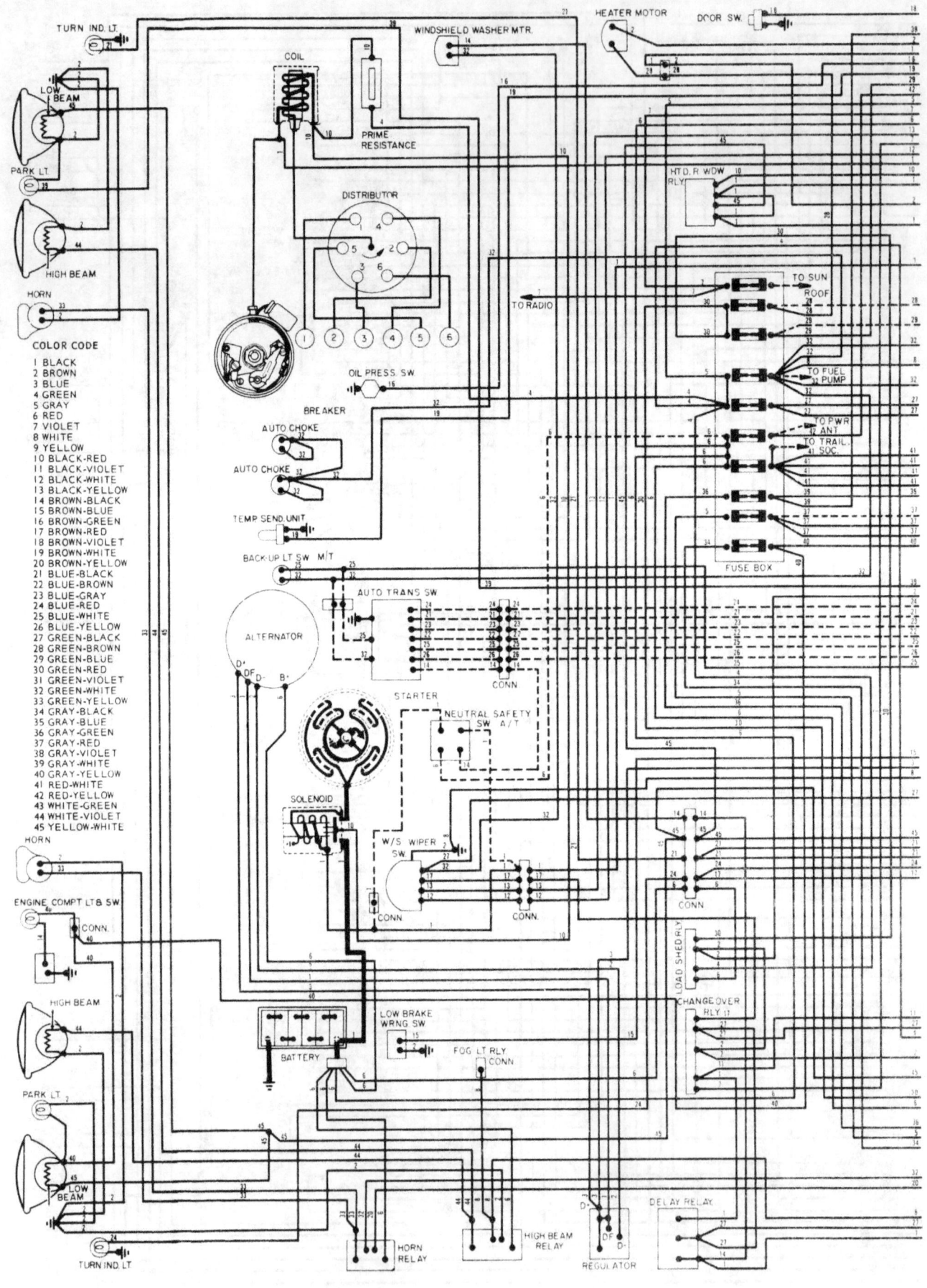

1970 & 1971 - 2800 CS

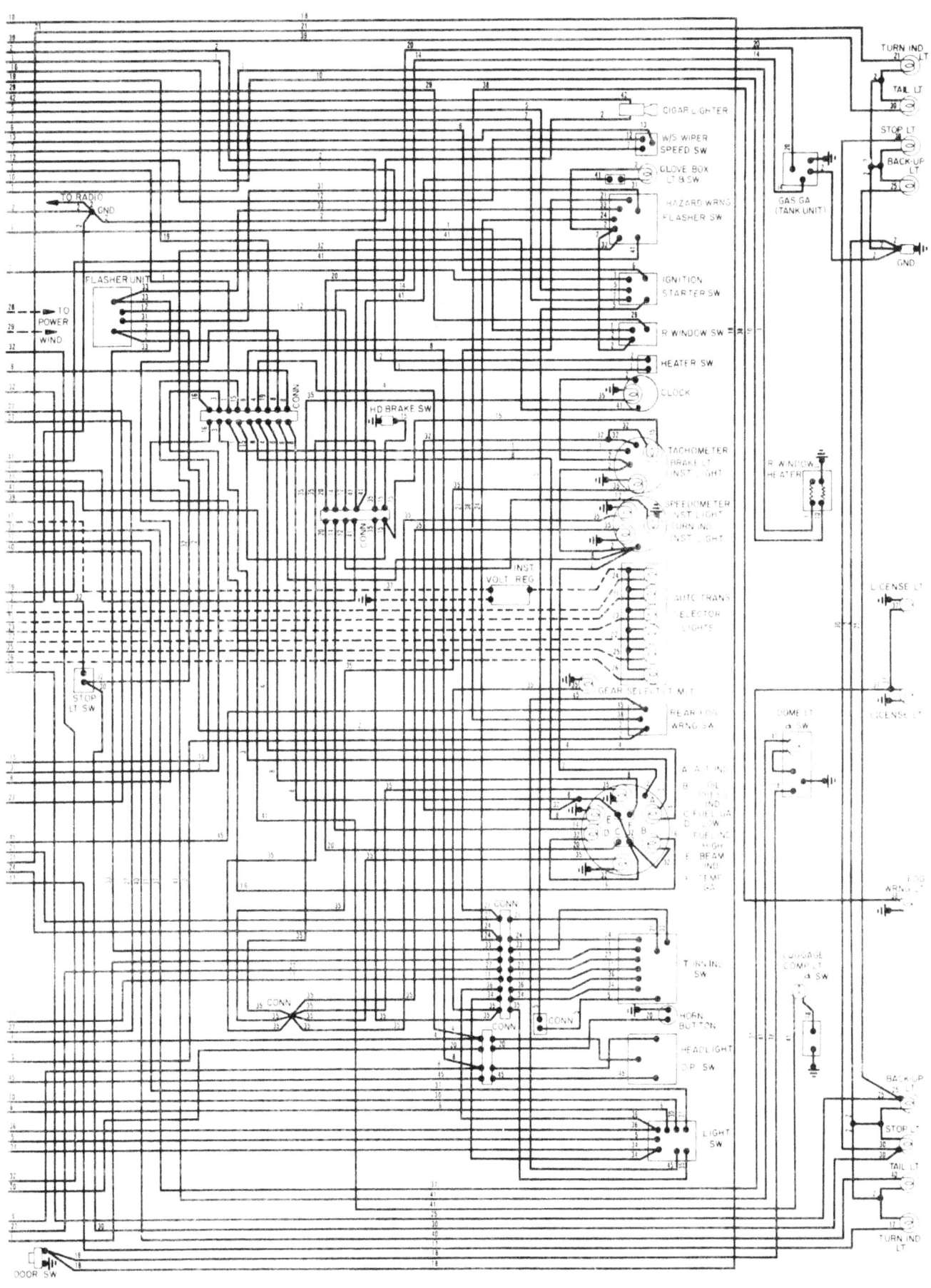

1972 - Bavaria

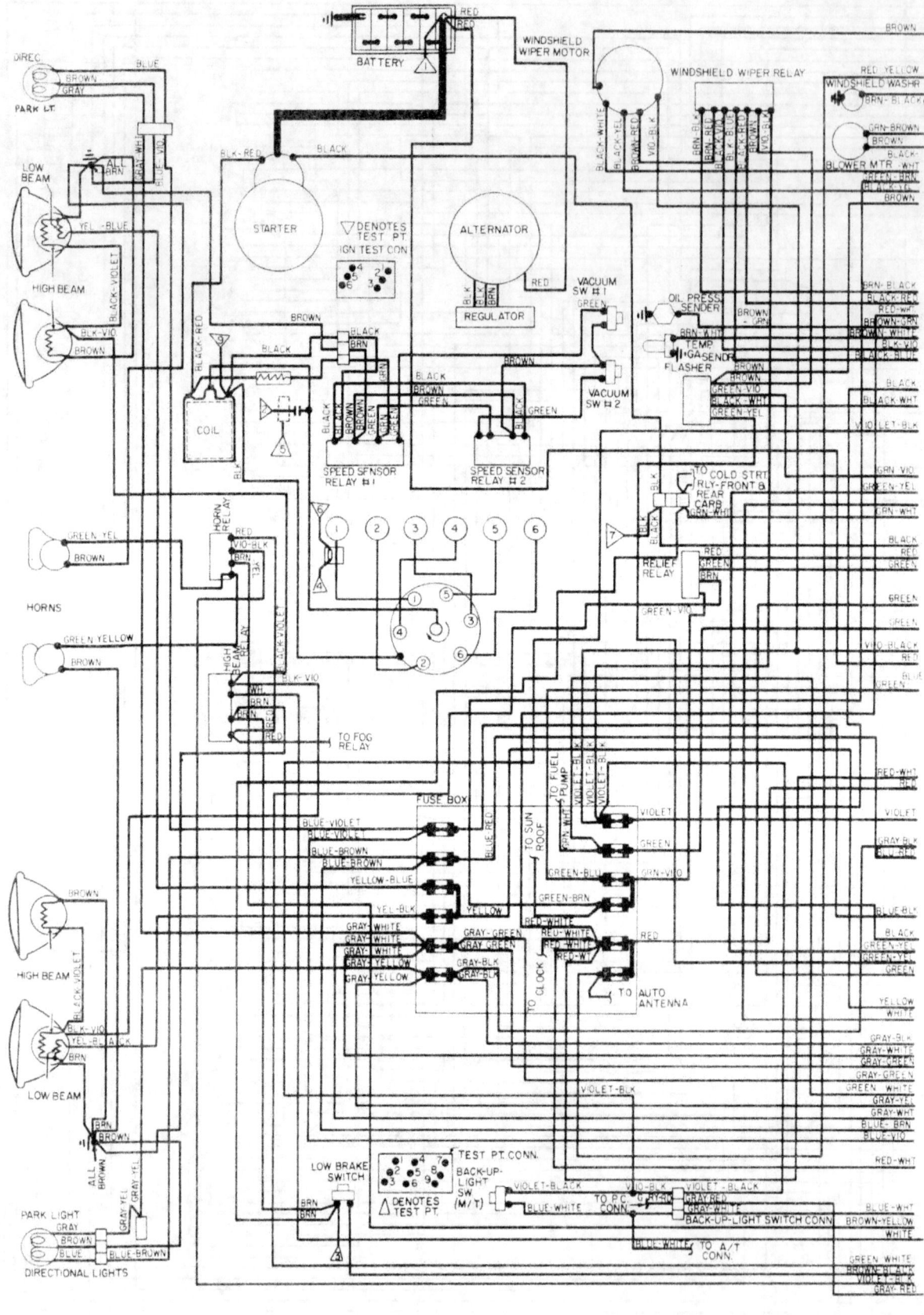

1972 - Bavaria

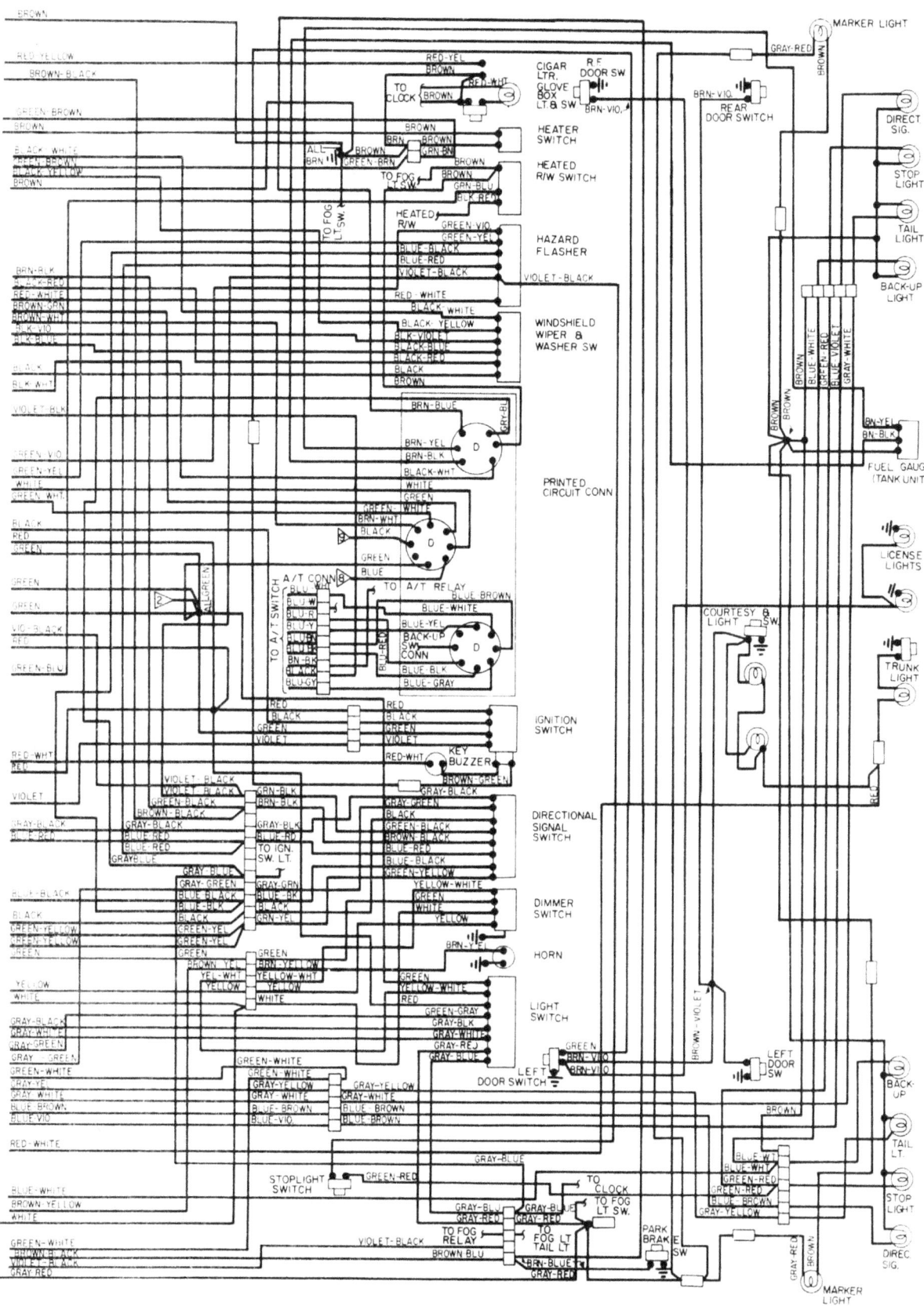

1972 & 1973 - 3.0 CS

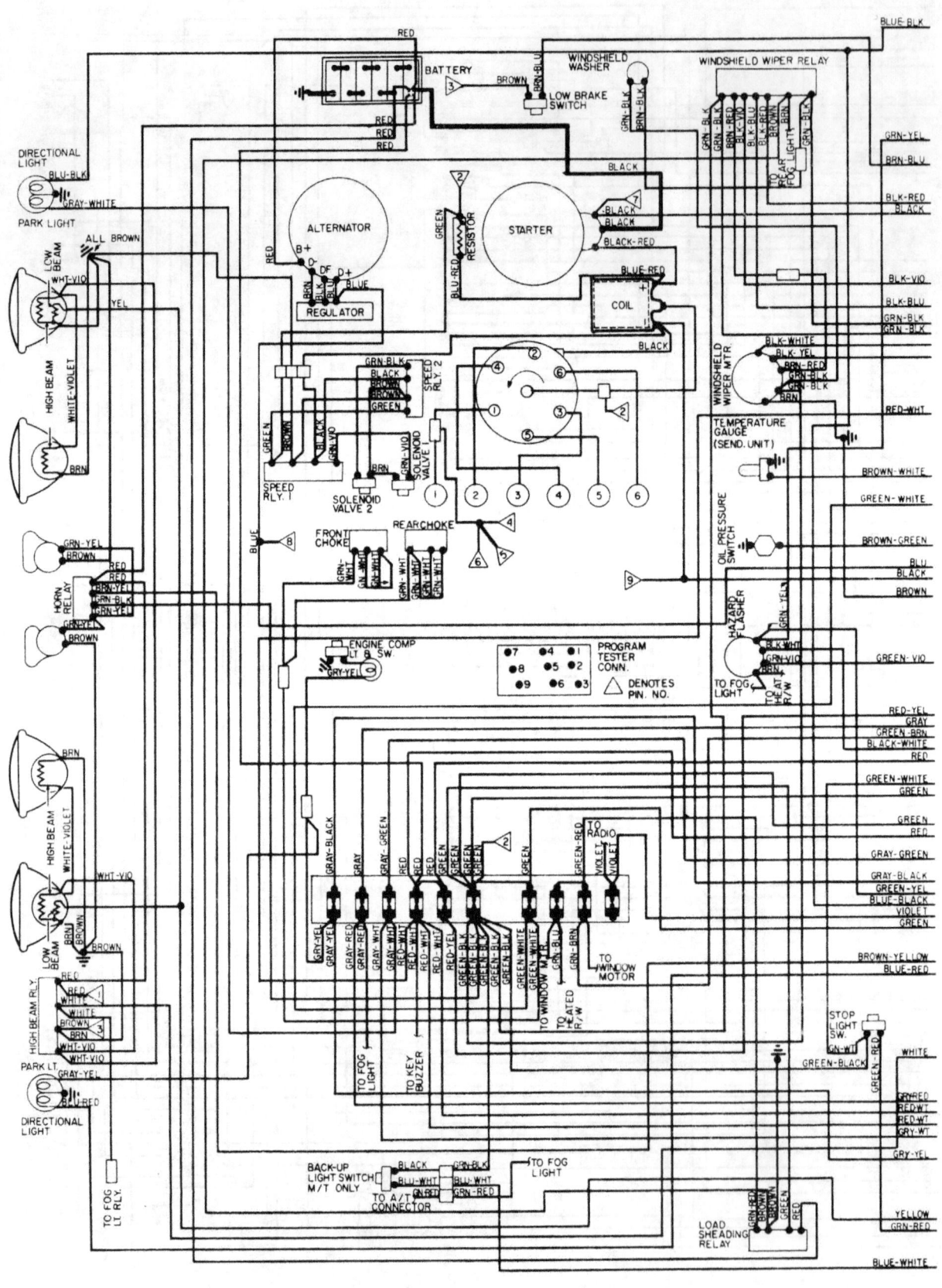

1972 & 1973 - 3.0 CS

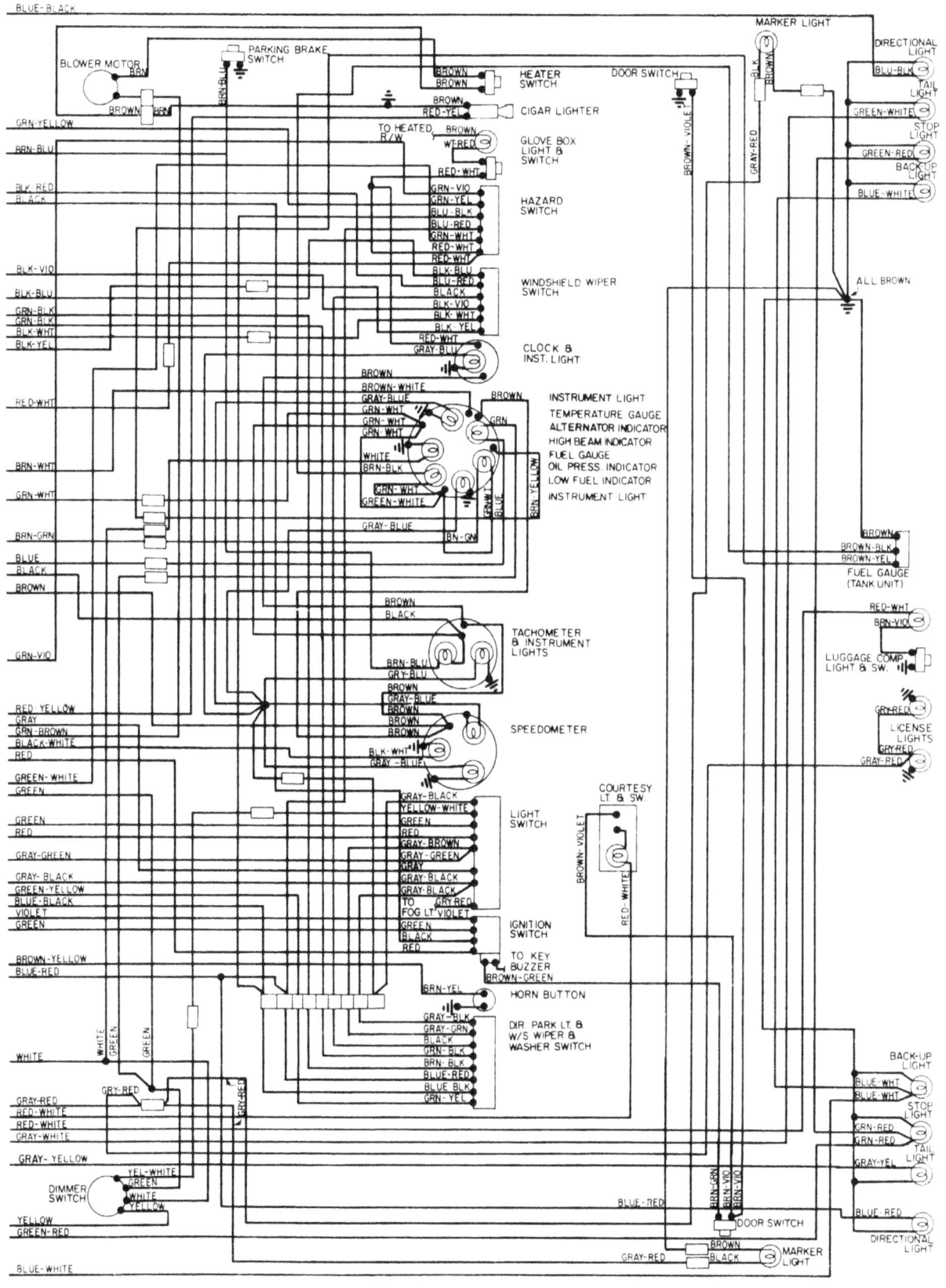

1974 - 3.0 Sedan & Bavaria

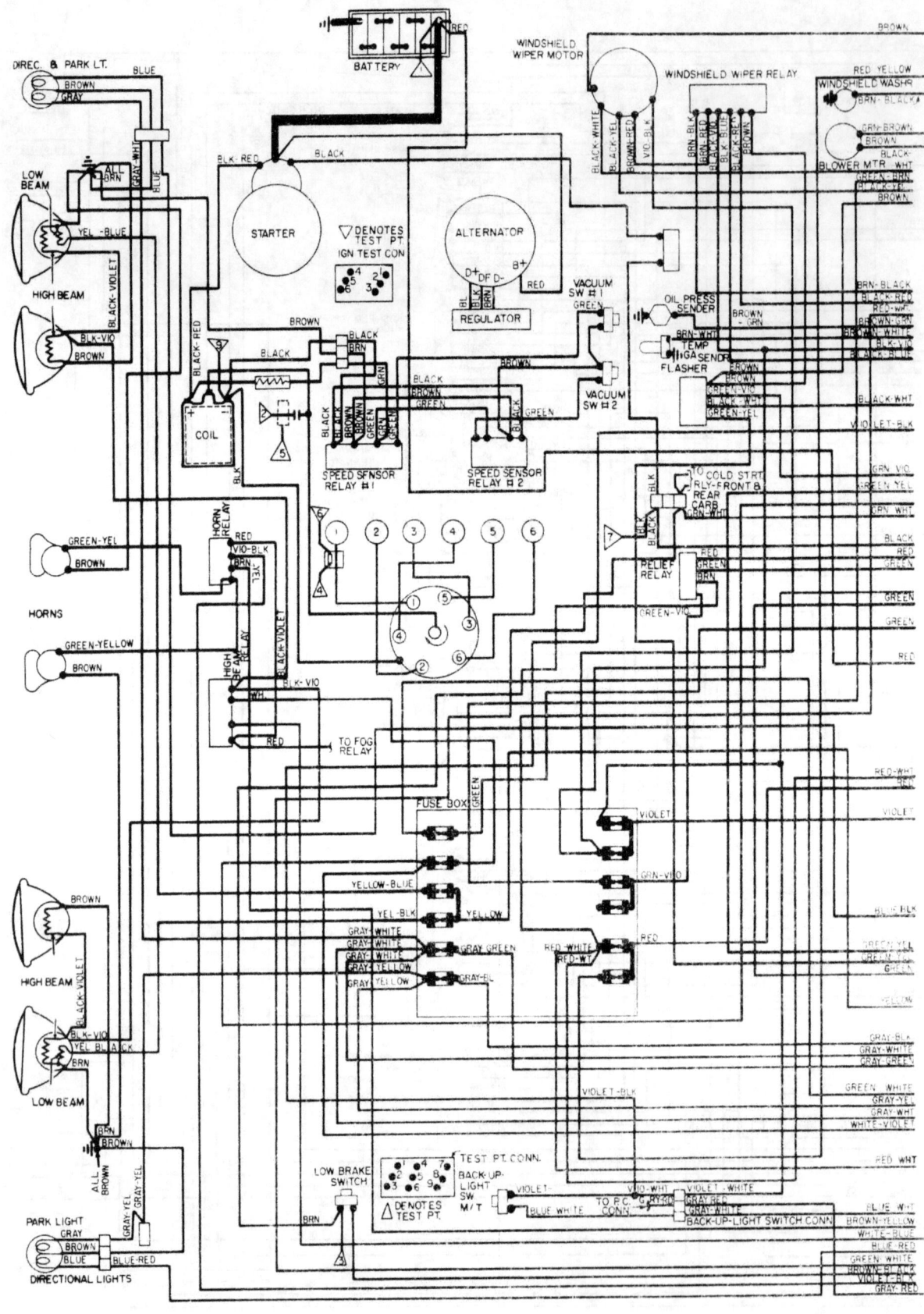

1974 - 3.0 Sedan & Bavaria

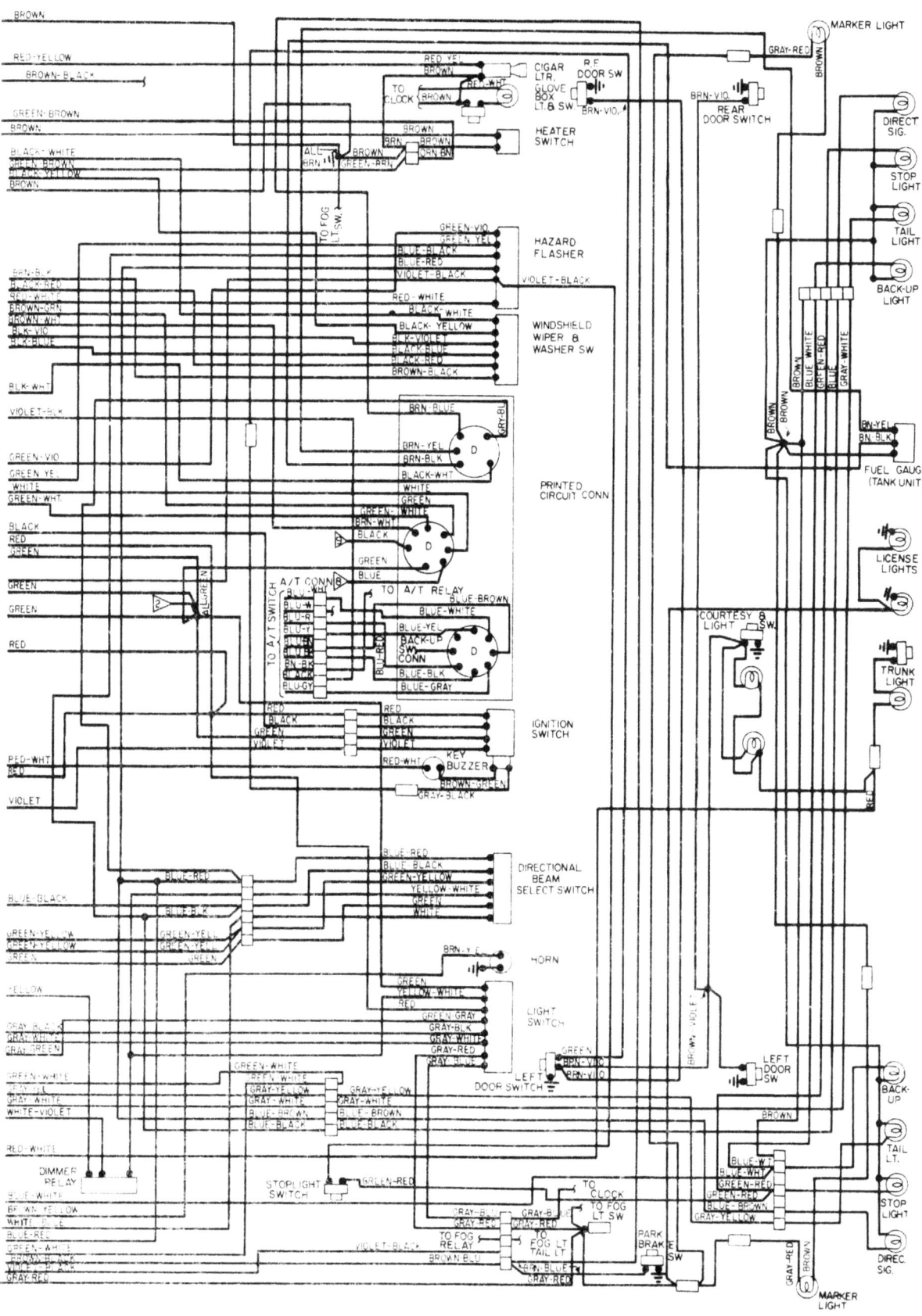

1974 - 3.0 Coupe

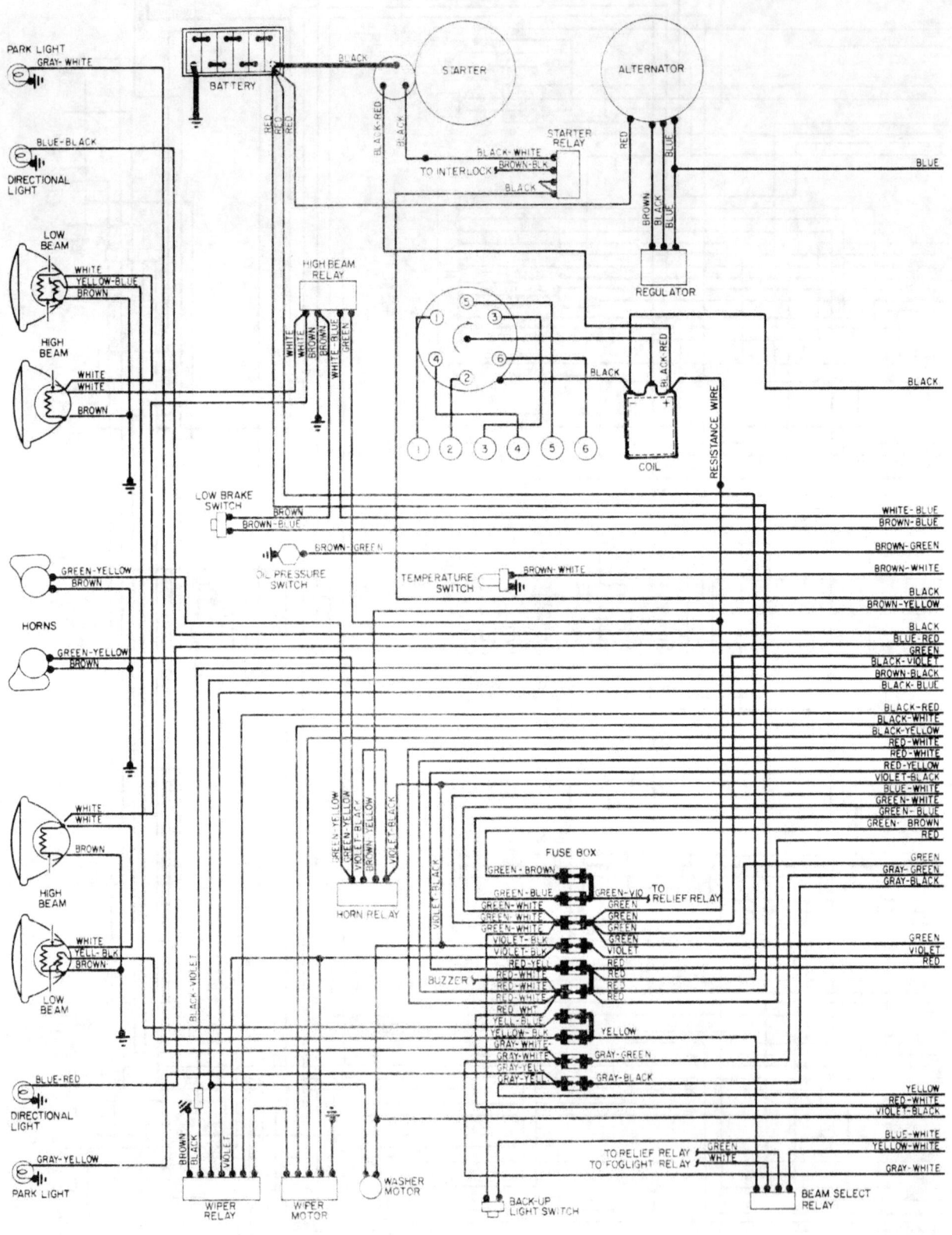

1974 - 3.0 Coupe

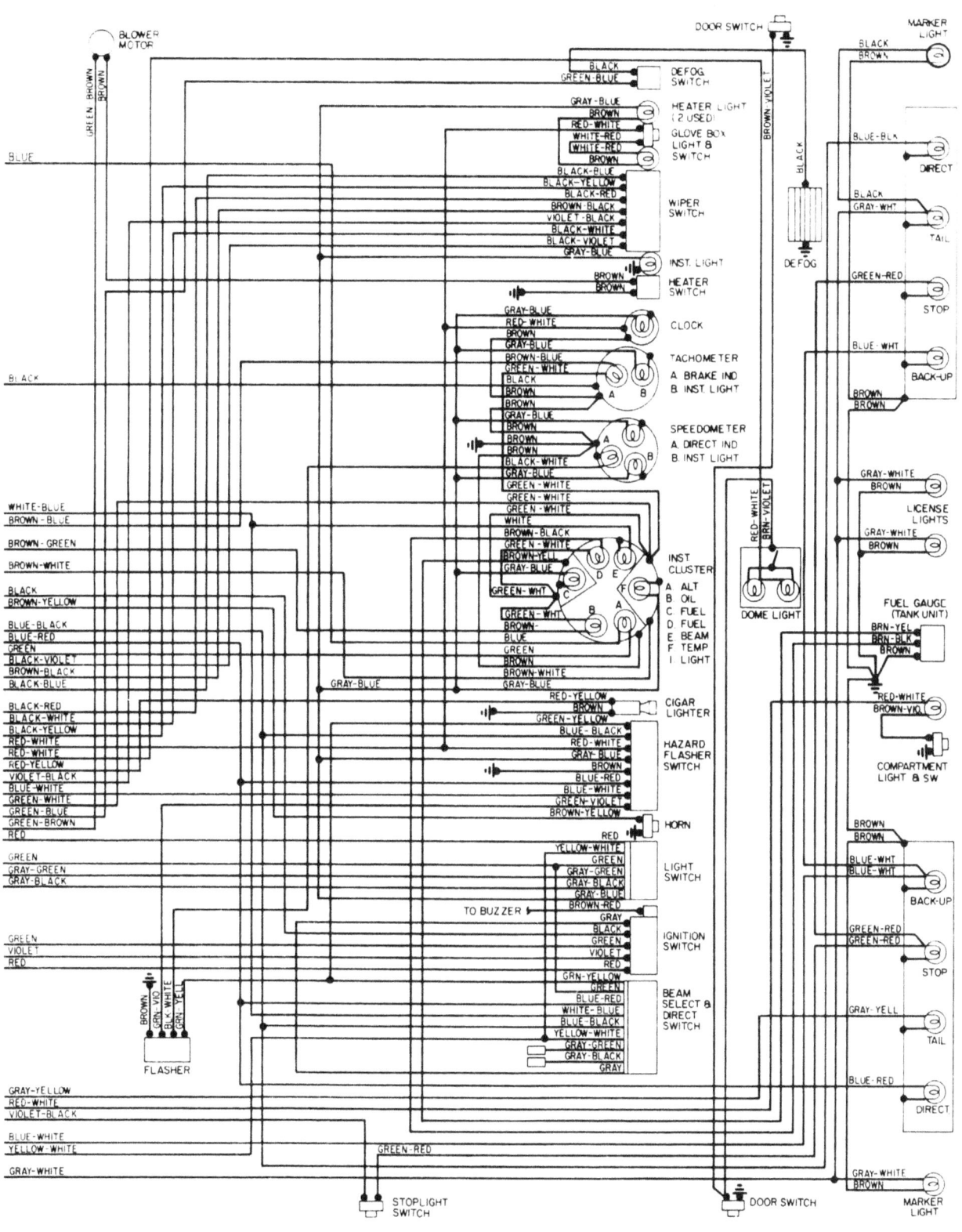

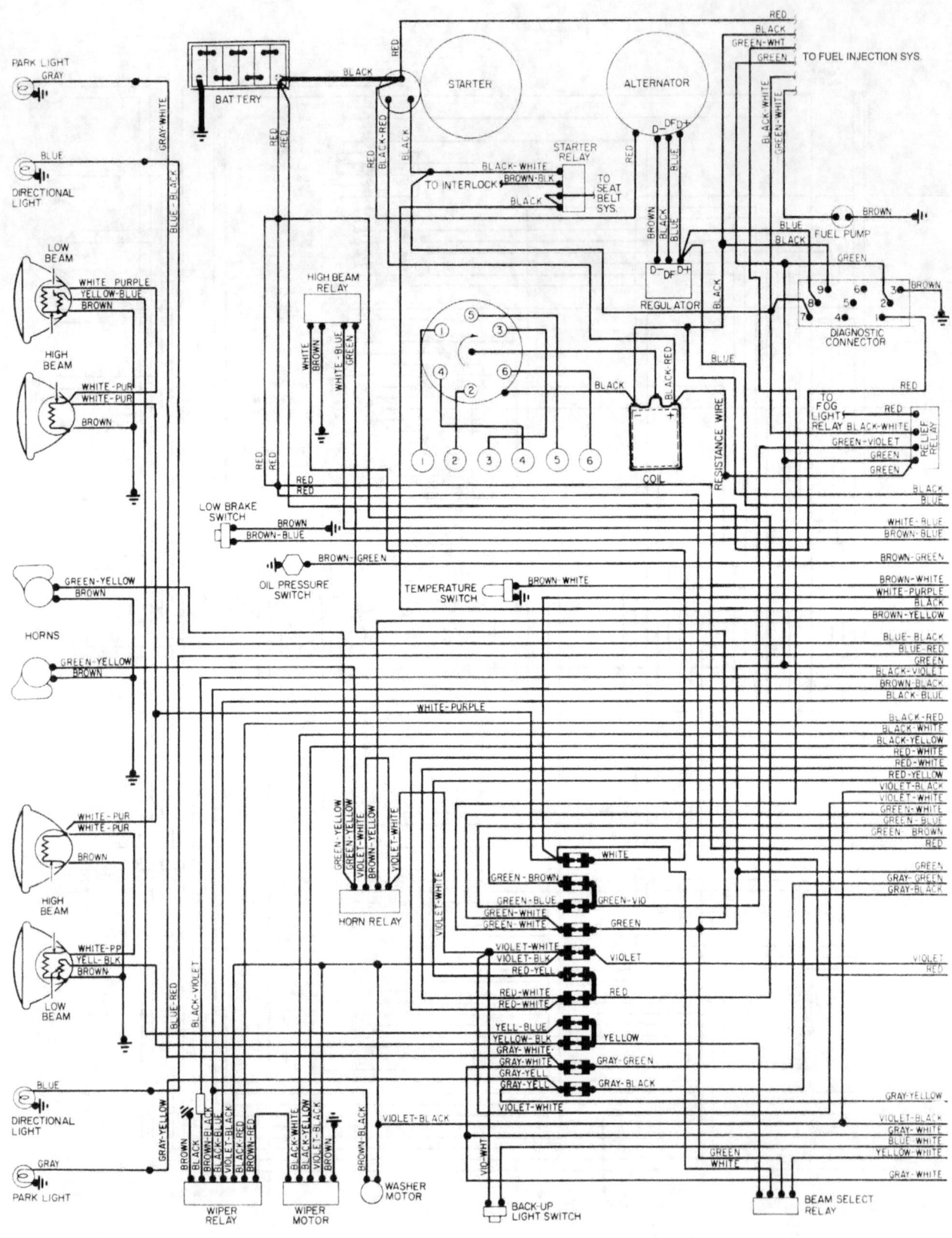

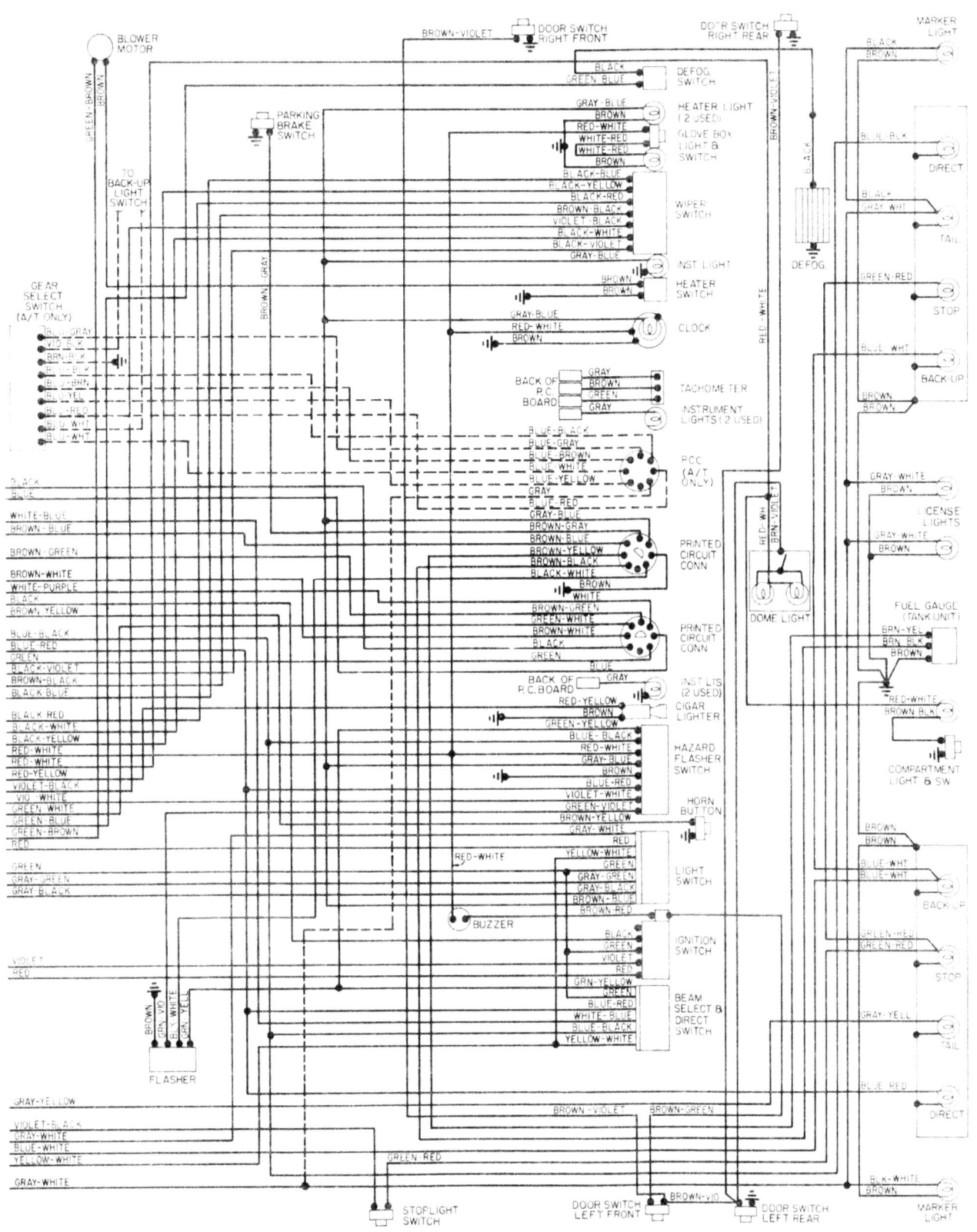

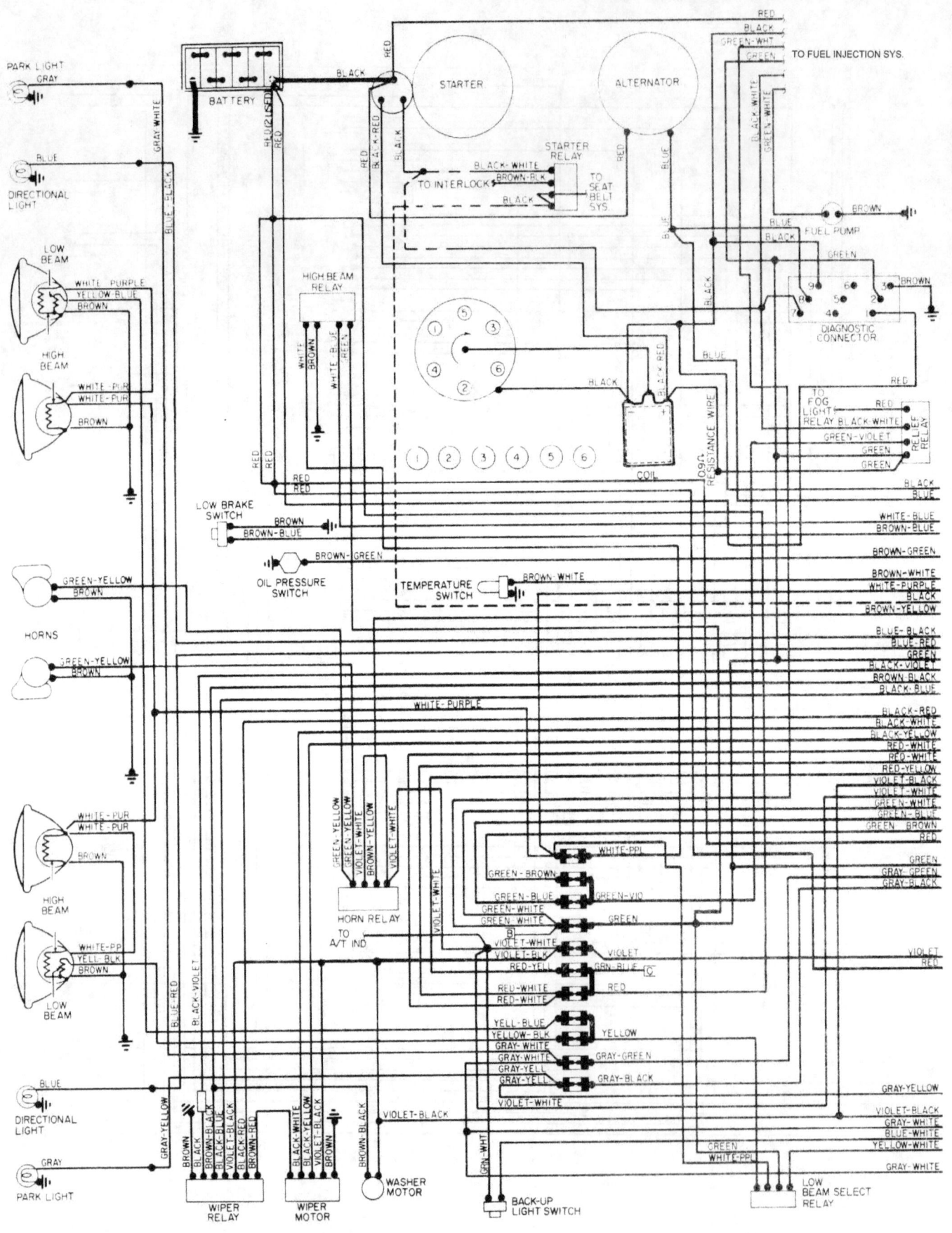

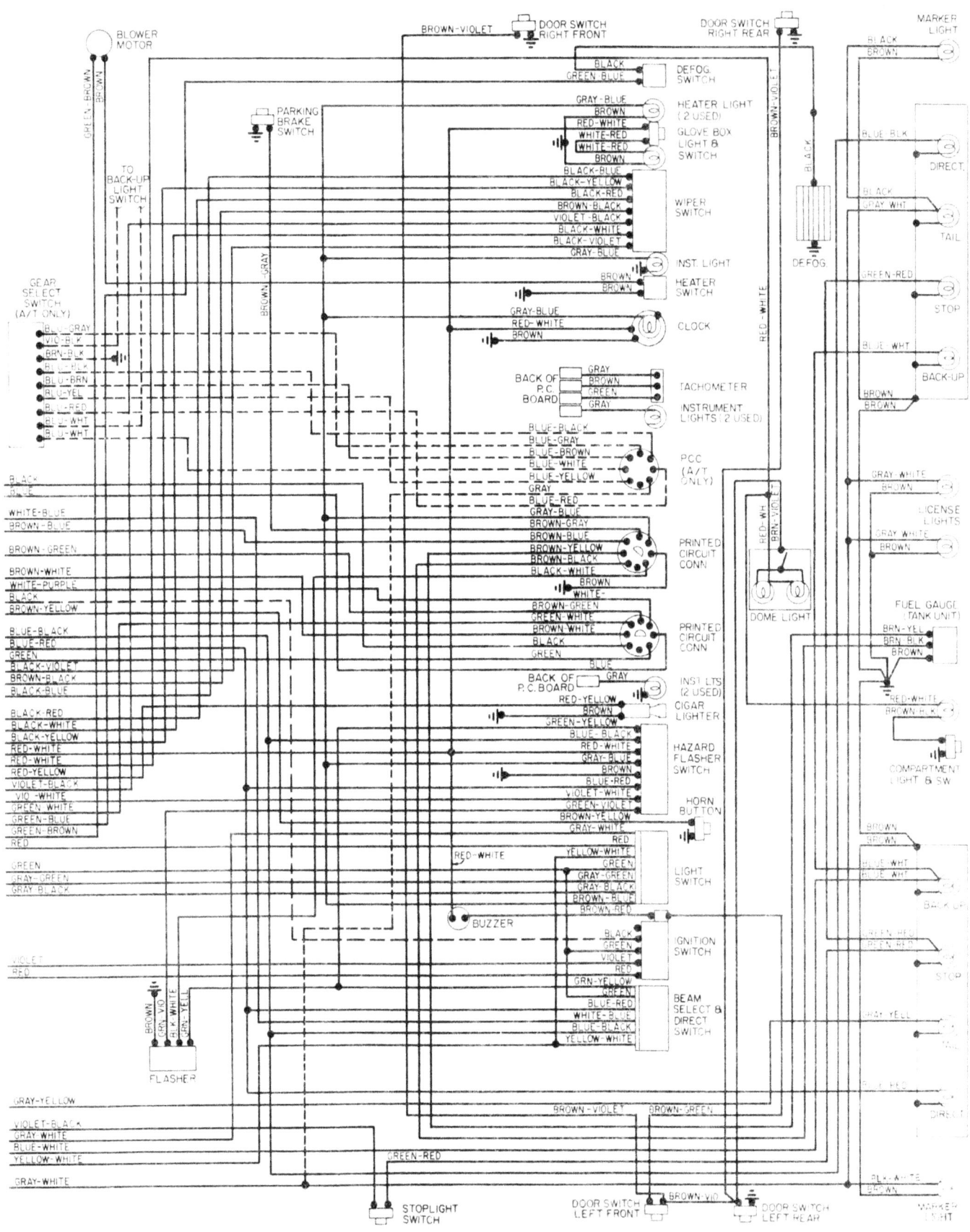

VELOCEPRESS MANUALS – AUTOMOBILE BY MAKE

ALFA ROMEO GIULIA WORKSHOP MANUAL 1300 TO 2000cc 1962-1975
ALFA ROMEO GIULIA TECH MANUAL CARBURETED CARS FROM 1962
ALFA ROMEO GIULIA TECH MANUAL FUEL INJECTED CARS FROM 1969
ALFA ROMEO GIULIETTA & GIULIA 750 & 101 SERIES 1955-1965 WSM
AUSTIN-HEALEY SPRITE & MG MIDGET WORKSHOP MANUAL 1958-1971
BMW 600 LIMOUSINE FACTORY WORKSHOP MANUAL
BMW 600 LIMOUSINE OWNERS HAND BOOK & SERVICE MANUAL
BMW 2000 & 2002 1966-1976 WORKSHOP MANUAL
BMW 2500, 2800, 3.0 & BARVARIA WORKSHOP MANUAL
CORVAIR 1960-1969 WORKSHOP MANUAL
CORVETTE V8 1955-1962 WORKSHOP MANUAL
FERRARI HANDBOOK ROAD & RACE CARS (SERVICE/SPECS) 1948-1958
FERRARI 250GT SERVICE & MAINTENANCE by JIM RIFF 1956-1965
FERRARI 250GT & 250GTE FACTORY PARTS AND REPAIR MANUALS
FIAT 500 FACTORY WORKSHOP MANUAL 1957-1973
FIAT 600, 600D & MULTIPLA FACTORY WORKSHOP MANUAL 1955-1969
JAGUAR E-TYPE 3.8 & 4.2 SERIES 1 & 2 WORKSHOP MANUAL
JAGUAR MK 7, 8, 9 & XK120, 140, 150 WORKSHOP MANUAL 1948-1961
METROPOLITAN FACTORY WORKSHOP MANUAL
MGA & MGB OWNERS HANDBOOK & WORKSHOP MANUAL
MG MIDGET TC, TD, TF & TF1500 WORKSHOP MANUAL
PORSCHE 356 1948-1965 WORKSHOP MANUAL
PORSCHE 911 2.0, 2.2, 2.4 LITRE 1964-1973 WORKSHOP MANUAL
PORSCHE 911 2.7, 3.0, 3.2 LITRE 1973-1989 WORKSHOP MANUAL
PORSCHE 912 WORKSHOP MANUAL
PORSCHE 914/4 & 914/6 1.7, 1.8, 2.0 LITRE 1970-1976 WSM
TRIUMPH TR2, TR3, TR4 1953-1965 WORKSHOP MANUAL
VOLKSWAGEN TRANSPORTER, TRUCKS & WAGONS 1950-1979 WSM
VOLVO 1944-1968 ALL MODELS WORKSHOP MANUAL

VELOCEPRESS TECHNICAL BOOKS - AUTOMOBILE

HOW TO BUILD A FIBERGLASS CAR
HOW TO BUILD A RACING CAR
HOW TO RESTORE THE MODEL 'A' FORD
MASERATI OWNER'S HANDBOOK
PERFORMANCE TUNING THE SUNBEAM TIGER
SOUPING THE VOLKSWAGEN
SOLEX CARBURETORS (EMPHASIS ON UK & EU AUTOMOBILES)
SU CARBURETORS (EMPHASIS ON UK AUTOMOBILES)
WEBER CARBURETORS (EMPHASIS ON ALFA & FIAT)

VELOCEPRESS BOOKS & GUIDES - AUTOMOBILE

COMPLETE CATALOG OF JAPANESE MOTOR VEHICLES
FERRARI 308 SERIES BUYER'S AND OWNER'S GUIDE
FERRARI BROCHURES AND SALES LITERATURE 1968-1989
FERRARI SERIAL NUMBERS PART I - ODD NUMBERS TO 21399
FERRARI SERIAL NUMBERS PART II - EVEN NUMBERS TO 1050
HENRY'S FABULOUS MODEL "A" FORD
MASERATI BROCHURES AND SALES LITERATURE

VELOCEPRESS BOOKS – AUTO RACING

CARRERA PANAMERICANA - MEXICAN ROAD RACE (BOOK OF)
DIALED IN - THE JAN OPPERMAN STORY
VEDA ORR'S NEW REVISED HOT ROD PICTORIAL

MOTORCYCLE OWNERS & ENTHUSIASTS ARE DIRECTED TO OUR WEBSITE
www.VelocePress.com
FOR A COMPLETE LISTING OF MOTORCYCLE MANUALS & BOOKS

www.ingramcontent.com/pod-product-compliance
Lightning Source LLC
Chambersburg PA
CBHW080733300426
44114CB00019B/2579